Globalisation, Governance and Human Rights

About the Editors

Dr. Anisur Rahman is currently Professor and Director, UGC-Human Resource Development Centre, Jamia Millia Islamia, New Delhi. He holds Masters in two disciplines—Economics (AMU) as well as Sociology, M.Phil and Ph.D. (JNU). Before he joined Jamia Millia Islamia in 1999, he worked at the Institute of Applied Manpower Research, Planning Commission, Government of India. His area of interest includes South Asian Migration and Diaspora, Gulf Social Demography, Issues of Higher Education and Minorities. He has published 5 books and over 50 Research Papers in Reputed Journals in India and abroad including his contributions as chapters in edited books by well known scholars. Dr. Rahman has presented over 70 Research Papers in several Conferences/Seminars/Workshops in India and Abroad. He has visited several countries like the USA, UK, France, Germany, Netherlands, Sweden, Denmark, Switzerland, Hong Kong, Saudi Arabia, and UAE. He visited Paris, France under Indo-French Social Scientist Exchange Programme thrice for research in 2010, 2013, and 2015. He has delivered over 100 invited talks at different institutions of higher learning in India and abroad. He is also a member of several academic committees, bodies and editorial boards. He may be contacted at arahman@jmi.ac.in, anis_1964@yahoo.co.uk

Dr. Niharika Tiwari is currently working as Assistant Professor at Department of Political Science, DDU Govt. P.G. College, Saidabad, Prayagraj, Uttar Pradesh, India. She did her B.A. (Hons., Political Science) and M.A. (Pol. Sc.) from Banaras Hindu University (BHU), M. Phil and Ph.D. from Centre for South Asian Studies, School of International Studies, Jawaharlal Nehru University (JNU).

She has qualified UGC-NET (JRF)) in Political Science and UGC-NET in Women Studies. She has taught at Kalindi College, University of Delhi for three years (2011-2014). She has developed MOOC courses for MHRD's SWAYAM platform. She has delivered many invited lectures. Her areas of interest are South Asian Studies, Good Governance and Human Development, Gender Studies and Multiculturalism. She has book, chapters in books, and articles in international journals to her credit.

Globalisation, Governance and Human Rights

South Asian Experiences

Edited by
Anisur Rahman
Niharika Tiwari

CONCEPT PUBLISHING COMPANY PVT. LTD.
NEW DELHI-110059

ISBN: 978-93-5439-056-2

First Published 2022

Published and Printed by

Since 1974

Concept Publishing Company Pvt. Ltd.
A/15-16, Commercial Block, Mohan Garden,
New Delhi-110059 (India)
T: 91 11 41101460, 91 11 25351460, 91 11 25351794
E: publishing@conceptpub.com, *W*: www.conceptpub.com

Cataloging in Publication Data--Courtesy: D.K. Agencies (P) Ltd. <docinfo@dkagencies.com>

Globalisation, governance and human rights : South Asian experiences / edited by Anisur Rahman, Niharika Tiwari.

pages cm

"... outcome of few selected papers presented at the international seminar held at Jamia Millia Islamia in April 2017. ... organized by the UGC Human Resource Development Centre, JMI in collaboration with the Institute of Kashmir Studies, University of Kashmir"--Page vi.

Includes bibliographical references and index.

ISBN 9789354390562

1. Globalization--South Asia--Congresses. 2. Human rights--South Asia--Congresses. 3. South Asia--Politics and government--Congresses. 4. South Asia--Foreign relations--Congresses. 5. Women in development--South Asia--Congresses. I. Rahman, Anisur, 1964- editor. II. Tiwari, Niharika, editor. III. Jamia Millia Islamia (India). UGC Human Resource Development Centre, organizer. IV. University of Kashmir. Institute of Kashmir Studies, organizer.

LCC DS335.G56 2022 | DDC 954 23

Preface

South Asia is one of the most significant regions of the World. In the past, it has been one of the oldest cradles of civilization and culture. Even today, it is considered to be one of the most viable and important regions from an economic, political and social point of view. This region has in fact enormous potential that can generate opportunities and careers for the people of the region if it is governed efficiently. The major challenges that region is facing are mass poverty, unemployment and corruption that need to be fought collectively. Although, South Asia is seen to be well compact region geographically, historically and geopolitically, but its internal divisions, deep mistrust among its states are significant factors that create impediments from realizing its potential of economic development, political empowerment and the cultural enrichment of its citizen. There is a need to draw a roadmap in order to achieve common economic frameworks that should be capable enough to eradicate poverty, hunger and barriers for utilizing its natural resources for the regional development. It is equally important to formulate the viable strategies to utilize regional resources in a sustainable and equitable manner that could enhance the growth and development of the region.

The volume provides a new perspective through which we would understand the issues and challenges that are plaguing South Asia. Challenging issues are like conflicts, human rights violations, poor governance, gender imbalance, low per capita income, poverty and unemployment that are in fact the major hurdles in the way of regional development. Envisioning a new South Asia which must be inclusive is the need of the contemporary times in order to eradicate, poverty, illiteracy, poor healthcare, regional disparity and conflicts, etc. These issues are common to all South Asian countries. The quality of education and healthcare in South Asia need to be improved substantially in order to fight these issues. All the time, we use to blame our colonial past for all the ills of South Asia. Now the time has come to change the mind-set of the people and focus on real challenges faced by the South Asian countries. For this, unity and cooperation not only between the Governments but also amongst South Asian peoples are required in order to reap the benefits from the forces of globalization for regional advantage. As globalization brings several benefits such as free flows of goods, services, finance, people and ideas, the South Asian countries would take advantage of these flows. There are changes in institutions and policies at national and international levels that would also positively affect the existing institutions in South Asian countries. Moreover, it is also important to identify common values, and shared aspirations and formulation of collective agenda for action for overall development of the region.

It is evident that nearly one-fourth of the global population lives in the region of South Asia. Imagining a better future for the region is the need of the day. For this, South Asian unity is necessary which is quite possible if concerted effort is made in this direction. It is also important to give primacy of human rights, democracy and governance for the establishment of a just society in the region. These institutions, such as democracy and governance, are interconnected and reinforce each other. Governance is understood as the instrument of the effectiveness of a society's institutions. Good governance implies that problems and challenges are managed effectively, efficiently and in response to vital needs of society. Ensuring human rights is one of the most important aspects of good governance in democratic society. This is true that the effective elected forms of governance rely on public participation, accountability and transparency. This is now important to strengthen these democratic institutions for growth and development in the region.

The regional diversity that needs to be celebrated should be considered as its strength for creating regional unity through developing socio-cultural understanding, economic integration and political accommodation in South Asian countries. This regional unity will have to be based on human values rather than politics. It will have to be a collective effort for ensuring human dignity, equity and social justice. People of the region, who have the legacy of a common civilization for a long time, want peaceful coexistence and development in the region. Peoples' aspirations need to be met by promoting regional cooperation, common brotherhood and friendly environment in South Asia.

This volume is in fact the outcome of few selected papers presented at the International Seminar held at Jamia Millia Islamia in April 2017. This was organized by the UGC Human Resource Development Centre, JMI in collaboration with the Institute of Kashmir Studies, University of Kashmir. I am grateful to Dr. Muslim Jan, the Coordinator of MA programme that was running at the UGC HRDC on account of MOU between Jamia Millia Islamia and the University of Kashmir. She was in fact the main person who deserves credit for holding the international seminar. Our special thanks go to the then Vice Chancellor of the University of Kashmir who provided funds for organizing this event for the benefit of South Asia MA Students. We are also thankful to all scholars who thoroughly revised and updated their papers for this volume.

We also extend our special thanks to Prof. Abdul Rahim P. Vijapur who provided all possible help in bringing out this volume. My sincere thanks and gratitude are due to Prof. Najma Akhtar, Vice Chancellor, Jamia Millia Islamia, New Delhi, for promoting her faculty by giving more freedom to do more academic work so that Jamia Millia Islamia could excel nationally and internationally. We are thankful to HRDC staff members who helped us a lot in bringing out this volume. Ms Shahla Tarannum and Mr. Faisal Farooqui deserve special appreciation who provided all support whenever required. Dr. Ansari P., PDF scholar, Mr. Waseem Ahmed and Naziya, Ph.D. scholars, West Asian Studies deserve special thanks and acknowledgement for their support and cooperation. We also would like to extend our heartfelt thanks to our colleagues, friends and well-wishers whose name has not been mentioned here but they helped me in this academic endeavour.

I am really indebted to my family Nargis (wife), Tabish (son). Tooba (daughter) who were indeed the sources of strength to me. I will fail in my duty if I don't mention the name of Dr. Rashda Siddiqui who helped us in many ways to complete this volume.

The last but not least, I owe to Dr. Niharika Tiwari, Asstt. Professor, Govt. P.G. College, Saidabad (Prayagraj, UP) who readily agreed to work with me as Co-Editor for bringing out this volume. Without her cooperation, this professional endeavour would never have been possible.

Finally, Concept Publishing Company Pvt. Ltd., New Delhi deserves appreciation for bringing out the book for the benefit of all stakeholders, especially South Asian scholars.

Anisur Rahman
Niharika Tiwari

Content

SECTION III

Bilateral Relations and Cooperation

SECTION IV

Socio-economic Development and Regional Diversities

SECTION V

Mainstreaming Gender and Minorities

List of Contributors

Ajulka Saxena, Research Scholar, Department of Political Science, Jamia Millia Islamia, New Delhi. She may be contacted at ajulka06@gmail.com

Amna Mirza, Assistant Professor, Department of Political Science, SPM College, University of Delhi. She may be contacted at amna.mirza786@gmail.com

Anil Dutta Mishra, Expert on Gandhi, New Delhi. He may be contacted at anilduttamishra@gmail.com

Anisur Rahman, Professor and Director UGC HRDC, Jamia Millia Islamia, New Delhi. He may be contacted at arahman@jmi.ac.in

Ankit Tomar, Doctoral Research Scholar, Centre for International Politics, Organization and Disarmament (CIPOD) (SIS), JNU. He may be contacted at ankittomar505@yahoo.in

Anusha Halim, Ph.D. Scholar, Department of English, Jamia Millia Islamia, New Delhi. She may be contacted at anushahalim22@gamil.com

Deepika Handa, Assist. Professor, Department of Political Science, Motilal Nehru College (Evening), University of Delhi. She may be contacted at hdeepika@yahoo.com

Khaikholen Haokip Assistant Professor, Centre for Studies in Society and Development, School of Social Sciences, Central University of Gujarat. He may be contacted at khaokip@gmail.com

Md. Aftab Alam, Associate Professor, Department of Political Science, AMU, Aligarh, U.P. He may be contacted at aftabamu75@gmail.com

Md. Badruddin, Professor, Department of Political Science, PES's RSN College of Arts and Science, Goa University, Ponda, Goa. He may be contacted at drbadar786@gmail.com

Md. Kalimuddin Ahmad, Professor, Department of Mathematics, Aligarh Muslim University (AMU), Aligarh. He may be contacted at ahmad_kalimuddin@yahoo.co.in

Md. Misbahuddin Ansari Ph.D. Scholar, Centre for West Asian Studies, Jamia

Millia Islamia, New Delhi. He may be contacted at mdmisbahuddin92@gmail.com

Naveen Kumar, Assistant Professor, Department of Law, North Eastern Hill University, Shilong. He may be contacted at naveenkr77@gmail.com

Niaz Ahmed, Ph.D. Scholar, Centre for West Asian Studies, Jamia Millia Islamia, New Delhi. He may be contacted at niazahmed487@gmail.com

Niharika Tiwari, Assistant Professor, DDU Govt. PG College, Saidabad, Prayagraj, UP. She may be contacted at niharikatiwari15@gmail.com

Nitin Malhotra, Assistant Professor, Department of Political Science, University of Delhi. He may be contacted at malhotra.k.nitin@gmail.com

S. Prabhakar, Joint Director in Parliament of India (Lok Sabha Secretariat), New Delhi. He may be contacted at s.sprabhakar_2000@yahoo.com

Sana Ahmed, Ph.D. Scholar, Centre for West Asian Studies, Jamia Millia Islamia, New Delhi. She may be contacted at sana.ahmed.jmi@gmail.com

Sana Beg, Assistant Professor, Centre for Management Studies, Jamia Hamdard, New Delhi. She may be contacted at sanasbeg@jamiahamdard.ac.in

Saiyed Md. Shahnawaz, Research Scholar (Ph.D.), Centre for West Asian Studies, Jamia Millia Islamia, New Delhi. He may be contacted at shahnawazsm.in@gmail.com

Shah Alam, Assistant Professor, Centre for Women's Studies, Aligarh Muslim University, Aligarh. He may be contacted at shahalamcws@gmail.com

Sheetal Kapoor, Associate Professor, Department of Commerce, Kamala Nehru College, University of Delhi. She may be contacted at sheetal_kpr@hotmail.com

Shikha Kapoor, Associate Professor, Department of Adult and Continuing Education and Extension, Faculty of Social Science, JMI, New Delhi. She may be contacted at skapoor@jmi.ac.in

Sreoshi Sinha, Ph.D. Research Scholar, Nelson Mandela Centre for Peace and Conflict Resolution Studies, Jamia Millia Islamia, New Delhi. She may be contacted at sreoshisinha10@gmail.com

Sudhir Singh, Assistant Professor, Department of Political Science, Dayal Singh College, University of Delhi, Delhi. He may be contacted at sudheer162000@gmail.com

Tabasum Firdous, Associate Professor, Centre of Central Asian Studies, University of Kashmir. She may be contacted at firdousazmat@gmail.com

Umesh Kumar, Ph.D. Scholar, Centre for West Asian Studies, School of International Studies, JNU. He may be contacted at umesh.bbauk@gmail.com

Wakeel Ahmed, Assistant Professor, Noida International University, UP. He may be contacted at wakeel ahmad_kalimuddin@yahoo.co.in

Introduction

Anisur Rahman and *Niharika Tiwari*

South Asian region has its unique identity at global level due to its potentials as well as limitations. The countries of this region have many things in common like common history, culture, literature and language etc. The political history and the evolution of the institutions of governance in South Asia are also similar to a certain extent as today's three major countries that is Bangladesh, India and Pakistan used to be a single political unit before the partition of India in 1947 and thereafter the partition of Pakistan in 1971. South Asia is the most populated region of the world. South Asia consists of eight countries, Afghanistan, Bangladesh, Bhutan, India, Maldives, Nepal, Pakistan and Sri Lanka. According to UNFPA's State of World Population Report 2019[1], India is the most populated country of South Asia with 1368.7 million, followed by Pakistan with 204.6 million, third position is occupied by Bangladesh with 168.2 million. Rest of the countries have relatively lesser population, viz. Afghanistan 37.2 million, Nepal 29.9 million, Sri Lanka 21 million, Bhutan 0.8 million and Maldives 0.5 million. The common feature of this region is that all the countries are state-centric and give much importance to the borders over the human security, have developing economies, low or medium level of human development and multicultural society. The region spends huge amount on the purchasing of arms and ammunitions instead of spending on health and education. Consequently, the region has been suffering from abject poverty, malnutrition, unemployment and many other challenges. The 'demographic dividend' seems to be an option that can be converted to an opportunity with prudent policy making and its successful implementation.

In contemporary international scenario, the geo-strategic importance of South has increased manifolds. For instance, due to increasing interest of China in South Asia owing to its Border Road Initiative (BRI) has made South Asia the hotspot of international politics and diplomacy. Apart from this, the economic importance of the region lies in the fact that it consists of a big middle-class giving rise to a big market for the multinational companies, developed nations and migrant workers of this region who serve in different parts of the world. Thus, South Asia has its specific relevance in international politics.

The book delves into the pros and cons of the interlinkages between globalisation, governance and issues of human rights in South Asia. The book is unique and panoramic as it deals with a range of issues covering almost all major aspects of globalization, governance and human rights and the scenario that develops after the confluence of these three concepts. The positive as well as negative aspects of globalization has been dealt with in detail. The issues of governance and human right have been analyzed through the spectrum of legislature, right based approaches to food, disability, child rights and consumer rights. The debates surroundings gender, minorities and socio-economic development of the region have been explored extensively. The rationale behind this book is to understand South Asia through a post-development perspective. Therefore, it becomes imperative to understand the conceptual aspect of these three phenomena discussed in this book.

The onset of *globalization* is an irreversible process. It might get shaped and reshaped but it cannot be eradicated from the discourses of the world politics. Globalization is a multidimensional process that is characterized by free flow of capital, goods, services and ideas whereby the boundaries of the sovereign nation-states are getting eroded gradually. According to Farazmand and Pinkowski[2], the idea of globalization can be understood as internationalization, border openness, a process, an ideology (freedom, individualism, free market enterprise, and plural democracy), a cause and effect phenomenon and as both a transcending phenomenon and a continuing process of capital accumulation. It integrates the people economically as well as culturally.

The proponents of globalization consider it as the best opportunity to converge the entire world politically, economically and ideologically. They also support values of market capitalism at economic front, political values of liberalism and individual freedom. Whereas, the opponents of globalization see to it as the process of monopolization and homogenization. They consider it a serious threat to the world of peoples, nation-states, cultures, governments, national sovereignty, democracy and self-determination, communities, individual freedom, and public administration.[3] The process of globalization has influenced the domestic as well as foreign policies of the sovereign countries. For instance, IMF and World Bank, the twin institutions of Bretton Woods Agreement are the pillars of globalisation and later on World Trade Organization (WTO) was also added to this series of the institutions of global governance. These institutions have drastically changed the domestic as well as international economic policies having its ramifications in the field of culture and politics as well.

The issue of *Governance* is closely connected to the globalization. Governance is a process whereby decisions are made to maintain the public order and peace and to distribute the available resources. The concept of governance has evolved over a period of time from institution-centric governance to people-centric good governance. According to Addink[4] (2019):

> Governance concerns a state's ability to serve its citizens. It involves the rules, processes, and behaviours whereby interests are articulated, resources are managed, and power is exercised in society. Despite its open and broad character, governance relates to the very basic aspects of the functioning of society and its political and social systems. It is described as a basic measure of a society's stability and performance. As this society develops a more sophisticated political system, governance evolves into the notion of good governance (Addink, 2019:3).

However, there are different mechanisms to implement the governance process. Broadly, it can be democratic, authoritarian or a blend of both. In contemporary discourse, the kind governance is appreciated where common people and their needs are given priority and the human rights of the people are secured and encouraged. Because human rights are necessary for the multidimensional development of the personality of the people.

In this globalized world, the issue of *Human Rights* is much discussed because of the fact that it is often violated by the fellow citizens, non-state actors and the state agency through ethnic conflicts, terrorism, religious fundamentalism, pseudo-nationalism, caste and gender etc. The idea of human rights is deeply rooted in the historical developments at international level. Its concrete form is available as the United Nations Universal Declaration of Human Rights[5] (1948). According to the Article 01 of this Declaration, "*All human beings are born free and equal in dignity and rights. They are endowed with reason and conscience and should act towards one another in a spirit of brotherhood.*" This Article can be interpreted as, all human beings are born free and equal but the unequal socio-economic, political and cultural structures of the society discriminate with them and undermine their worth and potential.

The protection of human rights of the people depends upon the system of governance to a large extent. In the absence of strong will-power from those who are at the realm of power human rights remain a mere rhetoric.

> The implementation of good governance and human rights in general, and economic, social, and cultural rights, to a great extent depends on the substantive principles of good governance. Human rights (and especially the legal provisions protecting these rights at all levels) correspond to or include different principles of good governance. So, in essence, we find the principles of good governance in the discussions about human rights, but often these principles are only recognized as human rights and not as principles of good governance (*ibid.*).

Globalization, governance and human rights all work in close proximity. Protection of human rights in a globalized world has become inevitable. This is achieved through International Laws and global as well as domestic mechanisms of governance. Globalized world has provided many new opportunities to the human beings in the form of increased mobility, enhanced choices and access to global ideas. For instance, the trade related human rights such as intellectual property rights etc. come under global laws governing intellectual property rights, whereby, a person and company can get benefited out of its innovations and creations. Globalization has internationalized the issues of human rights violation, therefore, International organizations like United Nations and International Council on Human Rights, Human Rights Watch and international tribunals etc. also take the issues at serious note. Thus, globalization has led to an increased concern about the responsibility of international actors to protect and promote human rights. Added to this, globalization has also insisted the states to control the behaviour on non-state actors operating from the territory of a particular state because liberal economic system requires peaceful environment to flourish the trade and economy.

However, it has given rise to many human rights and governance problems in the socio-economic and cultural field. Globalization has given rise to religious revivalism owing to the increased sense of insecurity and asymmetries. It has deepened the gap between developed countries and economies in transition leading to global economic meltdowns. Discriminatory nature of globalization has also given rise to powerful non-state actors creating the challenge of terrorism that violates the human rights of the people mercilessly.

South Asian countries have actively participated and supported the process of globalization and consequently their system of governance was influenced by the international laws and institutions. South Asian countries have opened up their economies for multilateral trade and their domestic and foreign policies and cultural norms also have the impact of globalization. Added to this, the issues of ethnic conflicts of this region reach to the international institutions. The ethnic crisis of Sri Lanka was discussed in the UN Human Rights Council. Similarly, when Malala Yousafzai was shot by the Taliban terrorist, the countries of the world came forward to protect her. Likewise, the rules and laws formulated by the International Labour Organisation (ILO) protect the rights of South Asian migrants, Poverty Alleviation Programmes of World Bank benefit South Asia and human rights organizations are constantly working to promote the human rights movements in this region.

This book elucidates the experience of South Asian countries *vis-à-vis.* the forces of globalization, issues of governance and notion of Human Rights. The book has been classified into *five* sections. All the five sections correspond to each other. The unique aspect of this book is that it deals with theoretical, legislative as well as pragmatic aspects of the issues. The issue of gender, minorities, role of media, electoral politics, human development, higher education, consumer rights, child rights and disability rights etc. have been contextualized in the conceptual framework of globalization, governance and human rights.

The *First section* of this book conceptualizes the various dimensions of globalization in general and in the context of South Asia in particular. Diverse ideological-theoretical perspectives and theoretical constructs to provide explanatory models to capture the contemporary global multidimensional processes have been discussed. The section also interprets "Deglobalization" *versus* "Reglobalization" the main ideas being debated in contemporary time, where there is no side which can claim absolute supremacy over the narrative. It also attempts to understand the relation between globalization and religio-cultural revivalism in India. The most important question discussed in this section is whether the religio-cultural revivalism can be seen as a response to the hegemonic Western value system which comes in the manner of homogenizing the world or as a consequence of the globalization in itself.

Second section of this book deals with the issues of governance and human rights in South Asia. The core issue of this section is the right based approach towards the institutions of governance. It explains the genesis of the concept of good governance. The interrelation between human rights and good governance has also been described. It deals with the role of the legislature, judiciary, and other institutions in protecting human rights by advocating the good governance practices to resolve the problems. The issues of children, differently abled people, consumers and human rights violations during armed conflicts have been analyzed exclusively.

The *Third section* delves into the bilateral relations among the countries of South Asia. It has been realized that economic regionalism could not flourish in full-fledged manner in this region due to certain historical baggages and misunderstandings casting shadow over the functioning of the SAARC. Therefore, it is imperative to comprehend the bilateral relations and its impact on other countries. This section discusses about Indo-Pak relations and reaches to a conclusion that peace is indispensable between the two for the development of this region. India's Triangular partnership with Bangladesh, Sri Lanka and Pakistan is also analyzed. Added to this, Plight of higher education and Islamic micro finance as a potential tool for poverty alleviation has also been talked over.

The *Fourth section* has explored the socio-economic development and regional diversities in South Asia. In this section new perspectives in development discourse have been elaborated. Challenges for human development in South Asia, Enigma of modernity, participation of non-governmental organizations in the social development of Nepal has been discussed. The nitty-gritties of Islamic micro finance as a potential tool for poverty alleviation in South Asia has been investigated in detail. Added to this, the plight of higher education as an obstacle for development in South Asia has been critically analyzed. In order to understand the dynamics of relationship among South Asian Countries, India's Triangular Partnership with Bangladesh, Sri Lanka and Pakistan has been examined.

In the *Last section* titled as *Mainstreaming Gender and Minorities,* women and minority rights have been analyzed in the context of governance and human rights. Comparatives method of research has been applied to find out the modalities that can be helpful in improving the conditions of women in South Asia. The political status and position of women in local self-governance in Jammu & Kashmir has also been discussed. This section explores women's participation in the political life of South Asian states, especially in India. It analyzes the nature of political participation of women in India, the government policies for the empowerment of women in the political sphere and the major factors responsible for the low level of women's participation in the political sphere have also been discussed. Scholars have further delved into the political usage of women's body while concentrating on reel and real life. It explores the relationship between gender and media and how media portrays gender in response to its construction and stereotype. Changing Discourse of Nationalism and the Status of Minorities in Bangladesh has been exclusively dealt with in detail.

The existing narratives of globalization, governance and human rights needs to be understood in terms of South Asia in order to bring economic prosperity, social cohesion and political stability in this region. More often than not, small issues get neglected amid meta narratives, therefore, this book has tried to select micro level issues to understand the macro level problems.

ENDNOTES

1. UNFPA (2019). State of World Population Report. UNFPA.
2. Farazmand Ali and Jack Pinkowski (2006). *Handbook of Globalization, Governance, and Public Administration*, CRC Press.
3. *Ibid.*
4. Henk, Addink (2019). *Good Governance Concept and Context*, Oxford: USA.
5. https://www.un.org/en/udhrbook/pdf/udhr_booklet_en_web.pdf

SECTION I

Conceptualizing Globalization

1
Governing the Global
Conceptual Explorations and Possibilities

Md. Aftab Alam

The Concept of Governance

The concept of governance is as old as human history. For ages, it was used along with its prescriptive term good governance to connote a particular way of administrative behaviour resulting into the satisfaction of common good and welfare of the society at large. But, since 1980s and 1990s, the term has become widespread in the development politics and occupies a prominent place in the international public policy discourse.

On theoretical plane, one group of thinkers use governance to connote a complex set of structures and processes both public and private while another group prefer to use it as a synonym of government referring to characteristics that are generally associated with a system of national administration.

The emergence of governance can be traced at the country level to a disgruntlement with the state dominated models of economic and social development prevalent throughout the socialist bloc and much of the Third World in the 1950s, 1960s and 1970s. At the international level, global governance can be traced to a growing dissatisfaction among students of international relations with the realist and the liberal-institutionalist theories that dominated the study of international organization in the 1970s and 1980s which then failed to capture adequately the vast increase in both numbers and influence of non-state actors and the implications of technology in an age of globalization.

Governance is the sum of the many ways individuals and institutions, public and private, manage their common affairs. It is a continuing process through which conflicting or diverse interests may be accommodated and cooperation may be taken.[1] It includes formal institutions and regimes empowered to enforce compliance, as well as informal arrangements that people and institutions either have agreed to or perceive to be in their interest.

The term governance is used to denote the command mechanism of a social system and its actions that endeavour to provide security, prosperity, coherence, order and continuity to the system. The concept of governance should not be restricted to the national and international systems but should be used in relation to regional, provincial and local governments as well as to other social systems such as education and the military, to private enterprises and even to the microcosm of family.[2]

Governance in this way encompasses the activities of governments but it also includes many other channels through which commands flow in the form of goals framed, directives issued and policies pursued.[3] The study of governance has become important and compelling as questions of public policy grow in complexity as the number and power of actors and interested parties within state including unsanctioned or non-authoritative agents—increase as states find themselves pinched between increasing public expectation and constrains or shrinking resources and as various kinds of transnational relations proliferate, unmediated by government. Since governance is not merely the preserve of government, the necessarily generous scope of these definitions embraced observable but often deep and intricate patterns of power relations in societies.

Governance is a social function centred on making collective choices regarding matters of common concern to the members of human groups. Governance comprises patterns that emerge from governing activities of social, political and administrative actors.

Governing can be considered as the totality of interactions in which public as well as private actors participate aimed at societal problems or creating societal opportunities, attending to the institutions as context for these governing interactions and establishing normative foundation for all those activities. Governance can be seen as the totality of the theoretical conceptions on governing.[4]

As the effective power of non-state groups has grown, the profile of what has come to be known as "governance without government" had a considerable impact on the thinking about public policy, on the developing relationship between public and private actors and on the limits of governmental power. The governments have lost or are loosing their power to govern or they have lost their pre-eminence and are assuming a place within various self-governing networks.

The control capacity of government is limited for a number of reasons: lack of legitimacy complexity of policy processes, complexity and multitude of institutions concerned. Government is only one of many actors that influence the course of events in a societal system. Governance is not synonymous with government. Both refer to purposive behaviour, to goal oriented activities to systems of rule but government suggests activities that are backed by formal authority by police powers to ensure the implementation of duly constituted policies, whereas governance refers to activities backed by shared goals that may or may not derive from legal and formally prescribed responsibilities and that do not necessarily rely on police powers to overcome defiance and attain compliance.

The governments have lost or are losing their power to govern or they have lost their pre-eminence and are assuming a place within various self-governing networks.[5] Governance is not synonymous with government. Both refer to purposive behaviour, to goal oriented activities to systems of rule but government suggests activities that are backed by formal authority by police powers to ensure the implementation of duly constituted policies, whereas governance refers to activities backed by shared goals that may or may not derive from legal and formally prescribed responsibilities and that do not necessarily rely on police powers to overcome defiance and attain compliance.

Governance in other words is more encompassing phenomenon than government. It embraces governmental institutions but it also subsumes informal, non-governmental mechanisms whereby those persons and reorganizations within its purview move ahead satisfying their needs and fulfil their wants. Governance is a system of rule that is dependent on inter-subjective meanings as on formally sanctioned constitutions and charters and works only if it is accepted by the majority, whereas governments can function even in the face of widespread opposition to their policies.

Globalization

Globalization is a combination of internationalization, political and economic liberalization and a technological revolution. Globalization can be conceived as a process or set of processes which embodies a transformation in the spatial organizations of social relations and transactions, expressed in transcontinental or inter-regional flows and networks of activity interaction and power.[6]

It is characterized by four kinds of changes. First, it involves a stretching of social, political and economic activities across frontiers, regions and continents. Second, it is marked by the intensification or growing magnitude of interconnectedness and flows of trade, investment, finance, migration and culture. Third, it can be linked to a speeding up of global interactions and process, as the development of worldwide systems of transport and communication increases velocity of the diffusion of ideas, goods, information, capital and people. And fourth, the growing extensity, intensity and velocity of global interactions can be associated with their deepening impact such that the effect of distant events can be highly significant elsewhere and specific local developments can come to have considerable global consequences.

Although, globalization is old in the sense that transnational or even global systems have existed for centuries—indeed for millennia—contemporary globalization has distinctive traits due to enhanced communication technology and the global spread of capitalism. Different historical forms of globalization can be identified including the epoch of world discovery in the early modern period, the era of European empires and the present era shaped by the neo-liberal global economic project. These different historical forms of globalization are characterized by distinctive spatio-temporal and organizational attributes and particular patterns of extensity, intensity, velocity and impact in global relations, flows, and networks, alongside different degrees of institutionalization, modes of stratification and reproduction.[7]

Five broad conceptions across a vast array of literature with overlapping but substantially different emphasizes have emerged. One common notion has conceived of globalization in terms of internationalization. From this perspective, globalization is simply another adjective to describe cross-border relations between countries and globalization designates a growth of international exchange and interdependence. Evidence of such globalization is purportedly also be found in enlarged movements between countries of peoples, diseases, messages and ideas.

A second usage has viewed globalization as liberalization. Here, globalization refers to a process of removing state imposed restrictions on movements between countries in order to create an open borderless world economy on these lines. In fact, globalization has become a pre-eminent catchword for describing the process of international economic integration. Evidence for such globalization in recent decades can be found in the widespread reduction or even abolition of regulatory trade barriers, foreign exchange restrictions and capital control etc.

A third concept has equated globalization with universalization. In this usage, global means worldwide and globalization is the process of spreading various objects and experiences to people at all corners of the earth.

A fourth usage has treated globalization as Westernization or modernization especially in an Americanized form. Following this idea, globalization is dynamic, whereby the social structures of modernity (capitalism, rationalism, industrialism, bureaucratism, individualism) are spread the world over normally destroying pre-existing cultures and local self-determination in the process. Martin Khor has similarly declared that globalization is what we in the Third World have for several centuries called colonization.[8]

A fifth approach identified globalization as respatialisation. Following this interpretation, globalization entails a reconfiguration of social geography with increased trans-planetary connections between people.

The contemporary globalization has been increasingly associated with a tendency towards de-territorialisation so that social space can no longer be wholly mapped in terms of territorial places, territorial distances and territorial borders.[9] It highlights the rise of super-territoriality in contemporary globalization.

Governance, Globalization and Global Politics

In its political domain, globalization has led to a paradigmatic shift in the patterns of international political interaction and the nature and form of political organization. The emergence of 'global politics' involving extensive forms of political networks and activities is the most distinct expression of current phase of political globalization. Political decisions, actions and events in one part of the world have the potential to acquire almost global character. At global level, due to enhanced communication, political events and decisions-making differently located can become linked into complex networks of political interaction. The idea of global politics challenges the traditional distinctions between the domestic and international, the territorial and non-territorial and the inside and the outside as embedded in conventional concept of the "political". It also highlights the richness and complexity of the interconnections that transcend states and societies in the global order.

The realm of global politics is no more embedded in traditional geo-political concerns and issues but now increasingly involves a large variety of diverse social, political, economic, ecological and security issues and questions. The phenomenal and demonic rise of international terrorism in past decades, the pressing issue of global climate change and its cruel ramifications, the rampant human rights abuses and violations, increasing ethnic conflicts and violence resulting into ungoverned and stateless societies, global spread of new communicable diseases constitute an increasing number of transnational policy issues which transcend territorial jurisdictions and current international political alignments. These cannot be limited to a particular national territorial boundaries and demand international cooperation for effective and efficient solution.

The increasing pace of technological revolution in the fields of information and communication has the potential to link nations, peoples and organizations beyond the traditional limits of state boundary systems. These advanced means of communication have dramatically altered the nature and mode of political communication at global level. This has led to shaking and rupturing of the intimate connection between physical setting, social situation and politics—a distinguishing feature of most of the political associations from pre-modern to modern times. The new communication systems create new experiences, new modes of understanding and new frames of political reference independently of direct contact with particular peoples, issues or events.

The development of new communication systems generate a world in which the particularities of place and individuality are constantly repressed and re-interpreted through regional and global communication networks. But the relevance of these systems goes far beyond this, for they are fundamental to the possibility of organizing political action and exercising political power across vast distances.[10] The expansion of international and transnational organizations, the extension of international rules and legal mechanisms—their constructions and monitoring—have all received an impetus from the new communication systems.

In this era of increased and rapid paced global political inter-connectedness, the role of sovereign state is under severe challenge. A vast network of international regimes and organizations have emerged to guide and manage transnational activities like trade and commerce, financial flows, development and reconstruction, global crime, diseases, environmental pollution etc. These collective policy problems require global response and are no more confined to the traditional purview of a sovereign state. The emergence and rapid growth of these transnational issues and problems has involved a spread of layers of political regulation both within and across political boundaries. It has been marked by the transformation of aspects of territorially based political decision making, the development of regional and global organizations and institutions and the emergence of regional and global law.

Political communities can no longer be thought of, if they ever could with any validity, simply as discrete worlds or self-enclosed political spaces, they are enmeshed in complex structures of overlapping forces, relations and networks. In particular, the idea of a political community of a self-determining collectivity can no longer be located meaningfully only within the boundaries of a single nation-state, some of the most fundamental forces and processes which determine the nature of life chances within and across political communities are now beyond the reach of individual nation states.

In all major areas of governmental policy, the enmeshment of national political communities in regional and global processes involves them in intensive issues of trans-boundary coordination and control. Political space for development and pursuit of effective government and the accountability of political power is no longer co-terminus with a delimited national territory. National communities themselves by no means make and determine decisions and policies exclusively for themselves. While deciding on such issues as the regulation of health, conserving the environment and combating terrorism, national governments by no means simply determine that is right or appropriate exclusively for their own citizens.

These new political circumstances present a unique challenge to a world order designed in accordance with the Westphalian principle of exclusive sovereign rule over a bounded territory and its associated geopolitical mechanisms for governing world affairs.

The contemporary context of political globalization has led to a situation of "global governance", a convenient theoretical construct to understand the new possibilities thrown by political globalization and grasp the potentialities of human societies to grapple with those problems and issues existing and emerging beyond the traditional limits of nation-states.

Several factors have encouraged this burgeoning discourse on global governance. First, the end of Cold War brought to close the era of the stalemate politics within the United Nations and associated agencies. This created the prospect of a more active and effective international governance. It also enabled a more inclusive form of multilateralism than had been feasible in a politically and economically divided world. Moreover, it contributed to the dwindling legitimacy accorded to hierarchical or hegemonic modes of regulating world order. These modes are contested by a diverse range of transnational pressure groups, social movements and protest movements.

Second, the intensification of globalization has increased the demand for multilateral corporation and the provision of global public goods include financial stability, the setting of common standards in ever more areas and environmental protection. A new infrastruction of global regulation has evolved reaching ever more deeply into the domestic affairs of states and societies and it remains central to the promotion and management of globalization.

Third, during the last three decades, there has been a significant reconfiguration of state power and authority governing has become a more complex and volatile process. Realizing cherished domestic political goals, delivery of core policy programmes and resolving domestic crises increasingly involve the state in a negotiated order between diverse agencies, both public and private, within and beyond the state.

Governance as a concept of analysis refers to this process of social coordination with a public purpose-process in which the state plays a strategic but not necessarily the dominant role. Given the absence of a world government, the concept of global governance provides a language for describing the nexus of systems of rule-making, political coordination and problem solving which transcend states and societies.[11]

It is particularly relevant to describing the structures and processes of governing beyond the state where there exist no supreme or singular political authority. Theoretically, it is much more than simply a descriptive term, it constitutes a broad analytical approach to addressing the central questions of political life under conditions of globalization, namely who rules in whose interests, by what mechanisms and for what purposes.[12]

As an analytical approach, global governance rejects the conventional state centric conception of world politics and world order. The principal unit of analysis is taken to be global, regional or transnational systems of authoritative rule making and implementation. At the analytical core of the global governance approach is a concern with understanding and explaining the political significance of global, regional and transnational authority structures.[13]

Those who are skeptical of the utility of focusing on global governance does not contest the assertion that these has been significant expansion of international regulation or that it involves a complex politics between states, civil society and international organizations. The rapid globalization of the world economy has elevated the governance issue to the top of the international economic agenda—the battle ground has become the entire globe and the types as well as the number of participants have greatly expanded to include states, international organizations and non-governmental organizations.[14] What the skeptics contest is the interpretation that global governance transcends geo-politics or that global institutions or transnational civil society are autonomous sites of power in world politics.

The global governance literature does not address the question of whether a globalized and globalizing world can actually be governed. The starting point for nearly all global governance perspectives is a recognition that power, authority and the capacity to affect significant outcomes is no longer the exclusive preserve of states and the global governance literature has already provided useful insights into the many ways in which state and non-state actors are variously configured to ensure at least the partial governance of specific areas—geographic or thematic.

Governance occurs on a global scale through the coordination of states and a vast array of rule systems that exercise authority in pursuit of goals that function outside national jurisdictions. Some of these systems are formalized, many consist, essentially of informal structures and some are still largely in choate, but taken together they cumulate to governance on a global scale.[15]

Much of the pioneering work on global governance has, therefore, focused on growth of institutions unique to transnational rather than territorial political spaces[16] and on the tensions and deficits opening up between governments and new or newly empowered sites of governance.[17]

What then is global about global governance? James N. Rosenan makes an important distinction to which the global governance literature largely conforms: there is a difference between governance of the world and governance in the world. The term global governance does not necessarily refer to a central authority. Rather global governance is a lot of governmental and non-governmental activities that occur in local places, the result of which contributes to the overall order of world affairs.[18]

In fact, global governance refers to patterns of polity-authority domains in the world and not only to forms of governance that are truly global. Global governance entails multiple perspectives on world politics and social life in an era of globalization.

In general, there are three principal explanatory accounts—with some variants of global governance—Liberal Institutionalist, Realist and Neo-Gramscian/Marxist. Although each has an interest in explaining pattern of governance beyond the state, there are considerable differences in their analytical and epistemological frameworks. These differences reflect underlying commitments to rationalist, historicist or reflectivist interpretations of the social world as well as to different ontological assumptions about the constituent elements of world politics—states, social forces or ideas. Liberal institutionalism argues that governance beyond state is endemic since it arises from the functional benefits which in an interdependent world, states can realise through the strategic coordination of their policies and activities. International institutions matter because they deliver important benefits to states and their absence would undermine the achievement of domestic objectives. Accordingly, they empower governments rather than shackle them.[19] They matter because they function as relatively autonomous mechanisms, mediating between the hierarchy of state power and global public policy outcomes.

For realism, geopolitics remains essential to understanding the conduct and dynamics of global governance. Governance beyond the state is largely contingent on the policies and interests of the most powerful states. International institutions are principally devoid of autonomous power and function largely as instruments for the advancement of the interests of the most dominant states or coalition of states.

Moreover, no convincing account of global governance can ignore even in a globalizing era, the centrality of the inequalities of power between states. The hierarchy of power moulds the architecture as well as substantive purposes and priorities of globes governance. In accounts given by realism, geopolitics retains a disproportionate role in shaping the structure, patterns and outcomes of global governance. Marxist and Gramscian theories share with realism an emphasis on geo-politics and US hegemony in explaining the pattern and significance of global governance. However, they consider that both these factors have to be understood in the context of the structural imperatives of globalizing capitalism.[20] Global institutions are an instrument for sustaining and expanding the pre-dominance of global corporate capitalism.

In this respect, the conduct and project of global governance is shaped by an unwritten constitution that structurally privileges the interests and agendas of global capital, often at the expense of the welfare of nations, communities and national environment.[21] However, the institutions of global governance serve more than a regulatory or managerial function for they also provide areas within which this unwritten global constitution is legitimized and contested. In this respect, they are sites of struggle with the potential for transforming world order.

Both realism and Marxism are highly critical of the unreflective nature of much of the existing literature on global governance. This skepticism arises from three principal considerations that the existing literature exaggerates the autonomous power and efficacy of global institutions and civil society organizations, that as an approach to understand how world order is managed, this literature is theoretically flawed in so far as it elides global governance with the effective source of international order and that in adopting a form of pluralist analysis, conventional studies of global governance fail to penetrate beyond the dynamics of global politics to the underlying structures of power.

For these reasons, the global governance perspective may be descriptively accurate but it is largely devoid of explanatory power, it is so far the most part little more than two concepts in search of a theory: Global and Governance.

ENDNOTES

1. *Commission on Global Governance: Our Global Neighbourhood*, Oxford: Oxford University Press, 1995, p. 2.
2. Alexander King and Bertrand Schneider, *The First Global Revolution: A Report of the Council of Rome*, New York: Pantheon Books, 1991, pp. 151-182.
3. James N. Rosenau, *Governance in the Twenty First Century, Global Governance* (1) 1995; p. 14.
4. Jan Kooiman, *Governing as Governance*, London: Sage, 2003.
5. R.A.W. Rhodes, "The New Governance: Governing without Government", *Political Studies*, vol. 9. No. 4 (September 1996), pp. 652-60
6. David Held, Anthony McGrew, David Goldblatt and Jonathan Perraton, *Global Transformations*, Cambridge: Polity, 1999.
7. David Held and Anthony McGrew (eds.) *Governing Globalization: Power, Authority and Global Governance*, Cambridge: Polity, 2002.
8. Martin Khor, *Globalization and the South*, Penang, Malaysia: Third World Network, 2001.
9. G.O. Tuathail, "Borderless World? Problematising Discourses of Deterritorialisation", *Geopolitics*, Vol. 4, No. 2 (Autumn) 2000, pp. 139-54.
10. R. Deibert, Parchment, *Printing and Hypermedia,* New York: Cornel University Press, 1997.
11. James N. Rosenau, "Towards an Ontology for Global Governance", in M. Hewson and T.J. Sinclair (eds.) *Approaches to Global Governance Theory,* (Albany: State University of New York Press, 1999.
12. James N. Rosenau, "Governance in a Globalizing World", in David Hetal and Anthony McGrew (eds.), *The Global Transformations Reader*, Cambridge: Polity, 2000.
13. James N. Rosenau, "Change, Complexity and Governance in Globalizing Space", in J. Pierre (ed.), *Debating Governance: Authority, Steering and Democracy*, Oxford: OUP, 2000.
14. Robert Gilpin, *Global Political Economy*, Princeton: Princeton University Press, 2001.
15. James N. Rosenau, "Change, Complexity and Governance in Globalizing Space" in Jon Pierre (ed.), *Debating Governance* Oxford: OUP, 2000, p. 182.

16. James N. Rosenau, *Along the Domestic-Foreign Frontier: Exploring Governance in a Turbulent World*, Cambridge: Cambridge University Press 1997.
17. R.A.W. Rhodes, *Understanding Governance: Policy Networks, Governance Reflexivity and Accountability*, Buckingham: Open University Press, 1997.
18. James N. Rosenau and E.O. Czempiel (eds.). *Governance without Government: Order and Change in World Politics*, Cambridge: Cambridge University Press, 1992.
19. Robert Keohane, *After Hegemony*, Princeton: Princeton University Press, 1984.
20. R.W. Cox (ed.), *The New Realism, Perspectives on Multilateralism and World Order*, London: Macmillan, 1997.
21. S. Gill (ed.), Gramsci, *Historical Materialism and International Relations*, Cambridge: Cambridge University Press, 1993.

2
Globalization: Myth and Reality

Anil Dutta Mishra

> "The real wealth of a nation is its people. And the purpose of development is to create an enabling environment for people to enjoy long, healthy and creative lives. This simple but powerful truth is too often forgotten in the pursuit of material and financial wealth." —*Human Development Report, 1990*

Introduction

Globalization has become the current Mantra or even panacea to solve all human problems. It is believed that the achievements of globalization would make the people all-over globe happy, prosperous and contented and that there would be no conflict, no poverty and inequality, no violation of human rights, no malnutrition, no illiteracy, and no disease etc. Each individual and community would be so integrated with the world that the benefits would flow both laterally and vertically so smoothly that no one would remain untouched by prosperity. There would be nation-state without boundary. It is said that global markets, global technologies, global ideas and global solidarity can enrich the lives of people everywhere, greatly expanding their choices. The growing interdependence of people's lives calls for shared values and a shared commitment to the human development of all people. This era of globalization is opening many opportunities for millions of people around the world. Increased trade, new technologies, foreign investments, expanding media and Internet connections are fuelling economic growth and human advance. All these offers enormous potential eradicate poverty in the 21st century. Today we have more wealth and technology—and more commitment to a global community—than ever before.

But reality is totally different. Recently, there has been increasing disillusionment among policy-makers in several parts of the world and some fundamental questions are asked. These are: Who want globalization? Globalization for what and for whom? Why is globalization of human resource not taking place? Do people want globalization? It is said that the issue of globalization is receiving considerable attention but no work is being done on the social costs involved (in terms of poverty, inequality, unemployment and tensions) nor on the growing marginalization of people in India as well as in other developing countries. The progress in areas like health, education and other social sectors are slowed by the diversion of precious human resources for national security and in combating terrorism and separatist movement. It is also said that the culture of consumerism is the product of globalization. Almost all the consumer items that are being promoted to sustain the economic growth have significant impact on nation and society directly or indirectly. The concept of globalization and the culture of consumerism are antithetical for all that Indian culture stands for. The new information technology and advances in telecommunications have tended to erode the heterogeneity of national lifestyles, social and economic values and even cultures. This is visible in the standardization of consumer tastes in favour of fast foods (evidenced by the omnipresence of McDonald's and Coca Cola) and American films and soap operas. Consumerism is based on domination, hegemony, exploitation, alienation, concentration of knowledge, wealth and power. On the Few top TNCs of the developed nations have increased their profits manifold, on the one hand, a very significant majority of people around the world are still struggling for their basic needs and existence. The people of Asia, Africa and Latin American regions are still not part of the globalization.

Globalization: A Conceptual Analysis

Globalization means different things to different people according to their ideology and perception. The word globalization is used in two ways. In a positive sense, it is used to describe a process of increasing integration into the world economy. In other words, it means the expansion of economic activities across national boundaries It is also used to prescribe a strategy of development based on a rapid integration with the world economy and view it as salvation. In other words, globalization is a process associated with increasing economic openness, growing economic interdependence and deepening economic integration in the global economy. In negative sense, it is seen as domination by developed nations over developing nations. In most of the countries, particularly those belonging to the developing world, liberalization policy has not been evolved indigenously. It has been adopted under World Bank-IMF combine conditionality of which internal and external liberalization policies are integral part.

Globalization is not new. Recall the early sixteenth century and the late nineteenth. But this era is different:

New markets —	Foreign exchange and capital markets are linked globally, operating 24 hours a day, with dealings at a distance in real time.
New tools —	Internet links, cellular phones, media networks.
New actors —	The World Trade Organization (WTO) with authority over national governments, the multinational corporations with more economic power than many states, the global networks of non-governmental organizations (NGOs) and other groups that transcend national boundaries.
New rules —	Multilateral agreements on trade, services and intellectual property, backed by strong enforcement mechanisms and more binding for national governments, reducing the scope for national policy.

According to the World Development Report (2000-2001), five actions are necessary:

- Promoting global financial stability and opening the markets of rich countries to the agricultural goods, manufactures and services of poor countries.
- Bridging the digital and knowledge divides, thus bringing technology and information to people throughout the world.
- Providing financial and non-financial resources for international public goods especially medical and agricultural research.
- Increasing aid and debt relief to help countries to take actions to end poverty within a comprehensive framework.
- Giving a voice to poor countries and poor people in global forums.

The key features of globalization are:

(a) *Economic features*: Growth in Trade; Growth in FDI and Capital Flows; Global Production and consumption; Global competition; Trade and Investment Liberalization Policies and

(b) *Non-Economic Features*: Loss of National Sovereignty; Standardization of values and cultures.

In other words, a major feature of globalization is the growing concentration and monopolization of economic resources and power by transnational corporations and by global financing firms and funds and globalization of national policies and policy-making mechanisms. National policies (including economic, social, cultural and technological areas) that until recently were under the jurisdiction of States and people within a country have increasingly come under the influence of international agencies and processes or of big private corporations and economic/financial players. This led to erosion of national sovereignty and narrowed the ability of governments and people to make choices from options in economic, social and cultural policies. Governments now have to implement policies that are in line with the decisions and rules of these international institutions. The key institutions concerned are the World Bank, the International Monetary Fund (IMF) and the WTO.

The other fundamental premise of globalization is the relatively unhindered flow of goods and capital (but not people) across national boundaries. There are three economic manifestations of this phenomenon—international trade, international investment and international finance. Globalization requires country's openness to the world economy. There are four elements that are conventionally considered in determining a country's openness to the world economy. There is, most importantly, (i) the proportion of a country's gross domestic product (GDP) that is involved in the international trade of goods and services. Than there is (ii) the related element of the level of tariffs, which speaks to the degree of protection accorded to local production against imports from the world economy. Beyond trade there is (iii) the element of the degree of transnationalization of production, that is, the extent to which exchange of capital takes place for purposes of production; for the less developed countries, it refers primarily to the import of foreign direct investment (FDI). Transnationalization of production stands on a different footing from international trade, even though trade is involved prior or subsequent to the production process. Essentially, while in the area of international trade during the era of globalization the relevant actors treat the world as a global market, in the internationalization of production the relevant actors treat the world as a global factory, the different constituent parts or division of which are located in several countries, yet from a single production system. Finally, but not unrelated to the previous elements, in (iv) the extent of state controls on capital movements.

It is very common to hear the words privatization, globalization and liberalization. In fact, privatization and globalization are inherent in liberlization. The theoretical foundations for the policy of liberalization including privatization are provided by several interrelated strands of literature mainly contributed by New Right Schools of Thought, Property Rights Literature, the Principal-Agent Relationship and Organization and Management Literature. In all there are four New Right Schools of Thought. These are (i) the Chicago School led by Friedman; (ii) the Austrian School led by Hayek; (iii) Public Choice School led by Buchanan, Tullock and Niskanen; and (iv) the supply side Economics School led by Laffer, Gilder and Wanniski. The New Right Schools of thought, in spite of intellectual differences, broadly maintain that state involvement leads to increasing monopoly, increasing budget and suppressing of entrepreneurial behaviour, limiting choice, overproduction of unwanted services and encouragement to waste and inefficiency. In view of this, the New Right has forcefully argued retrieval of the State as a regulator and producer. Therefore, deregulation/liberalization and privatization are amongst six-point reform agenda of the New Right. The other measures are the reduction of inflation, lower taxation, increasing role of market forces in the provision of public services and institutional and constitutional reforms. The aim of these reforms is to promote competition between rival bureaucracies, reduce the influence of interest groups and corporatist institutions and impose a constitutional upper limit on the public expenditure as a proportion of the gross national product.

The theoretical base of globalization is directly rooted in the principle of comparative advantage, specialization in the production of goods and services based on factor endowment and competition results in benefits to all countries in international trade. In the open economy model (i.e. economy having linkages with global market), international trade leads to factor price equalization and optimum pattern of resource allocation globally.

Globalization is a calculated imperialist design of hegemonization in economic, political, ecological and cultural terrains, threatening loss of economic, self-reliance and political sovereignty, erosion of democratic structures and damaging of plural cultural identities. Not only this, employment of protectionist policies, discriminatory trade-conditions, direct intervention in the domestic affairs of LDCs regarding their intellectual property right amount to virtual 'trade war' and destabilization of the fragile economies and strife-ridden politics of the latter. Globalism would remain an idle fancy in the absence of genuine 'inter-nationalism' that is, egalitarian interaction among nations.

As a culmination of the unbridled, unrestrained 'multi-national' capitals, globalization leaves the poorer counties behind in global competition, as the clear objective of capital mobility is profit, prestige and power for its owners and not the well-being of the people at large. This is confirmed by historical and empirical evidence. It is intrinsic to the nature of capital, as articulated by Lenin most vociferously, to move towards exploitable resources. As investments capital has moved and modernized, it has also in the process exploited people and natural resources and often left behind pollution, poverty, inequality, injustice, crime, corrupting and a general degradation of environment—a record not much different from the imperialist history of aggressive capitalism, obsessed with growth.

Globalization is a totalizing process interim of both hegemonization and homogenization, and extended and subtler American version of European colonial/imperialist ambitions of domination, expropriating and transforming the world in its own image. Ideologically also, it is a derivative of the earlier conceptualizations of 'progress' and 'modernization', premised on the West-centric view of civilization, materialism and economies glorification of the 'invisible hand' of the market, growth-observed industrial industrialism, objectification of nature and an instrumental treatment of humanity.

The spectre of mass resistance and political movements is on the anvil in a majority of Third World societies that have set out in the direction of globalization, constantly haunting and scaring to generate chaos and degeneration of whatever little is achieved by these societies. It appears that eventually globalization will prove to be a disaster for the developing societies that will push them into the oblivion of anarchy and instability reminiscent of the Hobbesean state of nature.

The Reality of Globalization

The end of 20th century witnessed ushering in of an epoch of New World Order in which the idea of globalization found expression and flourished under the auspices and blessings of Bretton Wood institutions—notably the World Bank and International Monetary Fund—paving a way for the neo-capitalist hegemony and subjugation in a more vigorous but civilized manner. As a matter of fact, globalization is a latest dream selling exercise on the part of U.S. promising a transparent, free and rational world order, which will ultimately culminate into an ideal Global Village.

Liberalization, privatization and globalization are the buzzwords in contemporary world. All goals end here. Privatization worldwide began in

1980s because of rising debt and low commodity prices. Eastern Europe, Russia, Ukraine, Argentina, Brazil, Hungary, Mexico, Poland have already gone through the process. In support of privatization it is said that direct state involvement in commercial activities conflicts with its other roles. The real picture of liberalization, privatization and globalization is quite different and complex.

Uruguay Round Agreement brought the WTO into existence. WTO agreements appears to be based on the hypothesis that liberalization is the panacea for all ills in the economy, trade and commerce for the society. The Uruguay Round Agreement not only reduced trade barriers—by an average of 40 per cent—but also laid down rules for what kinds of policies governments can make on matters such as intellectual property and investment, making its impact more complex, more expensive to employment and more difficult to predict. It is generally advocated that the free trade would lead to higher rates of economic growth. But the fact is that economic globalization and trade liberalization have concentrated power in the larger entities we know as transnational corporations. It is the TNCs which have benefited the most in the era of globalization. Small farmers are unable to compete in the global economy and are being driven off their land, leaving the door wide open to the corporations. Free trade has enslaved the hungry rather than freed them. Trade can help to achieve food security, but only if it is democratic and free from corporate control; only if it helps rather than hinders the poor. Further, about one-third of the global trade conducted by the MNCs is instrumental in liquidating national economies. In the political sphere, the nation-states find themselves increasingly constrained, as new enters of power emerge to delimit political sovereignty in terms of foreign aid, IMF loans, deregulation etc. Growing concentration of economic 'resources and political power' has also aggravated social schisms and conflicts.

The modern world has corporate-managed trade rather than free trade. The trade liberalization has failed the poor and stands in danger of giving trade as a whole a bad name. The poor are going hungry because of the way the trading system is working. Trade liberalization—'free' trade, trade without barriers—is harming, not helping them. The trade liberalization that the WTO oversees appears to be failing the poor, hindering rather than helping them, and handing power to transnational corporations.

India urged that developing countries be allowed greater autonomy in establishing and supporting domestic agricultural policy. A purely market-based approach might not be appropriate for developing countries, it said; for some countries, it might be necessary to adopt a market-plus approach, in which non-trade concerns such as the maintenance of the livelihoods of the agrarian peasantry and the production of sufficient food to meet domestic needs are taken into consideration… [W]hile it may not be possible to immediately ensure that developing countries are able to produce at least a minimum percentage of their annual food requirements, this is a goal that has to be pursued.

Globalization has an adverse effect on poor developing countries with an inadequate national capacity. Almost all the countries of the Third World have signed the WTO. While most have gained, the poorest, 800 million hungry people, have lost. Any society, national or international, will ultimately be judged on whether its systems, rules and regulations assist the neediest. By that criterion, the current international trade system is failing. People go hungry because they are too poor to grow enough or to buy enough food. On the other hand, in the late 1990s the world, as a whole, spent more than US $500 billion to combat the supposed 'millennium bug'—ten times more than rich countries give to the poor each year in development assistance. By contrast, the amount needed to have world hunger free by 2015—a target agreed at the 1996 World Food Summit—would be US $60 billion dollars over 15 years, or US $4 billion per year in increased spending, hardly an excessive amount.

Globalization is transforming trade, finance, employment, migration, technology, communications, entertainment, the environment, social systems, values, ways of living, patterns of thinking, cultures and patterns of governance. Unemployment, poverty, inequality and alienation are increasing, partly as a result of globalization. Crime, drugs, terrorism, violence, civil wars, diseases and environmental destruction are becoming globalized. Capital, technology and advanced skills dominate the more reality dispensable factors: unskilled labour and the environment. Cost reductions are carried out and labour and nature suffer. Globalization offers great opportunity for human advance—but only the stronger governance.

The globalization of production is weakening state-centric schemes for implementing economic, social and cultural rights, most dramatically in the wealthier countries of the Northern Hemisphere. It does not however seem to be creating viable alternative mechanisms. Semi-permanent unemployment, attributable in part to the development of increasingly global mechanisms of production and exchange, has already led to a modest shrinking of the welfare state in many countries in Western Europe.

In any case, the impact of globalization on economy, society and polity extends beyond external openness in respect of foreign trade, tariff levels, transnationalization of production and capital controls. The existing attraction of globalization as well as international pressures, such as from the WTO, encourage domestic policy changes in an effort to bring about greater institutional convergence with the more advanced economies. These policy changes in turn, are likely to have additional impact on economy, society and polity.

Globalization is very uneven process, with unequal distribution of benefits and losses. This imbalance leads to polarization between the few countries and groups that gain, and the many countries and groups in society that lose out or are marginalized. Globalization, polarization, wealth concentration and marginalization are, therefore, linked through the same process. A World Bank study finds that the poorest 40 per cent of people in developing countries have seen their incomes fall since liberalization began. The evidence is powerful and it discredits the claims of Western government ministers that trade liberalization lessens poverty. The rapid growth of the global economy in recent decades is perhaps most clearly shown by the fact that in 1970 the total number of Transnational Corporations (TNCs) was about 700, but grew by 1998 to at least 53,607 TNCs that were contracted with at least 4,48,917 foreign subsidiaries. The six largest corporations in the world (Exxon, General Motors, Ford, Mitsu, Daimler-Chrysler, and Mitsubishi) have combined revenues larger than the combined budgets of 64 nations that include 58 per cent of the world's population (including India, Indonesia, Brazil, Russia, Pakistan, Bangladesh, Nigeria, and Mexico). Only seven nations have budgets larger than Ford, Exxon or General Motors: namely France, the United Kingdom, Italy, China, Japan, Germany, and the United States. Size of individual corporations in comparison to nations is impressive. However, their growing influence based on their growing number makes them even more powerful.

The world has become more polarized, with the gulf between the poor and rich of the world widening in recent years. From 1970 to 2000, the share of the poorest 20 per cent rose from 70 per cent to 85 per cent. Uneven globalization is bringing not only integration but also fragmentation, dividing communities and nations. In the aftermath of liberalization, manufacturing by licence has given way to competitive manufacturing. Free trade is merely the global manifestation of the division of labour. The forces of global integration and technological advance can and must be harnessed to serve the interests of poor people. In 2000, of the world 6 billion people, 2.8 billion live on less than $2 a day and 1.2 billion on less than $1 a day. Six infants of every 100 do not see their first birthday, and 8 do not survive to their fifth. Of those who do reach school age,

9 boys in 100 and 14 girls do not go to primary school. These conceal extraordinary diversity and variations.

Globalization has divided the world into several factions that may be called Davos, Seatlle, Moscow, Beijing, Tehran and Okinawa factions. The Davos faction includes some 1000 state and corporate elites that annually meet at Davos, Switzerland, to chart the course of globalization. It represents the interests of the Global 1000 largest TNCs and OECD group of rich nations. The Seattle Faction consists of those in the advanced capitalist countries protesting against World Trade Organization in Seattle last year, because their lives have been dislocated by globalization. The Moscow Faction is composed of those countries that by reason of their own failures or discrimination are being left out of the globalization bandwagon. The Beijing faction consists of those countries that have more or less successfully jumped on the bandwagon in the hope of benefiting from its fruits. As a Crossroad of Japanese, Chinese, Southeast Asian, and Western civilizations, the Tehran Faction could be interpreted to include the Islamic militant movement protesting against the economic, political and cultural domination of a Western world order. The most eloquent spokesperson for its views happens to be but a secular Christian Palestinian nationalist, Edward said.

Globalization is thus affecting different categories of countries differently. This process can broadly be categorized as follows: growth and expansion in the few leading or fully participating countries; moderate and fluctuating growth in some countries attempting to fit into the globalization/liberalization framework; and marginalization or deterioration experienced by many countries unable to get out of acute problems such as low commodity prices and debt, unable to benefit from export opportunities. The UNCTAD report also warns of the risks, stating "the process of globalization and liberalization can also give rise to a number of potential negative consequences and challenges to development." It gives details of the following three problems: loss of policy autonomy (the range of policy instruments available to developing countries has narrowed as a result of economic liberalization policies and stringent multilateral disciplines); financial openness and the risk of sentiments of external investor; and the phenomenon of marginalization (in which some developing countries, specially LDCs, are unable to benefit from or meaningfully participate in globalization due to structural supply-side weakness and debt).

The uneven and unequal nature of the present globalization process is manifested in the fast-growing gap between the world's rich and poor people and between developed and developing countries, and in the large differences among nations in the distribution of gains and losses.

A large number of people in the developed and developing nations have strong reservations about the benefits of globalization to the poor nations and they have shown their resentment through protests on various occasions. In advance of Seattle meeting, more than 1,200 NGOs from nearly a hundred countries—from environmentalists to labour unions, Third World development groups to consumer organizations—signed a 'stop the WTO round' petition. The international trading system, said the petitioners, is 'inequitable, un-transparent and in conflict with national and international regimes that promote high environment and development standards. They proposed a fundamental review of the system, and the development of 'an alternative, humane and sustainable international system of trade and investment relations.' And they urged governments to 'move away from the habit of shaping their international trade policies around offensive interests of large Transnational Corporations'. The recent meeting of WTO in France was also protested by the large number of people.

India and Liberalization

The aim of structural reform programme was to attain a higher rate of growth on sustainable basis through efficiency and productivity originating from relaxation of government controls over production, investment and prices in the domestic economy and progressively opening up of the Indian economy to foreign trade, capital and technology. The structural reform measures constitute the core of the economic liberalization.

Liberalization in India has two dimensions—internal and external. The domestic liberalization policy encompasses all facets of the Indian economy. However, thrust areas are industry, public enterprises, taxation, financial and infrastructure sectors.

The industrial sector has witnessed far-reaching reforms. The New Industrial Policy, 1991 abolished compulsory licensing for all except a few industries. The reform has enabled the taking out of the licensing system for more than 90 per cent of the industrial sector. In case of existing units, all major expansions are exempted from licensing. The existing and new units are provided a new broadbanding facility with a view to enabling them to produce any article without an additional investment.

In the area of public enterprises five major reforms have been introduced. First, monopoly of the state sector has been drastically reduced from seventeen to four. That is, thirteen industries have been opened to private sector, which was hitherto monopoly of the state sector. This is known as disguised privatization. Within existing public enterprises, sweeping changes favouring increasing role of market forces are in progress. These include performance improvement through a memorandum of understanding (MOU) system, referring of sick enterprises to the Board for Industrial and Financial Reconstruction (BIFR) for the formulation of revival/rehabilitation schemes or closure and enhanced autonomy to select public enterprises for enabling them to become global and domestic players.

Privatization has not been explicitly referred to in the NIP, 1991. Initially, the word privatization, it seems has been avoided partly due to political considerations. In the first budget (1991-92) immediately after the announcement of NIP, 1991, limited selling of government equity under the name of disinvestment policies was mentioned. The selling of government equity below 50 per cent continued till late nineties. It is during October 1999 budget that a full-fledged privatization policy was announced. Under privatization policy, 13 public enterprises and 21 hotels owned by the government have already been privatized.

Based on the recommendations of Chelliah Committee and Rekhi Committee Tax Reforms comprise of moderate rate of taxation, broadening the tax base, simplification in compliance and extension of modified value added tax (MODVAT) to other areas. Financial sector reforms consist of slashing of Statutory Liquidity Ratio (SLR) and thus increasing the availability of funds with banks, allowing private banks to expand, encouraging new entrants, simplification and rationalization of the interest rate structure. The Government has also opened insurance sector to private sector. The capital market is undergoing similar reforms.

The infrastructure sectors particularly telecommunication, power and roads which were traditionally monopolies have also been opened to the private sector.

External liberalization (i.e. globalization) in India has covered areas such as trade, foreign exchange, capital and technology. The major initiatives include current account convertibility of rupee, allowing exchange rate of rupee to be determined by the market forces in foreign exchange markets, abolition of import through licensing except for consumer goods, drastic reduction in import duties overtime, automatic approval of Reserve Bank of India for foreign equity in select high priority industries, the provision of automatic approval for technology agreements in select high priority industries. In addition, Foreign Institutional Investors (FIIs) registered with RBI are permitted to operate in the capital market.

Large number of incentives are provided to Non-Resident Indians (NRIs) and Overseas Corporate Bodies (OCBs) to invest in India. Indian firms are also allowed to raise capital from International market through Global Depository Receipts (GDRs) and Foreign Currency Convertible Bonds (FCCBs).

Scarcity of income distribution data, obviously, makes it very difficult to arrive at precise assessment of the impact of Globalization on income inequalities, but it is clear that even after nearly one decade of advent of Globalization in India a vast gulf exists between the different income-earners with, as per World Development Report, 1999, top 20 per cent of the population accounting for 39.3 per cent of the total income while share of the bottom 20 per cent was only 9.2 per cent.

The point about retailing the foregoing data about persistence of individual-level poverty is that it gives rise to doubts about the positive pay-offs of Globalization as far as the regional inequalities also are concerned. While data sets about income inequalities at individual or percentile and decline levels are relatively scarce, a number of regional or inter-state inequalities data-sets have been generated making it possible to assess the impact of Globalization on real disparities.

According to *Economic Times* Research, the annual data show that over the period 1996 to 2000, 38 per cent of the companies declared losses at the net level in 2000 as compared to 16 per cent in 1996. In the period of economic reforms does the loss-making companies whose percentage has increased represent the cost of liberalization.

The cost of economic reforms is also reflected in the number of cases with the Board for Industrial and Financial Reconstruction (BIFR). BIFR till the year 1998 has compiled figures about sick companies on the edge of closure. A total net worth of Rs. 17,815.56 crore. has been wiped out two and half times over by accumulated losses amounting to Rs. 7,159.54 crore. Over 2,454 units across 19 industries are affecting around 15 lakh workers. The extent of human disaster is particularly acute in industries like textiles, metallurgy, jute etc.

The various Rounds of Surveys conducted by the National Sample Survey Organization (NSSO) reveal that the average annual growth rate of overall employment (in both the organized and unorganized sectors) was 2.73 per cent per annum in the period 1972-73 to 1977-78 but declined to 1.54 per cent per annum in 1983 to 1987-88 to 1993-94. As per the 55th Round (July 1999–June 2000) of the Survey on employment conducted by the NSSO overall employment grew by about 1 per cent per annum during 1993-94 to 1999-2000. Employment in absolute numbers has risen from

303 million in 1983 to 374 million in 1994 (2.04%) and to 397 million in 2000 (0.98 %). The labour force participation rate deceleration in the growth of the labour force from 2.29 per cent per annum in 1987-88 to 1993-94, to 1.03 per cent per annum in the period 1993-94 to 1999-2000.

A more detailed scrutiny of the inter-state variations in the growth-pattern (UNDP, 1999) shows that two states with high per capita income in 1980-1991, viz. Punjab and Haryana lost momentum in the nineties while Maharashtra and Gujarat overshot them indicating that during the Globalization era the Green Revolution lost steam while industry-based growth of Maharashtra and Gujarat was gathering speed. In case (and the probabilities of this being the case are high) economic momentum of Punjab and Haryana declines further the inequalities between the different states of the Indian federal system would certainly be aggravated significantly. In more specific terms, states like Tamil Nadu, Kerala, West Bengal, Madhya Pradesh, Andhra Pradesh and Karnataka would continue to stay at their current GNP ranks while Punjab and Haryana would decline and Gujarat and Maharashtra far ahead while Uttar Pradesh, Bihar and Odisha would continue to remain at the bottom unless those associated with "public governance" address this issue of persisting areal imbalances directly rather than letting the markets (read: MNCs) adopt their basic policy of "Betting upon the strong".

Thus, a worrisome aspect of the impact of Globalization upon the state economies is revealed by the fact there are not only wide-ranging areal differentials in terms of decline of poverty in India but the "Green Revolution" states are finding it difficult to sustain their (low) poverty-shares. While Punjab and Haryana had, till recently taken giant strides in poverty reduction, but, Haryana has already begun to slip with its BPL share in population rising from 0.92 per cent in 1983-84 to 1.83 per cent in 1987-88 and then dipping but still remaining higher at 1.37 per cent in 1993-94 than 1983-84; More recent Planning Commission data updated to 1999-2000 has shown that Haryana has regained its 'quit poverty' momentum but, in a paper prepared as recently as October 2001, Jeffery Sachs, Nirupan Bajpai and Annathi Ramiah have noted that following the Green Revolution high growth occurred in Punjab and Haryana and also, to a lesser extent, in other adjacent states of Rajasthan, Gujarat and Maharashtra, but populous eastern states like U.P. and Bihar failed to take advantage of Green Revolution and this factor can be regarded a cause of "divergence" or enhancement in inter-state inequalities during the Globalization process in India.

One of the most visible manifestations of what one might call a

"Globalization failure" pertains to the strategic front of inequalities, a failure which assumes great poignancy in the case of ROI since elimination of inequalities, individual as well as areal, was one of the most prominent items on the manifesto of its long "freedom struggle"; the Indian National Congress, which enjoyed pre-eminent dominance for the first four decades of the short ROI history and which is even now in control of as many as 14 states spread in all corners of its vast territory, is also committed to this goal making monitoring of the economic dispersion of the gains (and losses) of Globalization in terms of the territorial contours of the Indian political system an urgent necessity as the political parties which evolve the "correct" policies of public governance on this score is likely to gain better territorial acceptability.

Even the Father of the Nation Mahatma Gandhi, who was fond of and always emphasized for 'Swadeshi' set tone of globalization as early as in *Young India,* June 1, 1921, when he said that "**I do not want my house to be walled in an all sides and my window to be stuffed. I want the cultures of all lands to be blown about my house as freely as possible. But I refuse to be blown off my feet.**" But one can see the clear-cut difference between present day globalization and Gandhian concept of globalization.

Present day Globalization	Gandhian concept of Globalization
Alienation—man, society and nation	Integration—man, society and nation
Materialistic approach	Humanistic approach
Market-centric	Man-centric
Capitalism	Sarvodaya
Domination and conquest	Cooperation and change
Structural violence	Structural non-violence
Development	Sustainable development
Freedom	Swaraj
Dichotomy—man and nature	Harmony—man and nature

Mr. Manmohan Singh advocated greater interaction with the world and warned that "**if our economy is not equipped to absorb, assimilate, and to adopt this technical change which is taking place, all-over the world, I think we will be marginalized. Many developing economies are already being marginalized in the new global economic system that has emerged.**"

If the prevailing political and administrative environment continues, the possibility of recurring crises in the near future is not ruled out. The symptoms have already started appearing. Sluggishness in exports in spite of gradual devaluation of rupee *via* open market, increasing fiscal deficit, downgrading in international credit rating of India, bearish trend in the stock market, non-preparedness of the Indian people particularly the elite to pay more taxes etc. are signalling towards another crisis. Liberalization, privatization and globalization policies seem irreversible in India. India should strive to manage these mega trends to the best of its advantages.

Summing up

Human Development Report champions the agenda of the world's weak, those marginalized by globalization, and calls for a much bolder agenda of global and national reforms to achieve globalization with a human face. It cautions that globalization is too important to be left as unmanaged as it is at present, because it has the capacity to do extraordinary harm as well as good.

Liberalization, privatization and globalization policies have been exercising considerable influence on people and government. In developing countries like India, governance has responded both slowly and unevenly to economic liberalization. It is mainly due to the fact that liberalization policy in India has not evolved indigenously through the participation of political, bureaucratic and other institutions of governance. The liberalization policy is mainly adopted under the influence of World Bank-IMF combine. In case of India, the institutions of economic governance have responded very quickly to economic liberalization. The post-liberalization phase has witnessed amendments in many economic laws as well as introduction of economic laws to deal with changed environment.

Supremacy of economic institutions particularly finance ministry accompanied by erosion in the role of planning commission in economic policy making is another outcome of economic liberalization. Setting of new institutions such as Ministry of Disinvestments, Disinvestments Commission, Expenditure Commission and regulatory authorities in the field of telecom, power and insurance have increased the jurisdiction of economic administration in the Indian economy. Very fast growth of economic administration in response to liberalization, however, has not succeeded in achieving its goals such as a higher rate of growth on sustainable basis accompanied by improved efficiency and productivity in the Indian economy.

Further, these initiatives have covered mainly those services and areas, which cater to the elite. The areas of social concern such as poverty, unemployment, regional disparities and sectoral imbalance which have borne the burnt of liberalization policy have been kept out of these initiatives. This combination of coverage and neglect, if continued on the one hand would help the elite to consolidate its advantaged position and become partner of the ruling coalition of politicians and bureaucrats. On the other hand, it would alienate further the disadvantageous groups, sectors and regions from the mainstream.

Competitive markets may be the best guarantee of efficiency, but not necessarily of equity. Liberalization and privatization can be a step to competitive markets—but not a guarantee of them. And markets are neither the first nor the last word in human development. Many activities and goods that are critical to human development are provided outside the market—but these are being squeezed by the pressures of global competition. There is a fiscal squeeze on public goods, a times squeeze on care activities and an incentive squeeze on the environment.

In order to widen their policy options in the future and to strengthen their bargaining power, developing countries have to organize themselves to strive for a more democratic global system.

Greater collaboration among regional institutions of the South (for example, ASEAN, SAARC, SADC, Mercosur, Caricom etc.) especially in sharing of information and coordination of policies and positions, would be beneficial.

The developing countries should have more rights of participation in decision-making processes in the IMF, World Bank and WTO, which should also be made more accountable to the public and to the local and poor communities.

In the 21st century, much more focus has to be placed on changing economic policies and behaviour in order that the patterns of consumption and production can be made environmentally sound. What need to be discussed is not only the development model of the South but much more the economic model of the North and of course, to international economic order.

There is also a need to strive for governance at a national level that combines economic development, environmental concern and social justice. In both North and South, the wide disparities in wealth and income within countries have to be narrowed. In a situation of improved equity, it would be more possible to plan and implement strategies of economic adjustment to ecological and social goals.

As globalization becomes the new mantra of the powerful on the planet with the unholy Trinity—the IMF, the World Bank, and the WTO—claiming that it will solve all the economic problems of the world (including poverty and deprivation), it is time for the countries of Asia, Africa and South America to pause, take stock and critically appraise the whole process, examining the true and only options available to them.

The developing countries must be provided with a range of options regarding when, how and to what extent they should open their economics. For this, they must press their case in international forums and institutions where decisions on the global economy are made. Failure to do so would mean that they are subjected interminably to policies that further development prospects and options as well.

In the post-Covid-19 period, the entire notion of globalisation is threatened by the nation-states. Now the people believe in self-sufficient economy of the nation. Covid has already changed the people's behaviour and the way they think and live. Technology is recasting and reformulating man, society and the nation. Even the market and the concept of security is changing fast and domination of artificial intelligence and technology is increasing in every sense. We are aboard a train, which is gathering speed, racing down a track on which there are an unknown number of switches leading to unknown destinations. No single scientist is in the engine cab and there may be demons at the switch. Most of the societies are in the caboose looking backward.

REFERENCES

A.S. Bhalla (Ed.), Globalization, Growth and Marginalization, London, Macmillan Press Ltd., 1998.

Adarsh Kishore, "Globalization, Living Standards and Equity: Recent Progress and Continuing Challenges: National Experience–India", Paper presented at the Workshop for G-20 Members, Sydney, May 26-28, 2002. Mimeo.

Ahluwalia, M.S. "The Economic Performance of The States in The Post-Reform Period" in Rakesh Mohan (Ed.) *Facets of The Indian Economy,* New Delhi, OUP, 2002.

Alternative Economic Survey 2000-2001, New Delhi, Alternative Survey Group, 2001.

B.R. Nayar, *Globalization and Nationalism: The Changing Balance in India's Economic Policy, 1950-2000,* New Delhi, Sage Publications, 2001.

B. Ramesh Babu (Ed.), *Globalization and the South Asian State,* New Delhi, South Asian Publishers, 1998.

Beyer, P. (1994) Religion and Globalization, London, *Sage.*

Dieter Bos, *Privatisation: A Theoretical Treatment. Oxford: Clarendon* Press, 1991.

Dollar, David, *Globalization, Inequality and Poverty Since 1980,* Washington DC., World Bank, Mimeo, 2001.

Eisenstadt, S.N., *Modernization: Protest and Change,* Delhi, Prentice Hall, 1969.

Fukuyama, F., *The End of History and the Last Man,* New York, Free Press, 1992.

Hirst, P.Q. and Thompson. *Globalization in Question,* London, Cambridge, 1996.

Kurian, N.J., "Widening Regional Disparities in India: Some Indicators", *Economic and Political weekly,* February, 12, 2000:538-*550.*

Louis De Alessi, "*T*he Economics of Property Rights: A Review of the Evidence", *Research in Law and Economics,* Vol. 2., 1980.

Magdoff, Harry. (1992) *Globalization: To What End?* New York, Monthly Review Press, 1992.

Peter Aucoin, The New Public Management: Canada in Comparative Perspective, Montreal, Canada: Institute for Research on Public Policy, 1995.

Prahlad K. Basu et al., Governance and Government: Emerging Scenarios in the 21st *Century (Report for FCPC), New Delhi, 1996.*

*Roberet J. Holton, Globalizati*on and the Nation-State, Londo*n, Macmillan Press Ltd., 1998.*

*Ro*stow, W.W., The Stages of Economic Growth: A *Non-Communist Manifesto, London,* Cambridge University Press, 1960.

UNDP, 1999, *Diversity and Disparities in Human Development: Key Challenges for India,* New Delhi.

V.S. Sheth (Ed.), *Globalization and Interdependence: Africa and India,* Mumbai, Allied Publishers Ltd., 2000.

World Bank, *World Developmen*t *Report,* Washington DC., 2001.

3

Globalization and New World Order

India's Role in South Asia

Amna Mirza

Debating Globalization

Globalization is always being a buzzword for international politics. Though the narrative of globalization is talked by all, yet there is less debate on what it is actually about. Although global connections have an impact on all aspects of our lives, but this question remains complex for our times. While going into the roots we can find about Silk Road across Central Asia that connected China and Europe during the middle Ages or trading by European companies in many other colonies, it can be find out that the idea of trade and exchange did exist in the past as well. Though movement of goods and services, such interaction is not new, but the 'scale and nature' of interconnected today merits attention.

Since the end of Second World War, world has indeed become more interlinked through innovations, developments and advances in communication, science and technology. The neo-liberal policy and structural measures with it under the rubric of free trade, market capitalism promoted changes. However, there is other side of the coin as well where according to American Sociologist Immanuel Wallerstein in his perspective of world system, that capitalist and its related economic processes were paving way for development where rich grew at expense of poor. Further, we must note that changes—both positive and negative—that globalization brought affected social, political, and economic milieu and activities across national borders.

Anthony Giddens opines that globalisation involves a complex interaction of the dialectics of global and local-intensification of worldwide social relations that local and global are related.[1] The global politics witnessed a contrast—Globalization led to increase in opportunities and choices, efficiency, growth, profits etc. However, when gaps between rich and poor, inequality, injustice, insecurity, poverty, malnutrition, increase in rampant cases of non-traditional security dimensions like narcotics, terrorism, pandemics etc. then surely globalization has brought huge disadvantages also. It may have ushered unprecedented human advance for some but has also lethally reduced opportunities for others.

The Transition: Future of Globalization

The world is witnessing tectonic degree of change. Amidst the transition in world economics, finance, and power as the era of globalization is being interrogated, the centre of gravity with Brexit, Rise of President Trump's ideas of Make America Great Again, somewhere the idea of contract between citizens and government is being changed too.[2] In this turning point, there are debates that globalisation gave us benefits—free flow of money, people, goods, services ideas, but wealth inequality, imbalances in global economy cannot be ignored too.

Globalisation always faced a paradox that states valued own interests. The process of integration of world markets and interdependence oscillated between competition and cooperation. There are theorists who have presented alternative perspectives, like for innovative development as alternate to traditional ideological practices, need for justice in migration policies, working on pluralism akin to John Rawls ideas, amongst others.[3]

Deglobalization: Old and New Debates

Globalization was perceived as only acceptable way-out for nurturing ties. It may not be same for all but deepening and broadening of economic and social ties were inevitable and unstoppable. United Nations' Secretary-General Kofi Annan also remarked in 1999 that Globalization is an irreversible process, not an option. With narrative moving towards looking at isolating from others and blaming ravages of open transactions as cause for loss during trade-off and inter-change, phase of deglobalization has been observed.[4] Money is no more that mobile as it used to be with reports indicating towards. Foreign direct investment, Multinational companies' cross-border investments going below earlier levels due to pressures of deglobalization.

The idea of "deglobalization", was a scheme proposed by Walden Bello, in response to the Asian Financial Crisis of 1997.[5] It does not mean isolation, segregation and withdrawing from the world economy. It demands that world economic and political system should be restructured and reorganised in such a way that creates right condition to build the capacity of local and national economies. It signified the transformation of a global economy from one oriented towards the needs of transnational corporations to one oriented towards the needs of peoples, societies and nations. For deglobalization, diversity, miscellany and localisation are key tenets because grand narrative cannot answer these complexities. There is no "one size fits all" model.

Main ideas of deglobalization are namely—reorient national economies away from export production, implement policies that redistribute the sources of income and wealth, expanding public services in rural areas, de-emphasise focus on economic growth, recognise carrying capacity of the Earth, nurture participatory democracy, amongst others. At that time when approach of deglobalization was still under construction, no body imagined that it will be represented again, debated and joined with issues of future, that it is being looked as viable alternatives to the flawed system we have today by those very forces who are responsible.

The world history has seen protectionism earlier. Wall Street crash followed by Communism, regulation and controls, somewhat a similar degree of segregation is repeating now. Therefore, it is being opined that we are in a deglobalization period in the second wave. This brings us to next significant issue, what drives deglobalization? Which advocates that in globalization winners were few but those who lost were more.[6] The world saw the aftermath when Britain and the United States pull themselves out from the global trading system in 1930s, protectionism at the outset of the Great Depression—abandoning gold standard, devaluation, huge tariffs, uneasy terms or trade and ambiguities. These economic ruptures caused by political insecurities gave a breeding ground for Germany and Japan to pursue their own preferential policies and nativist politics.[7]

Seclusion and protectionism are being seen in policy stands taken by United States and this is also leading to speculation over consequences of a strong dollar. It is going in a notorious way—where at one hand there is fiscal stimulus in infrastructure while at the other hand one sees reports of closing borders, plans for border taxes just as an explanation to block cheaper imports. These economic links are a matter of concern and apprehension. There are more fears—as one can see that moving outside of an open border world or what one can say—going back or doing a U-turn on globalization—may just lead to negative impacts. It may cause inducement for greater inflation and thereby also cast an impact on investments and exchange rates. Movement towards protectionist policies have an impact on global financial flows and this further leads to risk of debt defaults and restructurings thereof.[8]

Re-Globalization

History has never been linear in its movement and progress. Similarly, globalization as a phase of history has had its ups and downs where it has been observed over several decades. If on one side it gave the world unprecedented benefits, then also at other side it was the cause of widening gap between the rich and the poor, schism between capital and labour. To critiques who say that it will be stalled soon, there is an alternative view that globalization will continue but with a different tenor and pitch. A narrative of a similar variant was echoed *via* idea of "reglobalization" wherein China at Davos World Economic Forum attributed great significance to make globalization and global governance work again.[9]

It is a matter of fact that globalization is in crisis and needs changes. Twists and turns of globalization have a bearing on Emerging world order. China is ready to dissent against any attempt towards containment. Through its ambitious strategy network build-up, infrastructure development, it is seeking to pursue agenda of globalization. It presented taking up the One Belt, One Road, a new global public good to sustain global governance.[10] Experts have dubbed this as '*Chiglobalization*'. This shall be defined by leadership, relevance and influence of China which will lead to a new vision for humanity, economic development, global and domestic governance, marked by a true sense of cosmopolitan culture with multiculturalism, inter-culturalism and pragmatism. So as United states abandons Trans-Pacific Partnership, this may help accelerate what we may say—Chiglobalization.

India and New World Order with South Asian Axis

Past attainments and sectoral collaboration cannot be the only basis of successful regional alignment. India must consider divergent approaches followed by its common neighbourhood. Geography, history, international context and domestic politics all account together to define politics of South Asia. Alongside porous borders, one must take in account—that state boundaries South Asia are new, where the paradox is that civilizations, languages, and beliefs are ancient. Excluding Pakistan, most of South Asian nations have been non-aligned. Globalization implied change and interdependence which lead greater integration in world economy in 1990s. South Asia is always analysed with reference to complexity in terrain, geopolitical and economic issue. With change being the only constant, it is important for South Asian region to develop a business framework and let it emerge as a global narrative. India with focus on ideas of digitization, empowering the indigenous macro-economy and then leap towards global economy can indeed play an important role in the debate of analysis of future of globalization.

Recent times have seen that the geopolitics of southern Asia has been intricate and erratic. There are several levels of the problem—greater involvement outside, rising competitions, unstable dynamics of India, Pakistan, China etc., contest what they all seek in economic development, regional and sub-regional cooperation, and security. At time of this ambiguity—where future is overwrought and the world seems less supportive of resurgent South Asia.[11] This requires what has been argued by experts that deeper engagement between politics, business and science.[12] Without this, India might not gain now of de-globalization and technological changes. India has a significant role to play in these churnings of power. It has gained much bigger stake which is growing with time. This puts the onus on India to ensure that world markets remain connected and open. Further it is its national interest also to see that the nation continues globalization. Recognising the significance of this idea, it even mooted the proposal for a coalition of middle-income countries to support for globalization at the time when political backlash is occurring in the United States and parts of Europe against free trade and investment.[13] At a time when globalization is being questioned, world is looking for new power centres, India can offer a new narrative by exploring avenues of regional cooperation in trade and energy. World needs sustainable energy avenues and India can surely set an example there.[14]

The global world is facing challenges and the erstwhile players are leaving it. Non-traditional security threats like narcotics, piracy and organized crime further add to complexities. At this juncture, emerging economies like India can help to re-write the story towards promotion of sustainable globalization, and build coalitions to counter issues like terrorism, pandemics, climate change. No doubt there are issues and global challenges which have been caused by globalization but India should take leap in South Asia to foster an open world economy, multilateral trade regime and facilitate healthy development of globalization further.

Globalization implied change and interdependence. Further South Asia is always analysed with reference to complexity in terrain, geopolitical, economic issues. With change being the only constant, it is important for South Asian region to develop a business framework and let it emerge as a global narrative.[15] India with focus on ideas of digitalization, empowering the indigenous macro-economy and then leap towards global economy can indeed play an important role in this debate of analysis of future of globalization.

South Asia's saga of globalization has not been good—as the costs of the recent phase of globalization were a burden on the poor while benefits were limited for limited section. Rise in productivity and ushering reforms, increase in global trade, finance and services never lead to any levelling of incomes. Governments may have opened their markets, but they ignored the abilities of people to keep pace with new forces of globalization. At this phase when globalization is itself exposed to new strains, countries like India can lead to voice concern for economic growth to be job-oriented, with labour and knowledge-intensive patterns of production and distribution.

Mechanisms of regional economic cooperation in South Asia have never had a stable routine. Its negotiating power in global forums also has not been united because of the political game play that prevail in the region. Market integration and capital was mobile, but it did not impact all equally, capital moved freely, but majority of unskilled and informal labour did not. Trade agreements were biased towards goods of interest for the West.[16] India should do a realistic assessment of the impact of globalization, analyse the harsh side that may have been ignored, revive and draw attention to the debate that if one wants more benefit from globalization, the need of the hour is work together. In the age of deglobalization, Brexit, foreign policy acquires heighted significance as against domestic policies because Politics with economics can lead to unforeseen consequences.

When the World faced the COVID-19 pandemic, which led to unprecedented crisis. Further, South Asian region with highly populated countries, witnessed new challenges in addition to existing ones. Amidst the health crisis and humanitarian issues within it, the role of India was factored in to be important. As an emerging economy, India can lead to betterment of itself, region and other countries also by putting forward the need for an ecosystem that thrives on innovation and translating problems into solutions.[17]

When China is fostering pan-Eurasian infrastructure initiative as a part of its grand plan for geopolitical domination, India must counter Hegemonistic designs which may be hidden under the presumed logic of connectivity and trade. It requires that India too attempts to re-globalize keeping its concern for sovereignty and territorial integrity, tap benefit of open borders by Striving for Asia-Africa Growth Corridor, linkages in Africa, which will go a long way as a strategy to overcome encirclement by hostile neighbour. At a time when globalization is being questioned, world is looking for new power centres, India can offer new narrative by exploring avenues of cooperation in trade, energy and achieving sustainable goals. World needs new perspective and India can surely set an example there.

The corona pandemic showed the world that there shall be tectonic shifts in global governance. There were remarks being made that we are entering a new world order. The prolonged economic slowdown dire to lockdown has affected stability of economy in many nations. Amidst this churning, dynamics of power and hierarchy of globalization are being challenged.

There are concerns as to who will be the next superpower and geopolitics has an important role to play in this regard. Also, with debates on changes in mode and context of globalization there are remarks about trade and domestic apparatus wherein technology and new sources of power like economic gains, development of human resources, knowledge economy, amongst others are important.

Instances of calls for "Quad plus", which includes India is important too for South Asian power dynamics. India has also called for important ideas like globalization with human face, need for continuing cooperation and humanitarian work with neighbours amidst crisis.

Any strategy of India with respect to China, is bound to be complex as the two nations have a lot of issues of debates as well as agreements for history, people, trade ties etc. Looking at the fact 'disruption' is a major feature of present-day world scenario, and herein India must recast its economic relation with China from trade oriented to larger blueprint based on industrialization, technology entrepreneurship etc. at a time when hegemony drives China, placing the need for Asian Unity at backburner, India must carve a bigger role for itself in recurring geopolitics and economic engagements in South Asia.

India needs to have right coordination of its domestic politics with industrial policies, to ensure it can cut across Chinese supremacy in trade agreement with Vietnam, Singapore, Asian India's cultural diversity, has ensured that it has a unique standing in South Asia. India has been reported to be most prepared tourist destination as against Maldives, Nepal, Sri Lanka etc.

Today when problems of World polity are complex where threats cut across the borders, and defy the conventional norms, herein an innovative approach is needed to cure ailing issues of global development. Further, doubts are being casted over monolithic and unidirectional way of globalization. The call to roll back forces of integration and interdependence is justified by the proponents based on inequities surrounding the myriad global processes. Taking the lead in issues of reform of globalization, India can offer a better narrative for South Asian politics.

The idea to let globalization sustain but with reforms, placing people over profits, can also enable India to present a new perspective for South Asian integration, based on cooperation, thereby defeating the expansionist dogmas. Such efforts will also be welcomed in global polity as the world is looking for paths to drive out of chaos.

South Asian neighbourhood is defined by great civilizational bonds, cultural affinity, heritages, yet with unequal geography and resources. Geopolitics of the region has an important link with global issues. If India can work to churn out new perspectives on need to revise global integration at a time when world polity is witnessing division based on globalization, de-globalization, and re-globalization, it shall not only be beneficial for global relations but also offer inputs on reworking of regional integration for other countries too.

Regionalism, regional integration has often been seen in contradiction with globalization. At one point, one is talking about interconnected markets and free world, while the other offers a picture of integration within a region only. However, one must understand the fact that both need common set of assumptions and support system to let it sustain—namely correct ideals, apt economic and domestic support. Further, today both globalization and regional integration are suffering on account of fallout of working of markets—wherein some gained, and many lost, or that giving primacy to only gains in sense of survival of the fittest. Interestingly, the need to re-engage on terms based on equity and inclusivity are panacea to reform both.

South Asia is one of the most populated regions in world, wherein with 1.5 billion people, it is home of 25 per cent of World population. These human resources asset need right blend of development, employment, sustainable energy, environment, which can be there with apt mechanisms of reforms in laws, right coordination of policies from. Education to industry, interdisciplinary perspectives to factor growth with humane element. India has the potential to unite and bridge the chords and with narrative of reformed globalization, that consolidates domestic strengths and lead towards integration in World apparatus based on rectifying mistakes of past and enable South Asia to play an important role in the global World.

ENDNOTES

1. Anthony Giddens, *The Consequences of Modernity*. Polity Press, Cambridge, 1991, pp. 71-75.
2. Michael O'Sullivan, *The Levelling: What's Next After Globalization*, Punlo Affairs, Hachette UK, 2019, pp. 2-8.
3. Alexander N. Chumakov, William C. Gay (ed.), 'Introduction', *Between Past Orthodoxies and the Future of Globalization: Contemporary Philosophical Problems*, Koninkjilke, BRILL, Netherlands, 2016, pp. 9-15.
4. Finbarr Livesey, why 2017 could be the year globalisation dies, Wired: United Kingdom, London, 17 May, 2017, link: http://www.wired.co.uk/article/finbarr-livesey-globalisation
5. Walden Bello, *Deglobalization: Ideas for a New World Economy*, Zed Books: London, 2004.
6. "We are in a deglobalization period: Business historian Geoffrey G. Jones", *Live Mind*, February 18, 2017, New Delhi.
7. Konrad Takabuski, "If you thought globalization was bad, just wait for deglobalization", *The Globe and Mail*, November 17, 2016.
8. Dambisa Moyo, US protectionism and deglobalisation spell inflation, February 6, 2017, http://blogs.ft.com/the-exchange/2017/02/06/protectionism-and-deglobalisation-spell-inflation-and-debt-defaults/
9. "Re-globalization Heralds an Emerging New World Order", *The BRICS Post*, January 9, 2017.
10. W. Jia, Now, "Globalization With Chinese Characteristics–Analysis", *Yale Global Online*, June 7, 2017.
11. Shivshankar Menon, "Brace Yourself, South Asia's Geopolitics Is Becoming More Complex, Less Stable", *The Wire*, 6 June, 2017.
12. C. Raja Mohan, "Raja Mandala: Battling de-globalisation", *Indian Express*, February 14, 2017, New Delhi.
13. "India Calls for Middle-income Country Coalition to Revive Globalisation", *Reuters,* 8 June, 2017.
14. Narottam P. Banskota, "Introduction", in *South Asia Trade and Energy Security: The Role of India*, Universal-Publishers, USA, 2012, pp. 9-10.
15. Shaista Khilji, and Chris Rowley Elsevier, *Globalization, Change and Learning in South Asia*, Chandos Publishing, Oxford, UK, 2013, pp. 2-10.
16. T.K. Rajalakshmi, "Globalisation in South Asia", *The Hindu Frontline*, Volume 19—Issue 09, April 27—May 12, 2002.

17. ORF Webinar, Technology, governance innovation and the pandemic: Discussing responses from South Asia and Africa, 26 June 2020, https://www.google.com/amp/s/www.orfonline.org/research/technology-governance-innovation-pandemic-discussing-responses-southasia-africa-67527/

4

Religio-Cultural Revivalism in India in the Era of Cultural Globalization

A Critical Analysis

Umesh Kumar

Introduction

The process of globalization has made entire world undoubtedly more connected and informed than before. In liberal normative imagination, globalization is considered as the carrier of modernity and democracy and emancipating entire world. However, the process of globalization itself has not been democratic in terms of lack of equal participation and representation of different cultures and nations. The various national and cultural identities are marginalized and not given proper representation and their due share in the process of globalization. It is claimed by the scholars that the Western cultures (European and American) have secured dominant position in the system of flow of wealth, and large interest and share of the benefits through the process of globalization goes to them. The critics to the globalization suggest that 'West' led by America is basically intended to the endorsement of the imperialistic interests through the process of globalization. When globalization is seen as a hegemonic process, it is argued that it serves the interests of global capitalist class and powerful states. Therefore, it has a negative impact on vulnerable people across the world and creating inequalities. It is frequently generalized that Western hegemony in the cultural sphere has threatened other cultures specially the global south. The Western domination over the process of the globalization has resulted in the radical responses from the non-Western world and demand for the democratization of the process of globalization (Gamage, 2016, Owolabi, 2001).

The responses in the cultural field have majorly come with the religio-cultural context in majority of the countries. It is argued that the globalization in its responses or consequences (it is the matter of contestation among scholars) has helped to the religious-revivalism. In India globalization, by the flow of the capital and technological development, helped majority religion and led to the increasing Hindu-religiosity among the burgeoning and largely middle class. It facilitated to the intensification of the Hindu-nationalist idea and expanded Hindutva and Brahmanical ritualistic practices across the India (Nanda, 2009). Luce (2011) and Singh & Haigh (2015) are of the view that process of globalization and new technology like television and Internet has resulted into nationalization of Hinduism. The Hinduism is becoming a unified religion and Hindu festivals are now celebrated across India. The conservative practices and caste affinity are loosening (Luce, 2011: 312-313, Singh & Haigh, 2015 cited in Singh and Aktor, 2015). In my observation, it is not the case that Hinduism is naturally being accepted by people across India rather it is marketization and consumerization of the Hindu practices and festivals by Brahmanical forces which dominate market spaces and the homogenization of Hindu culture is also being imposed over people by political power under the banner of Hindutva political ideology.

The expansion of Hindutva has threatened the local indigenous cultures, independent ideologies and worldviews and overall, it contradicts the idea of India as a modern nation which is based on the idea of 'unity in diversity'. The biggest contradiction in the context of Hindutva's interaction with globalization comes when the Hindutva project keenly show interest to participate in the economic globalization but at the same time reject the free cultural interaction. The Hindutva agenda rejects the Western cultures and education by projecting 'West' as the enemy and 'other' and asserts on the restoration of the so called 'Hindu ancient glory'. Contrary, the critics illustrate on the positive side of the cultural globalization that it promotes democratic norms and freedom that helps the marginalized classes and lower strata of the people to break the structure of the traditional slavery and opens the way up to emancipate them (it could be possible through the democratization of cultural globalization). It also helps culturally marginalized groups (Dalits, women, religious minorities, tribal communities and others) to search their independent identity and their 'self' or individual agency (Ilaiah, 2001). Therefore, the different arguments, perspectives, paradoxes and complexities about the cultural globalization have to be explained in detail and the religio-cultural revivalism in India in the form of Hindutva project has to be critically analyzed.

Understanding Globalization

Globalization is defined as the widening, deepening, and speeding up of worldwide 'interconnectedness'. Some argue that it is bringing about the demise of the sovereign nation-state. The global forces and institutions undermine the ability of governments to their own economies, societies and cultures (Scholte, 2000). In contrast, critics reject this idea and argue that states and geopolitics remain the principal agents and forces shaping world order (Gilpin, 2001). Whatever the case, but one thing could not be rejected that over the last three decades the sheer scale and scope of global interconnectedness has become increasingly evident in every sphere, from the economic to the cultural (Baylish *et al.*, 2011).

Though globalization is comprehended as an 'interconnectedness' paradigm, a trans-planetary process involving increasing liquidity and growing multidirectional flows as well as the structures (Ritzer, 2006), but in a critical observation, the flows are not the free flows which benefit everyone equally. It is understood as the project intended for the promotion of 'enlightenment modernity' across the globe led by the West with its neo-liberal agenda based on 'openness' that could help in the establishment and smooth functioning of the global capitalist market system (Lieber and Weisberg, 2002).

Today, this phenomenon is evident in almost every sphere of the life— economic, political and cultural. Even though the economic and political aspects of globalization have widely been written and discussed, the cultural aspect earned less attention from the academia. Culture is a primary carrier of globalization. Thus, the cultural side of globalization is termed as 'cultural globalization' which refers to the interchange of the ideas, values and meanings across the world (Lieber and Weisberg, 2002). The cultural globalization is deeply embedded in consumerism. It is a coherent set of practices, attitudes and values. It works on advertisement and mass media passing through whole social structure, which encourage perpetual expanding consumption of consumer goods and services. In the current form of market based culturally globalized world all spheres of social behaviour work interdependently towards the common goal of promotion and expansion of the global capitalist system. In the context of the economic and political realms, the global system has no need for an active inclusion of the global masses since only a small and exclusive group of elites steer the global economic and political processes. However, the global system encourages, demands, and indeed relies on the dedicated participation of the vast majority of global citizens in order to maintain a culture-ideology of consumerism (Sklair, 2002, Webb, 2005).

Sklair (2002) argued that the boundaries (national and local) do not matter for the main actors of the global capitalist system. They have total control in the production, delivery and marketing of the cultural ideology. It is characterized as the hegemonic consumerist culture which is spread by those who control this system (world media) as the lords of the so-called global village. In the contemporary neoliberal era, the global capitalist system tries to create a specific and relatively homogeneous global consciousness and a hegemonic 'common sense' by influencing the way the individuals perceive and approach their cultures and everyday lives. The 'culture-ideology' of consumerism is the life-blood of global capitalism. This culture-ideology of consumerism is circulated by the process of cultural globalization led by US and other Western forces (Webb, 2005). This led to what many argued, the 'Westernization' and particularly 'Americanization' of the world. The current era is described as "the global triumph of United States and its way of life." It is also called as 'Cola-colization' or 'Coca-globalization' (Foster, 2008), 'Disneyization', 'Wal-Martization' and 'McDonalization' (Ritzer, 2008).

The term 'culture' tends to be viewed often as the dependent variable. The materialist orientation of the literature has been accompanied by a notion that the social and cultural aspects are influenced by the world economy. Alternatively, cultural globalization is viewed by scholars as an autonomous process to reveal the importance of global cultural forces that play a crucial role in the process of globalization (Nijman, 1999:147-148). The Cultural globalization is defined as "acceleration in the exchange of cultural symbols among people around the world, to such an extent that it leads to a change in the local popular cultures and identities" (Nijman, 1999). In this context, the expansion of cultural globalization depends on two key elements: cultural symbols and their exchanges among people. The exchange of these cultural symbols depends largely on available communication technologies, ideologies and delivery systems (Jafari, 2007). Lieber and Weisberg (2002) observed that the culture is a primary carrier of globalization and it constitutes an important ground of contestation with regard to various existing identities; national and sub-national. When the various cultural forces or identities confront each other, here it is important to understand the concept of hegemony. Hegemony as a notion evolves through a continuous reciprocity of interactions between the dominant and the dominated cultures or entities (Harshe, 2006).

A group of theoreticians believe in a kind of contradiction between the global, national and local cultures. They uphold that the globalization results in homogenization that weakens the national and local cultures. In this regard, Latouche (1996) states that historical rise of the Western culture is willing to weaken other cultures. It led to the global uniformity of cultures and lifestyles. This made him conclude that the West wants to make the whole world Westernized and consequently threaten the Eastern cultures. Ritzer (2006) refers it as the process of 'McDonaldization', which is creating a homogenous global consumption culture with its roots in the American conception of culture. Therefore, it is the American conception of culture that has been introduced as the global culture and infiltrated into other cultures (Ritzer, 2006, 2004, Piri and Halim, 2011). Barber (1995) traces out a struggle between 'McWorld' (globalization and corporate control of political process) and '*Jihad*' (traditional value and theocracy). It occurred more vibrantly after the Islamic Revolution in Iran (1979) and in the same framework it became a major tension area between the global and native culture in a number of countries. Even, neither 'McWorld' nor the '*Jihad*' is supportive for the democracy.

In the view of the above discussed perspectives, the impact of globalization in the cultural sphere has been associated with the destruction of cultural identities. It is claimed that these identities are the victims of the accelerating encroachment of a homogenized, Westernized, consumer culture and Western cultural imperialism. The hegemonic imposition of Western culture (i.e. individualism, materialism, completion, hedonism, profit, greed, consumerism, commoditization, reductionism, and privatization) is breaking the indigenous values of other cultures and destroying their uniqueness. The powerful values generated and sustained by institutions and organizations with self-serving agendas are becoming preferences of the youth around the world.

There are also other different points of view on globalization, which contradict above arguments. Robertson (1992) does not consider globalization as a homogenization force alone, rather he considers it as homogenization and hetrogenization in a simultaneous manner. The native cultures and global cultures do not threaten one another, but rather there is a dialectical relationship between them. Peiterse (2004) also believes that not only globalization does not threaten the native cultures, but also it paves the way and opportunity for their development by reciprocal interaction. In fact, globalization is a sort of cultural 'hybridization' that rooted in the human history (Robertson, 1992, Piri and Halim, 2011).

Despite many contestations among the scholars of the globalization and the complex pictures of positive and negative understandings of the globalization there have been a serious concerns and responses to make the process of globalization more democratic and also many radical takes that tend to oppose it in its totality. Halliday (2007) is of the opinion that one of the most challenging questions on globalization is that of discovering the ways that lead to greater unification, homogenization of culture along with diversity, creativity or rejection of the dominant. There are many resistance movements in many forms termed as 'anti-globalization', 'anti-Westernization' and 'anti-Americanization'. In the economic field, by analyzing the neoliberal policies, Stiglitz (2002) argued that there are 'discontents' against neoliberal policies which are wrongly implemented by the market fundamentalist. The discontent or resistances is also evident in cultural sphere with its anti-hegemonic and anti-consumerist ethos.

Religio-cultural Revivalism in India

Today, when the flow of cultural globalization seems more rapid and dominant, it becomes important to discuss the relevance of religio-cultural revivalism in India and its relationship with the globalization and especially with the cultural globalization. It is important to see it as not only the source of resistance but to analyze it critically. The effects of the globalization in its cultural sense in India have been less in reality than it is perceived by the generalizations. The effects are also less in comparison with other countries. It may be because of the parallel ongoing religio-cultural revivalist Hindutva agenda as resistance or it may be because of the rigidity of socio-cultural setup that it did not allow other cultures to break its basic structure.

The movements of religious revivalism in India which connotes political and cultural defiance erupted in the early 1980s. Hindu religious militancy became increasingly powerful in India raised a forceful separatism against all that is alien (Saha, 1996). There is a debate as to whether Hindu-revivalist movements in recent decades were essentially cultural, political, class-oriented or social movements. What appears to be clear is that religio-cultural and political identity was of the paramount concern in the nation building process as designed by revivalist parties such as the Jana Sangh, Bharatiya Janta Party, the Rashtriya Swayam Sevak Sangh, Vishwa Hindu Parishad and others. These phenomena come with a keen interest in the 'Swadeshi'; national economic self-sufficiency, the use of Sanskrit, Hindi and Brahminic ritualistic practices in everyday cultural life. It is derived from the concern about restoring and reasserting a Hindu identity. Many revivalist parties and some religious groups employed the term 'Bharatvarsa' as a way of evoking not only the Vedic and Aryan background of the nation but also with the idea that the nation was based on religiously-dominated cultural values (Saha, 2001). It contradicts the concept of modern notion of nationalism which asserts that a modern nation-state cannot be built on the premise of religiosity.

For the better understanding of Hindu-revivalist claim one needs to comprehend the brief history of the origin and evolution of the Hindu nationalism. The Hindutva movement in modern history or contemporary times shapes the idea of Hindu nationalism and can be traced to 1925 with the foundation of the Rashtriya Swayamsevak Sangh (RSS) which has taken a task of 'propagating Hindu culture'. Prior to this the elements of Hinduism can be found in movements of Arya Samaj and the Hindu Mahasabha. However, these remained confined to religious aspects, and did not explicitly deal with politico-religious ones. The early religious movements were also confined to the regional cultural perceptions. As *Ramcharitmanas* was originated in northern belt and *Tantrik-Shakti* was confined to the Bengal. Contrary to it, recent religio-cultural revivalism is more widespread represented by many groups, missionaries and cultural-political organizations across the India. There is upsurge of Hindu religious sentiments even in the remote areas of Meghalaya in eastern India and Dravidian land of south India (Jaffrelot, 1999, Golwalker, 1939, Saha, 1996). For a long time, it was held that a close link existed between the modernization of a society and the secularization of the population. Consequently, it was argued that the influence of religion declined in modern society. Opposed to the modernization-secularization paradigm there is the view that the influence of religion in the public sphere has not declined, but in fact, has increased (Samajdar, 2015). The religious revivalism comes into view as a reaction to the globalization, but contrary to, it is propagated and intensified by the process of globalization (Annavarapu, 2015).

The revivalist idea of the Hindu state appeared to be conflicting and vague when it confronts with 'modern India' what Constitution of India holds. The founder of the concept of Hindu state Vinayak Damodar Savarkar saw the Hindu groups, including lower castes, as an imagined community having a common language, a common history, and the subjugation to common sovereign laws. Revivalist developed an idea that modern nationalism originated in the 'West' where the state was always a legal and political entity. In India, they argue, nation had been a cultural fact and used to be bound together by communities enduring religious and cultural values. Revivalists are of the view that modernization derived through the globalization is disintegrating the 'Hindu community' or ultimately the idea of 'community' in itself. To promote the Hindu cultural values RSS founded schools, hospitals, charities and urge people to give up 'wrong practices' and take up so-called 'pure Hindu practices'. The political organization like BJP mostly promotes upper strata of society into leadership. The revivalist groups objectify the Muslims as the enemies of Hindus. These groups promote Sanskrit and so-called 'pure Hindi' as unifying tool for the Hindu communities. Contemporary revivalists defended the common use of Sanskrit on a doubtful claim that it is the mother of all languages. For the political purpose these revivalists promote so-called 'pure Hindi'. Hindi is now a supra language, overriding several languages such as Avadhi, Bhojpuri, Braj, Marwari, Haryanavi, Maithili and Urdu across many Indian states. Hindi today seems to be growing as a new cultural identity (Saha, 2001). Recently, BJP led union government passed a law in which Hindi became the mandatory for the President and Prime Minister to deliver their speeches at the days of national importance.

The religio-cultural revivalism is found blended with the political fervor. There is an argument that political religiosity seems increasing all-over the world. As India is liberalizing and globalizing its economy there is a surge in popular religiosity among the burgeoning and largely Hindu middle class. It is evident from a boom in pilgrimage and invention of new and more intensified rituals. This religiosity is spread by state-temple-corporate complex that is replacing the more secular public institutions of the Nehruvian era. With the India's growing visibility in the global economy, Hindu religiosity is merging with feeling of national pride and propagates to become superpower. The economic success of the country is being attributed to the superiority of Hindu values, and India is seen as the great power status because of its so-called ancient Hindu civilization (Nanda, 2009).

In many ways this Hindu religio-cultural political agenda has succeeded in many achievements in the process of globalization through globalizing its Hindu symbols like Yoga, Sanskrit, so-called ancient Hindu glory and many other things. But for many reasons it could be critically analyzed. This may be beneficial for the capitalist agents of this religio-cultural politically derived self-serving project by ensuring its participation in globalization and benefiting itself by the global market. But it is equally dangerous for the sub-cultures of modern India, different worldviews and most importantly the modern democratic normative idea of India. Specifically, it is more dangerous to *Dalits*, minorities, tribes and women representing diverse cultures, identities and demanding their autonomy and agency. Ambedkar in his book *Pakistan or Partition of India* has asserted on the danger of what hc calls Hindu Raj. In his words: "If Hindu Raj does become a fact, it will, no doubt, be the greatest calamity for this country. No matter what the Hindus say, Hinduism is a menace to liberty, equality and fraternity. On that account it is incompatible with democracy. Hindu Raj must be prevented at any cost" (Ambedkar, 1946:358).

If Hindutva becomes assimilated to the global culture it becomes more dominant or hegemonic over other cultures and identities and tries to assimilate them into its fold and make the idea of Hindu nation a reality. The relative success of the Hindutva project is reflected in globalizing its symbols supported by the neo-liberal economic globalization which helped it to access global market. That is why BJP (at present ruling party in centre and in the states) one of the agent of this project never oppose economic globalization and market economy which is the also originated in 'West' but oppose cultural interaction and influence by promoting 'Swadeshi' and objectifying Western culture as alien (Brister: 2007).

In the field of culture, the nature of rigidity or the resistant capacity of the Hindutva could be understood by the arguments drawn from the empirical researches. The findings of one such research describe that in India despite of being heavy users of the new media, technology and flow of the global values such as freedom for individual and specially for women, increased autonomy for young people in choosing a spouse, cosmopolitan lifestyle, the changes in the gender culture and family structure of the large urban middle class have been relatively modest or unchanged. Despite the advent of globalization has introduced new cultural celebrations of autonomy and individual choice through the cable TV influences by global media and even Hindi-film emphasizes the search for the right partner, the restrains to the love marriages are not decreasing. The freedom to choose spouse by their own will for young people is still less prevalent (Derne, 2005). Contrary, the vigilantism led by Hindutva forces over the autonomy of girls and young people is getting legitimacy by popular mandate and support by large middle class to BJP in recent elections. And overall, the revival of the religious symbolism associated with the leaders is also supported by the large population. It could be seen as the clear sign of the relegio-cultural revivalism in cultural and political landscape of modern India.

The Hindu revivalist movement also asserted on the rejection of the modern science as catastrophic and manipulating human and natural world. In the replacement they assert on the path of ancient so-called 'holy science'. Many revivalists in that way accepted Mahatma Gandhi's interpretation. In his seminal work, *Hind Swaraj or Indian Home Rule* (1909), he by claiming epistemological evils of the modern science called on the nationalists to work for reconstruction of society on the basis of 'ancient science'. He predicted 'this civilization (scientific culture) is such that one only has to be patient, and it will be self-destroyed.' M.S. Golwalkar, Deendayal Upadhyaya who was associated with the revivalist movements, argued that science led development would bring 'man-made catastrophe' (Saha, 2001).

The revivalist ethos could be also found in what is described as anti-globalization protest in India. It could be linked with contemporary 'Swadeshi' movement (not the original Bengali 'Swadeshi' movement of the early twentieth century). India's contemporary 'Swadeshi' movement has roots in the 1970s and 1980s, when NGOs and action groups emerged to protest against various local issues related to perceived failures in the Nehruvian developmental model. The catalyst for the emergence of a more widespread and self-conscious anti- (or counter-) globalization social movement came with economic liberalization in the summer of 1991, which sometimes included opposition political parties as well. Most of the 'Swadeshi' campaigns of the nineties protest involved a small and consistent set of actors. These included both non-party action groups (NGOs), organized political parties, and research institutes. A handful of prominent activist leaders and a small number of cadre-based grassroots organizations were involved in almost every major anti-globalization or anti-foreign investment campaign. In spite of these small numbers, however, their short-term impact was significant enough to garner international attention, even if they failed to achieve their larger and longer term aims (Brister, 2007).

Baba Ram Dev's 'Patanjali' is another suitable example of the cultural revivalism as a form of resistance in the era of globalization. Patanjali has emerged as the real challenge to the MNCs. Its products attract Indian consumers by '*Desi*' symbolization on them. Patanjali has seen as the rejuvenation of the 'Swadeshi' movement against the '*Videshi*' products. The Patanjali is not only emerging as the major competitors of the many '*Videshi*' MNCs but also help revivalists' agenda of restoring so-called ancient glory and civilization. It works both the ways, the Sanskrit and Hindi naming of the products attracts Indians and also construct the minds of youth population in the favour of Hindutva agenda who have common tendency to be attracted by '*Videshi*' culture. Baba Ramdev promotes a distinctive vision of the Indian nation, invoking the principles of self-reliance and self-sufficiency. He asserts that Indians must free themselves from foreign influences, capital and products, and return to their cultural roots. He argues that India has been deprived of respect and recognition due to the hundreds of years of foreign colonization and weak post-colonial politics. Because of their lack of self-respect and pride in Indian culture, Ramdev says, Indians erroneously aspire to be like Westerners, wear Western clothes and use Western medicine; they have forgotten that India is the greatest and oldest civilization in the world, and most benefits of modern life have originated in India. He says that by restoring the Yoga and Ayurveda, we will restore the glory of India (Khalikova, 2017). In the name of national pride and 'Swadeshi' fervor it becomes easy to win the mind of consumers and attract them for buying the products.

Critical Analysis of Religio-Cultural Revivalism

The religio-cultural revivalists oppose Western culture as consumerist, corrupt and impure culture and assert to go back to the pure ancient culture. But critiques and many studies explain that this so-called 'pure' and 'holy' is itself consumerist and materialistic and has shown no artistic commitment towards the products produced by *Dalits* and hitherto *Sudra* communities (traditional producer class or lowest rank in the *Varna* system). The dominant capitalist and Brahmanical forces use their politically constructed hegemony over others. Eminent political scientist Kancha Ilaiah (2001) in an article argues, "in the cultural realm, globalization seems to have opened up a new channel of hope for the historically suppressed masses. Modern sociological studies have shown that the Brahmanical notion of 'purity' and 'pollution' in relation to ritual-culture, food habits and dress code kept a majority of India's masses as cultural slaves. Productive culture of hitherto *Sudras*, *ati-Sudras* (outcastes) and tribes was defined as impure and the ritual-consumerist Brahmanical culture constructed as pure and great. Even the concept of knowledge was defined in relation to a consumerist culture; while the productive knowledge was not accepted as knowledge." The knowledge was only considered as the ability to read the religious Sansktrit text which was not allowed for *Sudras* and *ati-Sudras* so the doors of knowledge were completely closed for them. The arts, skills and knowledge of *Sudras* and *ati-Sudras* were not considered as knowledge that they used in producing food building technological system, domesticating animals, constructing irrigation system. These all productive works were done by scientific thinking process and experience of people but were never considered as knowledge (Ilaiah, 2001).

In the process of diversification and democratization of modernity and globalization along with the cultural and counter-cultural forces who by the passes of time became the dominant identities, there are many subaltern groups who are asserting for their independent agency but those have either been ignored or not recognized in their independent agency. Now these subaltern discourses are being further suppressed in the battle of cultures at the national level. The subaltern cultural identities and their strength as alternative forces and as alternative normative moral vision of the modernity is crushed. In India, Phule and Ambedkar come from these subaltern groups whose discourses are suppressed by both the global Western cultural capitalist hegemonic agenda and its counter-cultural force like Hindutva or religio-cultural revivalism. These subaltern discourses have potential to be developed as the independent identities and world-views to establish alternative modernity in the process of democratization of globalization. The Hindutva forces promote Hinduization of the society in India with new flavor with the help of capitalist market (facilitated by economic globalization) which is actually not a new phenomenon but a tool in a new form to revive age-old Brahmanical structure of Indian society. At the cultural level Western consumerist culture and Hinduization may seem oppositional forces but at the economic level it goes hand in hand to suppress subaltern indigenous thinking.

These subaltern indigenous discourses are termed by Gopal Guru (2001) as 'Beyond' as an epistemological category. The category of 'Beyond' is distinctive from both the 'Swadeshi' and the 'derivative' (Videshi) as it seeks to characterize the nationalist imagination radically different. The thought which is made to exist in the 'Beyond' is different both in terms of style and substance. It is different in style as it expresses dissonance, difference and defiance to the revivalist agenda of the Hindutva. Such thoughts create interruptions in the conceptual stability and universal validity of the hegemonic thought and its capacity to resistance or to democratize process of globalization (Guru, 2011). The foundation of 'modern India' has not a homogenous thought process but the diversified thinking behind it where representation of various identities, thought processes, worldviews, ideologies should be ensured. The hegemonic Brahmanical revivalism either tries to assimilate various independent discourses or does not recognize their independent agency. The revivalists penetrate fear of the foreign Western culture in the minds of suppressed communities by objectifying it as enemy and try to assimilate them in the Hindutva fold. In the present debates RSS and BJP ideologues dominantly define Hindutva as the way of life and drastically include all the communities living at territory of Indian state in its fold.

Conclusion

The increasing globalization of the world society is the reality of today. The cultural globalization, however, has inseparable trait with economic globalization but also required separate attention in academia. The cultural globalization has affected world society in both negative and positive ways. The hegemony of dominant cultures has one side tried to homogenize the global culture but another side led to reactionary but gradually transformed as real assertion of the many national and sub-national identities at global and local level. It asserted the argument that equal participation of the various cultures and their representation must be ensured at global and national level. But the national cultures which are major actors of participation in the process of cultural globalization have failed in forming constructive resistance strategy to democratize the process of cultural globalization.

The globalization due to its more attention on market fundamentalism and promoting corporate elite friendly self-serving culture is diverted from its goal of promoting freedom and democracy in its real sense in India. It led to the revival of religious forces in new form helped by technology, media and market. These forces are rapidly attaining the legitimacy through spreading propaganda. In India, the religio-cultural revivalism in the name of resistance to Westernization constructs hegemony over the other local indigenous cultures and worldviews in India and questions their independent status and their direct participation in the process of cultural globalization and suppresses them by using material tools provided by the capitalist market system. These revivalist groups promote so-called 'ancient glory' like language (Sanskrit, pure Hindi), rituals, practices and social structures by using modern technology, media and communication. They target the large middle-class population of various sections of society and reassert the ancient traditional slavery in the new form. The electoral success and expansion of the revivalist party BJP in the various recent elections is the justification of the argument.

REFERENCES

Ambedkar, B.R. (1946), "Pakistan or Partition of India", in *Dr. Babasaheb Ambedkar: Writings and Speeches*, Vol. 8. Education Department, Government of Maharashtra. [Online] Accessed on 20 May, 2020, URL: https://mea.gov.in/Images/attach/amb/Volume_08.pdf.

Annavarapu, Sneha (2015). "Religious Nationalism in a Global Age: The Case of Hindu Nationalism". *Journal of Developing Societies, 31*(1), 125-146.

Baylish, John *et al.* (2011). *The Globalization of World Politics: An Introduction to International Relations*. New York: Oxford University Press.

Bhambhari, C.P. (2005). *Globalization: India, Nation, State and Democracy*. Delhi: Shipra Publications.

Brister, Thomas (2007). "Swadeshis in Competition: Enron and Indian's anti-globalization movement". *Contemporary Politics, 13* (4), 315-329.

Derne, Steve (2005). "The (limited) Effects of Cultural Globalization in India: Implications for Culture Theory." *Poetics, 33* (45), 33-47.

Foster, Robert J. (2008). *Coca-Globalization: Following Soft Drinks From New York to New Guinea.* USA: Palgrave Macmillan.

Gamage, Siri (2016). Hegemonic Globalisation and its Impact on the Global South: Sociological Perspectives and Anti Hegemonic Responses, [Online] Accessed on 12 June 2020, URL: https://www.researchgate.net/publication/303407405_Hegemonic_Globalisation_and_its_Impact_on_the_Global_South_Sociological_Perspectives_and_Anti_Hegemonic_Responses#:~:text=The%20hegemonic%20form%20of%20globalization,of%20access%20and%20equity%20issues.

Gilpin, R. (2001). *Global Political Economy*. Princeton: Princeton University Press.

Golwalker, M. (1939). *We or our nationhood defined.* Bangalore: Jagrana Prakashan.

Guru, Gopal (2007). "Social Justice: A 20th Century Discourse from the Quarantined India." in Sabyasachi Bhattacharya (ed.), *Development of Modern Indian Thought and the Social Sciences*. Delhi: Oxford University Press.

Guru, Gopal (2009). "The Idea of Ideal in Ambedkar", special lecture, delivered in an International Conference on Caste and Ambedkar. Organised by Institute of South Asian Studies, New York: Columbia University, 15 and 16 October.

Guru, Gopal (2011). "The Idea of India: Derivative, Desi and Beyond." *Economic and Political Weekly, XLVI* (37).

Halliday, Fred (2007). Culture and International Relations: Delusions of Difference. Paper presented in University of the Basque Country. Summer Programme on International Law and International Relations, Vitoria-Gasteiz.

Harshe, Rajen (2006). "Culture, Identity and International Relations." *Economic and Political Science Weekly, 41* (37), 3945-3951.

Ilaiah, Kancha (2003). "Cultural Globalization." *The Hindu*, February 22, 2003.

Jafari, Aliakhar (2007). "Two Tales of a City: An Exploratory Study of Cultural Consumption among Iranian Youth." *Iranian Studies,* Routledge, *40* (3), 367-383.

Jaffrelot, C. (1999). *The Hindu Nationalist Movement and Indian Politics.* New Delhi: Penguin Books.

Jun, Ho Jin (2003), *Religious Pluralism and Fundamentalism in Asia*, South Korea: Korea University of International Studies Press.

Khalikova, Venera R. (2017). "The Ayurveda of Baba Ramdev: Biomoral Consumerism, National Duty and the Biopolitics of 'Homegrown' Medicine in India." *Journal of South Asian Studies*, *4*(1), 105-122.

Kumar, Anand (2011), *Understanding Globalization and Emerging India,* New Delhi: Palm Leaf Publications.

Latouche, Serge (1996). *The Westernization of the World: Significance, Scope and Limits of the Drive Towards Global Uniformity*. Cambridge: Polity Press.

Lieber, Robert J. and Ruth E. Weisberg (2002). "Globalization, Culture, and Identities in Crisis." *International Journal of Politics, Culture and Society, 16* (2), 273-296.

Luce, Edward (2011). *In Spite of the Gods: The Strange Rise of Modern India*. London: Abascus.

Mahajan, Gurpreet and Jodhka S. Surinder (ed.) (2010). *Religion, Community and Development: Changing Contours of Politics and Policy in India.* New Delhi: Routledge.

Nanda, Meera (2009). *The God Market: How Globalization is Making India More Hindu*. Noida UP: Random House Publication.

Nijman, Jan (1999). "Cultural Globalization and the Identity of Place: The Reconstruction of Amsterdam." *ECUMENE, 6*(2), 146-164.

Owolabi, Kolawole A. (2001). "Globalization, Americanization and Western Imperialism." *Journal of Social Development in Africa*, *16* (2), 71-92.

Pathak, Avijit (2006). *Modernity, Globalization and Identity: Towards A Reflective Quest*. Delhi: Aakar Books.

Pieterse, J.N. (2004). *Globalization and Culture.* Lanahm, MD: Roman and Littlefield.

Piri, Daryoush and Halim Adina Ab (2011). "Diplomacy of Iran Towards Globalization: The Tension between Globalization and Islamization in Iran." *Cross-Cultural Communication*, *7* (1), 82-96.

Ritzer, George (2006). "Art, McDonaldization and Globalization of Nothing" in Ray Kiely and Samir Das Gupta (eds.). *Globalization and After*, New Delhi: Sage.

Saha, Santosh C. (1996). "Religious Revivalism among the Hindus in India: Ideologies of the Fundamentalist Movements in Recent Decades." *Indian Journal of Asian Affairs*, *9* (2), 35-54.

Saha, Santosh C. (2001). "The Idea of Hindu State (Rastra): Cultural Aspect in the Revivalist Movement in Contemporary India." *Indian Journal of Asian Affairs*, *14* (1/2), 45-61.

Salzman, Michael B. (2008). "Globalization, religious fundamentalism and the need for meaning." *International Journal of Intercultural Relations*, *32*, 318-327.

Samajdar, Arita (2015). "Religion in the Age of Globalization: Reflection on a Village in West Bengal, India." *Journal of Developing Societies*, *31*(1), 43-65.

Savarkar, V. (1969). *Hindutva: Who is a Hindu?*. Bombay: S. Savarkar.

Scholte, J.A. (2005). *Globalization—A Critical Introduction*. Basingstoke: Palgrave Macmillan.

Singh, Rana P.B. and Haigh, Martin J. (2015). "Hindu Pilgrimage and a contemporary scenario." In Stanley D. Brunn (Ed.) *The Changing World Religion Map*. New York and Dordrecht: Springer Science + Business Media B.V.

Singh, Rana P.B. and Aktor, Mikael (2015). "Hinduism and Globalization" in Brunn, Stanley D. (ed.) *Changing World Religion Map: Sacred Places, Identities, Practices and Politics*. New York, Springer.

Sklair, L. (1995). *Sociology of the Global System*. Baltimlore MD: Johns Hopkins University Press.

Starr, Amony and Adams, Jason (2003). "Anti-globalization: The Global Fight for Local Autonomy." *New Political Science, 25*(1), 19-42.

Zhuojun, Wang and Hualing, He (2014). "National Identity in the Era of Globalization: Crisis and Reconstruction." *Social Sciences in China, 35*(2), 139-154.

5
Globalization and Regional Cooperation in South Asia
Poverty Alleviation Strategies

Wakeel Ahmed

Introduction

South Asia has a large human capital capacity and it is dynamic in nature. Regional cooperation would be the mantra for the future trajectory of the region as a whole. If it is achieved through the integration of economies of the states then South Asia would be the significant player in the world. India's economic growth energized the region. As a result, it is changing and improving. South Asia would become the second largest economy in the world after China, even leaving behind the USA.[1] South Asia's trajectory from colonial to post-colonial to globalization is the reality. With the last quarter of the 20th century have seen enormous economic growth and developmental transformations relatively from its past experiences in the states of South Asia

In the sphere of human life particularly social, economic and political where the changes were taking place in the last decades of the past century, the challenges were posed before the government to redefine the concepts. This time was considered as the time of socio-economic transitions. There is no doubt that 21st century has been strengthening and increasing with a rapid pace towards the transitions. The governments had to rethink about their strategies of economic development because changes in the world economy pushed governments to do that. As a result, global and regional integration has been taking place. Through these strategies, institutions and partnerships can be developed and through this, economically viable and socially equitable societies can be built.[2]

Since the SAARC came into existence, there have been several meetings, agreements to the promotion of economic cooperation, poverty alleviation, and to combat terrorism in South Asia. It is broadly understood that peaceful and stable South Asia is crucial for regional development. One of the most crucial steps taken by South Asian countries, was the establishment of South Asian Association for Regional Cooperation (henceforth, SAARC) as a regional organization in 1985. The SAARC was designed to strengthen regional cooperation, stability, and welfare in South Asia. SAARC is an intergovernmental body at regional level, performing the task of promoting and achieving objectives and principles of SAARC. Its importance is seen in the process of resolving conflicts and sustaining peaceful relations among nations in South Asia. There is a vast opportunity for countries to cooperate in various sectors of the states.

Needless to say, South Asia is heterogeneous region. Geographical and historical proximity leads them to build cooperation to each other. South Asian region, which is located in southern part of Asian continent comprises of seven countries, later Afghanistan was included in 2007 namely, Afghanistan, Bhutan, Maldives, Nepal, India, Pakistan and Sri Lanka. To overcome the challenges, the efforts have been taken by politicians, diplomats, civil societies, multi-level agencies etc. in the sphere of concerned issues; these are significant stakeholders in domestic and foreign policy of member countries. Thus, the chapter would attempt to explore the opportunities of developmental issues and challenges coming in the way of regional cooperation in South Asia. The chapter has two sections except introduction and conclusion. The first is to understand regional organization and its regional dynamics in the context of globalization. The second has dealt with globalization and poverty alleviation efforts by states in the South Asia.

SAARC and Globalization

South Asian countries had sought a way, through which common agenda could be discussed and solved. It was materialized as SARRC, as other regional organizations in the world such as ASEAN in Southeast Asia, European Union in Europe. These regional groupings have integrated economies regionally as well as globally. SAARC was established to promote the welfare of the people of the region through active collaboration and mutual assistance in the economic, cultural, technical and scientific realm. India as the most populous country in the region has been playing an important role in SAARC activities and provides it with necessary direction for cooperation and development to make more peaceful and stable South Asia.

There was an integration agreement among states of European Union and ASEAN had inspired South Asian countries. Later, South Asia decided to form the SAARC as regional organization. Initially, the proposal for the organization was made by the president of Bangladesh and endorsed by other small countries, Nepal, Sri Lanka, Maldives, and Bhutan. Earlier, India and Pakistan were not ready to accept the proposal but later, both accepted the move. It was in mid-1985 year when the charter was embraced by all seven countries. SAARC is a driving force to integrate the region but has not been effective so far and lacking the adequate capacities.[3]

It is ineffective because there are several reasons for the slow progress of the organization such as India-Pakistan rivalry, internal and ethnic conflicts, imbalances in economies, are the challenges confronted by the earlier as well as the present governments of the states in South Asia. This kind of nature of the state of affairs of the region derailed the smooth functioning of SAARC in the globalized world.

Earlier, South Asian states followed protectionist policies and were dependent on the strategies more inclined towards closed economic system. But, in the last decade of the twentieth century particularly of 1990s, after the demise of Soviet Union, these countries opened their economies to the rest of the world. India begun liberalization, Pakistan, Bangladesh and Sri Lanka also liberalized their economies. It happened due to the pressure from International Monetary Fund (IMF) and World Bank (WB), and the success of ASEAN countries as well. In order to follow those policies, ASEAN countries encouraged countries in South Asia to pursue the policies of this kind. As a result, liberalization was increased and these trends inspired South Asia for the development of regional economic integration.[4]

Further, the integration of South Asian economies into world economy, there has been socio-economic transformations took place rapidly. Although, there have been unsatisfactory consequences of this process too, nevertheless Asia's reality is lack of a large infrastructure in the region which causes connectivity problem.

In the recent SAARC meeting, the main focus was on connectivity that demands infrastructure not only physical but also social or health and economic infrastructure so that flow of goods, services, capital, ideas, human resources must be exchanged smoothly without any hindrance. Such kind of connectivity through the development of infrastructure would pave the way for the socio-economic transformations in all spheres of human life of the countries of the region. While the most connected economies in Asia are able to solve their internal problems of underdevelopment and poverty but the experience on lower level of connectivity leaving them relatively isolated from the global economy. Regional transport cooperation efforts must be placed at the centre of connectivity. Enforcing sustainable policies are essential. The process of 'interconnectedness and interrelatedness of all aspects of society' is a process of globalization and can be substantiated by the quote below.

We cannot avoid the reality of the world as "*a series of complex, interdependent yet interrelated processes of stretching, intensifying and accelerating worldwide interconnectedness in all aspects of human relations and transactions— economic, social, cultural, environmental, political, diplomatic and security— such that events, decisions, and activities in one part of the world have immediate consequences for individuals, groups, and states in other parts of the world*".[5] In order to understand this process, it has to be noticed that which is embedded in a hierarchical system of power, exchanges and benefits which includes and excludes peoples and nations argued by James Pitras in his book; 1999.[6]

This process could have a serious impact on economic development within and on regional cooperation in South Asia. Despite the differences in the political systems, South Asian countries cooperate in many areas such as exchange of goods and services, development aid, humanitarian aid, and strategic domain as well. As a result, through these efforts, the welfare of the people gets promoted which improve the quality of life in South Asia. Today, communication is a strong feature that accelerates those connections and presents an image of a world unified by new technology and products.[7]

This view has been contended by some scholars that, as they argue that the phenomenon is not new itself, it occurred in earlier times too. However, there are some properties of it which is different in terms of speed and scale. South Asian countries have promoted mutual assistance in the technical and scientific field. Science and technology are one of the important sectors that are given primacy throughout the region. As far as economies of these states are concerned, it consists of agricultural, manufacturing, services. Investments in these sectors helped in the reduction of poverty and to boost up the overall economy and paved the way for further integration of these economies into global economy. Most of the states had accelerated their economic growth and social progress much better relatively.

Globalization and Poverty in South Asia

Despite the positive achievements, there is the other side of the same process too. In the first decade of the 21st century, poverty is still prevailing in South Asia. Where 1.4 billion people living, that is about one fourth of the world population and having 43 per cent poor people of the world, and in terms of world's GDP, it is only 2 per cent.[8] It is also said that South Asia is the largest poverty region in Asia.[9]

Despite the matter of the fact, is that, South Asian countries achieved progress, development, growth and reduced poverty from their own country and contributed to provide development aid and invested in neighboring country to one another. In case of India, it has succeeded well relatively since its Independence in South Asia. India is the largest in terms of its size, population and economy as well. Therefore, it is also important to increase and strengthen the cooperation among them as well as when states would interact at regional or international organizations to discuss their issues.

However, collective self-reliance among south Asian states could be promoted and strengthened. By addressing their internal problems as the larger population is still struggling to access institutions such as education, health services, and achieve human resource development as well as become from unskilled to skilled population. Due to which people understand and act in the world dominated by new technologies. Therefore, inadequate capacities of the states and ineffective organization could not be able to come forward to solve these issues. Self-reliant country in its natural and human resources, goods and services, technology would be able to help other country to make them independent but here independent opens the way of integration of national to regional and global economy. So, it can be said that globalization has increased the growth of economies in South Asian states.

For instance, we have some successful examples where growth along with the reduction in poverty due to the result of globalization like China and East Asian states. In these countries, governments played very significant role to manage industrial policies and took benefits from the international markets. The expansion of exports was the mantra of these countries, liberalized slowly not fastly. One important aspect of the success of China and East Asian Countries was that they did not follow the 'Washington Consensus' as it was directed but modified accordingly so that could work much in their own countries.[10]

As Joseph Stiglitz says, "the countries of East Asia grew because of globalization, but they managed it, shaped it, in ways that worked to their own advantage."[11] In case of China, Contemporary South Asian scholar, Ashutosh Varshney argues that China was among the biggest sufferers of 'globalization 1.0' and he analyzed his article to how 'globalization 2.0' has benefited China.[12] Education is one of the significant aspects of national development. Education has helped in the growth of the countries, like China (East Asia), South-East Asia, and South Asia. As China is one of the East Asian countries are in the top while South Asia is the last while South-East Asia stands in between. These are the important changes which took place in the current decade of the 21st century. While many countries have been experiencing lower levels of growth in the 21st century.[13]

Keeping the South Asia region poverty-free will depend on policies that promote balance and sustainable development and in turn, will keep economy sustainable. Globalization process is changing the contours of the Asian economies in general and South Asian economies in particular.

Another example like India, as India's Prime Minister, Dr. Manmohan Singh explains: *"India cannot prosper and progress without its neighboring countries also prospering and progressing, in equal measure...... [and] historically the South Asia region has flourished the most when it has been connected to itself, and to the rest of the world."*[14] It can promote and strengthen not only through cooperation, collaboration, and coordination to regional and global integration but also collective self-reliance in their own region. But the Prime Minister Singh also said that "we can't back on globalization, 'it' is here to stay."[15] However, India is also one of the countries which did not follow the way IMF's dictum of 'Washington Consensus'. As a result, India has also been able to reduce the poverty from its large population over the two decades but still challenges exist in Indian economy.

It is said that India's neighbouring countries for example Pakistan which has been a case of ethnic conflicts, military intervention in civilian affairs and unequal distribution of resources leads further to exclude the large section from the mainstream of Pakistan society and states, as Pakistan embraced globalization and liberalized its economy. As a result, there are economic consequences too and this can be understood from political economic perspective as well. One of the scholars from Pakistan, Akmal Hussain, *"Poverty in Pakistan is rooted in an acutely unequal distribution of productive assets and an associated asymmetric structure of power that distorts state markets and state institutions in such a way that they systematically discriminate against the poor with respect to access over resources, public services and governance decisions, which affects their immediate existence.*"[16]

Broad understanding of these common issues, when we talk about the illiteracy, low-life expectancy, and poverty, this region is characterized by these problems. Approximately, half of its child population is, being under-weight, compared with 30 per cent in Sub-Sahara Africa, and the region is most malnourished in the world. It is also least gender-sensitive and human deprivation, that is concerned, access to the health facilities, drinking water, sanitation, opportunity for work is lagging behind. Simultaneously, as far as security issues are concerned, this region is most militarized in developing world. The highest percentage of GDP is spent on military expenditures to contend the threat perceptions at the expense of improving the lives of people of these countries in South Asia.[17]

Due to these priorities of states of South Asia, some common agenda is lagging behind. Although, the process of consensus building, peaceful dialogue creates an international environment that develops trust. For accelerating regional cooperation, there is an urgent need in reenergizing SAARC. From the platform of SAARC, the efforts are taken to build cooperation among these states and address developmental problems as the most acute is poverty problem and resolving conflicts from South Asia.

Due to the prevailing conditions, the efforts were directed energizing the organization. As a result, the need for a social charter for South Asia was first expressed in the GEP report. The 10th SAARC summit held in Colombo in 1998 accepted in principle that a social charter be formulated: "which would focus on drawing-up targets with a broad range, to be achieved across the region in the areas of poverty eradication, population stabilization, empowerment of women, youth mobilization, human resource development, promotion of health and nutrition, and the protection of child."[18] Unfortunately, this charter was not implemented properly to address poverty problems in the region.

It was the twelfth summit in 2004, in which a decision to strengthen connectivity among countries in South Asia through the development of transport, transit and communication links. For this purpose, Asian Development Bank (ADB) is providing financial and technical support that has given to the member states, initiated the SAARC Regional Multimodal Transit Study (SRMTS) for enhancing connectivity.[19] In short, the chain of connectivity is to build infrastructure that would help in order to develop connectivity from one place to another that would be resulting social and economic development in South Asia.

Strategically, beyond South Asia, there are few countries, which were granted observer status in SAARC organization since 2005, namely China, European Union, USA, Australia, Japan, South Korea, Mauritius, and Myanmar.[20] Among these observers, China is showing keen interest, participating in SAARC summit. SAARC allows them in participating in the inaugural and closing sessions to make proposal for the development of SAARC. In 2010, Nepal submitted its proposal to include China as full member rather than observer but India did veto against this proposal. Among all SAARC nations, few small countries see China as balancing out India's strength within the organization.[21]

Some people see China would strengthen economic integration process because its sheer size, growth that would accelerate this process and this kind of alliance would increase the credibility of SAARC to the rest of the world.[22] Regional cooperation through SAARC must be based on mutual respect for the principles of sovereignty, equality, territorial integrity. India has some reservations as far as China's role in the region is concerned such as China's border with India, POK and 'One Belt and One Road' or CPEC are the most sensitive issues, these sometimes prevent the collaboration and cooperation in trades, goods and services, people to people contact through cultural exchange programme too among the members of SAARC. If one country interfere in internal affairs of another country which violets the principle of SAARC and weakens the whole region as a whole.

Economically, globalization has helped in the reduction of poverty and has increased employment opportunities although, this is the fact that globalization has affected the interests of South Asian countries adversely as well. South Asian countries are agricultural surplus but due to the textile and farm subsidies of EU and US that disturb these countries. The WTO quota in textile industry affected to the textile industries in South Asia's export capacities because quota is not abolished as yet. One said that, however, try to improve regional cooperation that has been increased but did not develop into 'effective operational mechanism.'[23]

However, in order to alleviate poverty, the independent South Asian Commission was established in 1991. During 17th SAARC summit in 2011, the attention was drawn mainly to eradicate poverty in South Asia. The Commission was to strengthen for this purpose. The member states of this Commission conduct an in-depth study on these diverse experiences. In the summit, there were strategies towards the poverty alleviation, health services, access to education, nutrition, social mobilization, agricultural development, labour-intensive, industrialization, human resource development.[24]

There are several connectivity projects and more than twelve integrated check-posts along with some countries such as Bangladesh, Nepal, Bhutan and Myanmar. These check-posts are in the process of making to facilitate trade and mobility along the borders of these countries. In spite of these efforts, there are implementation deficiencies and policy coordination challenges still remain. For instance, Bay of Bengal Initiative for Multi-Sectoral Technical and Economic Cooperation (BIMSTEC) or the Bangladesh, Bhutan, India, Nepal Initiative (BBIN), the Trilateral Highway and Kaladan projects, on the comprehensive Economic Cooperation Agreement with Sri Lanka and needed investments in regional institutions.[25] Recently, there was a meeting of SAARC countries in the time of Covid-19. At this platform, challenges were discussed by members of the organization; India has provided a large amount of financial aid to fight with the global pandemic.

Finally, it could be said that as far as the role of states in region is concerned, the progress of SAARC has been slow. The reasons for the slow progress are because of approaches of states towards South Asian region. It is also important to highlight that the different understanding and goals of geo-politics of states in the region. SAARC as regional organization emphasized to accelerate the role of the organization to contribute and increase cooperation in various sectors of the states for instance, scientific and technological sphere, builds a large infrastructure in South Asia. It is not only some states in the region but also other international organizations and platforms helped South Asian states to develop cooperation more in positive direction. But still disharmony in strategic domain and inter-conflicts between states have also stood in the way of regional cooperation.

Conclusion

South Asia has a potential with a large amount of human capital. It has gone a long from its independent past in terms of growth and development. Still the region has to go a long in future. The current global economic crisis is affecting most of regions in the globalized world. This crisis provides challenges and opportunities for the governments in South Asia as well. There is no dispute that South Asia is the outcome of colonialism. South Asian states started their trajectory of development and growth from as independent countries. Initial decades did pave the way for further developments. As with the demise of Soviet Union, however, in the 1970s, and 1980s, there were dramatic changes in the world and further was accelerated in 1990s. Then governments had to change their economic strategies by embracing global trends 'it' is globalization.

South Asian states formed regional organization to deal with the emerging situations called as SAARC in 1985. Since then, it has been working to achieve its objectives and principles in the region. This regional organization has not been successful as other organizations in different regions of the world such as European Union and ASEAN. The main reason for their success is, they have integrated their economies regionally as well as globally. China as one of the observer countries from East Asian region in the SAARC, has achieved development by reducing poverty, has provided employment for its large population and growth for the last few decades tremendously.

Similarly, India has achieved development and growth relatively in South Asia. India has also potential with human capital and large in terms of economy. South Asian states have accepted the reality of globalization and further liberalized their economies. Since then, globalization process has changed the contours of Asian economies in general and South Asian in particular. However, there are still challenges remain to address by the governments of the region. There are 'core' issues in strategic and economic domain which has to be solved by SAARC states.

It is understood that Asia as a whole is lacking infrastructure. In sub-region, due to the lack of infrastructure, there have been difficulties to integrate economies to each other. But in recent times, there are several connectivity projects and transport improved trade and services conditions along the border of Nepal, India, Bangladesh, and Sri Lanka in South Asia. SAARC as an intergovernmental organization has paved the way for the interaction of government to government but the role of international organizations cannot be denied as far as development issues are concerned such as poverty, illiteracy, malnourishment, women's empowerment. SAARC countries helped and invested in each other countries to address these issues by including them as common agenda of the organization.

Despite the achievements by states in their internal and external goals in South Asia, there are some strategic issues remained to be solved. Inter-state rivalry, terrorism, has stood in the way of regional cooperation. Regional cooperation can be understood as mantra for SAARC countries in the globalized world. For future prospects of this regional organization is that bitter memory of the past can be erased and differences must be solved peacefully for the development of mutual understanding, prosperity and welfare. As governments had to make a shift in their perspectives in policy arena1970s onwards. Now the time has come to rethink the role of states in South Asia.

ENDNOTES

1. Behra, N.C. (2012). "SAARC and beyond: civil society and regional integration in South Asia" in Sultan Hafeej Rahman, Sridhar Khatri, Hans-Peter Brunner (eds.), *Regional Integration and Economic Development in South Asia, Asia Development Bank (ADB)*, published by Edward Elgar, UK, p.3.
2. Gupta, D.S. (ed.). (2004). *The Changing Face of Globalization*, SAGE Publications, New Delhi, p.228.
3. Kher, P. (2012) "Political Economy of Regional Integration in South Asia", *UNCAD*, Regional Value Chains BACKGROUND PAPER no. RVC5, p.4.
4. Khan, H.A. and Larik, Z. *Globalization and Regional Cooperation in South Asia: A Political and Social Economy Approach. CIRJEF*-480 GSIS University of Denver Colorado 80208 http: // www.ed.tokyo.ac.jp/cirje/research/03 research 02 dp.html. p.21.
5. Kim, S.S. (1999). "East Asia And Globalization: Challenges and Responses", *Asian Perspective*, Vol. 23, No. 4, Special Issue on Globalization in East Asia, published by Lynne Rienner URL; http://www.jstor.org/stable/42704233 Accessed: 27-03-2017, p.17.
6. Pitras, J. (1999). "Globalization: A Socialist Perspective", *Economic and Political Weekly*, 20 1999, Cited in Introduction, samir Das Gupta (ed.), *The Changing Face of Globalization*, SAGE Publications, New Delhi, 2004, p. 20.
7. Cited in Samir Das Gupta (ed.), *The Changing Face of Globalization*, SAGE Publications, New Delhi, 2004, p. 228.
8. Khan, H.A. and Larik, Z. (2007). "Globalization and Regional Cooperation in South Asia: A Political and Social Economy Approach", p. 21.
9. Ibid.p.10.
10. Nayyar, R.T. (ed.), *Globalization and Politics in India*, Oxford India Paperbacks, 2020, p. 136.
11. Stiglitz, J. E. (2020). "The Overselling of Globalization" in Baldev Raj Nayyar (ed.), *Globalization and Politics in India*, Oxford India Paperbacks, p. 136.
12. Varshney, A. (May 4, 2020). "The new Capitalism", in *The Indian Express*, www.IndianExpress.comMonday, p. 8.
13. Kurien, C.T. (Feb. 15, 2020). "One Asia, Two Perspectives", in www.thehindu.com *The Hindu*, p.6.
14. Behra, C.N. "SAARC and beyond: civil society and regional integration in South Asia" in Sultan Hafeej Rahman, Sridhar Khatri, Hans-Peter Brunner (eds.), *Regional Integration and Economic Development in South Asia*, p. 5.
15. "Globalization is irreversible, skeptics have been proven wrong" https://m.economictimes.com/news/economy/policy/globalization, September 23, 2017.
16. Behra, C.N. "SAARC and beyond: civil society and regional integration in South Asia". p. 16.
17. Ibid., pp. 21-22.

18. Behra, C.N. (2012). "SAARC and beyond: civil society and regional integration in South Asia" in Sultan Hafeej Rahman, Sridhar Khatri, Hans-Peter Brunner (eds.), *Regional Integration and Economic Development in South Asia*, p. 29.
19. Ibid., p. 21.
20. Delimz,T. (2011). *SAARC— 25 Years of Regional Integration in South Asia*, KAS, International Reports, available at SAARC Secretariatehttp:saarc.sec.org/cooperation-with-observers/13 p.18.
21. Cited in Delimz, T. (2011). *SAARC— 25 Years of Regional Integration in South Asia*, pp.18-19.
22. Delimz, T. (2011). *SAARC— 25 Years of Regional Integration in South Asia*, p. 19.
23. Haider, A.K. and Larik, Z. (2007). "Globalization and Regional Cooperation in South Asia: A Political and Social Economy Approach", p. 31.
24. Shaheen, I. (2013). "South Asian Association for Regional Cooperation (SAARC): Its Role, Hurdles and Prospects", *IOSR Journal of Humanities and Social Sciences*, Volume 15, issue 6, Peshawar, Pakistan, p. 3.
25. Xavier, C. (Feb 06, 2020). "The quest for regional connectivity", in www.hindutantimes.com *Hindustan Times*, New Delhi, p. 16.

SECTION II

Understanding Governance and Human Rights

6

Indian Parliament and its Initiatives towards Human Rights and Good Governance

A Study of Parliamentary Inputs of 16th Lok Sabha

S. Prabhakar

Introduction

Human rights violations come in the form of prisoners deprived of their rights, women behind bars are treated badly, child sacrifice, domestic violence, cyber stalking etc. Police and human rights go hand in hand. Varied human rights violations find resonance in the corridors of Parliament. In India, we could see *Dalits* fighting for their rights; tribals fighting for forest rights; minorities fighting for their rights; atrocities against women are reported unabated forcing women to fight for their rights against such atrocities. According to the Supreme Court of India, even corruption is a violation of human rights. Corruption is rampant in our country. There is a need to erase corruption from the society. Good governance in the country, and with parliamentary initiatives and stricter laws, we are thinking of ending corruption activities.

Under Section 2 of the Protection of Human Rights Act, 1993, "human rights" means the rights relating to life, liberty, equality and dignity of the individual guaranteed under the Constitution or embodied in the International Covenants and enforceable by courts in India. "International Covenants" means the International Covenant on Civil and Political Rights and the International Covenant on Economic, Social and Cultural Rights adopted by the General Assembly of the United Nations on the 16th December, 1966.[1]

Indian Constitution and Human Rights

When Constituent Assembly was framing the Indian Constitution, it gave primary importance to human rights. It is to be noted that the Constituent Assembly incorporated the substance of the rights proclaimed and adopted by the General Assembly in the Universal Declaration of Human Rights. It states, "Human rights have been synthesized, as it were, not as an integrated fabric by the Preambular promises and various Constitution clauses of the National Charter of 1950."[2] This shows that India was receptive to the concept of human rights right from the beginning of our Independence and made efforts in that direction. We could see the discernible change concerning human rights situation in India but there are areas of concern in Jammu & Kashmir and the North Eastern Region.

Mid-April (7-18 April, 2008) witnessed the unfolding of a new international mechanism when the UN Human Rights Council's Universal Periodical Review (UPR) began to process of examining lots, the UPR Working Groups, in their first session, started with the human rights records of 16 countries including India, UK.[3] Earlier Commission of Human Rights was accused of scrutinising only a small number of countries. The Universal Declaration of Human Rights postulates that all human beings are born free and equal in dignity and rights and are entitled to enjoy all rights and freedoms set forth in the Declaration without discrimination of any kind. What is the reality? Are we moving in the right direction when it comes to ensuring basic rights and freedoms to our people? Over the years, many parliamentary initiatives were aimed at ensuring human rights to its citizen, about which, we would deal below.

Acts Related to Human Rights Passed by Parliament since 1st Lok Sabha

Parliament has a vital role in ensuring that human rights are protected and promoted in the country. Right from the 1st Lok Sabha in 1952, Parliament has enacted a number of laws for the protection of human rights in many spheres. These laws ensure human rights. For example, The Protection of Civil Rights Act, 1955; Suppression of Immoral Traffic in Women and Girls Act, 1956; Maternity Benefit Act, 1961; Dowry Prohibition Act, 1961; Equal Remuneration Act, 1976; Bonded Labour (Abolition) Act, 1976; Employment of Children Act, 1938 (Amended in 1985); The Child Labour (Prohibition and Regulation) Act, 1986; Juvenile Justice Act, 1986; Indecent Representation of Women (Prohibition) Act, 1986;

Sati (Prevention) Act, 1987; The Scheduled Castes and the Scheduled Tribes (Prevention of Atrocities) Act, 1989; The National Commission for Women Act, 1990; The National Commission for Minorities Act, 1992; The National Commission for Safai Karamcharis Act, 1993; The National Commission for Backward Classes Act, 1993; The Mental Health Act, 1993; The Protection of Human Rights Act, 1993; and The Persons with Disabilities (Equal Opportunities, Protection of Rights and Full Participation) Act, 1995.

These Acts serve the purpose of protecting human rights only if the Government of the day takes initiatives appropriate for ensuring human rights. Initiatives of Parliament and Government would be successful only if all the stakeholders in the field of human rights step in to preserve and protect human rights of those people who are deprived of basic human rights. Dr. Neera Bharihoke in his preface rightly brought out the crux of the issue concerning violation of human rights. He said, ".... demarcation between empowered and deprived is responsible for violation of human rights."[4] This cannot be farther from truth. He further stated that Human Rights are far more complicated phenomenon to which State-sponsored initiatives can only give a slight protection.[5]

Parliamentary Initiatives—Questions and Debates in the 16th Lok Sabha

Questions are very potent weapons or devices available to the Members of Parliament to seek information from the Government. In the 16th Lok Sabha, from 24.6.2014 till 25.7.2017, a little over three years, we could find only 16 questions on human rights were asked in Lok Sabha. Questions on State Human Rights Commission, violation of human rights, protection of human rights, human rights violation in the Middle East, World Human Rights Report, Human Rights Impact Assessment, Conference of National and State HRs Commission, protection of HRs in Sri Lanka were raised.

It is clearly evident that over the years, human rights violation questions have increased. For example, in response to a question[6] on violation of human rights, Minister of Home Affairs responded that cases registered with NHRC in respect of alleged violation of human rights during 2016-17, up to 5.3.2017, is 86,398, cases disposed of is 75,541, and pending cases is 10,857. This gives an insight into the human rights violations that are being reported in the country and the mechanism in place in the government machinery to deal with it. Much more needs to be done in this sphere to ensure that protection of human rights is put in place in letter and spirit.

When it comes to debates for the above mentioned 3 years, it was merely 23. Debates on Matter under rule 377, Private Members Bill on Transgender, HIV/AIDS and Compulsory Voting, Short Duration Discussions under Rule 193 on recent incidents in institutions of higher education in reference to JNU and Hyderabad Universities, and need to have stringent legislation to check increasing atrocities against women and children, discussion on special sitting on commitment to India's Constitution as part of 125th birth anniversary of Dr. Ambedkar, Demands of HRD and MHAs, violation of HRs of minority communities in Pakistan and Tibet, situation in Gaza due to alleged attack by Israeli forces on Palestine civilians, refusal of Visa to the UN investigation committee etc.

Debates in the 15th Lok Sabha show that there is a Human Rights Division in Army. Of late, it has been expanded down till Corps level. When complaints are lodged, Army takes suitable action to dispose of complaints in consultation with units/formations and other agencies concerned in the matter.[7] From 2010 till March 2013, a total of 178 complaints have been received by Human Rights Cell in the Army.[8] These complaints are from different States, including Jammu & Kashmir and North Eastern States. Such complaints indicate that human rights violations take place in Army. At the same time, Army is equipped with a mechanism to sort out human rights violations.

Likewise, if we go deep in the questions and the responses of the Government, in the 14th Lok Sabha, we could find the response of the Government about the Report of Amnesty International on Human Rights when the Member wanted to know the details of violation of human rights in Armed Forces of the country. The response of the Ministry of Home Affairs was, "Amnesty International is an International NGO based in London and is one among the many NGOs based outside India which bring out reports on alleged human rights violations from time to time all-over the world, including India. The methods used by such organizations to gather information have often been questioned, particularly as they are not free from bias. It is not the policy of the Government to react to such reports by International NGOs on international matters of India."[9] The Government stressed that it is committed to take all necessary measures to protect the human rights of all its citizens.

India's successful re-election to the United Nations Human Rights Council is surely worthy of celebration. This shows our continued commitment to the safeguarding of human rights.[10] This feat is a testimony of our efforts in protecting human rights. Parliamentary initiatives include the role of Committee. The Department-Related Parliamentary Standing

Committee on Home Affairs deals with the issue of human rights in entirety.

Department-Related Parliamentary Standing Committee on Home Affairs

'Human Rights' comes under the purview of the Department-Related Parliamentary Standing Committee (DPSC) on Home Affairs, which also deals with the Ministry of Development of North Eastern Region, is serviced by Rajya Sabha. As is the case with the functioning of the Parliamentary Standing Committee, the Committee, after detailed and thorough discussion among its Members and witnesses from the Ministry of Home Affairs and other concerned officials, comes out with its observations, conclusions and recommendations in the Report, which are looked into by the Ministry. Of late, many of the recommendations are accepted. As such, recommendations of the Committee are not mandatory on the part of the Ministry or Government to accept.

The Committee presents a Report to Rajya Sabha and the same is placed in Lok Sabha too. The Minister concerned lays a statement regarding the status of implementation of the recommendations contained in the Report of the Standing Committee on Demands for Grants pertaining to the Ministry of Home Affairs. This process would ensure that the recommendations, suggestions, observations of the Committee are taken serious note of by the Government which would result in redressal of grievances, streamlining of schemes, ensuring justice etc.

In the 16th Lok Sabha, Department-Related Standing Committee on Home Affairs was constituted on 1st September, 2014.[11] Initially when it was constituted, its Chairman was P. Bhattacharya. Now, this Committee is chaired by P. Chidambaram in the 16th Lok Sabha, with 21 Members from Lok Sabha and 10 Members from Rajya Sabha. Prominent Members are Sitaram Yechury from CPI(M), D. Raja from CPI, K. Rahman Khan and Mallikarjun Kharge from Congress, Kirron Kher, R.K. Sinha from BJP. Till now, it had presented about 23 reports to Ministry of Home Affairs and North-Eastern Region.

Other parliamentary initiatives, which indirectly contribute, and which give importance to the human rights in Consultative Committees of not only the Ministry of Home Affairs but also of various other Ministries of Government of India.

Consultative Committee of the Ministry of Home Affairs and Development of North Eastern Region

Functioning of the Consultative Committees of Members of Parliament for various Ministries is taken care of the Ministry of Parliamentary Affairs under the Government of India (Allocation of Business) Rules, 1961. In the meetings of the Consultative Committee, MPs get an opportunity to discuss informally issues concerning the Ministry with the Minister and senior officers of the Ministry. They would get to know about the policies, principles and programmes of the Ministry and the manner of their implementation. Discussions are held in a free and frank manner, and are confidential in nature. Minister himself chairs the meetings of the Consultative Committee of the Ministry.

In the 16th Lok Sabha, Consultative Committee of the Ministry of Home Affairs met 10 times. The latest being on 11.8.2017 on modernization of police forces; on 15.6.2017 on reorganizing Ministry of Home Affairs for the 21st century; and on 22.5.2017 on CCTNS & NERS (114) under the chairmanship of the Minister of Home Affairs, Rajnath Singh. Other Members are Haribhai Parthibhai Chaudhary and Kiren Rijiju, both Ministers of State in the Ministry of Home Affairs; 17 Lok Sabha Members; 12 Rajya Sabha Members; 2 ex-officio Members are Rajiv Pratap Rudi and Mukhtar Abbas Naqvi, both Ministers of State in the Ministry of Parliamentary Affairs.[12] On 12th November, 2014, the Committee discussed the state of Left-Wing Extremism.

There is a need to take up specifically protection of human rights as well as violation of human rights in the country by the Consultative Committee. Sincere efforts should be made by the Committee and the Members in this regard.

Though the Ministry of Home Affairs is part of the executive, but as the executive is accountable to legislature, we can very well say that they contribute to the parliamentary initiatives in the realm of human rights.

Ministry of Home Affairs

Ministry of Home Affairs has a Department of States which deals with human rights. It also has a separate Human Rights Division which deals with matters relating to the Protection of Human Rights Act and also matters relating to national integration, communal harmony and Ayodhya. Ministry has one of the broad responsibilities which involves coordination of policy relating to human rights.

Annual Report of Ministry of Home Affairs

If you go through the annual report, you would find whole range of issues being dealt with, for example, how to strengthen law enforcement response to trafficking, training and capacity building programmes, judicial colloquiums, issuing advisories to States/UTs on human trafficking, bilateral mechanism with Bangladesh, workshops were conducted in Bengaluru, Hyderabad, Ranchi, Jharkhand and Bhopal. Conditions in prisons were studied, research studies were conducted.

As we could see from the print media, complaints are received from Jammu & Kashmir against security forces personnel concerning violation of human rights. Annual Report states, "The Government attaches highest importance to human rights issue. It has repeatedly expressed its commitment to protection of Human Rights (HR) and prevention of HR violations in the country. The Security Forces are under instructions to respect the human rights of all people and work steadfastly with humane face while performing their day-to-day operational duties. Every reported case of alleged human rights violation is taken serious note of, investigations are made promptly in a transparent manner and taken to their logical conclusion.[13] Punitive action has been taken in 80 cases where complaints were found to be genuine.

Chapter 6 of the Annual Accounts of Ministry of Home Affairs for 2016-17 deals with Human Rights and National Integration. This Report conveys information about performance of NHRC. During 2016-17 up to 1.4.2016 to 31.12.16, 71,412 cases were registered, and 63,087 disposed. Transferred 16,382 cases to State HRs Commissions. NHRC recommended payment of interim relief in 344 cases amounting to Rs. 6,86,55,000.[14]

I am of the firm opinion that Parliament which is a place to legislative laws at the national level can bring about vast changes in protecting the human rights of the people. There is no dearth of institutions which protect human rights. We have National Human Rights Commission, which came into being in 1993. We can see the whole gamut of issues concerning human rights are addressed by the National Human Rights Commission, which is under the Ministry of Human Rights. In all the initiatives of Parliament, and to a great extent by the Ministry of Home Affairs, Ministry of Development of North Eastern Region, media play a very important role.

Parliamentary Initiatives—National Human Rights Commission (NHRC)

One of the major parliamentary initiatives towards protecting human rights came in the form of setting up of The National Human Rights Commission of India (NHRC) on 12th October, 1993 pursuant to the enactment of the Protection of Human Rights Act, 1993. Since then, considerable efforts have been made in ensuring human rights in the country. The NHRC has been making determined efforts to prevent violation or neglect of human rights occurring anywhere in the country coming to its notice. NHRC also started an Annual Journal in 2002 to create an important platform for building a body of high-quality scholarship on human rights. Research and spreading of awareness on human rights received a much-needed fillip with this endeavour. In 2010, it had focused on Millennium Development Goals, Human Rights in Conflict Situations, Role of Civil Society and Human Rights and Corporate Social Responsibility and Human Rights.[15] NHRC not only deals with all aspects for redressal of human rights but it also ensures spreading human rights awareness through their programmes like seminars, workshops, training etc.

NHRC is keen to see that State Human Rights Commission (SHRCs) is set up in every state. Though the onus is on the States, as per Section 21 of the Protection of Human Rights Act, 1992, to set up State Human Rights Commission, Government of India and the NHRC have been making efforts in this direction and with its constant efforts, States like Andhra Pradesh, Assam, Bihar, Chhattisgarh, Gujarat, Himachal Pradesh, Jammu & Kashmir, Karnataka, Kerala, Madhya Pradesh, Maharashtra, Manipur, Odisha, Punjab, Rajasthan, Tamil Nadu, Uttar Pradesh and West Bengal had set up SHRCs in 2009. By 2011, we could find 20 States setting up SHRCs have constituted State Human Rights Commissions. By February 2014, 23 States have in place SHRCs. It is also making recommendation to this effort. It also takes initiatives to hold interactions with the SHRC to explore and further strengthen areas of cooperation and partnerships. As on 21st March, 2017, 24 States have in place SHRCs.[16]

When it comes to filling up of vacancies in NHRC *vis-à-vis* SHRCs, NHRC is not affected by it but the pending cases—42,012 in number as of October 2014—bothers us.[17] There is a need to see that recommendations of the NHRC are complied with. The Chairperson of NHRC and former Chief Justice of India, K.G. Balakrishnan, in his article in *The Hindu* on the occasion of 66th anniversary of the adoption of the Universal Declaration of Human Rights—in 1948, the United Nations 'General

Assembly adopted the Universal Declaration of Human Rights—stated, "....concerned government authorities have complied with its (NHRC) decisions, the largely non-binding nature of the Commission's recommendations sometimes evokes the sentiment that perhaps such bodies are ineffectual."[18] This augurs well for ensuring human rights in the country. But there is a need to see that NHRC is made more effective with filling up of posts in various SHRCs. It is astonishing to note that Delhi is not having the State Human Rights Commission. Likewise, Mizoram, Meghalaya, Nagaland, Tripura and Arunachal Pradesh do not have SHRCs for the last 21 years. Even where SHRCs exist, we find Manipur, Himachal Pradesh, Jammu & Kashmir, Karnataka and Tamil Nadu remain headless and hence ineffective.[19]

This state of affairs needs to be changed. NHRC becomes an independent democratic institution. Extra efforts should be made to ensure that all the vacancies are filled up at regular intervals and no State Human Rights Commission is headless even for a day. With over 130 crore people, it is difficult to expect NHRC or SHRCs to ensure protection of human rights. There is a need for stepping in by other stakeholders like civil society, NGOs, media and the general public. While addressing on the occasion of Human Rights Day, Sumitra Mahajan, Speaker, Lok Sabha laid stress on the role of others in ensuring human rights. She remarked: "Human rights not the duty of NHRC alone. Protection and promotion of human rights is not the responsibility of the NHRC or government bodies alone."[20] It cannot be farther from truth. She further stated that it will not be sufficient to talk of human rights just on a particular day. We must become mutually sensitive towards each other's rights and duties for all times.[21] On the occasion, a theme or an idea of 'Human Rights 365' was unveiled, which means that everyday is a Human Rights Day and everybody at all times is entitled to all human rights.

Civil society has the wherewithal to check human rights violation. A vigilant civil society can bring about change in the prevailing human rights situation in the country. That is the reason why it is believed and said that civil society can play a vital role in preserving human rights in the country. "An empowered civil society can duly protect human rights and take efforts to redress victimization, on accountability of human rights violations."[22] NGOs have altered the state-centred approach of human rights protection and brought a sense of enthusiasm to promote human rights activism.[23]

State Human Rights Commissions face problems of unfilled vacancies. For example, Himachal Pradesh and Manipur SHRCs are functioning without chairperson since 2005 and 2010 respectively.[24] Another glaring episode of SHRCs is that Maharashtra Commission has not even prepared annual reports for more than 10 years.[25] This had been the case in spite of the clear mandate to place these reports before the Legislature every year. Many States lack resources to obtain information relating to human rights violations.

Being a signatory to the Universal Declaration of Human Rights, we can find many of the provisions of the Universal Declaration of Human Rights in the fundamental rights guaranteed to the individuals in Part III of the Indian Constitution.[26] Likewise, most of the economic, social and cultural rights proclaimed in the Universal Declaration of Human Rights have been incorporated in Part IV of the Indian Constitution.[27]

Human Rights and Media

Media not only highlights as to what is happening in the domain of human rights but also provides incisive and insightful coverage of various happenings leading to violation of human rights. Media has a major role in taking the happenings on human rights. Media has acquired the status of prime education, informative and catalytic agent to safeguard human rights.[28] One could see the news items relating to human rights violations in different parts of the country and the response of the Government or NHRC or the SHRCs. General public gets educated and aware of what is going on in the realm of human rights only through the media. Vice President, while delivering the Tarkunde (an eminent jurist and human rights activist) Memorial Lecture in New Delhi pointed out that people have a profound disenchantment with the state due to misuse of laws such as the Armed Forces (Special Powers) Act.[29] This amply conveys the status of human rights in the country. He also called for a fuller accountability into the system of governance at all levels so that the culture of impunity ends, and the state and its functionaries are held accountable for every act of omission or commission.[30]

It is a matter of concern to read that Haryana has the poorest human rights record when compared to Himachal Pradesh during the period 2012 to July 2014.[31] Media has to take up issues concerning defenders of human rights and expose those who come in the way of protecting and safeguarding the human rights. Only then can we expect activists, NGOs and defenders of human rights take up issues of violation of human rights and other issues in the fields of land rights, natural resources or environment, which have the bearing on the society. It is pertinent to point out here, "In Human Rights Council 2007 Report, the Special Representative of the United Nations Secretary General on the human rights defenders noted that defenders working on land rights, natural resources or environmental issues seem to be particularly at risk of attacks and violation of their rights.[32]

The extraordinary protest of Irom Sharmila against the AFSPA received much publicity only with the efforts of the Media. She was a volunteer at Human Rights Alert helping victims of violence, compiling cases and taking part in protest and peache marches, when the Malom massacre happened on November 2, 2000. Since then, she had come a long away. Misuse of AFSPA has caught the imagination of human rights activists for long. Even our Vice President recently made a statement to this effect. It is important to quote here the response of the Government in reply to a question in Lok Sabha. Ministry of Home Affairs, Government of India stated that there is no proposal to repeal the AFSPA or drastically amend it.[33] It also stated that Mr. Christof Heyns, the United Nations Special Rapporteur (SR) on Extrajudicial, Summary of Arbitrary Executions on his 12 days visit to India in March 2012 recommended in his draft report that AFSPA may be repealed or at least radically amended.[34] Her recent release in January 2015 and her arrest once again is a matter of concern.

It is reported in the Press that 50 per cent of human rights complaints are from Jammu & Kashmir. This is in response to the RTI application.[35] There was a huge hue and cry on appointing a retired IPS officer who was tainted as the Gujarat State Human Rights Commission.[36] It was reported widely in the Press that from complaints of eroding minority rights and religious intolerance to the crackdown against NGOs, women's rights to LGBT rights, Kashmir to Afrophobia—India's track record on human rights came under sharp scrutiny at the UN Human Rights Council in May, 2017 in Geneva. Several countries expressed concerns on India's FCRA [The Foreign Contribution (Regulation) Act], [The Foreign Contribution (Regulation) Act] laws, on rights of religious minorities and intolerance.[37] But the Attorney General, Mukul Rohatgi strongly defended the stand of the government by highlighting the efforts being made by the government to ensure protection of human rights and by stating that India is a secular state with no state religion.[38]

Another disturbing news brought by the media is that India tops world in slavery. India is placed behind China, Pakistan, Bangladesh, Uzbekistan. It is reported that India has the highest number of people in the world trapped in modern slavery with 18.35 million victims of forced labour, ranging from prostitution to begging, according to the 2016 Global Slavery

Index.[39] Amnesty International report cites the dark side of coal mining in Chhattisgarh, Odisha and Jharkhand where a pattern of human rights violations were mainly caused by displacement of *Adivasis* by different subsidiaries of the state-owned Coal India Limited (CIL).[40]

World Report 2017—India Events of 2016

If we go through the World Report 2017, we can know the real scenario of human rights prevailing in India. It seems by cursorily going through the said Report, it shows a stark reminder that still human rights violations continue unabated. I quote: "Security forces operating against Maoist insurgents continue to be accused of serious human rights violations, including sexual assault. Numerous tribal villagers have been arbitrarily arrested as Maoist sympathizers."[41]

Indian Government temporarily suspended the FCRA [The Foreign Contribution (Regulation) Act] status of the Lawyers Collective, and such other 25 prominent human rights NGOs invited lot of criticism. In June, three UN special rapporteurs released a statement raising concerns over the suspension and calling on the government to repeal FCRA.[42] It is pertinent to point out that in a joint statement following the India-European Union summit in March attended by Modi and the heads of the European Council and European Commission, the leaders "highlighted the need for efforts to ensure gender equality and respect for women and girls' human rights."[43] In October 2016, India hosted the BRICS (Brazil, Russia, India, China and South Africa) Summit wherein Prime Minister Modi spoke of partnering to address security challenges and economic uncertainties but there was no mention of working to uphold international human rights principles.[44]

Suggestions

At present, every year, Parliament Session meets for around 70 days a year. In the first three Lok Sabhas, we could see about 150 days of Session every year. In the last All India Whips Conference in Goa in 2014, Union Parliamentary Affairs Minister, M. Venkaiah Naidu while expressing concern over public perception of legislature, desired that number of sittings of Parliament would increase. With a single party receiving majority, we could expect smooth functioning of Parliament and its contributions would multiply in years to come with more sittings of legislatures on reaching consensus among political parties.

There is a need to make parliamentary debates and interventions more effective. Records prove the point that efforts have been made from time to time in this direction. Though parliamentary interventions by way of debates and discussions on human rights are not considerable, there is no denying of the fact that Parliament's efforts, as enumerated in some detail, is not negligible too.

Nevertheless, there is a need to bring more issues concerning human rights before Parliament for resolution. Growing awareness about human rights violations may lead to more and more issues concerning human rights would reverberate in Parliament which helps the Government to take note of and resolve them. Providing good governance is an Herculean task. Governments after governments have tried and faltered at providing the basic essentials to the poorest of the poor.

There is a need to ensure human rights to all. It is easier said than done. After 70 years of Independence, the scenario is not rosy to say the least. As stated in the chapter, huge mass of people is deprived of human rights. There should not be any differences between haves and have-nots. Everyone is entitled to human rights. Parliament through its initiatives has been making attempts to ensure over the decades that human rights are protected and there is good governance in the country. Much more needs to be done in the realm of participation by Members of Parliament by bringing in every aspect of human rights violation with a view to ensuring human rights to the deprived sections of society.

Conclusion

With the active participation of political parties with the feedback from the people and activists, parliamentary initiatives towards addressing violation of human rights as well as protection and safeguarding of human rights and ensuring good governance would become the order of the day which would see the end of human rights violation in the country.

The actions of Government are questioned and scrutinized by Parliament in its functioning. This advantage should be taken by the Members of Parliament in order to ensure protection of human rights of its citizens in the real sense of the term.

Nevertheless, there is a need to make parliamentary debates and interventions more effective. With a stable Government in place in the 16th Lok Sabha, with completion of three years, one should decide for oneself as to whether our country in regard to protecting human rights is moving in the right direction. Going by the human rights related issues brought before Lok Sabha for discussion, debate and redressal, no doubt there is an urgent need to bring more and more issues concerning human rights to ensure good governance in the country. There is a vast space to be filled in the domain of legislature which would go a long way in ensuring protection of human rights in the country. Efforts are being made from time to time in this direction. If one follows the parliamentary initiatives minutely, one would invariably conclude that it serves the national interest.

References

1. http://nhrc.nic.in Retrieved on 21.04.2017.
2. Patwaris, A.B.M., Mafizul Islam, 1991. *Fundamental Rights and Personal Liberty in India, Pakistan and Bangladesh,* 1st ed. New Delhi: Deep and Deep Publications, p. 63.
3. Sharma Mukul, 2010. "*Human Rights in a Globalized World—An Indian Diary*", New Delhi: Sage. p. 229.
4. Bharihoke, Neera, ed. 2010. "Human Rights–Content and Extent", *Preface*. New Delhi: Serials Publications.
5. *Ibid.*
6. Lok Sabha Debates. Unstarred Question No. 3011, dated 21.3.2017. http://164.100.47.194/Loksabha/Questions/QResult15.aspx?qref=49428&lsno=16
7. Lok Sabha Debates, 15th Lok Sabha, 2013, Unstarred Question No. 840, 10 December. http://164.100.47.132/LssNew/psearch/QResult15.aspx?qref=142882
8. *Ibid.*
9. Lok Sabha Debates, 14th Lok Sabha, 2008, Starred Question No. 2530, 16 December. http://164.100.47.132/LssNew/psearch/qsearch14.aspx
10. *The Pioneer*, 2014, 23 October. http://www.dailypioneer.com/rint.php?printFOR-storydetail&story
11. Rajya Sabha, http://164.100.47.5/webcom/MainPage.aspx# and http://164.100.47.5/webcom/typewize.aspx?type=DRSCRS
12. http://mpa.gov.in/mpa/ccms_rpt.aspx, 16.6.2017
13. Ministry of Home Affairs, Annual Report 2013-14, Ch. VI—Human Rights and National Integration, pp. 89-93.
14. Annual Report 2016-17, Ministry of Home Affairs, Government of India.
15. *Journal of the National Human Rights Commission*, India, Vol. 9, 2010, pp. viii.
16. Lok Sabha Debates, Unstarred Q.No. 3038, 21.03.2017. http://164.100.47.194/Loksabha/Questions/QResult15.aspx?qref=49433&lsno=16
17. *The Hindustan Times*, 2014, 9 December—http://www.hindustantimes.com/analysis/set-things/right-in-our-human-rights-bodies/article 1-1294923. aspx
18. *The Hindu*, 2015, "Universal Rights and Universal Violations", 11

December—Available online at—http://www.thehindu.com/opinion/op-ed/universal-rights-and-universal-violations/article6680008.ece
19. *The Pioneer*, "Cases Galore But no Human Rights Panel in Delhi", 6 November, 2014–Available online at—http://www.dailypioneer.com/nation/cases-galore-but-no-human-rights-panel-in-delhi.html
20. *The Hindu*, 2014, 11 December.
21. *Ibid.*
22. Mishra, Kaushlendra, 2011, *Human Rights in India—Historical Social and Political Perspective,* New Delhi: Navyug Books International, p. 57.
23. *Ibid.*, p. 57.
24. *The Hindustan Times*, "Set things right in our Human Rights Bodies", 10 December, 2014.
25. *Ibid.*
26. http://shodhganga.inflibnet.ac.in/bitstream/10603/6653/11/11_chapter%203.pdf, pp. 62-63. Retrieved on 21.11.2014
27. *Ibid.*
28. Gill, Dr. Rajbans, ed. *Human Rights—The New Awakening,* 2010, Chandigarh: Abhishek Publications, p. 11.
29. *The Hindu*, "End culture of impunity: Hamid Ansari", 23 November, 2014
30. *Ibid.*
31. *The Tribune*, http://www.tribuneindia.com/2014/20140920/nation.html#15
32. Sharma, Mukul, 2010, *Human Rights in a Globalized World—an Indian Diary,* "Ch. 11—Persecution and Persistence: Experiences of Rights Defenders", New Delhi: Sage. p. 68.
33. Lok Sabha Debates, 15th Lok Sabha, 2013, Unstarred Question No. 3488, 19 March.
34. *Ibid.*
35. Free Press Journal, 18 July, 2017 "50 per cent of human rights complaints from J&K: RTI".
36. *Statesman*, 13 July, 2017. "Encounter tainted cop made human rights panel chief".
37. *The Indian Express*, 5 May, 2017. "Minority rights, NGO crackdown raised at UN meet, India says freedoms secure".
38. *Ibid.*
39. *The Indian Express*, 1 June, 2016. "India tops world in slavery, says rights group".
40. *The Times of India*, 14 July, 2016. "CIL violating human rights, says Amnesty".
41. World Report 2017: India/Human Rights Watch. https://www.hrw.org/world-report/2017/country-chapters/india, Retrieved on 11.8.2017.
42. *Ibid.*
43. *Ibid.*
44. *Ibid.*

7
Human Rights and Good Governance
An Interface with Indian Judiciary

Naveen Kumar

Introduction

Human Rights movement has grown significantly in India, due to the wide gap between the articulation of international and national standards in national, regional and local settings. This gap demonstrates that there is an urgent need for good governance; a governance strategy that leads to the total sustainable development maintaining all the pillars of democracy. India needs stable and good governance practices based on public trust to enhance state capacity to fulfil the constitutional goal of equitable justices. Development of any country primarily presupposes protection of human rights and good governance and rule of law.

The timely needed intervention of judiciary is very important to deal with the problems of good governance. The role of judiciary can be understood by the large number of cases filed in the courts for the violation of basic human rights and the poor implementation of policies and programmes by the government. People approach courts with great expectations and institution of last resort to address their grievances under the Constitution. The judiciary has not hesitated in the past also on various occasions to remind the executives of their failures on the dynamic issues of adopting the good governance to protect the rights of the parties and also suggested best possible future strategies by issuing guidelines. Several times courts have filled the void of legislations looked at various international instruments and treaty for its effective implementation. Many legislations have been enacted by the Parliament and state legislature due to timely judicial intervention on the issue and also reminded the governments for the urgent need of the legislation on the subject to adopt good governance practices. There are large numbers of judgments passed by the courts where innovative methods adopted by the court to look at the very core of the problem of good governance and protection of human rights.

Genesis of the Good Governance and its Dimensions

It is a difficult task to give any precise definition to the term 'governance' with so many varied opinions between various schools of thinkers and scholars.[1] In such a situation, the World Bank[2] has attempted to define the term by taking a middle path in terms of the traditions and the institutions by which a country exercises its authority. According to World Bank in 1989 governance[3] means, "broadly as the tradition and institutions by which authority in a country is exercised. This includes the process by which governments are selected, monitored and replaced; the capacity of the government to effectively formulate sound policies; and the respect of citizens and the state for the institutions that govern economic and social interaction among them." Subsequently in 1992, this term has been explained in some larger context in the document[4], "the manner in which power is exercised in management of countries economic and social resources for development." As such, the usage of the term governance in varied forms covering numbers of both public and private organizations has become a widely used term in recent times. Initially, the freedom movement under the leadership of Mahatma Gandhi along with the aspirations connected with the framing of the Constitution of India was pivotal in shaping the road to the concept of governance. The quality and content of governance[5] of any nation is highly influenced by the national commitments and certain values present in the government and its citizens. Good governance is crucial for achieving proper economic growth and maximizing citizens' output of their investments. Good governance does not happen by chance. It is something that has to be demanded by the people and thereby be consciously and explicitly worked on by the nation. For achieving good governance, it is vital to encourage free participation of the citizens in the political process, competing for office, enjoyment of fundamental rights and civil liberties. Political leadership with accountability, sensible policy-making and ethical professionals in the civil services lead to the good governance. Good governance is a meaningful aspiration achievable through an independent judiciary with the presence of a strong civil society and a free press.[6] The term good governance has multiple facets and interdependent on various organs of government. To achieve the goal of good governance, all these organs of the government and non-government organization need to work in collaboration to protect the human rights of the citizen. In recent times, the term good governance implies an expanded connotation meaning to include more than multiparty elections, a judiciary and a parliament. The term has now become an elastic term rather than a mere concept.[7]

The Eleventh Five-Year Plan[8] envisioned certain goals of inclusive growth by reducing poverty and bridging the various strata of our society through significant improvement in the quality of governance. One way of defining good governance is to define it as accumulation of aspects of interface of individuals and businesses on one hand and the government on the other. The said Plan has laid down certain distinct dimensions of good governance:

- In a democratic country like ours, fair process of electing government at various levels as part of the constitutional right is a central feature of good governance.
- Accountability and transparency of government at all levels.[9]
- Efficiency in effective delivery of social and economic public services[10] as primary responsibilities with special attention to active role of the local governments with respect to health and education.
- Empowerment of local governments like the Panchayati Raj Institutions (PRIs)[11] by supporting them with sufficient funds and functionaries in the performance of their constitutional functions.
- Establishment of firm rule of law.[12] A present day society is an arrangement of complex relations and interactions between different private entities and businesses for whose balance clear legal rights and legal remedies are needed.

Finally, the existence of a fair and inclusive system in which the voices of the disadvantaged groups like SCs, STs, minorities and others[13] are heard and benefits ensured.

The concept of Good Governance has been useful for various walks of life to understand the problems of the efficient utilization of public and private resources of the country and it is very useful even to address the problems of protecting various human rights with economic, social cultural dimensions. This term has been used in various human right programmes and policies formulated by the United Nations[14] also. This concept becomes the necessity for the government to address the needs of the citizens and other stake-holders. Good governance is specifically linked to sustainable development.

E-Governance as a Necessary Tool of Good Governance

E-Governance is a new instrument or a tool for good governance. The efficiency of E-Governance depends upon the process reforms and process re-engineering through which Information Technology (IT) can be taken to the common man keeping in view the changing needs of the citizens and other stakeholders. The role of the government has transformed from a buyer or producer of Information and Communication Technology (ICT) service to that of a facilitator and a leader. Implementation of e-Governance means improving processes and outcomes in governance which further improves the delivery of public services to the citizens. Government's vital role in shaping and supporting e-Governance, e-Administration and e-Governance programmes are important for the improvement of governance. The technological advancements and the use of the internet create a platform for transforming the relationship between governments at all levels and citizens and the conduct of their business in new ways that lead to achieving good governance. E-Governance is more efficient and cost-effective for both citizens and government operations and public services.[15]

Good Governance and Human Rights

The recognition of the concept of human rights at the international level has always attracted political attention, both wanted and unwanted and raises serious questions as to theory and practice. Does a State's competence in dealing with its citizens mostly depend upon human rights or governance?[16] Does the economic development of a country or culture determine human rights? Is there any relationship between the rule of law, human rights and democracy? How human rights and democracy are related to economic and social development? On analyzing these questions, it is observed that there are no ready answers to them.

According to the United Nation's Commission on Human Rights, the main attributes of good governance include transparency, responsibility, accountability, participation and responsiveness to the needs of the people at large. Good governance is linked to a facilitating environment conducive to the protection of Human Rights and promoting equitable growth and sustainable human development. People from its Government expect that it would fulfil its necessary commitments and provides an equitable atmosphere, which is prerequisite to an individual's growth. It can also be understood that Good Governance entails effective participation in public policy-making, the dominance of the rule of law and an independent judiciary, along with a very robust system of institutional checks and balances. There is also some extent of horizontal and vertical separation of powers.

Prof. Yash Ghai in his article "Human Rights and Governance: The Asia Debate" has analyzed the understanding of human rights and governance differently in the West and Asian countries due to diverse socio-economic and cultural issues. The Asian realities need to be understood with some uniqueness due to different factors. He has observed that:

> "As per the Asian view of human rights, the contemporary debate is that it is different than the traditional approach of individual human rights, which developed in the West. The Asian view finds support as some leaders on various occasions have spoken of human rights as representatives of the whole continent. However, there is no homogeneity of Asian culture or Asian realities. The social and class positions in society have a great influence on the perceptions of human rights. A closer look at the picture reveals that the apparent uniform Asian perspective on human rights disclose it to be the perspective of a particular group, which is the ruling elites and they are usually able to gain publicity domestically and internationally. On the other hand, there are other Asian voices also, muted and oppressed voices of the marginalized and indigenous people. The path towards achieving better governance and democracy is undoubtedly a difficult and complicated involving different factors, namely the rule of law and liberal culture, democratic reforms and development of civil rights by means of extending other political rights, economic and social rights along with fairness and transparency in governance with a touch of marketization in some instances."[17]

One of the important factors hampering good governance is 'corruption'. The National Commission to Review the Working of the Constitution in its Consultation Paper[18] on Probity in Governance has observed:

> "The paradox of India, however, is that in spite of a vigilant

> press and public opinion, the level of corruption is exceptionally high. This may be attributed to the utter insensitivity, lack of shame, and the absence of any sense of public morality among the bribe-takers. Indeed, they wear their badge of corruption and shamelessness with equal élan and brazenness... Corruption today poses a danger not only to the quality of governance but it is threatening the very foundation of our society and the State."

Section 2(d) of the Protection of Human Rights Act, 1993 defines 'human rights' as "the rights relating to life, liberty, equality and dignity of the individual guaranteed by the constitution or embodied in international covenants and enforceable by the court in India."[19] The issues of corruption, whenever brought before a court of law has been viewed as a criminal offence and not as a human rights issue. It is the need of the hour to recognize corruption as one of the factors violating human rights. The anti-corruption initiatives should not be treated merely as violations of criminal law and tax law but as also a violation of human rights. There are numerous ways by which corruption can be presented in the trellis of human rights as it is by nature discrimination against people, it brings in unfairness in decision-making and it violates a whole class of civil and political rights.[20]

The right to know and make known is one of the crucial aspects indispensable to democracy in India. The right to know is seen as a docile right by itself. In India, there is a great need to depend upon activism, whistle-blowers, stings and investigative journalism to discover the truths affecting the democracy. As such, providing a certain degree of protection to journalists, activists or whistle-blowers is necessary.[21]

Right to development[22] is a recent addition to the classes of human rights. Development is another important aspect of good governance. Development may be described as a comprehensive economic, social and political process in which the realization of all rights occurs in due course of time when the realization of anyone right depends on the realization of all other rights. The promotion and protection of human rights are dependent upon the clarity of conviction and communication whose attainment is a human rights task by itself. It is a daunting task. Governance emerges simultaneously as a complex site of human rights practices of politics. Human rights values are non-negotiable for good states. According to the human rights approach, the states and its institutions are only the instruments for protecting, promoting and securing human rights for all. Many thinkers of human rights believe that the Universal Declaration on

Human Rights (UDHR) and its values form the basis of good governance. From a rights-based point of view, the concept of good governance has the function of supporting the endeavour of protecting economic, social and cultural rights of the people.[23] Although at times, human rights may not be seen as an integral part of good governance and good governance may be seen as a means for improving people's possibilities of claiming their human rights, still, good governance can offer something to human rights[24] and *vice versa*.

The Relevance of Judiciary for the Protection of Human Rights and Good Governance

The active role of the Judiciary in India is very crucial in the protection of human rights of the people and the process of good governance, which is indispensable to the proper functioning of the country. The Supreme Court, in the last few decades,[25] has given expanded interpretations to the fundamental rights, checking the threat from any agents of the State and also protecting the rights and dignity of the individual, thereby working towards good governance. The judiciary has played a very significant role in promoting and protecting human rights and strengthening the rule of law in the country. People are looking at the judiciary as a panacea of all problems of society. The courts try their level best to uphold the spirit of the Constitution for protecting the rights of the citizens. Even courts have not hesitated to issue directions and compelled the respective governments for promoting good governance practices. There are large numbers of cases where courts have even overstepped, in its approach traditionally, in the domain of executive to do justice with the people. On various occasions, the government has criticized the role played by the judiciary to even interfere in the matter of governance despite timely and needed interventions. Only some landmark cases have been analyzed to examine the impact of the judiciary for promoting good governance and protection of human rights. These judicial decisions have highlighted the importance of good governance in the country and also suggested the legal duty of the executive to deal with such matters. Lots of cases have been discussed to cover the various areas of governance so that the effective role can be understood.

In the matter of *Anjali Bhardwaj and others* v. *Union of India and Others*[26], the observation of the Supreme Court is as follows:

> "... the salient purpose which RTI Act is supposed to serve.

> This Act is enacted not only to sub-serve and ensure freedom of speech. On proper implementation, it has the potential to bring about good governance which is an integral part of any vibrant democracy. Attaining good governance is also one of the visions of the Constitution. It also has a vital connection with development. All these aspects are highlighted above. There is a definite link between the right to information and good governance. The RTI Act itself emphasizes on good governance and recognises that it is one of the objectives which the said Act seeks to achieve. The RTI Act would reveal that four major elements/objectives required to ensure good governance are:
>
> (i) greater transparency in the functioning of public authorities;
> (ii) informed citizenry for promotion of partnership between citizens and the Government in the decision-making process;
> (iii) improvement in accountability and performance of the Government; and
> (iv) reduction in corruption in the Government department."

In this case, the Supreme Court has analyzed the ambit of good governance. What are the essentials of good governance need to be understood by the executive? The matter was related to the appointment of Information Commissioner under Right to Information Act, 2005.

In the case of *State of Uttar Pradesh* v. *Raj Narain*[27], a Constitution Bench of this Court held that:

> "In a government of responsibility like ours, where all the agents of the public must be responsible for their conduct, there can but few secrets. The people of this country have a right to know every public act, everything, that is done in a public way, by their public functionaries. They are entitled to know the particulars of every public transaction in all its bearing. The right to know, which is derived from the concept of freedom of speech, though not absolute, is a factor which should make one wary, when secrecy is claimed for transactions which can, at any rate, have no repercussion on public security. To cover with veil secrecy the common routine business is not in the interest of the public...."

This landmark decision has established the right to freedom of information and done the groundwork for the enactment of Right to Information Act, 2005. It also strengthens the fundamental rights guaranteed under Article 19 of the Constitution. Without ensuring these rights democracy cannot function with its real strength.

In the case of *Reserve Bank of India* v. *Jayantilal N. Mistry* [28] where a Two-Judge Bench of the Supreme Court while upholding peoples' right to access information, made the following observations regarding the Right to Information that:

> "Because an informed citizen has the capacity to reasoned action and also to evaluate the actions of the legislature and executives, which is very important in a participative democracy and this will serve the nation's interest better which as stated above also includes its economic interests. Recognizing the significance of this tool it has not only been made one of the fundamental rights under Article 19 of the Constitution also a Central Act has been brought into effect on 12th October, 2005 as the Right to Information Act, 2005.... The ideal of 'Government by the people' makes it necessary that people have access to information on matters of public concern. The free flow of information about affairs of Government paves way for debate in public policy and fosters accountability in Government. It creates a condition for 'open governance' which is a foundation of democracy."

Further, in the case of *Manoj Narula* v. *Union of India*[29], the honourable Supreme Court has made some remarkable observation to analyse the very spirit of good governance and established with the citizens right, fundamental rights and constitutional values. The emphasis of the court was to make the decision making more transparent and accountable. The observation of the court is:

> "In a democracy, the citizens legitimately expect that the Government of the day would treat the public interest as the primary one and any other interest secondary. The *maxim salus populi suprema lex*, has not only to be kept in view but also has to be revered. The faith of the people is embedded in the root of the idea of good governance which means reverence for citizenry rights, respect for fundamental rights and statutory rights in any governmental action, deference for unwritten constitutional values, veneration for institutional integrity, and inculcation of accountability to the collective at large. It also conveys that

> the decisions are taken by the decision-making authority with solemn sincerity and policies are framed keeping in view the welfare of the people, and including all in a homogeneous compartment. The concept of good governance is not a Utopian conception or an abstraction. It has been the demand of the polity wherever democracy is nourished. The growth of democracy is dependent upon good governance in reality and the aspiration of the people is that the administration is carried out by people with responsibility with service orientation."

The concept of good governance has multiple dimensions. One of the important dimensions is the role of the executive in discharging their function as per the rule of law. The Bureaucrats are the pillars of the decision-making process, formulations of policies and programmes for the citizens and its execution without fear and favour. To resolve some inherent problems of Administration, the Second Administrative Reforms Committee (2008) was set up and a very detailed report was submitted by the Committee. For the implementation of this report, retired administrative officer filed the petition before the Supreme Court for its effective implementation to bring more transparency and adopt the practices of good governance.

The Report of the Second Administrative Reforms Committee (2008)[30] reads as follows:

> "A healthy working relationship between Ministers and civil servants is critical for good governance. While the principles governing the roles and responsibilities of Ministers and civil servants are well defined in political theory, in the actual working of this relationship this division of responsibility becomes blurred with both sides often encroaching upon the other's sphere of responsibility. In any democracy, Ministers are responsible to the people through Parliament and therefore, the civil servants have to be accountable to the Minister. However, an impartial civil service is responsible not only to the Government of the day but to the Constitution of the land to which they have taken an oath of loyalty. At the same time, implementing the policies of the duly elected Government is a core function of civil servants. That is why the division of responsibility between the civil servants and ministers needs to be more clearly defined. A framework in which responsibility and accountability are well defined would be useful."

The Supreme Court's decision in the case of *Maneka Gandhi* v. *Union of India*[31] was a vital breakthrough as it created a platform for future decisions dealing with the enforcement of social rights. In this case, the Supreme Court held that the right to life and personal liberty guaranteed under Article 21 of the Constitution of India must be given expanded interpretation to include a variety of rights which would give wider meaning to an individual's right to life of and boost his personality. Since then, the various decisions of the Supreme Court in PIL cases have shown the court's active engagement with almost every significant issue in India affecting public life. This in course of time has given birth to concepts like judicial creativity and judicial activism.

In the case of *Olga Tellis* v. *Bombay Municipal Corporation*[32], the Supreme Court dealt with the right to livelihood and housing of several hundreds of pavement-dwellers in Bombay. A journalist filed a petition pursuant to the decision of the Bombay Municipal Corporation of forcible eviction to build a freeway on the site. The Court held that the expression 'life' in Article 21 would necessarily include the right to livelihood and also held that though the state could not be compelled to provide means of subsistence to all its citizens, it could not deprive a citizen of the means to her livelihood.

In the landmark case of *Paramanand Katara* v. *Union of India*[33], the Supreme Court observed that certain hospitals were refusing to admit and provide emergency treatment to victims of accident and directing them to the hospital, which dealt with medico-legal cases. The Court held that the right to health was a fundamental right under Article 21 hence; no medical authority could refuse to provide immediate medical attention to a patient in need. This landmark judgment has created a new kind of right to health, which is not specifically guaranteed under the Constitution of India. The Court has harmonized the relation between the fundamental rights and the directive principle of state policy and various international treaties in the area of health rights.

The Supreme Court expressed anguish in the case of *Hussainara Khatoon* v. *Home Secretary, State of Bihar*[34], at the "travesty of justice" on account of under-trial prisoners spending extended time in custody due to unrealistically excessive conditions of bail imposed by the magistracy or the police and issued requisite corrective guidelines, holding that "the procedure established by law" for depriving a person of life or personal liberty (Article 21) also should be "reasonable, fair and just".

In the landmark case of *D.K. Basu* v. *State of West Bengal*[35], the Supreme Court found custodial torture "a naked violation of human dignity" and ruled that law does not permit the use of third-degree methods of torture on an accused person since "actions of the State must be right, just and fair, torture for extracting any kind of confession would neither be right nor just nor fair."

In the path-breaking case of *Vishaka* v. *State of Rajasthan & Ors.*[36], the Supreme Court said that "gender equality includes protection from sexual harassment and right to work with dignity, which is a universally recognized basic human right. The common minimum requirement of this right has received global acceptance. In the absence of domestic law occupying the field, to formulate effective measures to check the evil of sexual harassment of working women at all workplaces, the contents of international conventions and norms are significant for the interpretation of the guarantee of gender equality, right to work with human dignity.[37] This case has completely changed the direction of gender justice in India and laid the foundation of full-fledged law for the protection of sexual harassment at the workplace. This judgment delivered by the honourable Justice J.S. Verma, Chief Justice of India, during the period when there was no existing law to deal with the cases of sexual harassment at workplaces. He innovatively looked at the international treaty of CEDAW Convention to protect the rights of the victim and issued detailed guidelines for the future to fill the gaps of the law. This guideline has worked for a very long time to protect the rights of women. This guideline also helped in shaping the gender justice jurisprudence in India. Subsequently, the state enacted the law to deal with the problems of sexual harassment at the workplace.

In the case of *Shreya Singhal* v. *Union of India*[38], writ petitions were filed by aggrieved persons by the application of Section 66A of the Information Technology Act, 2000. Here, the arrest of two girls by the Mumbai police under section 66A of the said Act as they had expressed their displeasure at a *bandh* called in Mumbai in the event of the death of Shiv Sena Chief Bal Thackeray caused a lot of agony among the public. The Supreme Court has declared that Section 66A of Information Technology Act, 2000 as unconstitutional. This landmark decision can protect freedom of expression guaranteed in the Constitution under Article 19 of the Constitution.

In *Nabam Rebia* v. *Deputy Speaker*[39], the Court unanimously decided that "the Governor has no power to prep one and set agenda without the aid and advice of the Chief Minister. Governor has not been assigned any significant role, either in the executive or the legislative functioning of the state. Neither provision nor purpose of the framers was to assign to him a dominating position, over the state executive and the legislature. He cannot act as a super-constitutional authority."

In *Shayara Bano* v. *Union of India*[40], also known as the Triple Talaq case, there has been some confused thinking of the Court and wishes for law reform was expressed to prevent it to be used as a weapon against the women. The Court directed the legislature to make law in this regard. The Court took a different view to establish equity-based gender justice in society.

In *Justice K.S. Puttaswamy (Retd.)* v. *Union of India*[41], the nine-judge bench of the Supreme Court dealt with the question 'whether the right to privacy is a constitutionally protected value?' The Court held that "this reference is answered by stating that the inalienable fundamental right to privacy resides in Article 21 and other fundamental freedoms contained in Part III of the Constitution of India. M.P. Sharma (*supra*) and the majority in Kharak Singh (*supra*), to the extent that they indicate to the contrary, stand overruled. The later judgments of this Court recognizing privacy as a fundamental right do not need to be revisited."

In *Save Life Foundation* v. *Union of India*[42], a PIL was filed for the protection of good Samaritans like the by-standers or passers-by for rendering help to the victims of road accident by developing a legal framework to support them. The Court also approved two notifications for filling the existing legal gap through which immediate relief could be provided to the victims of the road accidents.

In *Rajbala* v. *State of Haryana*[43], the Panchayati Raj (Amendment) Act, 2015 was passed by the State of Haryana, which made matriculation as the mandatory prescribed educational qualification among other criteria for being eligible to contest in the Panchayat elections. The said amendment was challenged to be violative of Article 14 of the Constitution of India. The Court held that "the proclaimed object of such classification is to ensure that those who seek election to Panchayats have some basic education which enables them to more effectively discharge various duties which befall the elected representatives of the Panchayats."

In *Swaraj Abhiyan-I* v. *Union of India*[44], the Supreme Court took notice of the drought-like conditions in the States of Bihar, Gujarat and Haryana based on two PILs which heightened that the hesitation of these States in acknowledging the issue. Here, the Court directed "the Ministry of Agriculture, Government of India to hold a meeting within a week with the Chief Secretaries of these states to review the apparent drought situation and if so advised persuading the state governments to declare the drought."

In *Court on its motion* v. *State of Tripura*[45], one Keshab Debbarma wrote a letter to the Chief Justice of High Court of Tripura in which he brought to light the incomplete and pending status of construction of a certain road from Jagatpur to Hasermatha and the shocking disclosure that not one official had taken care to see the work for 10 years. The Court treated the said letter as a PIL and observed that it is the right of the citizens living in that area to have access to a road and so, the State is duty-bound to construct the road managing fund either from the existing scheme whether it is PMGSY or MGNREGA or from other sources. Also, it was directed that the construction should be completed within two years.

In *Laxmi* v. *Union of India*[46], the Supreme Court entertained the matter relating to the urgency of stringent regulations under the Poison Act, 1999 to check acid attacks on women. The Supreme Court directed "the Home Secretary, Ministry of Home Affairs and the Secretary, Ministry of Chemical and Fertilizers to convene a meeting to discuss the enactment of appropriate provisions for effective regulation of the sale of acid in the States/Union Territories; measures for the proper treatment, aftercare and rehabilitation of the victims of acid attack and needs of acid attack victims, and compensation payable to acid victims by state or the creation of a separate fund for payment of compensation to the acid attack victims." The Supreme Court further held that "the States and Union Territories which have not yet framed rules would do well to make rules to regulate the sale of acid and other corrosive substances in line with the model rules framed by the Central Government. The States which have framed rules that were, however, not stringent as the model rules framed by the Central Government, would make necessary amendments in their rules to bring them in line with the model rules."

In *Centre for P.I.L.* v. *Union of India*[47], it may be recalled that the Supreme Court had entertained the PIL relating to the allocation of 2G spectrum by the Government in terms of the Telecom Regulatory Authority of India Act, 1997. The Court had held that the allocation of the 2G Spectrum and the grant of Unified Access Service Licences (UAS Licence) with 2G spectrum on the principle of "first-come-first-served" and based on 2001 prices by invoking the theory of 'level playing field' is arbitrary and unconstitutional. Thereafter various applications came to be filed, which the Supreme Court disposed of while directing that the entire spectrum released as a result of quashing of the licences should be auctioned without further delay.

The careful examination of these cases has highlighted the proactive and visionary role played by the judiciary in promoting the goal of good governance in the administration of the country and safeguarding the human rights. The judiciary has also played an important role even in the law-making process. There are a large number of legislations which are enacted at the behest of the judiciary. These legislations have completely changed the overall perceptions of good governance. Moreover, Right to Information Act, Children's Free and Compulsory Education Act, 2009 and National Green Tribunal Act, 2010 enacted by the Parliament on the request and suggestions of the judiciary to have effective laws on the subject are the testimony of the role of judiciary in furthering the cause of good governance and protection of human rights. The impact of these legislations on governance is highly appreciated throughout the country.

Concluding Remarks

By way of summing up, it would be in the fitness of things to say that the implementation of good governance by the executive is indispensable for the protection of the rights guaranteed in the Constitution and other legislations to the citizens of India. The objective of sustainable development and protection of various human rights will remain only a paper tiger if it is not implemented in the letter and spirit. The judicial review of governmental action is essential for putting some checks and balances on it. The function of courts becomes very important to ensure people's basic inalienable rights. It is apparent from the cases discussed in detail above that the judiciary has significantly contributed in protecting the human rights of the people and also advocating for upholding the constitutional ethos and rule of law even in a testing situation. Further, it is necessary to highlight, by the way of conclusion, that the court on various cases discussed above made it compulsory for the government to adopt the good governance practice to uphold the rights of the parties to disputes. The judiciary has played a very effective role by entertaining public interest litigation on a large number of governance issues and decided the matter for the large section of society, which is otherwise not possible.

These cases are also describing the importance of timely judicial interventions to promote transparency and good governance in the decision-making process. A large number of human rights violations are also reality, which can be seen by the lots of cases decided by the High Courts and the Supreme Court. Human rights protections and good governance have other dimensions too that is beyond the domain of the judiciary. The courts have also explained that helplessness by making observations while adjudicating the disputes and suggested measures to the concerned stakeholders for the appropriate action. While analyzing the cases, it was also observed that approaches of courts to tackle all such problems changed in the last few years and judicial restraint had also followed selectively by the courts. This forms a subject matter of separate discussion and will be done on other occasion(s). Finally, it can be said that the judiciary has played a pivotal role in protecting human rights and good governance in the country.

ENDNOTES

1. Balmiki Prasad Singh, "Freebies and Good Governance", *Indian Journal of Public Administration*, Vol. LXII No. 4, 735-750 at p. 739.
2. World Development Report 2017, "Governance and the Law", World Bank Publications, The World Bank Group, 1818 H Street NW, Washington, DC 20433, USA available at http://www.indiaenvironmentportal.org.in/content/439193/world-development-report-2017-governance-and-the-law/ accessed on 05-04-2020.
3. World Bank Report on Sub-Saharan Africa, "From Crisis to Sustainable Growth", 1989, available at http://documents.worldbank.org/curated/en/498241468742846138/pdf/multi0page.pdf
4. O.P. Minocha, "Transforming India: From Good Governance to Sustainable Development via Millennium Development Goals", *Indian Journal of Public Administration*, Vol. LXII. No. 4750-760 at p. 752. For further details, see also, Amar Pal Singh, "Civil Society and Good Governance: Emerging Challenges", *Journal of Indian Law Institute*, Vol. 50., No. 1, 2008, pp. 80-93, World Bank Report on Governance and Development, 1992 available—http://www.gsid.nagoya-u.ac.jp/sotsubo/Governance_and_Development_1992.pdf.
5. See P. Sudha Rao, "India Governance Report 2012", *The Indian Journal of Public Administration*, Vol. LX No. 2, April-June 2014, pp. 380-386.
6. Balmiki Prasad Singh, "The Challenge of Good Governance in India: Need for Innovative Approaches", available at http://iasscore.in/pdf/yojna/1.%20The%20Challenge%20of%20Good%20Governance%20in.pdf accessed on 07-05-2017. Also see further, Balmiki Prasad Singh, "Freebies and Good Governance", *The Indian Journal of Public Administration*, Vol. LXII No. 4, October-December 2016, pp. 735-750.
7. Stella Ladi, "Good Governance and Public Administration Reform in the Black Sea Economic Cooperation (BSEC) Member States", *International Centre for Black Sea Studies*, Athens (Greece), Multimedia Ltd., December, 2008 available at https://www.researchgate.net/profile/Stella_Ladi/publication/242157028_Good_Governance_and_Public_Administration_Reform_in_Black_Sea_Economic_Cooperation_BSEC_Member-States/links/569e175708ae16fdf07b9c3b/Good-Governance-and-Public-

Administration-Reform-in-Black-Sea-Economic-Cooperation-BSEC-Member-States.pdf accessed on 07-05-2017.

8. Governance, Eleventh Five Year Plan, pp. 223-246 available at http://planningcommission.nic.in/plans/planrel/fiveyr/11th/11_v1/11th_vol1.pdfaccessed on 30-04-2017.
9. See Accountable Government Workstream: Study on Accountability in Public Works, Centre for Good Governance, Hyderabad, January 2014, available at https://cgg.gov.in/core/uploads/2017/07/Study-on-Accountability-in-Public-works.pdf accessed on 07-05-2017.
10. See Dolly Arora, "Ethics for Governance: Reinventing Public Services", (B.P. Mathur), *The Indian Journal of Public Administration*, Vol. LX No. 4, October-December 2014, pp. 960-962.
11. See, Rajni Kumari, "Devolution of Powers and Participation at Panchayat Raj Institutions: A Special Reference to Shri Mani Shankar Aiyar Committee Report", *The Indian Journal of Public Administration*, Vol. LXI No. 1, January-March 2015, pp. 177-190. Also see further, Amal Mandal, "Governance at Grassroots: Operation of Gram Sabha in Kerala and West Bengal", *The Indian Journal of Public Administration*, Vol. LXI No. 2, April-June 2015, pp. 303-318.
12. See, Jai S. Singh, "Ethical Governance: A Jurisprudential Study", *The Indian Journal of Public Administration*, Vol. LXI No. 2, April-June 2015, pp. 217-228.
13. See Kuldeep Fadia, "Reflections on Pressure Groups and Democratic Governance in India", *The Indian Journal of Public Administration*, Vol. LXI, No. 3, July-September 2015, pp. 55-564.
14. For Details see also, United Nations Development Programme, *Governance for Sustainable Human Development: A UNDP Policy Document,* ch. 1 (1997), Kofi A. Annan, "We the Peoples: The Role of the United Nations in the 21st Century", G.A. Res. 2000, U.N. GAOR, 54th Sess., at 22, U.N. Doc. A/54/2000.
15. P.K. Mohanty, "Using e-Tools for Good Governance and Administrative Reforms", the Second Administrative Reforms Commission, available at https://www.researchgate.net/publication/310835396_ICT_Good_Governance_and_Development accessed on 07-05-2017. Also see further, D.V.L.N. Murthy and A. Vijay Krishna, "e-Tools for Expediting Justice: A Case Study of APAT",*CGG Collected Working Papers*: 2003–Volume 1.
16. See B.M. Sharma and Abhishek Sharma, "Development, Good Governance and Human Rights", *The Indian Journal of Public Administration*, Vol. LX, No. 2, April-June 2014, pp. 209-234.
17. Yash Ghai, "Human Rights and Governance: The Asia Debate", *Australian Year Book of International Law*, http://www.austlii.edu.au/au/journals/AUYrBkIntLaw/1994/1.pdf accessed on 04-06-2017.
18. National Commission to Review the Working of the Constitution, a consultation paper on 'Probity in Governance', 21 August, 2001, Vol. II,

Book 1, New Delhi, India available at http://lawmin.nic.in/ncrw/finalreport/v2bl-12.htm.

19. The Protection of Human Rights Act, 1993, National Human Rights Commission, New Delhi.
20. C. Raj Kumar, "Corruption and its Impact on Human Rights and the Rule of Law: Governance Perspective" in C. Raj Kumar and K. Chockalingam (eds.), *Human Rights, Justice, and Constitutional Empowerment*, Oxford University Press, New Delhi, 2007, pp. 153-182.
21. Rajeev Dhavan, "Information and Democracy in India", *Journal of the Indian Law Institute,* Vol. 47: 3, July-September 2005, pp. 295-325.
22. Arun Sengupta, "The Right to Development and its Impact for Governance Reform in India" in C. Raj Kumar and K. Chockalingam (eds.), *Human Rights, Justice, and Constitutional Empowerment*, Oxford University Press, New Delhi, 2007, pp. 183-199. Also, see further, Mohammad Abdul Hannan, "Third Generation Human Rights and The Good Governance", *Hannan, M.A/ OIDA International Journal of Sustainable Development* 02:05 (2010) 41-50, available at https://papers.ssrn.com/sol3/papers.cfm?abstract_id=1717075 accessed on 05-04-2017.
23. See O.P. Minocha, "Transforming India: From Good Governance to Sustainable Development Goal *via* Millennium Development Goals", *The Indian Journal of Public Administration*, Vol. LXII No. 4, October-December 2016, pp. 751-760.
24. See Masoomeh Mostafavi, "Relationship between good governance and Human Rights", retrieved from https://papers.ssrn.com/sol3/papers.cfm?abstract_id=2136129 accessed on 05-04-2107.
25. Arim K. Thiruvengadam, "The Global Dialogue Among Courts: Social Rights Jurisprudence of the Supreme Court of India from a Comparative Perspective" in C. Raj Kumar and K. Chockalingam (eds.), *Human Rights, Justice, and Constitutional Empowerment*, Oxford University Press, New Delhi, 2007, pp. 264-309.
26. 2019 SCC Online SC 205.
27. (1975) 4 SCC 428.
28. (2016) 3 SCC 525.
29. (2014) 9 SCC 1 : 2014 SCC On Line SC 640 at page 50.
30. *T.S.R. Subramanian* v. *Union of India*, (2013) 15 SCC 732 : (2014) 3 SCC (L&S) 296 : 2013 SCC OnLine SC 980 at page 752, Para 15.1.3 of the Report of the Second Administrative Reforms Committee (2008).
31. AIR 1978 SC 597.
32. AIR 1985 SC 180.
33. AIR 1989 SC 2039.
34. AIR 1979 SC 1360.
35. AIR 1997 SC 610 17
36. (1997) 6 SCC 241.
37. Justice Y.K. Sabharwal, CJI, "Role of Judiciary in Good Governance",

available at https://highcourtchd.gov.in/sub_pages/left_menu/publish/articles/articles_pdf/goodgovernance.pdf accessed on 05-04-2017.

38. 2015(5) SCC 1.
39. 2016 SCC Online SC 694.
40. 2017 SCC Online SC 963,
41. 2017 (10) SCALE 1.
42. AIR 2016 SC 1617.
43. AIR 2016 SC 33: (2016) 2 SCC 445; also see *Yogendra Kumar Jaiswal* v. *The State of Bihar*, AIR 2016 SC 1474 (creation of special courts).
44. (2016) 7 SCC 498 at 50.
45. 2016 SCC Online Tri 441.
46. (2013) 9 SCALE 290.
47. (2013) 2 SCALE 357.

8
The Struggle for Human Rights and Rule of Law in a South Asian Periphery

Khaikholen Haokip

Introduction

Human rights movements produce a range of human rights movement organisations pursuing the cause of human rights. Over the years, rights movements have spawned the birth of several human rights non-governmental organisations (NGOs) or simply rights organisations. They seek to protect and promote human rights by playing myriad roles and discharging several functions. The traditional areas of intervention include, *inter alia*, exposing human rights violations, promoting rights awareness, and seeking changes in the legal system. They contribute towards keeping the political system open and accessible, thereby strengthening the cause of civil liberties and democracy. Predictably, the extant literature is replete with insights on the vital roles played by international NGOs towards the cause of human rights. Much of the achievements surrounding the spread and popularity of the ideas of human rights and the growing entrenchment of protection mechanisms at the national, regional and international levels have been attributed largely to the important role played by them.

However, literature on local rights organisations, operating within the geographical boundaries of a state or a region, is relatively thin despite the increasingly crucial role played by them in human rights movements. This chapter concentrates on the collective mobilisation for human rights in the Indian state of Manipur, located in the country's north-eastern corner. India's north-east is one of the most conflict-ridden regions of the country. Existing literature concerning rights issues in the region is largely in the form of reports produced by human rights activists and NGOs that detail the nature of rights violations in the region. Rights organisations and their roles in sustaining human rights movements in the region remain an important but largely unexamined phenomenon.

Towards filling this gap, this study examines the vital role played by local rights organisations in the specific context of Manipur. For this purpose, eight such rights organisations in the state were selected for the study: four of them are based in the Imphal valley and the other four in the hill areas of Manipur. The eight organisations are: Civil Liberties and Human Rights Organisation (CLAHRO), Centre for Organisation Research and Education (CORE), Human Rights Alert (HRA), Human Rights Law Network, Manipur branch (HRLN-M), Naga Peoples Movement for Human Rights (NPMHR), Kuki Movement for Human Rights (KMHR), Zomi Human Rights Foundation (ZHRF), and Sinlung Indigenous Peoples Human Rights Organisation (SIPHRO). These organisations provide insights into both the development of vibrant human rights movements in the state and how issues of public interests concerning human rights are placed in public discourse and demonstrate the success and limitations of human rights organisational activism.

The chapter is organised into two main sections. The first section is devoted to the background of Manipur to set the context for the evolution of the local rights organisations in the state. The second section examines the important agendas and areas of intervention of the organisations. Such focal areas are discussed under three main themes: Negative Rights violations under AFSPA, Positive Rights and Right to Self-Determination. These focal areas are deemed important as local rights organisations offer a window into how abstract universal human rights principles are interpreted, used and applied in local contexts.

The Context for Collective Mobilisation

Manipur is one of the 29 constituent states of the Indian Union located in the region called Northeast India. It is characterised by two distinct physical regions: the Imphal valley and the hill areas. Its population is classified as Tibeto-Burman speaking members of the Mongoloid race and can be clearly divided into two broad groups: the tribal and the non-tribal communities. While the dominant non-tribal communities, Meiteis and Meitei Pangals, predominantly inhabit the Imphal valley, the tribal communities traditionally inhabit the hill districts. The tribal communities or constitutionally known as Scheduled Tribes (STs) can further be divided into two broad ethnic groups: the Nagas and the Kukis (accounting for about 34% of the state's total population).

Conflicts in Manipur take place in three overlapping contexts: ethnic insurgency movements, counter-insurgency, and inter-ethnic conflicts. The demands of the insurgency movements range from political secession to greater political autonomy within the Indian state. Meitei insurgent organisations have the common objective of liberating Manipur (political secession) from the Indian state. The Naga insurgent groups demand an independent Naga homeland, called 'Nagalim,' which would bring together all Naga inhabited areas in India and Burma under a single political entity. The Kukis demand a separate state of their own within the Indian state. According to the New Delhi based Institute for Conflict Management, Manipur tops the list of insurgent organisations in Northeast India; there are about 32 insurgent organisations operating in the state.[1] A key feature of the crisis in Manipur is that in certain areas the writ of the insurgents is seen to be more effective than that of the state administration. They pose serious challenges to state authority, severely curtailing its capacity to enforce laws and to secure the rights of citizens.[2] They are also known to have indulged in flagrant abuse of human rights.[3] Likewise, the security forces, in the course of their counter-insurgency operations, have often been accused of committing egregious human rights violations.

India's treatment of the insurgency movements in the Northeast has been mainly through the prism of national security. This approach has led the Indian state to rely on its various coercive apparatuses to suppress the insurgency movements.[4] The region is heavily militarised with more than 55,000 Central Security Forces and about 14,000 state police forces operating in the state.[5] The armed forces are empowered with several special laws, specifically the Armed Forces Special Powers Act (AFSPA), 1958. The Act provides the legal framework for counter-insurgency operations in the region. It was first promulgated in the Naga Hills (present day Nagaland) and the hill areas of Manipur to tackle Naga insurgency. The whole of Manipur eventually came under this law by 1980 with the amplification of Meitei insurgency. At present, the AFSPA remains effective in the whole of Assam, Nagaland, Manipur (excluding municipal areas in Imphal valley) and certain pockets of Arunachal Pradesh.[6]

The AFSPA empowers members of the armed forces to shoot, even to the extent of causing death, on mere suspicion. It also allows for arrest without warrant of anyone who has committed or is likely to commit a cognisable offence. The most significant provision of the Act is that no legal proceedings can be instituted against any member of the armed forces without prior sanction of the Government of India (GoI).[7] The misuse of the AFSPA has assumed assorted forms. First, though the Act specifies that the declaration of a 'disturbed area' status is subject to review every six months, in practice the review has remained a routine bureaucratic exercise without objective assessment of the actual law and order situation. Such an arbitrary declaration of a disturbed area status is facilitated by the absence of a clear definition of a 'disturbed status' under the Act. The Act has been in force in Manipur for the last 60 years amounting to a localised form of indefinite emergency rule. Second, under Section 3 of the AFSPA, the armed forces are meant to be deployed in 'disturbed areas' for supplementing the local civil administration in the maintenance of law and order. More often than not the armed forces have been accused of supplanting the local civil administration in such notified 'disturbed areas.' Third, given the legal immunity enjoyed by the armed forces under the Act, allegations of human rights abuse largely go unchallenged.

Apart from insurgency related violence, Manipur has also experienced inter-ethnic strife and conflicts around the issues of, *inter alia*, identity, territorial control, and access to and control over state resources. Ethnic strife and conflicts in the state have developed around two main cleavages: between the valley-based Meiteis on the one side and the hill-based STs on the other; and between the various ethnic tribal groups. The involvement of insurgent organisations in such conflicts in the past had led to large scale loss of life, destruction of property, and displacement of people. The violent Kuki-Naga conflicts, the Meitei-Pangal conflicts, and the Thadou-Paite conflicts of the 1990s are cases in point. The preponderance of insurgency, counter-insurgency and conflicts around ethnic cleavages in the state has had, and continue to have, spillover effects prejudicial to human rights. This has made the region a key terrain for a concerted human rights movement.

Against this backdrop, a host of human rights NGOs emerged to champion the cause of human rights. They emerged in the backdrop of ethno-nationalist movements, counter-insurgency operations and ethnic conflicts. In the specific context of Manipur, they emerged primarily as a response to specific human rights abuses by the state coercive agencies. Khaidem Mani, a prominent lawyer and human rights activist in Manipur, notes:

> The complete disregard and contempt for human rights on the part of the various security agencies of the Indian state was the key factor that contributed to the formation of rights organisations in the state. Rather than acting as the protector and guarantor of peoples' rights, the military has become an instrument of oppression. Having experienced life under the jackboot and

> witnessed recurring human rights violations, the people became endeared to the idea and power of human rights and eventually mobilised themselves into launching a sustained human rights movement in the state.[8]

Overall, human rights movement organisations in the state have evolved broadly in two main phases, covering the decades of the 1980s and the 1990s, with each phase characterised by relatively different socio-political contexts and dynamics. The context for the emergence of rights organisations in the first phase (1980s) was provided by the ascendancy of Meitei and Naga insurgency organisations. And the second phase (1990s) was marked by the ascendancy of the insurgency movements of cognate Kuki tribes.

Focal Areas and Agendas

Rights organisations usually focus on a range of human rights issues. Their roles and focal areas are, however, contingent upon their objectives, ideologies, expertise, influence, resources and the environment in which they operate. Notwithstanding the fact that categorisation of rights is leaky and fraught with ambiguities, the focal areas of rights organisations may be classified as falling in the realm of three commonly categorisation of rights: civil and political rights; positive rights; and right to self-determination. Although, some of the organisations have one of these human rights issues as their primary focus, many of them generally combine all these issues in their agendas.

AFSPA and Human Rights Concerns

Civil and liberty rights encompass negative rights, such as, *inter alia*, right to life, fair trial, equality before law, and freedom of speech and association that requires protection from state's (or others) interference. Since their formative years, rights organisations in Manipur have predominantly focused upon these negative rights. This could be attributed to the fact that most of the rights organisations in the state emerged to campaign against the burgeoning human rights abuses during state's counter-insurgency movements.

Human rights excesses committed by the armed forces—fake encounters, extra-judicial executions, enforced disappearances, torture, arbitrary arrest, custodial deaths and rape, among others—are framed as stemming from misuse of powers under the AFSPA.[9] The draconian nature of the Act, as already discussed previously, is seen as providing the legal context and protection for such abuses. The standard *modus operandi* of the armed forces is to arrest a person without an arrest warrant; on mere suspicion of being a militant; torture or eliminate in stage-managed fake encounter; and then brand the fallen victim as a militant or a terrorist by claiming that weapons have been recovered from the victim. In this regard Namdithiu Panmei, Programme Coordinator of CORE, observes:

> It is too good to be a coincidence that most of these so-called armed-encounters invariably happened in isolated locations, are marked by absence of any casualty on the part of the security forces, and a recovery of a small arm or a hand grenade.[10]

The Imphal-based HRA, known for documenting cases of alleged fake encounters, maintains that certain provisions of the Act, such as those that enjoined armed forces to work in cooperation with local administration (and not as independent entity) and to hand over any arrested person to the nearest police station, have been honoured more in the breach than in the observance.[11] The elephant in the room concerning AFSPA, however, is the provision of legal immunity granted to members of the armed forces. In practice, this is seen as tantamount to foreclosing any remedy for human rights violations. In the absence of remedy, rights organisations reason, human rights do not meaningfully exist. This is corroborated by the fact that ever since the promulgation of the AFSPA, not a single case of request for sanction to prosecute accused members of the armed forces has been granted by Government of India.

The prolonged application of AFSPA, rights organisations argue, is seen as generating a 'climate of impunity'. A pointer to this is how state police forces, despite being not covered by the Act, indulge in torture and extra-judicial executions with impunity. Laifungbam Roy of CORE explains this as a reflection of the 'trickle down' effect.[12] An instance of this deep-rooted culture of impunity is evident in the killing of a former cadre of an unarmed Meitei insurgent organisation by the Manipur Police Commandos in Imphal in July 2009 in a busy market place in Imphal. The incident, to recall, had provoked a massive public outcry in the state. The sequence of the murder was captured on camera by a journalist of a New Delhi based print media house *Tehelka*.[13] At the time of the incident, the AFSPA was not in operation in the Imphal Municipal Council area.[14] The HRA maintained that the incident bore testimony to the fact that the security forces, whether covered by AFSPA or not, enjoyed absolute power without any semblance of accountability.[15]

Premised on broader human rights principles, campaigns against the AFSPA have been advanced on three interconnected grounds: as a legal issue, political issue and racial issue. First, as a legal issue, the Act is seen as contravening certain fundamental rights enshrined in the Constitution of India. By empowering the armed forces with the power to shoot to kill on mere suspicion, the Act is deemed to be contravening the fundamental right to life of a person (Article 21). The legal immunity enjoyed by the armed forces under the Act is seen as contravening citizens' right to constitutional remedies (Articles 32 to 35). The Act is also seen as contravening international human rights norms, particularly the International Convention on Civil and Political Rights (ICCPR) and the International Convention on the Elimination of All Forms of Racial Discrimination (ICERD), to which India is a signatory. The imposition of the Act is seen as akin to using emergency powers without resorting to the relevant provisions of the ICCPR.[16]

Inherent in this view is that if the Indian state considers the situation in Manipur as grave enough to warrant the imposition of AFSPA, which derogates certain rights, it should do so by declaring a state of emergency under Article 4 of the ICCPR. In such a situation, the state has the obligation to inform other treaty members of the 'provisions from which it has derogated and of the reasons by which it was actuated' and the date when such derogation would be terminated. The purpose of such a notification is to 'enable better monitoring of the emergency situation by international bodies and states'.[17] By imposing the AFSPA without a formal notification under the provision of the ICCPR, the rights organisations argue, the Indian state is actually resorting to an undeclared state of emergency in Manipur. Even if an emergency were to be imposed under the provision of the ICCPR, certain fundamental rights, such as, *inter alia*, the right to life and freedom from torture, are non-derogable.

Second, as a political issue, rights organisations see AFSPA as stemming from the Indian state's erroneous perception of the region's insurgency problems as a law and order problem. They argue that insurgency in the region is a political problem and that the approach to resolving it must also, essentially, be political in nature (as opposed to militaristic solution). The Act is also seen as fuelling insurgency in the region rather than acting as deterrence. The rising spread and intensity of insurgency in the region is an indication that the fight against insurgency without any regard for human rights is ineffective and counter-productive.[18]

Third, the Act is seen as a visible symbol of racial discrimination by the Indian state against the people of Northeast India—known as India's Mongoloid belt. It has been questioned on the ground that the Act has not been promulgated in areas affected by Maoist insurgency—touted as the biggest threat to India's internal security.[19] The Act is thus seen as providing a legal framework to enforce discrimination based on race.

The position of rights organisations on pre-empting cases of egregious human rights violations is that the state must view peoples as rights-bearing beings. The enactment of AFSPA and the culture of impunity it generates are aberrations of the principles and practices of rule of law and democracy. Security forces ought to comply with the law of the land and ensure that the fundamental rights of citizens are always protected. They argued that any arrest of a person should be done with production of 'arrest warrant' and be handed over to the nearest police station. Also, that effort should be directed towards securing conviction in law courts rather than engaging in torture and summary executions of the arrested persons. They demand that India should revoke the AFSPA, sign and ratify the United Nations Conventions Against Torture (UNCAT) and that independent humanitarian and human rights organisations should be allowed access to all interrogation and detention centres for independent investigation.

Positive Rights

In general, ESC rights or positive rights have traditionally been at the margins of the agenda of rights organisations (local or international). Their marginality is majorly a function of the fact that positive rights have continued to be debated on ideological terms. Despite the burgeoning recognition of the importance of positive rights since the promulgation of the ICESCR, liberal discourse on human rights—which places a premium on negative rights—continues to have a sway within global human rights discourse. In this line of argument, the moral imperative of positive rights—say, mitigating poverty and securing public health—is less weighted than the moral imperative of, say, stopping torture or arbitrary killing of human beings. The proffered argument is that positive rights reflect 'aspirations'; that their realisation is contingent upon the resource capacity of a state; and that their elevation as legal rights (justiciable) is unrealistic.[20] This hegemonic liberal narrative has been instrumental in shaping the rights agenda and functioning of rights organisations and donor agencies. Likewise, rights organisations in Manipur have also been preoccupied with civil and political rights. Their professed belief in the indivisibility of rights has not really gone beyond rhetorical invocation of positive rights; adhocism continues to define their advocacy efforts in this domain.

Aside from this, the neglect of positive rights by rights organisations in the state could also be attributed to three main factors. First, rights organisations are mostly ethnic in character formed in the backdrop of armed ethno-nationalist movements. Primarily formed with the agenda of exposing state abuse of human rights during counter-insurgency operations, they have never really placed positive rights at the centre of their agendas. Second, advocacy for positive rights requires relatively greater organisational capacity and expertise as it requires aiding the State or government with technical assistance concerning, *inter alia*, allocation of resources or particular trade off amidst competing demands—at times involving the choice of a particular positive right for codification to render it enforceable.

The methodology that rights organisations have traditionally used to hold the State accountable to its human rights conduct has largely been suitable for negative rights, whereas such methodology need not necessarily work for positive rights. This is because State can generally take refuge in the argument that it lacks the requisite resources. The relegation of certain positive rights to Part IV of Constitution of India, entitled *Directive Principles of State Policy*, which are non-justiciable, for instance, was a premeditated conscious choice keeping in mind the resource capacity of the Indian state. Further, in the case of positive rights, it is not easy to clearly establish whether a situation amounts to human rights violation, establish who the violators are, and clearly prescribe its possible remedy. In the absence of any clarity in these realms, the effectiveness of rights organisations to shame the government to remedial action is limited.[21]

Notwithstanding these limitations, from the mid-1990s, rights organisations in Manipur began to advocate for positive rights, more generally in the intersection of welfare needs and human rights. This belated broadening of their mandate can be attributed to the political space that the ongoing peace parleys (since the mid-1990s) between the Indian state and the Kuki and Naga ethno-nationalist movements have opened. The peace process has led to a relative decline in army and police atrocities, thereby giving the rights organisations the opportunity to direct their attention to positive rights. The outbreak of ethnic conflicts in the mid-1990s and the initiation of large-scale development projects, and increasing concern over land and identity, among others, have opened the space for advocacy efforts towards the fulfilment of basic socio-economic needs of the people. This shift in focus indicates that ideology does not always determine the activities and scope of rights activists or organisations.

In focusing upon positive rights, rights organisations in Manipur have been primarily associated with the welfare state, including healthcare, proper rehabilitation, education, housing, and food provisions. The focus on cultural rights has been associated with land rights, multiculturalism, language rights. Catering to these rights is seen as critical for realising individual freedom. It reflects what Jerome Bickenback says about the intimate connection between negative and positive rights: 'the value of negative freedom must be derivative from positive freedom'.[22]

All the organisations (both in the hills and the valley) have periodically taken up cases of public grievances relating to healthcare, primary education, denial of minimum wages, and distribution of essential commodities under the public distribution system in the rural areas of the state. Using the strategy of naming and shaming and fact finding committees, they have highlighted and exposed government's apathy towards securing minimum livelihood needs like food, water, clothing, shelter, and proper healthcare and educational service.[23] For instance, at the height of *Mautaam*[24] famine, the ZHRF, in partnership with the *Manipur Hill Journalists Union*, conducted a fact-finding team to ascertain the extent of hardships faced by the people. It had also played a pivotal role in the formation of the *Committee on Mautaam Famine Aid* to help with famine-relief efforts.[25] However, by and large, advocacy efforts for livelihood needs are episodic in nature, marked by a general absence of sustained campaigning.

Tribal rights organisations share a common concern over the need to protect tribal land, identity, and culture from what they perceive as hegemonistic policies and practices of the state government and the dominant Meitei community. These concerns have a background and are examined as follows. Tribal communities in the state have been governed by traditional tribal customary laws and institutions.[26] For instance, regarding land-use and ownership system, community landownership is common among the Nagas, while it revolves around chieftainship systems among the Kukis. However, post-Independent period has seen the enactment of several laws and the creation of institutions that undercuts or fail to safeguard tribal customary laws and practices. Prominent amongst these are: (i) Manipur (Village Authorities in Hill Areas) Act, 1956; (ii) Manipur Land Revenue and Land Reform Act (MLR&RA), 1960;

(iii) Manipur Hill Areas (Acquisition of Chiefs' Rights) Act, 1966; Manipur (Hill Areas) District Council Act, 1971; Hill Areas Committee (HAC).

The Manipur (Village Authorities in Hill Areas) Act), 1956 seeks to put in place an elected village authority village with the chief acting as ex-officio chairman sans any financial power.[27] The Manipur Hill Areas (Acquisition of Chiefs' Rights) Act, 1966 sought to strip tribal chiefs of all their powers. It was an attempt to appropriate the traditional authority of the chiefs, including control over land and vest the same in the government. The MLR&RA is concerned with the introduction of a system of land revenue administration in the state, except for the hill areas which were under the purview of the customary law.[28] Under section 158 of the Act, transfer of landownership from tribal to non-tribal is restricted. However, subsequent amendments have incrementally detached the various protective clauses for tribals from the Act. As a result, more than 100 tribal villages in the hill areas of the state have come under the ambit of this Act. In these villages where the Act has been extended, village chiefs can no longer afford to take refuge in customary laws in claiming the land; rather they would be treated as encroachers.[29]

The Manipur (Hill Areas) District Council Act, 1971, and subsequent amendments to it, envisaged to provide a measure of self-government to the tribals in the state (but outside the purview of the Sixth Schedule to the Constitution of India). The HAC is a statutory body created under Article 371C (inserted in the Constitution of India in 1971) having as its members all elected members of the state legislature from the hills. Ostensibly created to function as a 'consultative body' on matters concerning the administration of hill areas, the HAC has hardly been instrumental in safeguarding the rights and welfare of tribals as it has been routinely bypassed or manipulated by the government of the day.[30]

Predictably, the broader advocacy efforts of tribal rights organisations around these reflect the broader tribal struggles against the dominance of non-tribal Meiteis over the tribals and the perceived discrimination meted out to them by the state. The enactment of these discriminatory laws and the failure of HAC to carry out its constitutional roles, as alluded to above, are framed as a deliberate plan by the dominant Meiteis to usurp tribal land and customary practices. The KMHR and ZHRF, for instance, maintain that the tribal chiefs are the 'Lords of the Soil' and any attempts to tinker with their traditional landownership rights and authority system would entail permanent loss of tribal territory and identity.[31] T. Lunkim of KHMR, for instance, says, "The Kukis [tribals] enjoy a minimum level of social and economic security by dint of their control over land and resources".[32] Despite the fact that landownership revolves around Kuki chieftainships, he further discerns, the people are endowed with various usufructuary rights. The NPMHR has the slogan: "Our land is the only space from where our freedom springs. We are slaves without it".[33]

As a part of their broader struggle for land and identity, tribal rights organisations have also focused upon the implications of development projects for indigenous tribal peoples. While the state sees development projects as a vehicle for integrating marginalised indigenous peoples with the mainstream, the latter sees it as a form of 'adverse inclusion' wherein state's pursuit of inclusionary projects can be disadvantageous to them. An instance of this crusade against state sponsored development projects in Manipur is the Tipaimukh Dam that is sought to be built across the river Barak, located in the ecologically fragile, biodiversity rich region of the newly created Pherzawl district in Manipur. A coalition of rights organisations in the state under the banner *Committee against Tipaimukh Dam* (which includes SIPHRO, NPMHR, and other ethnic civil society groups) has been campaigning against its construction. The proposed project is seen as posing a threat to the land, identity, and culture of the already marginalised tribal population, as these would entail displacement of thousands of people from their traditional habitat, cause irreversible environmental destruction, promote influx of immigrants upsetting local ethnic balance, and further militarisation of the region.[34] It is against this backdrop that rights organisations have been vocal in their demand for implementation of the provisions of the Sixth Schedule to the Constitution of India[35] in the hill areas of Manipur.

Right to Self-Determination

Rights organisations in Manipur hold self-determination as vital for the full protection of all categories of rights. They all advocate the self-determination rights of their respective ethnic constituencies/groups. In articulating their demands, they draw on the moral and legal authority of global human rights regimes, such as, *inter alia*, the United Nations Declaration on the Rights of the Indigenous Peoples (UNDRIP), UDHR, ICCPR, and the ICESCR. However, it is noteworthy here that the broader polemic debate surrounding the meaning and application of the concepts 'indigenous peoples' and 'right to self-determination' is manifested in their advocacy for collective rights.

A central issue concerning the term 'indigenous peoples' is the question: to whom the term applies? Academic debates and the texts of intergovernmental organisations (various UN bodies) have not been able to generate a uniform conceptualisation of the term. Without elaborating the debate on the subject, and at the risk of oversimplification, one may say that there are certain criteria that inform the conceptualisation of indigenous peoples. It refers to (i) autochthonous peoples, i.e. descendants of those who were original occupants of the land; (ii) peoples who govern their own life as per their own customs and traditional institutions rather than by the institutions of the country of which they now are part; (iii) peoples who were victims of colonisation, and (iv) the non-dominance or marginalised character of their existence with no control of their national government.[36]

In the context of Manipur, the question of who is indigenous in terms of 'autochthon city' is a matter of intense debate as the region constitutes a setting wherein migratory traits had been integral to the population of the region. The highlands of India's northeast, for instance, has been known as a zone of refuge for recurrent waves (both small and large scale) of state-evading migrants over the last two millennia.[37] The attendant process of settlement and usurpation, assimilation, amalgamation, or reformulation of identities over a very long stretch of time is a pointer to the complexity of designating anyone community as unequivocally autochthonous. This complexity is well-captured in the response of Asian countries, including India, on the question of the applicability of the concept 'indigenous peoples' in the sense of autochthon city to their national minorities. They are opposed to the concept by giving a practical argument that 'after centuries of migration, absorption and differentiation, it is impossible to say who came first' and that any attempt to impose is a 'form of neocolonialism'.[38] However, at least at the theoretical level, the notion of indigeneity in terms of common historical experience as victims of colonialism and current marginality has its relevance to the diverse ethnic groups in Manipur.

Further, an associated problem with indigeneity is the question of self-determination. While the question of self-determination rights of indigenous peoples in the context of colonialism has been by and large a settled issue, its applicability in the context of decolonization (or post-colonial situation) is mired in controversies. In fact, India's position, on the concept 'indigenous peoples', as alluded to above, is informed by its perceived threat that a recognition of its national minorities (or STs) as 'indigenous peoples' would entail legitimizing their self-determination claims, particularly the external aspect of self-determination. India's longstanding position has been that the idea of self-determination applies only to independent states and that it can only be answerable to allegations of meddling with the self-determination status of independent states.[39]

Notwithstanding this enduring debate and contestations, rights organisations in Manipur have defined their respective ethnic constituencies/groups as 'indigenous peoples'—endowed with the right to self-determination under global human rights regimes. However, in the backdrop of competing territorial claims, the use of the term 'indigenous peoples' as a frame for self-determination campaign has been fraught with contestations. They tend to use the term selectively for the construction and articulation of ethnic identities to affirm or perpetuate boundaries between the self and the other, contextually and strategically, to serve specific political purposes. For instance, in the hill areas of Manipur, the NPMHR and other Naga organisations use the term 'indigenous peoples' to denote only the Nagas, to the exclusion of all others, particularly the cognate Kuki tribes who co-inhabit the hill areas. This subliminally delegitimises the self-determination claims of the Kukis. The implicit argument is that the Nagas are the only autochthonous tribes who have the first claim on the territory they now inhabit.[40] The KMHR and other Kuki organisations have strongly contested the Nagas' narrative. As indigenous peoples who had been victims of colonialism and having stood up against the colonial British regime during the *Anglo-Kuki War* (1917-1919)[41], the assertion goes, they are entitled for the right to self-determination.[42]

Further, and intriguingly, for the purpose of distinguishing the tribal communities of the state from the more dominant, non-tribal Meitei community, the tribal organisations cutting across ethnic lines liberally use the term 'indigenous peoples' to denote the tribal communities to the exclusion of the Meiteis. Given the tendency to equate the term 'indigenous peoples' with STs in India, the Meitei-centric, valley-based organisations assert Meitei indigenousness by seeking to be reclassified as STs.[43] This is evident in the increasing intensity of Meitei mobilisation recognition as STs.[44] They argue that the Indian Government's classification of the people of Manipur as tribals and non-tribals is an artificial one, that it constitutes an attempt by the government to divide the indigenous peoples of the state, and that the Meiteis too need to be recognised as STs.

The claim for the right to self-determination ranges from external self-determination to internal self-determination. All the organisations overwhelmingly project the right to self-determination as entailing the unconditional right of the indigenous peoples to freely determine their political status including secession. The claims for self-determination in the case of the NPMHR and the valley-based organisations by and large centre on external self-determination. For instance, the NPMHR has a publicly stated position that the Indian state should affirm and honour the Naga plebiscite held in 1951 that had voted for Naga independence.[45] The valley-based organisations, too, support the call of leading Meitei insurgent organisations for a plebiscite.[46] The restoration of the independent political status of Manipur after the end of British suzerainty in India is the major demand of Meitei ethno-nationalist groups. The mobilisation campaigns of the KMHR, ZHRF and SIPHRO, however, centre on internal self-determination in the form of special autonomy, ranging from separate statehood status to a Sixth Schedule status within the Indian union.

Concluding Remarks

The decades of the 1980s and 1990s marked the ascendancy of Meitei, Naga, and Kuki insurgency movements. The socio-political landscape of the state during this period was also marked by intense ethnic conflicts, rising ethno-national consciousness, and the pervading counter-insurgency operations that all engendered a poor human rights climate in the state. Against this backdrop, rights organisations of all hues emerged in Manipur.

These rights organisations have focused upon a range of human rights issues: AFSPA, civil rights and liberties, positive rights including cultural rights, and the issue of self-determination. In focusing on these rights, they not only evoke domestic and global human rights norms but also offer their interpretations of these norms and their relevance for application to local issues that affect the routine lives of the peoples. They locate the violations of civil and liberty rights within the legal framework of the AFSPA. This Act has been held to be unconstitutional and contravening global human rights norms, particularly in empowering the State to take away non-derogable basic rights, with legal immunity, and in nurturing a climate of impunity—not to mention of its role in supplanting local civil administration. From the initial preoccupation with state abuse of human rights that fall in the realm of civil and liberty rights, rights organisations have shown a capacity to adapt to a changed situation. They have been able to make a transition from having a minimalist approach to a more inclusive approach to rights. This is particularly evident in the advocacy efforts of tribal rights organisations that have increasingly embraced positive rights. State neglect of positive rights—such as, *inter alia*, social security needs, cultural rights to land, identity, and language—have all been framed within the broader framework of discrimination and marginalisation.

In advocating for right to self-determination, rights organisations frame their claims to this right based on indigeneity assertions. Inherent in their claims is the interpretation that indigenous peoples have the absolute right to self-determination, involving both external and internal aspect of this right. In advocating for self-determination right, they function within the limited framework of their own ethno-nationalism (involving competing demands) at times perpetuating or legitimising the 'communal situation' so intrinsic to the state. This is well-reflected in the recognition of self-determination claims of their own ethnic group sans a corresponding acknowledgement of the same right for others. This is notwithstanding their common historical experiences of being victims of colonialism. As these organisations operate as a sub-set of their own respective ethno-nationalist movements, the broader human rights movements in the state have been reduced to a site of ethnic contestations—particularly on issues pertaining to land and self-determination rights. Notwithstanding these challenges, there is no question that these rights organisations in the state have managed to carve out a distinct space wherein the rights of peoples assume centre stage.

ENDNOTES

1. See South Asian Terrorism Portal (SATP), 'Insurgent or Terrorist Groups in Manipur', http://www.satp.org/ satporgtp/countries/india/states/manipur/terrorist_outfits/index.html (Accessed May 23, 2020).
2. Sajjad M. Hassan, *Building Legitimacy: Exploring State-Society Relations in Northeast India* (New Delhi: Oxford University Press, 2008), 35-36.
3. Rani Pathak Das, 'Militancy in Manipur: Origin, Dynamics and Future', *Asia Europe Journal*, 6, no. 3 (2008): 561-574.
4. H. Srikanth, 'Insurgency and Counter-Insurgency: Agenda for Peace in India's Northeast', in *Polity and Economy: Agenda for Contemporary Northeast India*, ed. C.J. Thomas (New Delhi: Regency Publications, 2005).
5. Committee on Human Rights Manipur, *Submission of Committee on Human Rights (COHR), Manipur on Human Rights Situation in Manipur (India) to OHCHR* (Imphal: Committee on Human Rights, Manipur, 2008).
6. See 'What is AFSPA? Where is it in Force', *The Hindu*, April 23, 2018.
7. Ministry of Home Affairs, 'The Armed Forces (Special Powers) Act, 1958', http://www.mha.nic.in/sites/ upload_files/mha/files/ArmedforcesAct1958-290813.pdf (Accessed May 19, 2020).
8. Khaidem Mani (Lawyer and Human Rights Activist), in discussion with the author, Imphal, April 17, 2010)
9. See, 'Human Rights Defenders' Statement of Manipur', *Press Release*,

December 10, 2010, by a conglomerate of human rights organisations in Manipur.

10. Namdithiu Pamei (Programme Coordinator, CORE), in discussion with the author, Imphal, June 23, 2009.
11. See Babloo Loitongbam (Executive Director, Human Rights Alert), in discussion with the author, Imphal, June 17, 2009.
12. Roy Laifungbam (President, CORE) in discussion with the author, Imphal, June 25, 2009.
13. Teresa Reshman, 'Murder in Plain Sight', *Tehelka*, August 8, 2009, http://archive.tehelka.com/story_ main42. asp?filename=Ne080809murder_in.asp (Accessed May 23, 2020).
14. The AFSPA was temporarily lifted from the Imphal Municipal Area in the wake of violent public uprising against the killing of Manorama Devi in 2004.
15. Human Rights Alert, 'HRA Statement on BT Road Fake Encounter', *News release*, August 15, 2009.
16. See Babloo Loitongbam, 'Northeast India Experience', Paper presented at Session 5 of the *International Court of Justice's International Commission of Jurist's Eminent Jurists Panel: Terrorism, Counter-terrorism and Human Rights Sub Regional Hearing: South Asia*, 27 and 28 February, 2007.
17. Rodrigo Lobardini, 'Emergency Situations,' in vol. 2 of *Encyclopaedia of Human Rights*, Ed. David P. Forsythe (New York: Oxford University Press, 2009), 131.
18. Civil Society Coalition on Human Rights, 'India: Status of Human Rights in Manipur', http://lib.ohchr.org/HRBodies/UPR/Documents/session13/IN/JS13_UPR_IND_S13_2012_JointSubmission1 3_E.pdf (accessed November 2, 2012).
19. Rahi Gaikwad, 'Naxalism the greatest internal threat: Manmohan', *The Hindu*, October 12, 2009.
20. For an extended discussion on this, see 'Fiona Robinson NGOs and the Advances of Economic and Rights: Philosophical and Practice Controversies', *International Relations*, 2003, 17 (1): 79-96
21. For an extended discussion on the practical difficulties faced by rights organisations in the protection and promotion of ESC/positive rights, see Kenneth Roth, 'Defending Economic, Social and Cultural Rights: Practical Issues Faced by an International Human Rights Organization', *Human Rights Quarterly*, 26 (1): 63-73.
22. Jerome Bickenback, *Physical Disability and Social Policy* (Toronto: University of Toronto Press, 1993), 37.
23. See, 'Naga Blockade Pushes Manipur into Economic Crisis', *The Hindu*, May 11, 2010; Centre for Organisation Research and Education, *Manufacturing Poverty* (CORE, Imphal, 2005); KMHR, *Memorandum to Governor of Manipur on the Plight of Kuki Villagers*, Dated March 22, 2007.
24. *Mautaam* is a local term connoting Bamboo flowering which after drying up falls on the ground and become a source of food for rodents, giving rise to

rodent population. The rodents in turn feed upon rice and other agricultural products thereby causing scarcity of food supply, to the extent of causing famine.

25. See Zomi Human Rights Foundation, *ZHRF's Campaign for Human Dignity* (Lamka: ZHRF, 2008);
26. UA Shimray, 'Land Use System in Manipur Hills: A Case Study of the Tangkhul Naga' in *Land, People and Politics: Contest Over Tribal Land in Northeast India*, Eds. W. Fernandes and S. Barbora (NESRC and IWGIA, Guwahati, 2008), 88-112.
27. T.T. Haokip, 'Critically Assessing Kuki Land System in Manipur', in Ch. Priyoranjan Singh (Ed.) *Tribalism and the Tragedy of the Commons: Land, Identity, Development: The Manipur Experience* Akansha Publishing House, New Delhi, 304-328.
28. Dena, Lal (2011): 'Land Alienation and Self-government in the Hill Areas of Manipur', *Manipur Online*, 9 March,http://manipuronline.com/features/land-alienation-self-government-hill-areas-manipur/2011/03/09 (Accessed May 16, 2020)
29. Dena, Lal, 'Historical Perspectives of the Process of Marginalisation: A Study of Hill Peoples' Experience in Manipur', Paper Presented at a Seminar on the *Marginalised Indigenous Hill People in Manipur: Problems and Opinions*, New Delhi, 8-9 December 2006.
30. Sangeeta Barooah Pisharoty, 'In Manipur, Growing Tension between Hill and Valley', *The Wire*, September 27, 2015, https://thewire.in/politics/in-manipur-a-growing-conflict-between-hill-and-valley-people (Accessed April 17, 2018).
31. Zomi Human Rights Foundation, *The Zo People and the Zomi Human Rights Foundation in Respect of Manipur, Northeast India* (Zomi Human Rights Foundation, Lamka, 2008), 7.
32. T. Lunkim (Chairman, KMHR) in discussion with the author, Imphal, April 11, 2010.
33. Raile Rocky Ziipao, *Infrastructure of Injustice: State and Politics in Manipur and Northeast India* (Routledge, New York), 2020.
34. See *Joint Memorandum of NPMHR and SIPRHO to Prime Minister of India*, September 8, 2008; Also see, Chakka Bandh on September 18 against Tipaimukh Dam, *Imphal Free Press*, September 17, 2008.
35. Sixth Schedule, as per Article 244 of Indian constitution, provides autonomy in tribal self-administration in four north-eastern states, excluding Manipur.
36. See, Virginius Xaxa, *State, Society and Tribes: Issues in Post-Colonial India* (New Delhi: Pearson, 2014); B. G. Karlsson, 'Anthropology and the Indigenous Slot: Claims to and Debates about Indigenous Peoples' Status in India', *Critique of Anthropology*, 2003, 23 (4): 403-423.
37. The upland Northeast India is a constitutive part of James Scott's Zomia. See James C. Scott, *The Art of Not Being Governed: An Anarchist History of Upland Southeast Asia* (Yale University Press, New Haven, 2009).

38. Benedict Kingsbury, 'Indigenous Peoples' in International Law: A Constructivist Approach to the Asian Controversy' in: *The Concept of Indigenous Peoples in Asia: A Resource Book*, ed. Christian Erni (IGWIA/AIPP, Chiangmai, 2008), 124.
39. Dilip Gogoi, *Unheeded Hinterland: Identity and Sovereignty in Northeast India* (New Delhi: Routledge, 2009).
40. See, S.R. Tohring, *Violence and Identity in Northeast India* (Mittal Publications, New Delhi, 2010), 110; Also see 'Naga bodies ask Kuki armed groups not to create identity crisis', *The Peoples Chronicle*, July 2, 2018.
41. Anglo-Kuki War refers to the three-year Kuki uprising against the colonial rule. The uprising has been variously described as the "Kuki Rising", and "Zou Gaal", depending upon the social location of the writer. Colonial historiography and other locally dominant literature have however predominantly term it as "Kuki Rebellion", informed largely by the politics of representation.
42. Chongloi, S., *Nationalism and Political Consciousness: Problems and Prospects* (Imphal: KMHR, 2005).
43. P. Singh, *The Problem of Change: A Study of North-East India* (New Delhi: Oxford University Press, 1996), 153.
44. Rahul Karmakar, 'ST demand for dominant groups fuels campaign in Assam, Manipur', *The Hindu*, March 28, 2019.
45. NPMHR, 'Naga Plebiscite,' http://www.unpo.org/article/620#sthash.x1YFr4O2.c7goXBXo.dpuf (Accessed March 15, 2018).
46. See, *Summary of the Proceedings and Resolution* of the National Convention on the Legal and Political Implications of the Abduction and of Sanayaima, November 4, 2010, held in Imphal. The convention was organized by a conglomerate of rights organisations based in Imphal.

9

Right to Food during Armed Conflicts

A Challenge to International Human Rights

Sreoshi Sinha

Introduction

It is interesting to note the pivotal position that Right to Food holds in today's context among all the basic human rights enshrined in the 1948 Universal Declaration of Human Rights. The right to adequate food as a human right was first formally recognized by the United Nations in the Universal Declaration of Human Rights (UDHR) from 1948, as a part of the right to a decent standard of living. In the UDHR Article 25(1) it was stated that:

> "Everyone has the right to a standard of living adequate for the health and well-being of himself and of his family, including food, clothing, and housing and medical care and necessary social services, and the right to security in the event of unemployment, sickness, disability, widowhood, old age or other lack of livelihood in circumstances beyond his control."[1]

It was further recognized in Article 11 of the International Covenant on Economic, Social and Cultural Rights, a binding instrument for those states having ratified it, that "recognize the right of everyone to an adequate standard of living for himself and his family, including adequate food, clothing and housing...". In paragraph 2 of the same article, the States Parties to the Covenant recognize the fundamental right of everyone to be free from hunger and list measures to be taken individually and through international cooperation in order to bring hunger to an end.

In a way, right to food also finds a place as Article 27 of the "Convention of the Rights of Child", 1989 where "States Parties recognize the right of every child to a standard of living adequate for the child's physical, mental, spiritual, moral and social development."

Multiple legal instruments along with the international conventions, regional treaties and national legislations further emphasizes the importance of this right as a part of The Right to An Adequate Standard of Living. With all these legislations and declarations, we, as the international community, have made it clear that we strongly believe that every human being, irrespective of any attribute such as ethnicity, religion or gender, is born with this inherent Right to Adequate Food and the Right to be Free from Hunger and Starvation. But yet, in spite of these binding legislatures it is observed that in times of distress this solemn promise of not letting any of our fellow humans go hungry has miserably failed.

The Right to Food is one of the most fundamental human rights that every living human must possess along with our Right to Dignity as human beings. No human being deserves to starve to death due to inaccessibility of food. Before the conventions and the treaty laws had come into existence, the Right to Food was still seen to be a moral right, strengthened by customary laws. Morality, although inherent in human beings, is not seen to be strictly 'legally binding' on the state and non-state actors. The advent of International Human Rights and Humanitarian Law has filled this void and has made the perpetrators of human rights violations answerable before international courts in the past such as the International Criminal Tribunal for the Former Yugoslavia, United Nations International Criminal Tribunal for Rwanda and more recently, the International Crimes Tribunal (Bangladesh). International Human Rights Law, in this sense, is the defender of these basic rights and dignity of humankind.

Protecting human rights is a complex task and requires a host of institutional frameworks, but during the times of conflict the task of protecting human rights of the civilians becomes extremely difficult. With the breakdown of the law and order machinery, the common man has nowhere to go for seeking justice and asking for the enforcement of his legal rights such as the Right to Food. The administration, in several instances, is incapacitated to assist the victims owing to the ensuing chaos. In other circumstances, the state itself perpetrates these excesses as has been the case in former Yugoslavia. It is in such circumstances that the international community has progressively attempted to intervene and provide humanitarian assistance to the affected people.

The international community has now perceived the upholding of basic human rights such as the right to food as a basic responsibility. This century saw the developments of recent public international laws such as the 2012 Food assistance programme, as a major step towards the fulfilment of such a goal. The United Nations agencies such as the World

Food Programme (WFP), the Food and Agricultural Organizations and other International Humanitarian assistances from Organizations such as the Red Cross, and nations have contributed their financial resources, personnel, food supplies and other essential commodities to international humanitarian missions in an attempt to help the vulnerable local civilians trapped in a civil war. However, several factors including the volatile security situation as well as budget shortfalls and inaccessibility of those trapped civilians, limit their ability to deliver aid to the most affected places in the world.

The Guarantee to the Right to Food in the Face of an Armed Conflict: Current Position of the Right to Food in Public International Law

International Human Rights, historically, has faced its worst blows at the hands of armed conflicts, both of international and internal nature. From the end of Second World War to the present date, civil wars have witnessed the worst forms of atrocities against the human race as a whole. Belligerent parties to a conflict of such a nature, on many occasions, starting from the Iran Crisis of 1946 to the ongoing Yemeni Civil War, have committed such excesses.

In the context of the food crisis in the ongoing Yemeni Civil War, Ms. Hilal Elver, the United Nations Special Rapporteur on the Right to Food had said, "The deliberate starvation of civilians in both international and internal armed conflict may constitute a war crime, and could also constitute a crime against humanity in the event of deliberate denial of food and also the deprivation of food sources or supplies."[2]

The gravity of this issue is perhaps apprehended from the aforementioned statement when one realizes that the denial of Right to Food is an international crime of such a grievous nature that the perpetrators may be tried for committing a War Crime and a Crime against Humanity. It is imperative, at this point, to comprehend the developments in International Law to this date in this area.

Article 14 of the Additional Protocol-II (1977) to the Geneva Conventions has prohibited the use of starvation of civilians as a combat tactic. Consequently, the destruction or damage of essential objects indispensable for the civilian population including but not limited to foodstuffs, agricultural areas, crops, livestock and irrigation works as a method of warfare constitutes a War Crime in any armed conflict including civil wars.

Moreover, instances of starvation of the civilians in the civil wars in

Nigeria and Sudan have been strongly condemned by several countries and intergovernmental organizations.

However, despite the treaty laws and the protocols in place, this grave crime continues to be perpetuated to this date. Such a travesty of humanity is nothing less than a blot on our efforts to make this world a more just and humane place for all of us. The 'Solemn Promise' is somehow broken in the event of a civil war and as a result, millions of people die of hunger and even more stand on the verge of food insecurity. More robust enforcement of these basic rights, in particular, and International Humanitarian Law, in general, is the need of the hour.

More often than not, during an ongoing civil war, we are more concerned about its politico-strategic outcome. During a humanitarian situation, which is often in conjunction with a civil war in today's world (as has been the case with the United Nations Missions in Somalia and presently, in South Sudan), the majority of the resources and personnel of the contributing nations is utilized for military and allied purposes. While such an approach is not outright wrong, inadequate attention is paid to the degrading living condition of the civilian population in these conflict zones.

With the outbreak of hostilities on both sides, the international media starts broadcasting the advances made by the international peacekeeping operation or conversely, the day-to-day losses suffered by the mission. Analysts, international agencies, and prominent personalities spring into action to analyze the state of affairs and comment on its implications. Meanwhile, the respective countries evacuate their nationals from the war zone as soon as possible. But, the international community often overlooks one of the most significant stakeholders in such a conflict: the local inhabitants. What the state actors need to be reminded of today is that apart from their own evacuated nationals, the peacekeeping force personnel, and the on-ground UN officials, the utmost protection and safeguarding of human rights is warranted by the local civilian population as well. Leaving aside the International Law, humanity itself warrants us to protect the human rights of the local population.

Noting this inherent responsibility on the part of the international community, the UN Special Rapporteur on the Right to Food Ms. Hilal Elver had once warned the belligerents in the Yemeni Civil War that "The right to food does not cease in times of conflict, indeed it becomes more crucial as a result of the acute vulnerabilities in which individuals find themselves. Parties to the conflict must be reminded of their obligations under international humanitarian law to ensure that civilians and prisoners of war have access to adequate food and water during armed conflict."

However, in order to gauge the adverse conditions in the civil war zones adequately, it is indispensable to conduct a case-by-case analysis of the status of human rights in three civil wars in recent history that illustrate cases in point of violations of the Right to Food by the involved parties and how the international response to such situations has evolved over decades.

Ongoing Conflicts and Food Insecurity

In 2014, just over 170 million people were estimated to be directly affected by ongoing, armed conflict, a number that has probably risen as conflict has escalated in the Middle East and South Sudan.[3] Today, ongoing conflicts in Syria, Yemen, and South Sudan are causing enormous social and economic devastation and levels of food insecurity that are, to use the Global Hunger Index term, "extremely alarming". Each of these conflicts reflects its own perfect storm of political confrontation, economic collapse, and human suffering. Further, violent conflicts instigated by non-state actors—the Taliban, Al Qaeda, ISIS, Boko Haram—are spilling across borders. The story of conflict and food insecurity in Afghanistan, briefly recounted here to frame the challenges of the coming decades. Food insecurity has been an important element in each, both as a result of the ongoing violence and as an accelerant that has contributed to civil unrest. Dealing with the fall-out from these conflicts requires coordinated, comprehensive interventions in security, diplomacy, development, and humanitarian assistance.

Coming to food security in South Asia, decades of war, civil unrest and natural disasters have taken a huge toll on Afghanistan. Despite recent progress, millions of Afghans still dwell in severe starvation and poverty, with a crumbling infrastructure and a landscape suffering from rapid environmental changes.

According to the World Food Programme[4], around 39 per cent of Afghans live below the poverty line, with huge differences in living standards between those living in cities and those in rural areas. The country has some of the world's highest infant, child and maternal mortality rates, and many thousands of children die needlessly each year because they lack access to adequate food and nutrition. Around 41 per cent of Afghan children under the age of five are stunted, with low height for their age, while 10 per cent are acutely malnourished.

Around 33 per cent of Afghans are food insecure—around 9.3 million people—and some 3.4 million of them are severely food insecure. Unemployment is high and economic growth slow, with gender-based violence and access to healthcare and education adding further problems.

Physical security is a major concern, and insurgent activity and military operations continue to affect food security in some areas. Along with other issues such as illegal logging, uncontrolled grazing and deforestation, this undermines humanitarian efforts. Nearly 7,50,000 conflict-affected people required humanitarian food assistance in 2016.

Apparently, the United States, who was the largest source of funding in Afghanistan, strongly promoted the objective of state-building, but the central and regional governments of Afghanistan remain, by all accounts, weak, corrupt, and unable to meet citizens' needs for their food, health and well-being. A reduction of the international military force in 2014 has led to a resurgence of the Taliban and the re-emergence of a host of conflicts among various ethnic groups, warlords, and political figures as they vie for resources and control. Levels of violent, armed aggression and civil unrest have remained high.

The withdrawal of foreign troops contributed to an economic collapse. Funding and jobs that had been associated with military-related construction, procurement, or other services dried up. An increase in insurgent activities destroyed infrastructure and made it difficult to travel for work. Many Afghans have moved to informal settlement cities in search of employment opportunities where housing conditions are precarious and jobs have proved to be scarce. International development and humanitarian assistance efforts have continued, but security constraints have reportedly curbed their effectiveness. Competition for resources continues to fuel the corruption that exploded during the war and poor households fall prey to local politics and constrained resources.[5]

A 2014 study of urban poverty, food security, and nutrition in Afghanistan's large cities provides intimate portraits of families displaced to informal settlements, where they exist at the margins of society and the national economy.[6] In spite of relatively high levels of food production and imports at a national level in 2014, the poor families interviewed in the study related stories of their food concerns. Accessing food is the main challenge that urban households face on a daily basis. Food security in the city is a question of income and access to stable employment, both particularly challenging for households with addicts, female-headed households, and households with low levels of education. Low and unreliable income often necessitates reducing the quantity of food in the household on a regular basis. More importantly, it means sacrificing food diversity, as many food items become unaffordable. It also causes high levels of anxiety as the income each day will determine both the nature and amount of food the household will consume. A focus group of women in Kabul summed up their situation: "We have no money to buy wheat, oil, flour or beans. We try to borrow but we have asked for credits so many times to the shopkeepers that they will not let us do that anymore. There is no community support because everyone is poor here; we cannot even help each other. We just buy food when our men bring back money."

World Food Programme (WFP) in Action

The World Food Programme (WFP) is an agency of the United Nations that has been at the forefront of food assistance in conflict situations since its inception in 1961. It is the largest humanitarian organization that is devoted to the purpose of upholding the Right to Food and promoting General Food Security.

WFP has been operational in Afghanistan since 1963, helping to tackle the country's nutritional, educational and environmental problems, and supporting vulnerable people to improve their livelihoods. Active in all 34 provinces, WFP has shifted its focus in recent years from emergency assistance to rehabilitation and recovery. According to a relevant news source, on September 2nd, 2016, the U.N. The World Food Programme (WFP) has warned that 40 per cent of Afghanistan's population—or 11.3 million people—are food insecure, while chronic malnutrition affects more than 40 per cent of Afghan children under five years old. WFP Executive Director Ertharin Cousin issued the warning after the conclusion of her four-day maiden visit to the war-ravaged country, during 2016, the first by a WFP chief in 13 years, to "implore" the donor community to continue their support despite the squeeze on funding because of new global crises.

"This is not the time for the international community to turn away from the needs of the people of Afghanistan", she had told reporters then in Kabul. While WFP has already reached almost two million of the most vulnerable Afghans with food and cash assistance, Cousin said, the organization needs $50 million in donor funding to reach another 1.6 million people through the end of this year.

"It is the funding challenges and a turning away of the international community, or reduction in support by the international community for the activities here in Afghanistan, which will limit our ability to perform the work that is required", Cousin said, when asked about the biggest concern for WFP's Afghan mission. She noted that the 3.6 million Afghans whom the WFP is trying to help do not include thousands of refugee families who have returned or are in the process of returning home from neighbouring Pakistan this year. "Many of them come across with nothing, without the ability to meet the food-assistance needs of their families", said the WFP head, adding that her organization is working with other partners to meet the needs of returnees. Cousin admitted that increased instability and conflict in some Afghan areas has forced WFP to suspend programme operations periodically throughout the year. "The answer to terrorism and conflict is hope and opportunity provided by sustainable, durable economic opportunity and prosperity where every parent can access the food that they required to feed their children", she said. Afghanistan's Northern provinces are traditionally inaccessible for aid deliveries during winter months, and the spread of fighting to those areas in recent months has added to the challenges facing aid groups.

However, despite such commendable efforts, the WFP is limited in its ability to provide humanitarian assistance to the required number of people due to funding shortfalls. This has left severely food insecure Afghans, children, pregnant mothers and conflict-stricken refugees and internally displaced persons without adequate aid. According to a report by The Amnesty International[7], **"My Children Will Die This Winter: Afghanistan's Broken Promise to the Displaced",** due to the Taliban led insurgent attacks a staggering 1.2 million people are internally displaced in Afghanistan today, a dramatic increase from some 5,00,000 in 2013. Afghans already form one of the world's largest refugee populations, with an estimated 2.6 million Afghan citizens living beyond the country's border. "Even after fleeing their homes to seek safety, increasing numbers of Afghans are languishing in appalling conditions in their own country, and fighting for their survival with no end in sight", warned Amnesty's South Asia Director Champa Patel. Despite the promises made by successive Afghan governments, internally displaced people (IDPs) in Afghanistan continue to lack adequate shelter, food, water, healthcare, and opportunities to pursue education and employment, according to Amnesty International's findings. Despite the assertion that IDPs have a right to request and receive food, water and adequate clothing in the 2014 policy and their obligations under international law, the Afghan government has failed to provide reliable accessibility to basic living necessities. People are forced to make long, daily trips to gather water and struggle to find one daily meal.

"Food is a luxury here, no one can afford it", Raz Muhammad, a community leader in Kabul's Chaman-e-Barbak camp said. "We mostly live off bread or spoiled vegetables from the market. The last time we received food assistance was ahead of last winter when we got three sacks of wheat." Civil conflict and weather-related shocks have severely stressed food security in Afghanistan during 2016, increasing the need for food assistance, according to a FAO report.[8] Acute food insecurity affects more than 8 million people in Afghanistan and their numbers are likely to increase with the return of around 6,00,000 refugees from Pakistan before the end of 2016.

Lesson Learnt

Afghanistan, thus, is a case in point that demonstrates that our responsibility does not end at the point where we merely provide for the formal rationing of food at a distribution depot. In fact, ensuring the unhindered and safe access to the depot for the collection of the ration by the civilians and safeguarding the depot with the requisite number of armed personnel is equally important.

Food Insecurity in Sri Lanka in Times of Conflict: The most direct impact of conflict on well-being is loss of human life. In addition to the immediate distress this causes, loss of life has a direct impact on household's welfare. The loss of able-bodied members in the household limits the households earning capabilities and deprives its members of the most basic necessity, which is the access to food. In North-Eastern Sri Lanka where civil conflict raged for around two decades, one of every twelve households reported that one of their family members has been killed as a result of the conflict and as a consequence their economic ability to consume food have been diminished or extinguished. In some cases, the poorest and the most vulnerable are more likely to become combatants and risk loss of life. When people are compelled to leave their homes during the times of conflict, they are cut-off from their usual sources of income and food and become very vulnerable to food insecurity. In refugee camps they are often subjected to overcrowding, poor sanitation and inadequate food supplies. The living conditions in the refugee camps facilitate the spread of infectious diseases, which jeopardize food security through poor food absorption. The disruption of markets, roads, crops, livestock and land that warfare brings also has an immediate and long-term impact on the income of those in the affected areas and as a result on their economic access to food. In Sri Lanka the situation had been the same during the civil war. Persistent hunger and starvation became more eminent due to the absence of social institutions and other service providers. Schools are destroyed during civil wars, teachers are killed in long lasting civil wars, which in turn affects the economic ability of the citizens and has a negative impact on the access to food in the long run. Health care services are also greatly disrupted, deliberate destruction of healthcare facilities have been widely reported during conflict in Sri Lanka, which in turn have affected food security adversely. The impact of conflict on hunger gives rise to an even more dangerous conflict in return. Regression estimates suggest that halving the income of a country during a civil war doubles the risk of an upcoming civil war. Again, Racism and Ethnocentrism in Asia Pacific countries contributes significantly to food insecurity of millions of people today. Sri Lanka suffers from social stratification in terms of racism and ethnocentrism and in turn also faces considerable poverty and food insecurity emanating from different forms of racism and ethnocentrism.

Sri Lanka's civil war from 1983 to 2009 was concentrated largely in the northern and eastern portions of the country. During the war, farming and fishing, the two of the main livelihood sources in the region, were affected by myriad factors, including embargoes, transport difficulties, insecurity and breakdown of market systems. The rural economy collapsed in many areas in Northeast province (Peace and Conflict Monitor 27/02/2012). The effects of the war are still felt on the local economy. (http://reliefweb.int/, 2017)

Hence, the preliminary findings of a 2012 comprehensive food security assessment (CFSA) by WFP, indicated that 44 per cent of households in the five districts of Northern Province are food insecure (37% moderately food insecure and 7 % severely food insecure). A similar survey by WFP and the government in 2011 found over 60 per cent of households in Northern Province were food insecure (46 % moderately food insecure and 15 % severely food insecure).

"While there have been improvements, without doubt, food insecurity continues to be a serious cause for concern across pockets of the north. People there are really struggling", said Julia Vasconcelos, head of WFP's area office for Northern Province, citing rising food prices, lack of job opportunities, and high levels of poverty as contributing factors. Among the 3,800 households interviewed across eight districts in the north and east—Jaffna, Kilinochchi, Vavuniya, Mullaitivu, Mannar, Trincomalee, Batticaloa, and Ampara—food insecurity was particularly pronounced in Jaffna.

At present 55 per cent of Jaffna residents are food insecure (44% moderately food insecure and 11 % severely food insecure). Of the 1,11,457 families now classified as food insecure in the five northern districts more than 65 per cent, or 73,404 families, are in Jaffna. While overall poverty levels across the north have dropped in the past year, 55 per cent of households in Jaffna continue to live under a poverty line of less than US$1 per day per person, the findings revealed. Fruit, vegetables, and other food are readily available in the local market, but "People simply do not have the money [to buy enough food]", said Rashkarn Marthraja, a butcher in Jaffna. The price of rice, a staple part of the Sri Lankan diet, has remained largely stable, but prices for dairy products, meat and other items have seen a dramatic increase. "Last year a kilo of meat cost 700 Sri Lankan rupees (US$5.23). Today it costs 1,100 rupees ($8.22)", he said[9].

6.7 per cent of Sri Lanka's population are unable to meet a daily calorie intake of 2,030 kcal due to low income. Northern Province: 10.7 per cent. Central province: 6.5 per cent. Eastern province: 10.8 per cent (2012) (World Bank 08/2015) and Sri Lanka has one of the highest rates of wasting prevalence in the world, at 19.6 per cent, with 23 per cent of the population (4.7 million people) undernourished (WFP 31/01/2017; WFP 14/02/2017). 15 per cent of children under five are stunted (2012) (Global Nutrition Report 2014).

World Food Programme in Action

Sri Lanka graduated to lower middle-income country status in 2010 thanks to the adoption of effective development policies. However, the country continues to struggle with the effects of a 27-year civil conflict that resulted in significant economic and social damage. Improvements in human development and the nutritional status of children, women and adolescents have remained stagnant. The increased frequency of natural disasters such as drought and flash floods further compounds food and nutrition insecurity. Nearly one person in four is undernourished, and underweight and anaemia affect almost a quarter of children and women. As per WFP's most recent Cost of Diet Analysis, 33 per cent of the population cannot afford the minimum cost of a nutritious diet. The World Food Programme (WFP) has been present in Sri Lanka since 1968, providing both emergency assistance in response to natural and human-made disasters (i.e. tsunami, droughts, floods and civil war), and in developmental programme such as school meals and nutrition interventions. WFP supports the efforts of the Government of Sri Lanka towards achieving Sustainable Development Goal to end hunger, achieving food security and improved nutrition and promoting sustainable agriculture by 2030.

Way Ahead

In International Law, conscious efforts have been made since 1945 to recognize and protect the Right to Food as an inherent right of every human being. The 1945 Constitution of the UN Food and Agriculture Organization (UN FAO) proclaimed the crusade for humanity's liberation from hunger. The moral obligation involved on the part of the state and non-state actors for protecting this right is considerable, to say the least. However, the legal obligations cannot be neglected either. The 2012 Food Assistance Convention, which is currently in the process of being adopted by different countries and already ratified by at least 5 signatories, is the first step of this century in this direction.[10] As the only legally binding international treaty on food aid, it has an important role to play in the forthcoming decades. It is definitely a reassuring action which underlines the increasing importance of the Right to Food in International Human Rights Law.

Conclusion

It is hoped that institutional and legal steps, combined with a strong social initiative from the non-governmental aid organizations and conscious global citizens, are slowly but steadily taking this world towards a brighter future free from hunger and malnutrition, a world where people in a civil war will not starve to death as a result of inaction on the part of their authorities and a world where children will not go undernourished by reason of an ongoing conflict in their country. The day every human being is able to have "physical and economic access" to food supplies and the UN won't have to act on another Security Council resolution to send thousands of soldiers to protect the food shipments in yet another civil war-torn country, this world will have become a better place for all of us.[10]

It is with such ardent hope and desire for change that thousands of selfless humanitarian aid workers are striving to deliver assistance to conflict-ridden people in Afghanistan and Sri Lanka among other places of not only South Asia, but the entire world. They have re-strengthened our conviction in the belief that humanity strives to serve all and neglects none.

ENDNOTES

1. Office of the UN High Commissioner for Human Rights. (2010). Right to

Adequate Food, Fact sheet No. 34. United Nations Office (Geneva). Retrieved from http://www.ohchr.org.

2. Office of the UN High Commissioner for Human Rights News Centre (2015, August 11).
3. Alex De Waal, "Armed Conflict and the Challenge of Hunger: Is an End in Sight?" Global Hunger Index, ch. 3, 2015, http://ebrary.ifpri.org/utils/getfile/collection/p15738coll2/id/129685/filename/129896.pdf.
4. "World Food Programme." Rome, 2014.
5. Paula Kantor and Adam Pain, "The role of social resources in securing life and livelihood in rural Afghanistan," Bath Papers in International Development, 2011.
6. Samuel Hall, "A study of poverty, food security and resilience in Afghan cities," Urban Poverty Report for the Danish Refugee Council and People in Need, 2014.
7. Amnesty International, *My Children Will Die This Winter: Afghanistan's Broken Promise to the Displaced*", 2014.
8. Food and Agricultural Organization of the United Nations, "Crop Prospect and Food Situation", Quarterly Global Report, 2019.
9. Food and Agricultural Organization of the United Nations.
10. Choi, K.; Beladi, H.; Schmitz, A.; Kennedy, P.L.; Schmitz, T.G. (2015). *Food Security in an Uncertain World: An International Perspective*. Emerald Group Publishing, Bingley, U.K.

REFERENCES

Gul, A. (2016). 40 Per cent of Afghans Are Food Insecure, WFP Warns. Islamabad: www.voanews.com.

(2017). http://reliefweb.int/. Start Network, Acaps.

International, T.A. (2016). "My Children Will Die This Winter": Afghanistan's Broken Promise to the Displaced." Kabul: The Amnesty International.

(July, 2012). IRIN News. Jaffna: Irin.

Mukherjee, A. (2012). *Food Insecurity in South Asia*. Sage Publications.

Nations, F.A. (2016). Ongoing conflicts continue to intensify food insecurity. Rome.

(2014). World Food Programme. Rome.

10

Exploring the Disability Rights in South Asia

Reflections on Policy-Provisions in India and Bangladesh

Nitin Malhotra

Introduction

There is fair degree of plausibility on the presumption that Disability is a global phenomenon affecting the people of the entire world. It is not true of a specific country, creed, gender, age, or race but instead cuts across all political entities and social identities world-wide. Anyone can become a victim to physical, visual or mental dysfunctionality at any point of time in life (Jaeger and Bowman, 2005). Global estimates indicate that at least ten per cent of the world's population lives with some form of disability. In the present industrially and technologically oriented society, people are far more likely to succumb to disabilities. Moreover, most people are not born disabled except a few. They acquire disability at some point later in life on account of accidents, international wars or natural disasters: floods, famine drought, earthquakes etc.

According to World Report on Disability (2011), jointly prepared by World Bank and World Health Organization (WHO), there is a close affinity between disability and poverty. Disability causes poverty and poverty accentuates the chances of disability. It implies that people with disabilities are among the poorest and most vulnerable and they experience high rates of poverty, poor health, low educational achievements along with few employment opportunities. This finding signifies a shift in perceiving disability from medically proven problem within an individual body to a socio-economic construction. The efforts to address challenges to development such as unequal distribution of income, unemployment, lack of services like health, and education play a critical role in overcoming hardships caused by disability. Thus, there is a growing realisation that disability should be established as a developmental agenda. It is generally emphasized that this segment of society should not simply participate and contribute to the process of national development but also have share in national resources. In such a state of affairs, the differently abled section could benefit from the fruits of development and exercise all basic rights and liberties at par with others.

Despite being a reality the world over, disability has not featured directly in the efforts towards achieving global development. This is evident in the fact that rights of the people with disabilities did not find any place in the United Nations Millennium Development Goals (MDGs, 2000) which intended to massively reduce poverty from the face of the world by the year 2015. Endorsed by 189 countries, MDGs are a collective set of developmental objectives addressing the needs of the world's poorest and most marginalized people. It is both ironical as well as disheartening to note that Disability empowerment has not been incorporated as one among the eight Development Goals to be achieved in the new millennium (21st century) (Conrad Grebel University College, accessed 05-04-2017, at 20:19 hours). In this way, the issues of people with disabilities have either been largely overlooked or underemphasized in development discourse allround the globe and more so in the developing countries of South Asia. Since power creates a visible and audible discourse, and the disabled people lack power, they are often not heard and remain unnoticed. In this context, it is very aptly stated that "persons with disabilities have always been in but not part of society" (Rimmerman, 2013: 9).

In comparison to developed nations, the situation of disabled persons is further exacerbated in developing countries of the world. In South Asian Region, a vast number of people are disabled and lack basic support such as access to social safety nets, education, health services, and gainful employment. In fact, the incidence of disability are increasing by virtue of conflicts, disasters, malnutrition and the diseases like cancer and HIV/AIDS pandemic. Disability issues are given low priority and many forms of disability are difficult to capture in statistics, often due to under-reporting. Therefore, it calls for a regional cooperation to alleviate poverty and take initiatives to accelerate the rate of progress in a way such that there are lesser probabilities of disability occurrences and persons with special needs could enjoy an improved standard of living.

In South Asia, both India and Bangladesh are relatively identical in terms of the condition of disabled population lacking basic services of education, health, employment opportunities etc. They had shared a common colonial past and had once coincided in geographical territory. Unlike India which is multi-lingual multi-religious and multi-ethnic society, Bangladeshi people are integrated and more or less homogenised through a common language, i.e. Baangla. These countries have placed an emphasis on protection and promotion of rights of disabled. However, it is evident that the rate of progress on disability policy and its magnitude varies greatly from country to country in the region.

It is, therefore, pertinent to deal with disability policies introduced by Indian state and people's Republic of Bangladesh that serve as a chief source of legal recognition of their rights. Such rights would simply remain a mere claim without socio-political recognition. The present chapter provides a comprehensive account of policies and legislative enactments initiated by the two, namely Persons with Disabilities Act (1995), National Policy for Persons with Disabilities (2006), the Rights of Persons with Disability (RPWD, 2016) Act, etc. in India and Bangladesh gave effect to legislations: Disability Welfare Act (2001) and National Action for Disability (2002). This chapter has tried to locate rights of the disabled people within the broader policy framework of both the countries under purview. Comparative analysis of diachronic or synchronic nature might be adopted as research method. This work is stimulated by the following objectives:

- To set disability rights as a developmental agenda in South Asia.
- Present a vivid description of rights provisions enumerated in disability policies of India and Bangladesh.
- If possible, make comparative analyses of disability enactments prevalent in both the countries.
- To uncover the gaps and propose alternatives or reforms to policy provisions.

The Prevalence of Disability in Bangladesh and India

No comprehensive empirical study has been conducted at present to determine the incidence and prevalence of disabilities in Bangladesh. The few studies that have been conducted reflect a medical rather than a social model of disability, and they are also limited in geographical coverage. While no reliable national data exist, anecdotal information and a number of micro studies generally suggest a disability prevalence rate of between 5 to 12 per cent. This is close to the WHO estimate, which states that 10 per cent of any given population can be considered to have some or other form of disability. Ignorance and wrong beliefs surrounding disability, compounded with a negative and derogatory attitude of the community (including family members) have contributed to the marginal development in the disability sector in Bangladesh.

On the other hand, the fifteenth Indian Census (2011) has presented an articulative data estimate on disabled population in the country. As per the Census, about 2 to 3 per cent suffer from any kind of disability. The categories of disability have been increased from 5 to 8 with inclusion of 3 new categories. An increase in proportion of disabled population in both rural and urban areas was observed. Moreover, the prevalence of disability has also increased among males and females of the country.

Disability-oriented Policy Framework and People's Republic of Bangladesh

The National Constitution of Bangladesh, 1972, has numerous provisions that obligate the government to protect the rights and dignity of all citizens of the country equally and without any bias whatsoever. Part II enshrines provisions on fundamental principles of state policy and Part III elaborates on fundamental rights to be guaranteed to the entire citizenry comprising disabled segment as well. Section 28 of Part III prohibits any form of discrimination on such grounds as caste, race, sex etc. The Constitution also allows room for additional provisions to ensure that citizens who do not have access to all the public amenities are able to obtain such services. As per section 28 (3) "no citizen shall, on grounds only of religion, race, caste, sex, or place of birth be subjected to any disability, liability, restriction or condition with regard to access to any place of public entertainment or resort, or admission to any educational institution" (Bangladesh's Constitution of 1972, 2020, p. 16). This vision has given the government ample opportunities to adopt legislative and policy frameworks for the development of full potentials of persons with disabilities in the country.

As early as 1993, the Government established a National Coordination Committee on Disability under the Ministry of Social Welfare which later adopted the National Policy on Disability in 1995 to ensure equal participation and pave increased opportunities for persons with disabilities. The concerned law has been approved in tune with all national and international commitments or obligations and the provisions of National Constitution. This policy embodied the first official recognition of disability issues by the government as part of development agenda. The policy was given legal support when the National Parliament enacted the Disability Welfare Act on 4 April, 2001.

This law provides the first ever national definition and classification of disability in the country. The Act defines disability as a condition in which any person becomes physically crippled or mentally imbalanced either congenitally or as result of disease, even being a victim of accident, or due to improper/maltreatment. In such a case of full or partial incapacity, he/she is unable to lead a normal life. The document broadly enlisted 6 categories of disability: visually impaired, physically handicapped, hearing impairment, speech impairment, mental disability and persons with multiple disabilities.

Part IV of this Act accounts for education of disabled citizens of Bangladeshi state. For this purpose, establishment of Specialised Education Institutions to cater to the different needs of the children with disabilities is deemed necessary. It was also realised that specialised curriculum should be designed and developed and special textbooks to be written. The introduction of Special Examination System had been recommended, if situation demands. Provisions are laid down to create opportunities for free education to all children with disabilities below 18 years of age. In order to make it a reality, books and equipment free of cost or at low-cost are to be provided. As per legislation, Endeavour is to be made to create opportunities for integration of students with disabilities in the usual class set-up of regular normal schools wherever possible. To achieve this goal, training for the teachers and other employees working with the disabled should be arranged. Besides, there was declaration to undertake programmes for imparting vocational training for the disabled. It was resolved to arrange easy transport facilities for up-down journey to school for the students with disabilities.

Part VI emphasized on Rehabilitation and Employment of the Persons with Disability. It was desired to undertake appropriate Schemes including Credit-Support programmes for rehabilitation of the persons with disabilities. Establishment and maintenance of Rehabilitation Centres, both at Government and Non-Government level considered crucial. It has been agreed to Design and Develop Training Manual for Vocational Training of the PWDs and carry-out such Training Programmes according to the Manual so developed. Identification of appropriate job/employment areas for the disabled and creation of employment opportunities has also been an essential goal. It was intended to ensure equity of opportunities for employment while recruiting employees in the government departments, statutory bodies and local authorities for suitably qualified persons with disabilities. In this connection, actions be taken to relax the prescribed minimum age limit for recruitment of PWDs in the concerned jobs. The appropriate governments shall ensure reserve quota in the recruitment of posts to the government departments, statutory bodies and local authorities and disseminate information on job-opportunities for them (Bangladesh Persons with Disability Welfare Act, 2001).

Part VII has dealt with access to Transport Facilities. For this purpose, appropriate transport facilities at all buildings and establishments are to be set-up including government departments, statutory bodies and private organizations to facilitate easy movements and communications for the PWDs. Appropriate measures should be taken to adapt toilets at rail compartments, water-vessels, bus-terminals and waiting rooms so that the persons with disabilities can also use it like others. Installation of auditory signals at all main road-crossings in the cities was proposed in the document. So, attempts were made to devise suitable signs and symbols to facilitate safe and hazard-free mobility of persons with disabilities. Under this legislative enactment, easy access and movement of the wheel chair users is facilitated by making appropriate curb cuts and slopes and ramps at public buildings. The persons with disabilities carrying duly issued Identity Card are to be permitted to travel by train, buses, water-vassals, Airways along with an escort at concessional fare and also to make arrangement for carrying portable luggage alongside (Bangladesh Persons with Disability Welfare Act, 2001).

The Prime Minister's office issued an executive order in 2002 to put this law into force. A National Coordination Committee on the Rights and Protection of Persons with Disabilities (responsible for coordinating all disability initiatives by the Government of Bangladesh) then formulated and adopted a National Disability Action Plan on 24th September, 2006 to implement the National Policy on Disability and the Disability Welfare Act. The Action Plan is very comprehensive, involving forty-six Ministries and divisions of the government to undertake specific activities for persons with disabilities. The government has also appointed a focal person in every division of the Ministries (forty-six focal persons) who can provide the persons with disabilities the opportunity to avail services from the government easily.

In 2013, the Rights and Protection of Persons with Disabilities Act came into force, repealing and replacing the Disability Welfare Act of 2001. The new law has, to an extent, adopted the provisions of the UNCRPD and marks a transition to a more rights-centric approach than the earlier welfare-based approach of the 2001 Act. The Act not only has a broader definition of the nature of disabilities but also sets out the rights of persons with disabilities in more detail covering the fundamental rights as well as the cultural, social, economic and political rights. Furthermore, the Act vests duties on various committees for better protection of rights of persons with disabilities in a regional and national level and the Schedule of the Act lists out the State's obligations for establishing.

Policy Initiatives in the Republic of India

No doubt, the Constitution provides chief source of policy framework of any state and India is no exception to it. Chapter 3 and 4 of the Constitution of India on fundamental rights and directive principles of state policy respectively, sets out basic vision towards its citizenry. The fundamental rights guaranteed in chapter 3 of Constitution of India (right to equality, freedom, life and liberty, religion and cultural and educational rights) are uniformly applicable to all citizens alike, whether disabled or non-disabled. This fundamental law of the land secures prohibition of discrimination, equality of status and of opportunities for all including the disabled.

However, it is an undeniable fact that disability has not been recognised as an important factor of discrimination under the anti-discrimination clause as it is the case with caste, race, sex, religion, place of birth etc. The access needs of particularly the differently abled people have not been given special weightage. Yet, it is equally true that the provisions with regard to general access to public spaces for everyone including disabled are enumerated in compliance with universal design principle. In this context, the constitution under "Article 15(2) states that no citizen (including the disabled) shall be subjected to any disability, liability, restriction or condition on any of the above grounds in the matter of their access to shops, public restaurants, hotels and places of public entertainment or in the use of wells, tanks, bathing *ghats*, roads and places of public resort maintained wholly or partly out of government funds or dedicated to the use of the general public" (Bhattacharya, 2014: 102). Likewise, with a similar purpose, Article 19 of the Constitution of India guarantees 6 basic freedoms for all citizens inclusive of the persons with disabilities, subject to reasonable restrictions. More importantly, Article 19(1) clause D holds that "All citizens shall have the right to move freely (physical movement) throughout the territory of India" (Bakshi, 2002: 33). This signifies free and easy mobility for everyone to access and explore places in States and Union Territories throughout the country.

Chapter IV of the Constitution contains the Directive Principles of State Policy (DPSP), which reflect the aims and objectives for the State to comply with. These directives have acknowledged the obligation of the Indian state to provide better education and employment opportunities for weaker section including disabled. Under Article 41, it is directed that the State shall make provisions for ensuring the right to work, education and public assistance in case of unemployment, old age, sickness and disablement. Additionally, Constitution of India also acknowledges general state obligations to Pawed in the State List of federation under the title: "Relief of the disabled and unemployable" (Bhambhani, accessed on 23/9/2018, p. 1).

Though, initial few decades since Independence did witness some initiatives to address employment and educational concerns of disabled such as special schools, vocational rehabilitation centres (VRCs), special employment exchanges etc. But, yet there was hardly any substantial policy legislation to address their over-all access needs. India happened to be the signatory of Proclamation on Full Participation and Equality of Persons with Disabilities in Asia and Pacific and Biwako Millennium Framework for Action Towards an Inclusive, Barrier-free and Right-based Society. It was deemed necessary to reflect the obligations under these agreements at the national level and give effect to the Proclamation through legislations in disability sector.

India expressed its commitment to the cause of creating a disabled friendly environment through the legislation of 'persons with disabilities (equal opportunity, protection of rights and full participation) Act (PWD)' in 1995. The Act came into force on 1st January, 1996 and extends to the whole of India except the State of Jammu & Kashmir. The legislation has defined disability under seven categories such as blindness, low vision, leprosy-cured, hearing impairment, loco motor disability, mental retardation, mental illness. It provides provisions for securing the right to education, employment, creation of barrier free environment, rehabilitation and social security of disabled etc. Composed of 14 chapters, this law on disability has been enacted under Article 253 of the Constitution of India read with item No. 13 of the Union List.

Chapter V of the Act is devoted to the cause of education for the children with disabilities. It is stated that The "Appropriate governments and the local authorities shall ensure that every child with a disability has access to free education in an appropriate environment till he attains the age of eighteen years" (PWD Act, 1995, Section 26). Section 28 put forth provisions to initiate research by official and non-governmental agencies for the purpose of designing and developing new assistive devices, teaching aids, special teaching materials necessary to give a child with disability equal opportunities in education. Section 30(A) provides for transport facilities to the children with disabilities or alternative financial incentives to parents or guardians to enable their children with disabilities to attend schools. Section 30 (Clause B) of the legislation emphasized on the removal of architectural barriers from schools, colleges or other institution and imparting vocational and professional training. With a view to make examination process accessible the Act recommends suitable modification in the examination system to eliminate purely mathematical questions for the benefit of blind students and students with low vision. In this context, also mentioned that "all educational institutions shall provide amanuenses to blind students and those with low vision" (PWD Act, 1995, Section 31).

Chapter VI is concerned with employment of the differently abled. It has laid down provisions for 3 per cent reservation in every government and public sector establishment. Section 38 provides that appropriate governments and local authorities shall formulate schemes to ensure the relaxation of upper age limit in jobs. Provisions are made for "Health and safety measures and creation of a non-handicapping environment in places where persons with disabilities are employed" (PWD Act, 1995, Section 38).

Chapter IX of this policy document entitled 'non-discrimination' has made provisions for their equal access to physical environment in the areas of transport, roads or outdoors and public places. Section 44 is concerned with removing barriers in transport sector. It is committed to take special measures such as adapting rail compartments, buses, vessels and aircrafts in such a way as to provide easy access to disabled persons, in general and adapt toilets in rail compartments, vessels, aircrafts and waiting rooms so as to allow the orthopaedically handicapped persons to use them conveniently.

In order to develop access to roads or out-doors Section 45 has incorporated provisions for installation of auditory signals at red lights in the public roads for the benefit of persons with visually handicap, causing curb cuts and slopes to be made in pavements for the easy access of wheel chair users, engraving on the surface of the zebra crossing for the blind or for persons with low vision, engraving on the edges of railway platforms for the blind or for persons with low vision, devising appropriate symbols of disability and warning signals at appropriate places etc.

For building up accessible environment in public spaces, it is proposed that "the appropriate Governments and the local authorities shall provide for—ramps in public buildings, adaptation of toilets for wheel chair users, Braille symbols and auditory signals in elevators or lifts and ramps in hospitals, primary health centres and other medical care and rehabilitation institutions" (PWD Act, 1995, Section 46).

In 2006, The National Policy for Persons with Disabilities has recognized that Persons with Disabilities are valuable human resource for the country and seeks to create an environment that provides them equal opportunities, protection of their rights and participation to the fullest in society. The National Policy identified nine key areas of state intervention, viz. barrier-free environment, education of persons with disabilities (PWD), employment, Human Resource Development (HRD), social protection, Sports, Recreation and Cultural activities etc. According to this policy document, for creation of barrier-free environment, many strategies were to be adopted. "Public buildings (functional or recreational), transport amenities including roads, sub-ways and pavements, railway platforms, bus-stops/terminals, ports, airports, modes of transports (bus, train, plane and waterways), playgrounds, open space etc. were to be made accessible" (National Policy for PWD, 2006, Section 51). It was also required that "Modification of Curriculum of Architects and Civil Engineers will be undertaken to include issues relating to construction of barrier-free buildings. In service training will be provided on these issues to the government architects and engineers. Effort will be made to ensure adoption of the bye-laws and space standards by all the states, municipal bodies and Panchayati Raj Institutions in the country.

India happened to be one of the signatories to U.N. Convention on the Rights of Persons with Disabilities (UNCRPD) which the country ratified on 1st October, 2007. In order to reflect the commitment of and give effect to UNCRPD at national level, Indian parliament enacted the Rights of Persons with Disabilities (RPwD) Act on 28th December, 2016. This enactment was also regarded as extension or contemporary version of the PWD Act (1995).

Chapter II of this legislative document is devoted to rights and entitlements of persons with disability. The enactment authorizes appropriate governments to ensure whole gamut of such rights as right to equality, live with dignity and respect on equal basis with others, right to inheritance of property, to safety against risk of human emergency, armed conflicts, and natural disasters, protection from torture, inhuman, cruel or degrading treatment, rights against all forms of abuse, violence and exploitation, accessible voting right, right to access courts, tribunals, commissions or other judicial authorities, accessibility of information regarding reproductive and family-planning etc. (RPwD Act, 2016, Sections 3-15).

Critical Appraisal

A review of the disability policy framework of India and Bangladesh would inform us that, by and large, the legislative content of these countries is almost identical. Both share the priority areas belonging to the policy documents, i.e. education, employment, rehabilitation, accessible environment for them and so on, except minor differences. However, the way these target areas are to be achieved or the specified plan of action to attain those objectives regulated by the state is often dissimilar. This is evident in the fact that while Indian PWD Act, 1995 has fixed three per cent reservation across all grades of posts guaranteeing right to work for disabled, whereas, in Bangladesh, Disability Welfare Act, 2001 sets 10 per cent quota in grade 3 and 4 and 1 per cent of reservation in group 1 and 2 in public-sector employment respectively. Besides, though India has pursued a rights-oriented approach in its policy initiatives, whereas policy provisions in Bangladesh are driven by a pro-welfare agenda based on the notion of need.

Policy initiatives on disability issues in these two countries only remain on paper and lacks implementation at the level of ground reality. Policy legislations are formulated but hardly yields the expected and desired results. It seems that these policies are devised out of international pressure rather than political will of the concerned states. An examination of their political history shows that very seldom disabled persons have been treated as human resource and are able to contribute to national development. Yet, it cannot be denied that India has progressed far more in disability policy interventions and has even surpassed Bangladesh. The reason is delayed liberation of Bangladesh in 1971 due to political turmoil and instability in East Pakistan.

Though policies are formulated to cater to the needs of each and every member of target group. In the process, they eventually contribute to the common good of society at large. In fact, this is not the case with policy measures meant for the disabled in Bangladesh and India. These policies are formulated with a preconception of disability as a monolithic category and do not consider inherently varying needs of each sub-segment within the disabled. When executed, they serve the interests of one inter-sections or another within the disabled for example literate and economically well off persons amongst visually and orthopaedically disabled. In this way, some disabled are benefited at the cost of other whether it is learning needs, information, employment or right to franchise. It thus poses a problem of lacunae or bias in policies on rights and welfare of disabled persons. For example, the Bangladeshi persons with Disability Welfare Act, 2001 has its inherent gaps and it is flawed in the sense that there was no mention of punishment for violence against persons with disabilities.

In these South Asian countries, although the rights of differently abled community are legally recognised. But having said that, there is a discrepancy between formal guarantee and actual enjoyment of their rights. Rights of persons with disabilities is one of the most misunderstood areas of the development arena in Bangladesh, and also one of the most commonly forgotten development agenda. They are not exercised by the disabled ones, owing to inaccessible environment in education, health, employment, transportation, voting process.

Concluding Remarks and the Way Forward

Both Bangladesh and India have expressed their obligation to the international treaty by becoming parties to UNCRPD in the same year (2007). They have contributed to disability rights discourse through legislative measures. Nonetheless, conservative mindset and poverty-ridden population accentuate the chances of disability as a growing regional phenomenon. This poses hindrance to the protection of their rights along with full and effective participation in all activities of life like the rest. It is quite evident that India has an edge over Bangladesh in terms of the rate of progress on disability policy and the magnitude of rights guaranteed. In a report on disability rights prepared by national grassroots and disabilities organization and National Council for Women with Disabilities of Bangladesh, it is conveyed that despite of being signatory and party to the U.N. convention, it has not obliged to submit a report on current status of disability rights in the country till date. The report also adds that employees with disability tend to be paid lesser wages than the non-disabled, are often subject to harassment at workplace and even lacks access to basic services like health and education etc. (NGDO and NCWD, Bangladesh Report, 2015).

In view of the above challenges, certain recommendations and proposals are inevitable to develop alternative policy matter or to reform the existing policy framework. In the first place, it is the sense of necessity or national political will and not international compulsion/imposition that is supposed to be the guiding force behind policy interventions in these countries. In addition, a shift of focus from welfare approach to rights-based paradigm of disability in true sense is urgently required. Further, a more strong and viable monitoring mechanism should be the order of the day to effectuate the legislative provisions and enable disable persons actually enjoy their rights in the best possible way. In other words, legislative and policy framework is to be complemented with reasonable degree of practical observance and supervision.

According to a report of Disability Rights Watch Group, entitled 'State of the Rights of Persons with Disabilities in Bangladesh', one of the major reasons for people with disabilities not enjoying their rights and entitlements are the general inaccessibility of infrastructure. Thus, in holistic sense, to bridge the gap between policy recognition of rights and its practical manifestation, collective action of removing barriers to educational services, employment opportunities, rehabilitation, transportation, built environment, and healthcare is indispensable. Unquestionably, some studies demonstrate that poverty is intricately linked to disability and *vice versa*. Therefore, more emphasis must be laid upon poverty alleviation programmes with an outlook to integrate disability into the mainstream of development agenda of both India and Bangladesh.

Last but not the least, the conservative perception of disability as an outcome of the sins committed in the previous life has to be changed and disability, rather, is to be viewed from the lens of being a socially constructed reality. This is materialized provided the social engineering programmes are adequately promoted in both the republics of South Asia. As a result, a spirit of social acceptance of disabled persons as equal partners in the process of nation building and socio-economic progress is deemed critical. After all, the so-called policy-makers/bureaucrats stem from similar social setting and are exposed to share same attitudes towards persons with disabilities.

In a nutshell, the disability population is scattered throughout the world and do not constitute a homogeneous or collective voice like that in gender and racial identities. The rate of development is also uneven in South Asia. Lesser the degree of underdevelopment and greater would be the chances of disability empowerment. So, in a nutshell, it is pertinent that the rights of differently abled citizens ought to be made a vital component of development agenda which will surely pave way for a disability-inclusive development strategy in South Asian region.

REFERENCES

Bakshi, P.M. (2002). *The Constitution of India*. Delhi, India: Universal Law Publishing Corporation Pvt. Ltd.

Bangladesh's Constitution of 1972, Reinstated in 1986, with Amendments through 2014. (February 4, 2020). Retrieved from http://www.constituteproject.org/Banngladesh_2014.pdf 23:41 hours, Accessed on 2nd May, 2020.

Bhambani, Meenu and Officer (2006). Policies and Institutions for Persons with Disabilities in India. Retrieved from http://web.worldbank.org/images_pdf

Bhattacharyya, Rajib (May, 2014). "Disability Laws in India: A Study". *International Journal of Research (IJR)*, 1 (4), pp. 99-115.

Conrad Grebel University College, Ontoreo, Canada: University of Waterloo (accessed on 05-04-2017) Disability Discourse in South Asia and Global Disability Governance. Retrieved from https://uwaterloo.ca/grebel/disability-discourse-south-asia-global-disability-governance.

Disability Rights Watch Group and National Forum of Organizations Working with the Disabled (NFOWD) (December, 2009). State of the Rights of Persons with Disabilities in Bangladesh. Dhaka, Bangladesh: Government of Bangladesh.

Henderson, G. and Bryan, Willie V. (Eds.) (2011). *Psycho-Social Aspects of Disability*. Oklahoma: Charles C. Thomas Publisher, LTD.

Jaeger, Paul T. and Cynthia Ann Bowman (2005). *Understanding Disability, Inclusion, Access, Diversity, and Civil Rights*. London: Praeger Publishers.

Ministry of Law, Justice and Company Affairs (1995). The Persons with disabilities (Equal Opportunities, Protection of Rights and Full Participation) Act. New Delhi: Government of India Publications.

Ministry of Law and Justice [Legislative Department], (28th December, 2016). Rights of Persons with Disabilities Act. New Delhi: *Gazette of India Extraordinary*, Government of India.

Ministry of Social Justice and Empowerment (2006). *National Policy for Persons with Disabilities*. New Delhi: the Government of India.

Ministry of Social Welfare (1995). *National Policy on Disability. Dhaka: Gazette Notification*, Government of Bangladesh.

Ministry of Social Welfare (2001). Bangladesh Persons with Disability Welfare Act. Dhaka, Bangladesh: *Gazette Notification*, Government of Bangladesh.

Ministry of Social Welfare (2013). The Rights and Protection of Persons with Disabilities Act. Dhaka: Government of Bangladesh.

National Grassroots and Disabilities Organization, National Council for Women with Disabilities, and Bangladesh Legal Aid and Services Trust (2015). Current Status of Rights of Persons with Disabilities in Bangladesh: Legal and Grassroots Perspectives. Dhaka: Government of Bangladesh.

Office of General Registrar and Census Commissioner, (2011). Census of India, *Data on Disability*. New Delhi: Government of India.

Rimmerman, Arie. (2013). *Social Inclusion of People with Disabilities: National and International Perspectives*. New York: Cambridge University Press.

The Prime Minister's Office (24th September 2006). *National Disability Action Plan*. Dhaka: Government of Bangladesh.

United Nations (October, 2003). *The World Bank and Disability in South Asia: A Portfolio Review*.

World Bank and World Health Organisation (2011). *World Report on Disability.* New York: United Nations.

Acronyms and Abbreviations

PWD: Persons with Disabilities, **RPWD:** Rights of Persons with Disabilities, **UNCRPD:** United Nations Convention on the Rights of Persons with Disabilities, **WHO:** World Health Organization, **NGDO:** National Grassroots and Disabilities Organization, **NCWD:** National Council for Women with Disabilities, **BLAST:** Bangladesh Legal Aid and Services Trust.

11

Child Rights and Governance in South Asia

Some Reflections from India

Shikha Kapur

> "There can be no keener revelation of a society's soul than the way in which it treats its children." —*Nelson Mandela*

Introduction

Children are the most important human resource and the future of any nation. They have to be nurtured in an environment that leads to their overall physical, mental, social, educational, emotional and economic growth. Neglecting children means loss to the society as a whole. A deprived childhood will lead to impediments in the growth and development of a nation, compromising its peace, security and social stability. Children are the future citizens of a country and every government is committed to undertake appropriate legislative and administrative measure to ensure protection of children and their rights.

Biologically, a child is a human being between stages of birth and puberty (American Heritage, 2011). Legally a child refers to a minor, below the legal age of majority. According to the universally accepted definition of United Nations Convention on the Rights of the Child (UNCRC) every human being below the age of eighteen years is known as 'child' unless the age of majority is attained earlier under the national legislation. Till then it is the family, as a fundamental group of society that should be responsible for the growth and well-being of all its members especially the children.

In 1924 for the first time, the rights specific to the children were recognised and responsibility of adults towards children was reiterated. The Geneva Declaration (1924) became the first International Human

Rights document in the history of mankind to address the issue of child rights. It was United Nations Convention on the Rights of the Child (UNCRC) (1989) which set out the first international instrument that covered the full range of human rights, viz. the civil, political, economic, social, health and the cultural rights under child rights irrespective of any race, colour, sex, language, religion, political or other opinion, national or social origin, property, birth or other status. The Convention on the Rights of the Child has 54 articles in all. Articles 1 to 42 broadly cover *Right to Survival, Right to Protection, Right to Development* and *Right to Participation*. Articles 43-54 address how adults and governments should work together to make sure that all children get all their rights. They emphasise that children are entitled to special care and assistance and family is the fundamental group of society and is responsible for providing natural environment for the growth and well-being of children, so that they can take responsibilities within the community. Ratified by 195 countries across the globe with the exception of United States and Sudan, the CRC is the most widely ratified and accepted human rights treaty (CRC, 2017).

South Asia: Child Rights and Child-Friendliness of Governments—Key Features

Afghanistan, Bangladesh, Bhutan, Maldives, Nepal, India, Pakistan, and Sri Lanka form the countries of South Asia. These countries vary in terms of geography, population size, internal and external socio-political factors, and systems of governance. The region is diverse. It hosts the highest mountains in the world as well as small island atolls. Bangladesh, Pakistan and India are among the ten most populous countries in the world, while Bhutan and Maldives barely account for half a million people each. About 30 per cent of South Asians live in urban areas. The countries in this region are vulnerable to disasters and a political upheavals and internal and external tensions and conflicts.

South Asia today is witnessing gradual change as governments are taking important steps to acknowledge and implement children's human rights. They are often in collaboration with and influenced by a range of non-state actors.

Around 27 years have passed since the Convention on the Rights of the Child (CRC) was launched by the United Nations. The key features of the Report of Child friendliness of Governments in South Asian region (2013) reveals very interesting results:

1. Domestic legislation in South Asia has in the recent years, incorporated key aspects of the CRC and child-related ministries, committees and other entities for children. In some cases, very progressive pieces of legislation have been enacted. In spite of laudable laws, policies and institutions enacted by governments, the mechanisms of implementation have not always been effective.
2. Limited human and financial resources and low priority given to children's issues make implementation extremely difficult or impossible and limits opportunities for success.
3. Children and young people are increasingly making use of the skills, platforms and opportunities in a number of settings to realise their participatory potential but there have been many *ad hoc* initiatives by governments to support children's participation. There is a need for a systematic effort by governments to involve and support girls and boys in school governance, in the community, in family-level decision-making and, especially, in local and national governance.
4. The data on health, education and protection of South Asian children shows that in spite of many advances there is still a need for concerted action from governments and other stakeholders to prevent malnutrition, deaths from preventable diseases and to ensure proper sanitation facilities. Too many children are out of school, there is shortage of skilled teachers and access to quality education. Further high levels of violence against children persist in the region with no legal and social support for children and their families to seek redressal once abuse has occurred.
5. The legal and policy reforms in South Asia have to be backed by child-related budget allocations. South Asian children issues need to be integrated in national planning and financing processes and discussed at the highest levels of government.
6. The Report also reveals increased and fruitful interaction and synergies between governments and other child rights actors, non-governmental actors, children and their families. They are pushing and expanding the child rights agenda in spite of intermittent tension and a tendency of governments to limit the space for civil society when they feel their interests are challenged.
7. Overall, Sri Lanka has the highest score in the child-friendliness index.

8. India has done the most towards establishing an enabling legal and policy framework for children, closely followed by Nepal, Bangladesh and Sri Lanka.
9. It is important to note that all countries, including Afghanistan and Pakistan, have made important progress in almost all parameters covered by the report.

Child in India

India is located in South Asia. With an area of 32,87,263 km^2 it is the third largest country in Asia, and the seventh largest country in the world in terms of its size and area (Kapur, 2016). India is home to 1.21 billion people (Census of India, 2011), the second largest population after China in the world. Each year, 26 million children are born in India. They constitute 20 per cent of the world's infants. The Census further estimates that children up to 18 years comprise 39 per cent of the total population. The percentage distribution of children between 0-18 years further reveals that there are 9.7 per cent children between 0-4 years, 9.2 per cent children between 5-9 years, 10.5 per cent children are between 10-14 years while there are 9.5 per cent children between 14-18 years (Census of India, 2011). Gender-wise distribution of children between 0-18 years shows that 52 per cent are males while females are 48 per cent. The sex ratio in India is 933 per 1000 males. India is a young nation since 41 per cent of India's population is below the age of 20 years. Mean age in India is 29 years. India is ranked at 130 (out of 188 countries) in the 2015 Human Development Report (HDR) in the medium human development category with a Human Development Index (HDI) score of 0.609.

Child Rights in India

The Constitution of India—the highest legal document of the land protects rights of every Indian citizen including the children. It includes all rights covered under the Convention of Child Rights.

- *Article 21 A:* Provides Right to free and compulsory elementary education for all children in the 6-14 year age.
- *Article 24:* Right to be protected from any hazardous employment till the age of 14 years.
- *Article 39(e):* Right to be protected from being abused and forced

by economic necessity to enter occupations unsuited to their age or strength.

- *Article 39(f):* Right to equal opportunities and facilities to develop in a healthy manner and in conditions of freedom and dignity and guaranteed protection of childhood and youth against exploitation and against moral and material abandonment.
- *Article 45:* Right to early childhood care and education to all children until they complete the age of six years.

Just as any other adult male or female, children too have rights as equal citizens of India. These rights are:

- Right to equality (Article 14).
- Right against discrimination (Article 15).
- Right to personal liberty and due process of law (Article 21).
- Right to being protected from being trafficked and forced into bonded labour (Article 23).
- Right of minorities for protection of their interests (Article 29).
- Right of weaker sections of the people to be protected from social injustice and all forms of exploitation (Article 46).
- Right to nutrition and standard of living and improved public health (Article 47).

The Constitution is the supreme law of India. It came into effect on 26 January, 1950. It encompasses most rights UNCRC as Fundamental Rights and Directive Principles of State Policy. The government has the flexibility to undertake appropriate legislative and administrative measures to ensure children's rights.

State of Child Rights in India

Child Rights in India is rather a neglected area because of the sheer size and population, rampant illiteracy and poverty that rampantly plague our country. Children are subjected to all forms of inhuman treatment and violence, denied access to healthcare and education; they are beaten, abused, abandoned, raped, turned into sex slaves and sold over and over across the world-meeting unimaginable ill-fate ever possible. Their childhood is a far cry from anything but beautiful, peaceful and loving! They can be easily dubbed as 'Children of the Lesser God'.

A review of State of Child Rights in India clearly indicates that children face many challenges here. The first challenge is the debate emanating over the very definition of Child. We as a country have yet to decide as to 'who is a child?' Different Acts and statutes have different definitions of a child. In the Indian Majority Act (1875) age of child is 18 years while in the Child Marriage Restraint Act (1929) it is 21 years for males and 18 years for females. It is 15 years in the Factories Act (1948); 14 years in the Apprentices Act (1961), Child Labour (Prohibition and Regulation) Act (1986); 16 years in the Immoral Traffic (Prevention) Act (1986) and 18 years in The Juvenile Justice Act (2001) which has now been replaced by the Juvenile Justice (Care and Protection of Children) Act, 2015 where the children between 16-18 years can be tried as adults for heinous crimes. Those indulging in heinous offence can get a minimum of seven years imprisonment under any existing law, serious offences will lead to imprisonment between three to seven years and for petty offences can be penalized with up to three years imprisonment. As per the Census of India, any person below the age of 14 is a child. Every state has its own definition and different age limits for a child.

A further look at the vital statistics pertaining to status of children in India ring many alarm bells. Children in Indian continue to lose their lives to vaccine-preventable disease like measles, which remains the biggest killer. Child malnutrition continues to be a serious problem in India, despite India's booming economy, it is home to one in three malnourished children in the world (HAQ, 2008). One out of every five children who die of diarrhoea worldwide is Indian (MedIndia, 2007). The Infant Mortality Rate (IMR) is 47.57 infant deaths under one year old in a given year per 1,000 live births (Census of India, 2011). According to the Rapid Survey on Children (2014), 38.7 per cent children under 5 years are 'stunted' while 15.1 per cent are 'wasted'; only 65.3 per cent Children between 12-23 months old are fully immunized; 69.5 per cent children between 6-59 months have anaemia (NFHS-3, 2006); 44.7 per cent adolescent girls aged 15-18 years have low Body Mass Index (BMI) (<18.5) (low weight).

The National Commission for Protection of Child Rights has reported 2404, 3281, 3340 and 2270 cases of violation of child rights in 2012-13, 2013-14, 2014-15 and 2015-16 (till 30.06.2015) respectively. The violation of child rights includes violations under the Right of Children to Free and Compulsory Education Act, 2009 and violation under the Protection of Children from Sexual Offences Act, 2012. Child rights violations are also related to displacement, violence, trafficking etc. The actions taken by National Commission for Protection of Child Rights include conduct of summon hearings and giving directions to concerned officials, giving recommendations to State Governments (Jadhav, 2015).

Despite the United Nations Child Rights and several countries constituting laws against it, child labour is prevalent all through the globe even today. India has the largest number of child labourers under the age of 14 in the world. One in every 11 children in India is working and part of the labour force. It is estimated that more than 120 million children between ages 5 and 14 across the world are involved in child labour (Gwalani, 2015). Of these 10.13 million are in India. Adolescents between 15 and 17 years of age doing hazardous work form 62.8 per cent of the overall child labour population as compared to almost 25 per cent of adults work in hazardous conditions.

The number of children who go missing and remain untraced has increased by almost 84 per cent between 2013 and 2015 (Damodaran, 2016). In India, according to estimates, 180 children go missing on an average everyday. The number of untraced children keep piling year on year. According to the National Crime Records Bureau (2014) report every 8 minutes a child goes missing in India. 40 per cent of them are never found. They are taken from their homes and sold as labour, beggars and for sexual exploitation. West Bengal had the highest number of missing children with more than 12,000 missing in 2011 (Shah, 2011). Kidnapping and abduction comprise 42.3 per cent crimes against children (NCRB, 2014). Barring a few states, the police in India do not register first information reports (FIRs)—the first step to an investigation—for missing children. So no formal case is even filed. They only make an entry into the list of missing persons at the police station where the child is reported missing so in-depth investigations are rare. In Delhi following the Noida serial murders (also Nithari serial murders, Nithari Kand) after 24 hours, if a child is not found, a case of kidnapping has to be filed by the police (Shah, 2012).

The Protection of Children from Sexual Offences Act, 2012 (POCSO Act) was passed in an effort to address growing rates of child sexual abuse and poor rates of conviction. The Act provides for care and protection measures for victims, child-friendly procedures during investigation, evidence-recording and medical examination, establishment of a special court, appointment of special public prosecutors (SPPs) and compensation. The trials have to be completed within specific timeline. This Act has been touted as the panacea for crimes against children. Despite such dramatic reforms, "Crime in India 2014" reveals that the conviction rate under the POCSO Act is a measly 24.6 per cent and the pendency rate at an alarming 95.1 per cent. A year after the implementation of POCSO, a RTI application filed by NGO Pratinidhi in Delhi alone reveals that of the 792 cases received under this Act 750 (94.69%) cases were pending with all the courts even after lapse of one year. Of the decided cases, only 14 accused had been convicted (Mathur, 2013). According to the Delhi State Legal Services Authority (DSLSA) the rate of conviction in cases of sexual offences against children was alarming conviction rates in POCSO matters for 2014 was 16.33 per cent, 19.65 per cent for 2015 and 18.49 per cent till July 31, 2016 (*Indian Express*, 2016).

The Way-Out

The governance plays a very vital role in protecting its citizens especially children and their rights. A committed government, sensitized policy makers, alert legislature, curious administration, a watchful community, empowered education system, trained police and judiciary, implementation of laws and acts and rehabilitation of children when and where needed.

The **right to survival** can be achieved through Child-survival programmes. A relatively high infant and child mortality rate has to be reduced. Nutritional status of mother and children needs to be enhanced and anaemia eliminated. Immunization coverage has to be enhanced. The fully immunized children still only constitute a minority of the children. Declining sex ratios is a matter of worry and the girl child has to be allowed to be born.

The **right to protection** has to recognize child labour as a malaise assuming menacing proportions. The problem of tackling child labour requires a holistic approach by weaning child away from the work, educating the parents and the society about the disastrous effects of child labour. The futility and inadequacy of child labour in fulfilling the social and economic needs of the family at the cost of nation's development has to be driven home. Child sexual abuse especially child rape, child trafficking and child prostitution is assuming alarming proportions in the country. There is need for separate provisions for dealing with the offenders, stricter punishments and speedy disposal of cases is a must. Children in conflict with law have to be provided with juvenile homes and protection homes with suitable environment. The purpose of these homes is to bring reform in children and not turn them into hardcore criminals.

Right to development can only be ensured by giving opportunities to children for access to education. Their enrolment and retention have to be improved and adequate infrastructure available to them by way of well-equipped playgrounds, laboratories and libraries.

Right to participation or Child participation should take place at every level. In the families, in schools, in the administrative and judicial set up as it is essential to prepare children for responsible life as an adult, especially in a democratic country like India. Child participation is the obligation of every country that has ratified the CRC. The children are encouraged to make their views known. Adults and parents have to start listening to children involve them in decision making process.

Conclusion

In spite of the Constitution of India—the highest legal document of the land protects rights of every Indian citizen including the children and the fact that India is also a co-signatory to the Convention on the Rights of the Child (CRC) a lot still needs to be done for the protection of Child Rights. Directive Principles of State Policy in Indian Constitution (Article 39) empowers the state to direct policies so that the tender age of the children are not abused and childhood are protected against exploitation and moral abandonment. So it is the government's duty to ensure the fundamental rights of children in India are protected and honoured. It is necessary that all duty-bearers for children promise... a childhood which does not include begging on streets, working in agricultural fields and construction sites, be trafficked, raped, abused and forced to work as sex slaves but be given an environment of love, hope, peace and learning.

REFERENCES

Census of India (2011), Government of India.

Kapur, Shikha (2016). "Rural Tourism in India: Relevance, Prospects and Promotional Strategies." *International Journal of Tourism and Travel*, Vol. 9, No. 1 and 2, pp. 40-49.

National Family Health Survey (NFHS)-3, 2005-06: India: Volume I. Mumbai: IIPS.

NCRB (2014). *Crime in India 2014*. Ministry of Home Affairs.

Rapid Survey on Children (2013-2014). Ministry of Women and Child Development, Government of India.

Raykar, N., Majumder, M., Laxminarayan, R. and Menon, P. (2015). *India Health Report: Nutrition 2015*. New Delhi: Public Health Foundation.

The South Asian Report on the Child-friendliness of Governments (2013). Save the Children, HAQ: Centre for Child Rights, Plan International, CRY: Child Rights and You, Terre des Hommes, Germany.

NET RESOURCES

Census of India, (2011). Child Populaton in India. Retrieved April 14, 2017 from http://www.census2011.co.in/literacy.php

Census of India, (2011). Vital Statistics. Retrieved April 14, 2017 from http://www.censusindia.gov.in/vital_statistics/srs_report/9chap%202%20-%202011.pdf

Child. (n.d.) *American Heritage® Dictionary of the English Language, Fifth Edition*. (2011). Retrieved April 14, 2017 from http://www.thefreedictionary.com/child

Child. (n.d.) Oxford University Press. Retrieved April 14, 2017 from https://en.oxforddictionaries.com/definition/child

Constitution of India. Retrieved April 14, 2017 from http://haqcrc.org/child-rights/constitution-of-india/

CRC, (2017). Retrieved on April 14, 2017 from http://www.ohchr.org/EN/ProfessionalInterest/Pages/CRC.aspx

Damodaran, Damodaran (2016, May 20). 180 Children Go Missing In India Every Day. Most May Never Be Found. *The Huffington Post*. Retrieved on April 14, 2017 from http://www.huffingtonpost.in/dipin-damodharan/180-children-go-missing-e_b_10114654.html

Failure to provide forensic reports delaying child abuse cases: Delhi HC told (November 22, 2016). *The Indian Express*. Retrieved on April 14, 2017 fromhttp://indianexpress.com/article/india/india-news-india/failure-to-provide-forensic-reports-delaying-child-abuse-cases-delhi-hc-told-4390037/

Gawalani, Payal (2015, June 14). Every 11th kid in India a part of the labour force: Study. *TNN*. Retrieved on April 14, 2017 from http://timesofindia.indiatimes.com/city/nagpur/Every-11th-kid-in-India-a-part-of-the-labour-force-Study/articleshow/47659827.cms

HAQ (HAQ: Centre for Child Rights). 2008. Still out of Focus—Status of India's Children. New Delhi, p. 87.

HDI (2015). 'India ranks 130th in 2015 Human Development Index: UNDP'. December 15, 2015. Retrieved March 09, 2016 from *website: http://currentaffairs.gktoday.in/india*-ranks-130th-2015-human-development-index-undp-12201528950.html

Jadhav, Radheshyam (2015, July 31). 2270 cases of violation of child rights in 2015. TNN. Retrieved on April 15, 2017 from http://timesofindia.indiatimes.com/city/pune/2270-cases-of-violation-of-child-rights-in-2015/articleshow/48298582.cms

Mathur, Aneesha (2013, October 31). 750 of 792 child abuse cases pending in courts. Retrieved on April 15, 2017.

MedIndia. 2007. Diarrhoea Claims Nearly 1000 Children In India Everyday. *Indian Health News*. Retrieved September 19, 2007 fromhttp://www.medindia.net/news/Diarrhoea-Claims-Nearly-1000-Children-inIndia-Every-Day-Report-26603-1.htm

NCRB (2014). *Crime against children.* Retrieved on April 15, 2017 fromhttp://ncrb.nic.in/StatPublications/CII/CII2014/chapters/Chapter%206.pdf

No need for special POCSO courts: Government *The Indian Express*. Retrieved on April 14, 2017 from http://indianexpress.com/article/cities/delhi/750-of-792-child-abuse-cases-pending-in-courts/

Shah, Shreya (2012, October 16). "India's Missing Children, By the Numbers". *The Wall Street Journal*. Retrieved on April 15, 2017 fromhttp://blogs.wsj.com/indiarealtime/2012/10/16/indias-missing-children-by-the-numbers/

UNCRC. (1989). Retrieved on April 15, 2017 fromhttp://www.ohchr.org/Documents/ProfessionalInterest/crc.pdf

12
Consumer Rights in South Asia

Sheetal Kapoor

Introduction

Globalization has led to borderless world where the dramatic advancement of the ICT industry (telecommunications and internet) has played significant role in providing new opportunities for consumers and businesses. In the same way, greater openness in the economies of the region in the face of current trends towards globalization and regionalization offers promising opportunities for infusing greater dynamism into their domestic, economies. Since the consumer cannot check or verify the claimed features of the product or service by the website it has to rely on the representation of the e-portals and many times makes payment before receiving the product. Further, the consumer has very less knowledge about the address of the seller and sometimes has no means to verify the address mentioned on the website. There are increasing cases of Online Fraud, ATM Data Leak, websites containing fake information, someone impersonating us on Social Media—all pose huge problems to consumers and breach of privacy many times happens in case of online transactions. The present study entails studying the level of consumer protection in South Asian countries comprising India, Pakistan, Nepal and Bangladesh, and has been divided into five Sections.

Consumer Protection in India

The Indian consumer market has gone through a drastic change with the advent of digital technologies, rapid penetration of e-commerce, smart phones, cloud and internet since 1986. The Consumer Protection Act, 1986 being the foremost legislature for protecting the rights of the consumer and providing relief to them through compensation, has now become archaic and does not consider rapid changes in the consumer marketplaces, especially those dealing with online shopping, teleshopping, product recall, unsafe contracts and misleading advertisements and therefore, it was felt to replace it with the Consumer Protection Act, 2019.

With the growing number of pending cases in the consumer courts and huge delays in providing speedy justice to the consumers for petty amounts, the need of the hour was to bring in a new legislature to empower the consumers. The Consumer Protection Act, 2019 (No. 35 of 2019) was passed by Parliament and received the assent of the President on 9th August, 2019 and provides for the protection of consumers and provides fast track alternatives so that justice reaches to the aggrieved consumers immediately. The New Act, repeals and replaces the older Consumer Protection Act, 1986 and provides mechanisms for making the consumer complaint system more robust. It envisages to remove anomalies and numerous problems faced by consumers in delay in timely disposal of complaints, e-commerce, product liability misleading advertisements. Innovative methods such as mediation, Central Consumer Protection Authority, class action suits would be a part of the Consumer Protection Act, 2019. Since the rules of the New Consumer Protection Act, 2019 are yet to be framed and implemented it is time to look at what the New Act would deliver and draw a comparison with CPA, 1986.

Shortcomings in the Consumer Protection Act, 1986

After 30 years of enactment of the CPA, 1986, it is time to revisit its objectives and organisational structure and enlist its shortcomings in the present era. In 1986 when the Consumer Protection Act was enacted a key milestone in consumer advocacy was achieved in India, which provided a legislative framework for better protection of the interests of the consumer by creating a formal but quasi-judicial dispute resolution mechanism exclusively for consumers. This progressive legislation established a three-tier quasi-judicial consumer dispute redress machinery at the National, State and District levels aimed at providing simple, speedy and affordable redress to consumers. The consumer courts were established with the twin objective for speedy redressal of consumer complaints and to establish quasi-judicial authorities unlike civil courts to provide compensation to consumers. But over the years there have been heavy pendency of cases in various consumer courts. Some of the lacuna of the Consumer Protection Act, 1986 are:

(a) The Consumer Protection Act, 1986 although a benevolent legislature whose sole purpose was to protect the rights of the consumers has become outdated and does not consider rapid changes in consumer market places, especially those dealing with online, teleshopping, product recall, unsafe contracts and misleading advertisements.

(b) Section 13(3A) of CPA, 1986 states that "every complaint shall be heard expeditiously as possible and endeavour made to dispose of complaint within a period of three months from the date of notice by the opposite party and five months if it requires testing of commodities." But it is seen that due to heavy pendency of cases and frequent adjournments delay in getting justice takes place (The Consumer Protection Act, 1986).

(c) The consumer commissions have been overburdened with pending cases and the buyer-seller contract is tilted in favour of the seller. Further, the procedures are becoming expensive and time consuming.

(d) The Presidents and Members of the Consumer Courts constitute the backbone of the consumer dispute redressal system. They play a major role in enhancing the faith of the consumers in the redressal mechanism. But it has been seen that there are more than 400 posts of President and members in various Consumer Forums which are lying vacant. The State Governments do not show any interest in immediately filling up the vacant posts and the issue of consumer protection is not a part of any political parties' agenda.

(e) Consumer Commissions are functioning with staff deputed from other departments who do not have any experience in judicial practices. It is necessary to provide intensive training to the members of the Consumer Courts before putting them on the job. The present practice is to provide training after assuming charge as a member.

(f) Many times, it is seen that the award given by Consumer Commissions is very meagre and petty and the consumer has to run from pillar to post to get the orders implemented.

(g) There has been lack of proper coordination among the President and members of the consumer commissions, for timely adjudication of cases and many times around ten or fifteen adjournments are allowed.

(h) The President of the National Commission or State Commission are not empowered to take up *suo motu* action in consideration of the damages affecting a sizable number of populations, e.g. misleading advertisements.

Analysis of the Cases Disposed by Consumer Courts

According to the data available from the Department of Consumer Affairs more than 4.3 lakh cases are pending in the various consumer courts, which is an alarming figure. When the consumer courts were formed their main purpose was to provide inexpensive and speedy redressal to consumers, where a consumer could itself plead case in the consumer courts. Since the law was complex in nature, many consumers started hiring lawyers and there were frequent adjournments which were given by these consumer courts which started delaying the entire adjudicatory process.

Table 12.1: Total Number of Cases Disposed by Consumer Forums Since Inception (Update on 5-7-2018)

Sl. No.	*Name of Agency*	*Cases filed since inception*	*Cases disposed of since inception*	*Cases Pending*	*% of total Disposal*
1.	National Commission	122042	103520	18522	84.82
2.	State Commissions	788463	678124	110339	86.01
3.	District Forums	3903706	3605673	298033	92.37
	Total	**4814211**	**4387317**	**426894**	**91.13**

Source: www.ncdrc.nic.in

Analysis of data regarding number of cases disposed by consumer courts shows that on 5th July, 2018, at National, State and District level, a total number of 48,14,211 cases were registered out of which 43,87,317 cases have been disposed. Thus, there is an astounding figure of 4.3 lakh cases which are still pending in various consumer foras and the disposal rate is 91.13 per cent. Table 12.1 depicts that 1,22,042 cases were registered since inception up to 5th July, 2018 with the National Commission out of which 84.82 per cent cases were disposed of, while 11 per cent were still pending with the National Commission. In case of State Commission 7,88,463 cases were registered since inception up to July 2018 and 86.01 per cent cases were disposed of. A staggering number of 39,03,706 cases were registered throughout the District Consumer Forums in the country and performance of District Consumer Forums was better as 92.37 per cent cases were disposed of. Justice delayed is justice denied, therefore, the huge number of pending cases in various consumer forums is a major drawback of the CPA, 1986. For petty amounts such as getting compensation in case of defective products, deficiency in service consumers have to wait for years to get justice.

Consumer Protection Act, 2019

The objective of the Act is to provide for protection of the interests of consumers and to establish authorities for timely and effective administration and settlement of consumers' disputes.

Some of the highlights of the Consumer Protection Act, 2019 are:

(a) The definition of 'Consumer' would include both offline and online consumers. The expressions "buys any goods" and "hires or avails any services" would include offline or online transactions through electronic means or by teleshopping or direct selling or multi-level marketing.

(b) Establishment of the Central Consumer Protection Authority (CCPA) to promote, protect and enforce the rights of consumers, to investigate and intervene when necessary to prevent consumer detriment arising from unfair trade practices, and to initiate class action including enforcing recall, refund and return of products. Thus CCPA can act on:

   1. Complaints of unfair trade practices,
   2. Issue safety guidelines,
   3. Order product recall or discontinuation of services,
   4. Refer complaints to other regulators,
   5. Has punitive powers such as imposing penalties,
   6. Can file actions before consumer commissions, and
   7. Intervene in proceeding in matters of consumer rights or unfair trade practices.

   The Central Authority will have an Investigation Wing headed by a Director-General for the purpose of conducting inquiry or investigation under the Act. For false and misleading advertisements CCPA may issue a penalty up to Rs. 10 lakhs on a manufacturer and endorser and includes online marketing. For a subsequent offence, the fine may extend to Rs. 50 lakh. For every subsequent offence, the period of prohibition may extend to three years. However, there are certain exceptions when an endorser will not be held liable for such a penalty. The CCPA has the authority to direct the removal of a misleading advertisement.

(c) The pecuniary jurisdiction of adjudicatory bodies increased in case of District Commission to Rs. 1 crore, in case of State Commission between Rs. 1 crore to Rs. 10 crore and National Commission above Rs. 10 crore. Further simplification of procedure for filing of complaints and online filing of complaints.

(d) The Bill also lists punitive actions against those who are found manufacturing, storing, distributing, selling, or importing products that are spurious or contain adulterants.

(e) Provisions for "product liability" action for or on account of harm caused by or resulting from any product by way fixing the liability of a manufacturer to a claimant.

(f) Provision for "mediation" as an alternate dispute resolution (ADR) mechanism which aims at giving legislative basis to resolution of consumer disputes through mediation, thus making the process less cumbersome, simple and quicker. This will be done under the aegis of the consumer fora.

(g) Several provisions aimed at simplifying the consumer dispute adjudication process in the consumer fora are envisaged. These include, among others, enhancing the pecuniary jurisdiction of the consumer disputes redressal agencies, increasing minimum number of members in the consumer fora to facilitate quick disposal of complaints, power to review their own orders by the state and district commission, constitution of 'circuit bench' to facilitate quicker disposal of complaints, reforming the process for the appointment of the president and members of the district fora, enabling provisions for consumers to file complaints electronically and file complaints in consumer fora that have jurisdiction over the place of residence of the complainant, and deemed admissibility of complaints if the question of admissibility is not decided within the specified period of 21 days.

(h) E-commerce guidelines would be mandatory under consumer protection law which would include 14-day deadline to effect refund request. It would mandate e-tailers to display details of sellers supplying goods and services on their websites and moot the procedure to resolve consumer complaints. The e-commerce companies would also be required to ensure that personally identifiable information of customers are protected. Display terms of contract between e-Commerce entity and the seller relating to return, refund, exchange, warranty/guarantee, delivery/shipment, mode of payments, grievance redressal mechanism etc. to enable consumers to make informed decisions.

The Consumer Protection Act, 2019, it is believed that with its innovative changes would help in empowering consumers and provide justice to the needy in time.

Consumer Protection in Bangladesh

Bangladesh has enacted Consumer Rights Protection Act, 2009 to deal with protection of consumer rights. The Law is an addition to 61 other relevant laws in the country which deal with the consumer rights and their protection mechanisms in a sporadic way. The Consumer Rights Protection Act, 2009 ensures consumer protection by providing quality goods and services at fair prices. It also highlights consumers' right to information regarding quality, quantity, standard and value of the goods and services.

To fulfil the objectives of the Act, a National Consumer Right Protection Council has been established. A Director General of the Consumer Rights Protection Council is appointed under the Act to oversee the consumer rights practices throughout the country. To facilitate the functioning of National Consumer Rights Protection Council, a district committee in every district named District Consumer Rights Protection Committee has been constituted.

The Consumer Rights Protection Act bans the sale of commodities at high price, checks adulteration, fake products, forgery in weighing goods, selling expired items and misleading advertisements. These are considered as serious crimes, and the law also spells out punishment for such offences.

According to the Act, any businessmen found guilty under the law would be penalised with a punishment ranging from one year to three years imprisonment and minimum Tk 50,000 to Tk 2,00,000 as fines. There are provisions for at least 20 types of crimes ranging from hoarding, flouting of packaging rules to over-charging for products. The law stipulates formation of a National Consumer Protection Rights Council headed by the Commerce Minister and branches at the district level.

The Consumer Rights Protection Tribunals have been set up in districts and sub-districts to check unfair practices related to consumers' goods. Consumers are allowed to take legal steps individually. They can file complaint through e-mail, fax or other sources to the Director General concerned regarding such crimes.

Seeking Redressal

Consumers in Bangladesh face a number of specific problems, such as: adulteration, product inconsistent with price, deceptive advertising, deceptive packaging and branding, false information about goods and services, cheating in weights and measures, false date, fraudulent production process and selling.

Complaints about any anti-consumer rights practice under this Act have to be filed by any consumer to the Director General or any person authorised by the directorate within 30 days of the incident. The authority upon receiving a complaint shall immediately investigate or inquire into such a complaint. If such a complaint is proved to be true after investigation, the Director General or any officer authorised by him may, in his administrative action, impose fine upon the guilty person. If any fine is imposed and realised, 25 per cent of such realised fine shall immediately be paid to the complainant concerned.

If any regular criminal case is filed in a court or in a special tribunal under The Consumer Rights Protection Act, 2009 and if the accused is fined upon found guilty and if the fine is realised, 25 per cent of the realised fine shall be paid to the complainant concerned. Any person may make complaint by examining the matter of adulteration or copying of goods in a public or private laboratory at its own initiative.

Need for Harmonisation of Consumer Protection Laws

Overlapping of laws is a problem for Bangladesh to implement measures against criminality associated with violation of consumer rights. Different Laws on the same subject, different types of punishment for the same offence under different Laws, court fees for filing a suit for compensation, delay in proceedings, investigation procedure left to the police instead of independent authorities, lack of monitoring mechanism have been observed by experts as potential impediments to enforcement. On the other hand, there are some controversial and conventional laws in existence in the country. These laws are so outdated that little or no protection is provided to the consumer's interests. The enforcement mechanisms of the consumer rights are not praiseworthy as no individual complaint can be entertained by the Court without written permission of the Director General of the Consumer Rights Protection Department (Ahamuduzzaman and Hussain, 2009).

Some of the steps in this direction could be:

(a) Educating the consumers by creating awareness through multimedia programmes and advertising;
(b) Establishing a separate court for addressing consumers' specific complaints;
(c) Enacting a law with all provisions to promote and protect the rights of consumers and repealing the backdated laws or provisions thereof;
(d) Taking effective measures for fair pricing and quality products by establishing market-control authorities;
(e) Monitoring prices of essential commodities, checking standards of various articles and ensuring safety products to the consumer;
(f) Constituting a 'consumers' complaint redress authority;
(g) Exempting consumers of court fees for filing a suit on the protection of consumer rights;
(h) Allowing individual consumers to lodge complaint directly with the police or criminal Court and increasing the involvement of civil society organisations; and
(i) Giving exact definition of various products increasing mobile court operations.

Consumer Protection in Pakistan

The first Consumer Protection Law was prepared by Iqbal Haider, who introduced the first Consumer Protection Law in Islamabad. The NWFP established its Consumer Protection Law in 1997, followed by Baluchistan in 2003. In 2005, Punjab followed suit. Consumer courts were approved in 2006 and became functional in 2007. These courts are in 11 districts of Punjab and any person belonging to other districts can appeal to a nearby district court. If consumers have any complaint about a product, services or a company they may contact these courts. By writing an application, attaching a copy of receipt and submit it to the District Consumer Court.

If the Consumer Court is satisfied that the product or service complained against sufferers from any of the defects specified in the claim, it may direct the manufacturer or service provider to remove the defect, to replace the products with new products, to reimburse to the claimant the price of the product, to pay reasonable compensation and to award actual costs of the legal proceedings.

Redressal Mechanism

(1) The Authority formed by the Islamabad Consumer Protection

Council, is responsible for receiving the complaints of consumers and those made on behalf of the Council, their investigation and determination. The Police, Capital Development Authority and other agencies of the Federal Government and Islamabad Capital Territory Administration Act in aid of the Authority for Performance of the functions under this Act.

(2) Under the Consumer Protection Act of Punjab Province, consumer courts and councils are established at divisional level and district DCOs are also authorized to hear public complaints, impose fine upon unruly manufacturers or refer their cases to consumer court/council. In addition to action on public complaints, CPC can also act *suo motu*.

(3) In Sindh Province, Government has set up a 15-member Consumer Rights Council (CRC) in September 2005, with a jurisdiction restricted to Karachi city only. However, the government has not been able to adopt a formal law so far and establish the necessary infrastructure and consumer courts across the length and breadth of the province.

(4) The NWFP Assembly adopted a Consumers Protection Bill in 1997, which was amended in 2005. This law provides for the setting up of a provincial council for protection of consumers' rights. However, the provincial government has not enforced this Bill so far.

(5) The Consumers Protection Bill of Baluchistan was adopted by the Provincial Assembly on October 30, 2003. A provincial council for protecting consumer rights has been constituted under this law, however district councils are yet to be formed. The law empowers judicial magistrates to hear consumer complaints instead of establishing special consumer courts.

Lack of Political Interest

In Pakistan, the laws clearly define the guidelines to protect consumer interests, but as the old saying goes, "laws are not enforced, they will never be obeyed". Lack of political will to enforce laws, like most other laws, the consumer protection laws have been totally ignored, both by manufacturers and the government and remain ineffective.

Due to the lack of consumer protection laws and the lack of government support, there are very few Consumer Organizations that are working on consumer issues. According to Islamabad Consumer

Protection Law where any right of consumer is infringed, the person responsible for such infringement shall be punished with imprisonment which may extend to two years, or with fine, or with both. Any misleading advertisement through print or electronic media or by chalking on walls or in any other manner in contravention of the Act, the manufacturer or service provider shall be punished with imprisonment which may extend to two years, or with fine, or with both. The Authority may order for payment of compensation to the consumer to the extent the consumer has suffered any damage or loss through any unfair trade practice. The Authority may, where it deems necessary for protection of the right of other consumers, order for confiscation of any goods or material or direct for their destruction.

Section IV: Consumer Protection in Nepal

In Nepal, the Act is known as "The Consumer Protection Act, 1998". It came into force on 13 April, 1999. It has 30 sections in total and establishes the Consumer Protection Council. The functions of the Council are:

(a) Advising the government on matters relating to the protection of rights and interest of consumers.
(b) Prices, quality and purity of consumer goods and services.
(c) Disseminating information.
(d) Conducting various studies.

The Act regulates the powers of Inspection officers to inspect and investigate where there are reasons to believe that products and services which are not safe or of proscribed standards are being produced sold or supplied.

The Government of Nepal is introducing a revised Consumer Protection Act to ensure the consumers' rights and make the market monitoring more effective. The New Act would make the government at the central, provincial and local levels more responsible to monitor the market and control artificial price hikes of goods and cartel. The monitoring agencies did not take action against the culprits on the spot due to weaknesses in the existing Consumer Protection Act, therefore, the new legislature would take care of the e-commerce transactions and problems and challenges faced by the consumers due to online purchases.

Currently, there are number of institutions which are liable to look after consumers' rights in Nepal. Among them, Department of Commerce,

Supply and Protection of Consumers, Department of Food Technology and Quality Control, Nepal Bureau of Standards and Metrology, Department of Drug Administration, District Administration Office, local governments and National Human Rights Commission are the authorities which conduct market monitoring and receive complaints from the consumers. In theory, these authorities are supposed to look after the welfare of consumers but in reality, they avoid the duty. The concerned authorities often blame either the shortfall of resources or the weak laws when it comes to safeguarding the consumers' interests.

Conclusion

An efficient consumer protection legislation not only protects and promotes the privileges and happiness of its consumers, but also enhances socio-economic targets of its macro-economy, such as scarcity alleviation, competent, fair and translucent market method, good governance and beyond all, socio-economic impartiality for its citizens. It is an established fact that consumers are the largest stake in any country and have the power to make or break a brand. In India, the Consumer Protection Act, 2019 with its innovative measures takes into account both online and brick and mortar transactions and also empowers the Central Consumer Protection Authority (CCPA) to take *suo motu* actions to protect the rights of the consumers. But unlike India, in Bangladesh, Nepal and Pakistan, the consumer protection laws are archaic. For speedy redressal of the consumer complaints, there should be active support from the government and implementation of the law should be in letter and spirit which is missing in these countries. Outdated laws, poor implementation and lack of awareness amongst masses are some other reasons why timely justice is not available to the poor and needy consumers of these countries.

REFERENCES

Aggarwal V.K. (2015). *Consumer Protection: Law and Practice*, Bharat Law House, Delhi.

Ahamuduzzaman *et al.*, *Consumer Protection Law*, July 2009, pp. 123-124.

Constitution of Bangladesh, the Ministry of Law, published by the Parliament.

Consumer Protection Judgements (CPJ) relevant cases.

G. Borrie and A.L. Diamond. *The Consumer, Society and the Law*, New York, 1983, p. 9.

G. Ganesan and M. Sumathy (2012). *Globalisation and Consumerism: Issues and Challenges*, Regal Publications.

George, S. Day and A. Aaker (1970), "A Guide to Consumerism", *Journal of Marketing*, Vol. 34, pp. 12-19.

Goodwin Cathy, *Recognition of a Consumer Right, Journal of Public Policy and Marketing*, Vol. 10, No. 1, 1991, pp. 149-166.

Kapoor, Sheetal (2019). *Consumer Affairs and Customer Care*, 2nd Edition, Galgotia Publishing Company.

L. Kabir, *The Penal Code, 1860*, Dhaka, 2009.

M. Humayun Kabir Chowdhury, *et al.*, "Consumer Perceived Value Formation in Bangladesh: A latent Structure Approach," *ASA University Review*, Vol. 1, Issue No. 1, pp. 1-4.

Misra, Suresh, (August 2017). "Is the Indian Consumer Protected? One India One People."

Mizanur Rahman, "Consumer Protection in Bangladesh: Law and Practice" (1994) 17(3), *Journal of Consumer Policy,* 349.

Rao, Rajyalakshmi (2012). *Consumer is King*, 3rd Edition Universal Law Publishing Co., Delhi.

The Consumer Protection Act, 1986 (Bare Act).

The Consumer Protection Act, 2019 (The Gazette of India).

The Protection of Consumer Rights Act, 2009. Published by the Bangladesh Government on April 6, 2009.

Ulf Bernitz and John Draper, *Consumer Protection in Sweden, Legislation, Institutions and Practice*. Stockholm, 1986, p. 11

www.cda.gov.pk

www.consumeraffairs.nic.in

www.consumereducation.in

www.ncdrc.nic.in

www.ncdrc.nic.in

SECTION III

Bilateral Relations and Cooperation

13
Plights of Higher Education as an Obstacle for Development in South Asia

Mohammad Kalimuddin Ahmad

Established in 1985, the South Asian Association for Regional Cooperation (SAARC) comprises eight member states: Afghanistan, Bangladesh, Bhutan, India, Maldives, Nepal, Pakistan and Sri Lanka. This is the most populous and the most densely populated geographical region in the world; comprising over 1.7 billion people which is about 21 per cent of the world's total population [WP]. South Asia is lagging behind in terms of education, employment and health services.

The following is the estimated (e) and forecasted (f) analysis of real GDP at market prices for South Asian countries available as of April 7, 2020 [WB]. It may be pointed out that during the COVID-19 pandemic, the economy of these countries are fluid enough and changing day by day.

Table 13.1: GDP at Market Prices in Per cent

Country	*Fiscal year*	*2019 (e)*	*2020 (f)*	*2021 (f)*	*2022 (f)*
Afghanistan	December to December	2.9	-5.9 to -3.8	3.3 to 3.9	5.2 to 6.2
Bangladesh	July to June	8.2	2.0 to 3.0	1.2 to 2.9	2.8 to 3.9
Bhutan	July to June	3.9	2.2 to 2.9	2.0 to 2.5	3.1 to 3.5
India	April to March	6.1	4.8 to 5.0	1.5 to 2.8	4.0 to 5.0
Maldives	January to December	5.2	-13.0 to -8.5	6.3 to 7.3	5.0 to 5.5
Nepal	mid-July to mid-July	7.1	1.5 to 2.8	1.4 to 2.9	2.7 to 3.6
Pakistan	July to June	3.3	-2.2 to -1.3	0.3 to 0.9	3.2 to 3.3
Sri Lanka	January to December	2.6	-3.0 to -0.5	0.2 to 1.2	2.0 to 2.5

Out of the many objectives outlined in the SAARC Charter, one of the main aims is *"to promote active collaboration and mutual assistance in the economic, social, cultural, technical and scientific fields."*

Spending on Education

The World Bank report shows that the spending on education (in terms of percentage of their GDP) for these countries is quite low [WE]. *These countries must set education as their national priority and invest more in education so that their future generation could compete globally. In the absence of advanced labs and better educational setups, affluent and meritorious students are going to the advanced world and getting settled there, a big loss in terms of a 'brain drain' for these nations. Whereas on the other hand, the meritorious and poor students are deprived of better facilities, and again the nations are at loss. We have examples of South Korea, Taiwan, Malaysia and Singapore in our neighbourhood who have transformed their status from a third world country to an advanced industrial one in a short time with reasonable funding on education. Therefore, we must evolve a master plan for scientific and applied research with specific goals, realistic implementation and continuous education. The South Asian University (an international university established by the eight member nations of SAARC with the headquarters in New Delhi) is doing some ground work in this direction but it should be augmented by developing research infrastructure to help researchers attain specific goals.*

SAARC Universities in QS World Rankings

As per the recent QS World University Rankings [QS], which assess performance of institutions across four areas: teaching, research, employability and internationalization, no SAARC institution could figure in the Top 100 slot whereas there are 25 institutions from Asia in this slot (Breakup of 25: China 6, South Korea 5, Japan 5, Hong Kong 5, Singapore 2, Taiwan 1, Malaysia 1). However, three institutions IIT–Bombay, IIT–Delhi, and IISc–Bangalore from India could find a place in the 100-200 slot at 152, 182 and 184 places respectively. So the question is: from where to start? Since schools are the feeder of higher educational institutions, it is urgently required to invest more in the primary sector of education, especially in terms of infrastructure development by increasing budgetary allocation.

It is important to mention here the weightage of parameters adopted in the ranking. They are: Academic reputation (40%—survey based), Employer reputation (10%—survey based), Faculty/student ratio (20%), Citations per faculty (20%), International faculty ratio (5%) and International student ratio (5%).

Table 13.2: Universities/Institutions of SAARC Countries that Figure in QS World Ranking of Universities

Country	*University/Institution*	*Ranking 2020*
Bangladesh	Bangladesh University of Engineering and Technology	801-1000
	University of Dhaka	801-1000
India	Indian Institute of Technology, Bombay	152
	Indian Institute of Technology, Delhi	182
	Indian Institute of Science	184
	Indian Institute of Technology, Madras	271
	Indian Institute of Technology, Kharagpur	281
	Indian Institute of Technology, Kanpur	291
	Indian Institute of Technology, Roorkee	383
	University of Delhi	474
	Indian Institute of Technology, Guwahati	491
	Six Universities/Institutions	601-800
	Nine Universities/Institutions	801-1000
Pakistan	Pakistan Institute of Engineering and Applied Sciences	375
	National University of Science and Technology, Islamabad	400
	Five Universities/Institutions	501-1000
Sri Lanka	University of Peradeniya	801-100

In many of the advanced countries, the conventional use of black boards is supplemented with computer based technology. Our problem: how to address the needs of the rural area with the changing technological advancement in the urban area? *It is true that a section of population of these countries is tuned to the development and adapting to technology in imparting education to students, but a large section of the population does not commensurate with the development—partly because of lack of infrastructure and non-availability of well trained teachers*. Right now, the adaptation of technology in school education is moving at a snail's pace, while the world outside is speeding at a supersonic rate. The challenges before us are to prepare the children of today for a world that has yet to be created, for jobs yet to be invented, and for technologies yet un-dreamed of.

SAARC Universities in QS Asia Rankings

Since 2009, the **QS Asia University Rankings** highlights the top universities in Asia each year. The methodology used to create the ranking is similar to that used for the QS World University Rankings, but with some additional indicators and adapted weightings. *This set of criteria, developed in consultation with regional experts and stakeholders, is designed to reflect key priorities for universities in Asia, drawing on as much available data as possible*. They are as follows: Academic reputation (30%—survey based), Employer reputation (20%—survey based), Faculty/student ratio (10%), International research network (10%), Citations per faculty (10%), Papers per faculty (5%), Staff with Ph.D. (5%), Proportion of international faculty (2.5%), Proportion of international students (2.5%), Proportion of inbound exchange students (2.5%), and Proportion of outbound exchange students (2.5%).

Based on these criteria, if we try to find SAARC institutions in the Top 100 slot of Asian universities/institutions, we find eight (8) from India and one (1) from Pakistan. However, in the top 200 slot, there are twenty (20) Indian universities/institutions, seven (7) from Pakistan and one (1) each from Bangladesh and Sri Lanka.

Parameters in These Rankings

If we look at parameters in these rankings, we find that about 50 per cent of weightage in the ranking is survey based which is unfair for the institutions which are not so famous. The elite institutions grab the lion's share in surveys. However, it would be in the interest of institutions if we increase the proportion of international students and international faculty through exchange programmes with top institutions. The teachers of institutions may be encouraged to publish only in quality journals so that it may be taken into account by the rankers.

NIRF: A Suitable Ranking Measure for SAARC Countries

National Institutional Ranking Framework (NIRF) is an initiative of the Ministry of Human Resource Development (MHRD), Government of India, to rank educational institutes across the country based on teaching standards, research work, placements and outreach programmes, among other parameters. The ranking parameter and their weightage are as follows: Teaching, Learning and Resources (30%), Research and

Professional Practice (30%), Graduation Outcome (20%), Outreach and Inclusivity (10%), and Perception (10%) [IN]. *This can be a suitable ranking measure for the institutions of SAARC countries.*

Institutions of Eminence (IoE): An Indian Initiative

Taking in view that no Indian university/institution figure in top 100 list of world ranking of institutions, government has recently come up with a plan to select 20 Institutions of Eminence (IoE) in September 2017 [IE]. The Ministry of Human Resource Development (MHRD) has selected 20 institutions (naming them IoE), providing certain autonomy/funding so that they could find place in top 100 global institutions in 10 years. Only those institutions who figure in 500 global ranking or in top 50 NIRF ranking of MHRD are eligible to apply for eminence tag. *Therefore, it is imperative for the government of SAARC nations to come-up with a concrete plan like this, so as to address the needs of our future generation.*

Success Story of Higher Education in Western Countries

In the year 1990, Prof. (Dr.) Helmut Neunzert, the Head of the Department of Industrial Mathematics of the University of Kaiserslautern, Germany, visited Aligarh Muslim University, Aligarh, where I was pursuing Ph.D. in the Department of Mathematics. Till then, we were doing Mathematics for the sake of mathematics, without knowing its real beauty. We learned from Prof Neunzert that "mathematics is behind all industrial development in Europe" and in fact he encouraged us to apply for a Master programme of Industrial Mathematics. This programme had few scholarships sponsored by the German industries for the students from developing countries. Though I was a good student of the Department of Mathematics, AMU but when I joined this master programme at the University of Kaiserslautern in 1991, it was altogether different and difficult for me. Professor told us that there are three legs of Industrial Mathematics: "Mathematics, Technique and Computer Science and you have to do justice with all of them." It is to be mentioned here that students in this programme were from different disciplines. *We were adequately given theoretical lectures by the senior professors of the department but the beauty of this programme was the tutorial classes and Modelling Seminar.* During lectures we were given problems and were asked to submit answers in a week or so. Further, there was threadbare discussion on those problems in separate tutorial classes. This way, we learnt the theory properly.

The Mathematical modelling seminar was a thing to be cherished; a group of two-three students were given a problem from the Industry and a mentor was allotted to work under his supervision. Here we understood how mathematics can help us to model these problems. It was not an easy task: you never know which mathematics will be used, whether your model will be well-posed, whether you can get numerical solution by the well known numerical methods or you have to find the other way out to simulate the model on the computer screen. Altogether a lot of work, and lot to learn and develop depending upon the problems.

To get the problems and finance from the industry was not easy those days. As described by Prof. Neunzert, "many times managers or supervisors of Industrial houses were reluctant to speak or share their problems with mathematicians. They considered only engineers or computer scientists to be useful to them." *The efforts of Prof. Neunzert brought a big change in a decade or so he established an Institute for Technical and Industrial Mathematics (abbreviated as ITWM in German language) which later in the year 2000 became Fraunhofer ITWM.* For the detailed overview of this institute, I refer to the book edited by Neunzert *et al.* [HN1] which was published by Springer in 2015. The articles therein would be of real motivation to the younger generation to go for the modelling career.

Neunzert *et al.* [HN2] rightly mentioned, "Only recently the 3rd world began to receive the message of Industrial Mathematics. Therefore, there is an acute shortage of properly educated mathematicians. There are, of course, some excellent pure mathematicians and quite a number of good applied mathematicians in the traditional British sense. But their work is mainly "method driven" ("I do, what I am able to do"), but not problem driven ("I do, what should be done"). Academic careers make this attitude necessary: One has to belong to a scientific family (even if it is very small), one has to publish (even if it is a generalization of a generalization) in order to be promoted. Who dares to work on a modelling problem, when he/she does not know, which kind of mathematics is needed, what the result will be, where it should be published, who (besides may be a company) will be interested in? However, Real career jumps need surprising results, new problems and new ideas—all that could not be expected without taking a risk! Moreover, senior professors do not need a security belt when working on new problems; they could go ahead and give the young scientists a chance and some credit to work on industrial problems. Obviously, the pressure comes from outside: Governments press scientists to contribute to the economic welfare of their countries. Does this really mean a cultural loss? Once more: The very few very best have some right to maintain that—and it is the duty of the many others to protect them, to protect them by proving that their ideas and mathematics as a whole is one of the most useful and valuable technologies."

Mathematics as a Modelling Tool

Since ages, mathematics has been used in Modelling and interdisciplinary studies. Knowingly or unknowingly people used mathematical models in religious and daily activities. During ancient or medieval times, modelling was performed in various parts of the world independently as there were no or least interactions those days but in recent times the power of internet has made whole world a global village. So the modelling as such is not new but the tools used are continuously evolving with the passage of time. It is getting more refined with better precision. At this point of time, no discipline can ignore the use of mathematics in their subject field. *Mathematics is the future technology, it must be realised by the academics of SAARC nations. Mathematics has changed advanced the world by its applications in every field from engineering, computer science, and humanities to day to day affairs.*

As an illustration, I mention here some of modelling and interdisciplinary approach that shaped the real world problems in different ages.

Whether it is conditional proposition and syllogisms of Ibn Sina [IS], the work of many other logicians or the work of Nobel Laureate of literature, Bertrand Russell in Mathematical logic, these all lead to modern day fields of artificial intelligence, Computer Science and fuzzy logic; Mathematics has been enriched through this interdisciplinary approach. The Arabs even produced, in Omar Khayyam, a great poet and a great Mathematician who classified equations of the third degree into 25 categories and then attempted to solve them.

To ascertain an auspicious moment for his daughter's wedding, Bhaskar-II (1114–1185), an Indian mathematician developed a mathematical model. He nailed a small hole at the bottom of a cup and allowed it to float in a vessel filled with water, arranged so that the cup would sink at the beginning of the propitious hour.

Hellenistic mathematics (in the regions of Egypt, Greece, Mesopotamia) had a number of great exponents, including Euclid, Archimedes, Apollonius, Diophantos and Ptolemy. Euclid's *Elements* was the foundation of systematic geometry and remained the cornerstone for the teaching of the subject until recent times. Ptolemy's *Mathematical Treatise (al-Majisti in Arabic and Almagest in Latin)* is the most complex account of geocentric system, which places the earth at the centre of universe. The Arab scholars inherited the Hellenistic Sciences and they would have certainly benefited out of this treasure.

The importance of Mathematics can also be gauged from the *commentary of Proclus*, who lived sometime in fifth century AD: "Mathematics arouses our innate knowledge, awakens our intellect, purges our understanding, brings to light the concepts that belong essentially to us, takes away the forgetfulness and ignorance that we have from birth, sets us free from the bonds of unreason; and all this by the favour of the god [Hermes?] who is truly the patron of this science, who brings our intellectual endowments to light, fills everything with divine reason, moves our souls towards Nous [the highest form of knowledge], awakens us as it were from our heavy slumber, through our searching turns us back upon ourselves, through our birth pangs perfects us, and through the discovery of pure Nous leads us to the blessed life." (*Proclus: A Commentary on the First Book of Euclid's Elements*, translated by Glenn R. Morrow, Princeton University Press, 1970, p. 38).

So to say, mathematics not only awakens our intellect but sets us free from the bonds of unreason.

But unfortunately there are instances in history that describe the interference of religion in science. Galileo who is often called the "father of modern physics", was put under house arrest until his death (8 January, 1642), when he had contradicting views with the Church. Further, the tragedy of the demolition of the last observatory in 1580 (also known as the Istanbul Observatory) established by Taqi al-Din, exemplified the victory of the Clerical faction over science.

Concluding Remarks

The education system of SAARC countries is mostly degree oriented; it is required to establish a link between academia and industry. There are shifting trends in every research field, so the education system has to be adapted accordingly. We may send our bright students under the student's exchange programme to some centres of excellence in Europe or America that are in forefront for interdisciplinary research. The huge population of this region could become a boon if their potential is properly utilised by making them skilled. In this way, they can become an asset to the nation rather than becoming a burden on the taxpayers of the country.

REFERENCES

[WP] https://worldpopulationreview.com/countries/saarc-countries/

[WB] https://www.worldbank.org/en/region/sar/overview

[WE] https://data.worldbank.org/indicator/SE.XPD.TOTL.GD.ZS?locations=8S

[QS] https://www.topuniversities.com/university-rankings/world-university-rankings/2020

[IN] https://www.nirfindia.org/About

[IE] https://www.ugc.ac.in/ioe/

[HN1] H. Neunzert, D. Prätzel-Wolters (eds.), *Currents in Industrial Mathematics*, Springer-Verlag Berlin Heidelberg 2015. DOI 10.1007/978-3-662-48258-2_2.

[HN2] H. Neunzert, A.H. Siddiqi, *Industrial Mathematics–Ideas and Examples*, Report No. 177, 1997, Department of Mathematics, University of Kaiserslautern, Germany.

[MKA] M.K. Ahmad, *Science, Technology and Development*. pp. 382-390, 2020, appeared in the Book "Higher Education, Good Governance and Development-Issues, Challenges and Prospects" (ed. by A. Rahman), Concept Publishing Company Pvt. Ltd., New Delhi.

[IS] Ibn Sina, Abu Ali, al-Shifa al-Qiyas (ed. by S. Zayed), Cairo 1964, 229-425. *The lithographed edition of al-Shifa*, published in Tehran in 1886 AD includes only the Physics and Metaphysics (in two volumes).

14
India's Triangular Partners
Bangladesh, Sri Lanka and Pakistan

Md. Badruddin

Introduction

The triangular partnership of India with Pakistan, Bangladesh and Sri Lanka continues to remain a debated topic during the age of globalisation and economic liberalisation. The issue of religious fundamentalism (India and Pakistan), undocumented migrants (Bangladesh), and ethnic cleansings (Sri Lanka) are not easy to tackle. The height of mistrust, suspicion and strategic insecurity continue to encircle the geo-political scenario. The mindset of Pakistan has not changed, Bangladesh blames India for not accepting UN Refugee Conventions while Sri Lankan Tamil Tigers are still unhappy as they are largely living under fear and social insecurity. Historic facts, intellectual foundation, and poorly circulated literature, particularly about the status of refugees from Bangladesh, and ethnic nationality from Sri Lanka still remain the fundamental problem in various policy matters despite continuous efforts of cooperation and peace. Similarly, misinterpreted version of Islam and censorship of Indian media are widely discussed subjects. Radical Indian minds got too much indulged in political issues and saffron agenda rather than promoting secular democratic system and giving focus on 'China Economic Model', a lesson for the whole world. Therefore, India has to create new alternatives both in the form of problems as well as solutions.

Liberation of Pakistan, creation of Bangladesh, and demand of separate Tamil Land in Sri Lanka have greater impact on policy agenda and security matters which cannot be easily ignored. Empowerment of narrow theocracy, interreligious chauvinism, persisting huge regional imbalances, and political exploitation completely failed to produce effective leadership and governance ability between all four governments: India, Pakistan, Bangladesh and Sri Lanka. International human rights agencies, therefore, became alert to monitor the ongoing developments among ideologically conflicting South Asian Tigers and falsely proclaim civil societies. India's lust for vote banks from migrants, refugees, ethnic minorities and political contractors were designed for democratic power. Bargaining Actors despite constrains and inadequacies, often tried to impress the humanitarian agencies by imposing forceful law. American policy to play a dual diplomacy in form of Global Policeman and misinterpreted version of Islam are well-known to the world community. Then why should Bangladeshi and Pakistani Muslim refugees and terrorist organizations in India be kept in hitting list which remain to be understood in the context of secular democratic law. Politically dictated version of censured media and rightist forces of ruling *Moditva* ideology raise serious doubts and uncertainties for India's future. Alignment of Bangladeshi Refugees and Pak Muslims in India with ISI activities is nothing but to widen the gap between the various religions just for political benefits. The output will not bring any concrete solution rather it will result in social disarray, and political instability if New Delhi, Islamabad, and Dhaka officials do not use rational thinking on these sensitive issues. In short, India's Triangular Partners: Pakistan, Bangladesh and Sri Lanka continue to remain debated subject in academic circle. All three suspicious partners should work together on the core issue of economic development, inter-state trade, and collective social security to promote social partnerships.

Indo-Pak Relations

Ever since 1947 when Pakistan was freed from India, the relations between the two neighbouring countries have remained far from satisfaction. It is rather a complicated issue to come out on a particular result without going into deeply rooted history, partition of India, division of natural resources, and demarcation of boundaries. Prominent issues like territorial aggrandizement, sharing of river and marine water resources, communal riots, migration factors, self-determination in Jammu & Kashmir (J&K), Pakistan's nuclear duplicity, and geo-political complications in Siachin Glacier aggravated Indo-Pak Relations; all are important dimensions. Furthermore, Pakistan's nexus with Islamic Fundamentalism, trans-border smuggling, discriminatory trade barriers, role of Indian *vs.* Pakistani media, and attitude of young Indians against Pakistan do not hold logical ends. Whereas, the fundamental issues of both countries have domestic roots, the projection of the superpowers in South Asia severely complicated these problems by exacerbating tensions between India and Pakistan rather escalating tension and promoting peace agenda.

Engagements of major powers like USA, China and Russia need to play effective role of peace rather than promoting dubious game to end ideological competition, political rivalry and geo-strategic interest. Pakistan's inclination towards the oil rich Gulf and power nexus with US and China, whereas India's policy of non-alignment and 'no first use' are not justified on many grounds. Pakistan's too much dependency on power bargainers and imports of arms ammunitions from USA, and India's propaganda against Pakistan at every excuse are simply based on false perceptions and imaginary evidences in several references. Washington's stand about 'military aid diplomacy' for India to sign non-proliferation treaty has never suited to Indian policy-makers. Neither India nor Pak will roll back or cap their nuclear programmes thereby reducing the prospects of Confidence Building Measures (CBM). With well-known facts, US-Pak Military Alliance sharpened Indo-Pak tensions, escalated and found Pakistan as a trustworthy partner to serve its national interest. For varied reasons, the US found a golden opportunity to escalate *Kashmir* dispute and its reference in the UN to establish its strategic interests in the region at the pretext of peace building. Thus, the invention of US amidst Indo-Pak Relations serves as ideological victory at various pretexts. Since Modi Government came into power in 2014, both media as well as policy-makers played damaging role by patronizing the Indian Muslims as anti-nationalists. Sizeable Muslim community are kept under maximum pressure to compromise with Hindu Majority agenda, politically manipulated issues of *Triple Talaq*, Love *Jihad*, lynching cases, cow-goat meat politics, temple-mosque controversy, worship at disputed sites and censorship of media have worsened Indo-Pak relations.

Historical Milestones: Peace or Confrontation

India and Pakistan continue to face serious challenges since the creation of Jinnah's Two Nation Theory and the subsequent partition in 1947. The root causes have been border disputes, distribution of water, religious differences and cross-border terrorism. Questionably, Indo-Pak history is marred with revulsion, mistrust and political hostility rather than promoting developmental agenda. Indeed, peace between India and Pakistan is the prerequisite for achieving stability and economic development in South Asia. In the past, efforts were made at bilateral and multilateral levels to normalize the relationship between two South Asian Tigers. Strategic culture of unpleasantness, sense of insecurity, mistrust, and the divergent geo-political interests of the great powers have also contributed to the environment of distrust and antagonism. Consequently, peace and democracy remain a distant dream for the people of Indian Subcontinent. The legacy of communal antagonism, regional variations, uncomfortable environment and territorial disagreement—all go through the historical roots of 'Divide and Rule' and 'Two Nation Theory' of Jinnah, which raised serious controversy on repeated interval. Pakistan ever since looked India, as a 'Hindu State' by ignoring the secular character and the existence of Islamic state like Pakistan was bound to raise misgivings against India.[1]

There have been odd developments as the history is full of volumes about Indo-Pak Relations. During the year 1962, Sino-Indian war took place where Pakistan occupied Kashmir (PoK) at the pretext of China was the beginning of conflict and confrontation. It was the historic start of rivalry between two partners. It led to serious repercussion in March 1971 when East Pakistan was renamed as 'Bangladesh'—resurgence of migration and refugees became the bone of contention. Indian forces played crucial role to free the East Bengal Region. Subsequent political developments resulted in the influx of undocumented refugees from Bangladesh to India of diverse categories, especially *Chakmas* (Buddhists), Bengalis (Muslims), Christians and large number of unidentified Hindus. In July 1972, Shimla Peace Agreement was signed to respect the doctrine of *Panchsheel* (non-aggression, peaceful coexistence, territorial sovereignty, integrity and international peace). It was the legacy of Nehru, India's first Prime Minister and the architect of Non-Aligned Conference that was held at Bandung, Indonesia (1956). It was a comprehensive blueprint for good neighbourly relations between India and Pakistan. Under the Simla Agreement both countries undertook to abjure conflict and confrontation towards the establishment of durable peace, friendship and cooperation.

During March 1983, Establishment of Joint Commission to promote tourism, industry, education, health, IT sector and scientific developments, was the first successful sign of peace effort. Joint Diplomatic initiative of Indian Prime Minister Indira Gandhi and Pak President General Zia-ul-Haq during 1983 added several prominent areas. General Zia's 'Cricket Diplomacy' has often been exemplified as a mark of gesture and love towards India. In December 1983, Indo-Pak Nuclear Deal under the banner of SAARC worked as the mark of regional security. Several initiatives like Peace Negotiation on the issue of *Siachin* Glacier (March 1986), Establishment of Confidence Building Measure (CBM: March 1986) and

Agreement for the respect of each other's nuclear facility (January 1991) were the successful peace attempts. During November 1992, Second Level of Diplomatic Initiative on *Siachin* Glacier during Narsimha Rao (Indian Prime Minister) and Ghulam Ishaq Khan (President of Pakistan) as an independent affiliation, was successful diplomatic mission to India. However, there were major changes in Indo-Pak Relations during Deve Gowda Ministry in March 1997 when both rival partners agreed to normalize Economic Relations with Pak President Farooq Leghari. During Atal Bihari Vajpayee Ministry, Comprehensive Review of Bilateral Relations was signed in March 1999 but the issues of terrorism in J&K became serious business. As a result, extension of ceasefire in J&K in May 2001, Vajpayee Ministry was forced to formulate a fresh peaceful dialogue in January 2002 during the initial phase of Pak President Pervez Musharraf. In May 2003, 'No War Pact Agreement' was signed between Zafarullah Jamil and Vajpayee, the Prime Ministers of Pakistan and India respectively.

Dr. Manmohan Singh, India's diplomat, economist and then Prime Minister signed Secretary Level Promotion of Exchange with Pak Premier Shauket Aziz in August 2004. After a gap of ten years, Delhi-Lahore Peace Bus Journey was restarted in February 2005, a pact signed between Manmohan Singh and Pak Prime Minister Shauket Aziz. In September 2008, Pak Prime Minister Yousaf Raza Gillani and Manmohan Singh agreed to establish 'Anti-Terror Group' to normalize cross-border terrorism in J&K. In April 2012, both India and Pak supported Second Proposal for MFN (Most Favoured Nation) Clause through bilateral dialogue. But the issue of Indo-US Non-Nuclear Civilian Peace Pact with George Bush (Jr.) remained detrimental; leaving many doubts of uncertainties for Pak. Advent of Modi Phase in India in May 2014 brought dramatic changes in Indo-Pak Relations. During December 2015: Modi's surprise visit to Pakistan marked as gesture of cultural exchange during Prime Ministership of Nawaz Sharif.

Since Prime Minister Narendra Modi came into power in May 2014, controversies moved around about the use of public exchequer spend during foreign visits. Modi's visit to Pakistan has four implications: Pak and Terrorism, nuclear blackmail, issue of self-determination in J&K, and historical ties with Pakistan. Both countries continue to make allegations against each other on the issue of terrorism. On 25 February, 2017, *Al Jazeera,* an Arab Channel described India and Pakistan as the for ever rivals on Kashmir problem as described by Shashi Tharoor, an independent writer and ex-India's Minister for External Affairs. On 14 February, 2019, a convoy of vehicles carrying security personnel on the Jammu Srinagar National Highway was targeted by a vehicle-borne suicide bomber at Lethpora in the Pulwama district in J&K. The attack resulted in the deaths of 40 Central Reserve Police Force personnel. During the month of July 2020, Chinese intrusion in Ladakh by violating Line of Actual Control (LAC) near the Galwan Valley and Pak's virtual silence exalted fresh tension between the three countries. In political dilemma, it is rather difficult to arrive at a particular consensus as who is the real culprit or innocent: India, Pakistan or China.

Pakistan's Nuclear Duplicity: Options before India

Since the beginning of Atomic Age (Hiroshima-Nagasaki Disasters on 6 August, 1945), the mankind has faced horrifying threat and challenges. Role of international organisations, disarmament conferences, regional associations and NGOs have been partially successful in fulfilling the accomplishment of world's nuclear programme as full of horrors.[2] Pak's dream to be a symbolic super power and the major rival of India has acquired the Weapons of Mass Destruction (WMD) through active collaboration of China and North Korea, and thereby promote militant nationalism. Gradual strategic considerations co-opted with Islamic sentiments to design Jihaad (Holy War), Pak also decided to align with power blocs (USA and Saudi Arabia) by ignoring the principles of non-alignment, *Panchasheel,* International Atomic Energy Agency and partly South Asia Association of Regional Cooperation (SAARC). It certainly proved disadvantaged for India believing in the principle of 'No First Use' or 'Never Use' War Doctrine. It is widely understood that the entire 'Nuclear Episode' worked under supervision of Dr. Abdul Qadir in collaboration with Pakistan Atomic Energy Commission (PAEC). Pak opposed the signing of Non-Proliferation Treaty (NPT) and explored the new possibilities of Islamic Bomb, and thereby distanced from India. In fact, it was the strategy of Pak's Development Model agenda and technology power, never liked by India about Pak's model of peace that reached to height during 9/11 Episode. Modi Government remains the most sensitive on issue of terrorism ever since June 2014 highlighted during his hundreds of foreign visits. In fact, American Policy of favouring democracy, high reputation of Indian knowledge workers in USA, acknowledging India as a rising power and advanced nuclear technology have provided strong outlcok. Only meaningful dialogues can promote mutual understanding with aid of Peoples' Forum for Peace and

Democracy, Peoples of Asia Forum, India Pakistan Friendship Society, Travelling Seminar, NAM Media & SAARC Committee, and all are increasingly important.

Terrorism in J&K: Issue of Self-Determination and Statehood

Although the problem of J&K began in 1972 after the failure of Simla Peace Agreement between India and Pakistan, another serious demand of Khalistan, a separatist movement in Punjab in 1984 following the death of Sikh Militant Jarnail Singh Bhindranwale who propagated hateful speech. It is the core issue around which J&K and Pak Diplomacy revolves. It has been a suspicious and complicated issue for complete independence (*Azadi*). It was raised through the leaders of secessionist and separatists' groups like All India Hurriyat Conference, and J&K Liberation Front that openly blamed the Government of India for ignoring "Self-Determination" which proved a misnomer or failure. The issue was raised internationally time and again through the UN General Assembly Resolution, Security Council and International Covenant on Civil and Political Rights. The matter was seriously taken by the United Nations to tackle the problem between India and Pakistan. UN Security Council was compelled to intervene in the matter on 1st January, 1948 and considered Kashmir as the disputed region. After due deliberation, the UNSC passed a resolution and appointed the United Nations Commission on India and Pakistan (UNCIP). It started working in June 1948 and gave proposals on 11th December, 1948 which came into force on 1st January, 1949. However, Pakistan neither withdrew troops from Kashmir nor respected the norms of UNCIP. Hence, the wishes of the people of J&K to determine their self-autonomy remained in whirlpool. The UNCIP's recommendation, Mc Naughton Plan (1950), Dixon Proposal (1954), Graham Mission (1955) and Jerring Mission (1957) were recognized under the auspices of High Officials only but all proved fruitless.[3] The Simla Agreement (June 1972) proved highly volatile under which Pakistan agreed to withdraw troops from all its strategic positions. But the issues of PoK, so-called *Azad Kashmir,* that was forcefully captured by Pakistan in 1948, still remains unsettled. Now PoK has its own constitutional law since 1974, with Prime Minister and President appointed by Federal Government at Islamabad. It broadly includes the terrorist prone Zone called as Giligit, Baltistan, Hunze and Chitzal probably among the most interior regions beyond the reach of a common man.

J&K is a direct victim of sponsored cross-boarder terrorism. Probably

Pak's dream to annex J&K that occurred in 1965 (Indo-Pak War), 1971 (creation of Bangladesh) and 1999 (Kargil War) remain far from satisfaction. In 1970, General Zia and Pak's ISI, concocted the strategy of Pak sponsored terrorism known as 'Operation Topak' where financial assistance were required for training, weapons and other assistance that significantly helped the terrorist. It gave the birth of hundred of terrorist organizations like Hizbul Mujahid, Harkatul Ansar, Lashkar-e-Toiba, JKLF, Al Burq, Hizabullah, Jamaat-Ul-Mujahiddin, Al-Jihad, Kashmir Liberation Front, Al-Fatah, Jamat-e-Islami, Islamic Students League and other small non-identified organizations are active in J&K Valley. Most of these groups are equipped with ultra-modern communication and possess deadly weapons like AK 47, AK 56 Riffles. For varied reasons, Pak officials identified them as 'Freedom Fighters' rather than falsely claimed terrorists. India's initiative through diplomatic and another bilateral means to convince the Rulers of Pak hardly fulfilled the UN mandate. Pak President, General Parwez Musharraf often maintained double standard on J&K issue while UN officials are committed to enforce the right of self-determination through bilateral dialogues between the two countries. Unfortunately, India's diplomatic initiatives do not suit to the interest of Islamabad officials who threaten to use nuclear weapons against India. India is not willing to repeat the experience of Kargil War that brought immeasurable casualties both moral as well as material. At several pretexts, India also started Sadbhavana Yatra (Goodwill Bus Journey) between New Delhi and Lahore at periodical intervals, but every time it failed to earn any benefit for either party. Politically motivated abruption of Articles, 370 and 35A, by Modi Government, the issue of 'Self-Determination' remains detrimental. Since August 6, 2019, the clauses of 370 ceased to operate when J&K was declared as a union territory by Government of India under direct control of President where local Assembly will have no claims. Even large number of prominent leaders like Farooq Abdulla, Omar Abdullah, Mehbooba Mufti and Sajjad Gani Lone were kept under house arrest including several activists, free thinkers, intellectuals, academicians and local politicians. But how far such subversive policy of India is going to help the situation in Kashmir, remains to be answered in the context of accountability, transparency and judicial system.[4]

Indo-Pak Relations: A Critique

It is right and high time to look into the matters seriously by India's neighbours. Indo-Pak bilateral talks on the matter of terrorism by no means are well-known principles. They make news even when they mark a mere resumption of dialogue without durable results. Why not both India and Pak take affirmative decision to uproot terrorism from the soil of South Asia let UN work as a mediator. Some sensible critiques have suggested 'Indo-Pak Kashmir Peace Model' for prosperity and happiness in South Asia. India has to adopt a common consensus on the issue of terrorism without giving due attention to a particular cause. A greater transparency of defence build-up is an important parameter of Indo-Pak Relations. Peaceful approaches like welfare of the peoples of South Asia, Economic growth, social progress, cultural development to realize their full potential, encouragement with international and regional organizations with similar aims and purposes are increasingly important.

Indo-Sri Lanka Relations

Indo-Sri Lanka relations are built upon a legacy of intellectual, cultural, religious, linguistic and geographical foundations. However, these links have been deeply affected by the question of legitimate rights, welfare of Tamil minority and fishing boundary dispute. Despite odds and challenges, India cannot distance from Sri Lanka due to disturbing strategic connotations for its national security and commitment to maintain peace over mainland Sri Lanka facing ethnic conflict since 1985. Three factors: geo-political differences, ethnic issues and fisherman crisis need to be understood in context of Indo-Sri Lanka Relations.

Geo-Cultural Issues

Sri Lanka (formerly Ceylon) officially Democratic Socialist Republic of Sri Lanka, an island in the Indian Ocean with area of 65,600 sq. kilometre, is situated at the Southeastern Coast of India. It is a multiethnic society with 75 per cent local Sinhalese followed by 15 per cent Tamils and mixed minorities. Ethnic Sri Lankans practice Buddhism, Hinduism, Islam and Christianity. Predominantly an agriculture-based economy, Sri Lanka is undergoing ethnic conflict between Tamils and Sinhalese since 1980s.[5]

For last several decades, Sri Lanka has maintained cordial relations with India. During recent years, Sri Lanka's membership with Non-Aligned Movement and close association with South Asia Association of Regional Cooperation (SAARC) are the key factors to understand the relations between two countries. Sri Lanka continues to face serious challenges due to cross-ethnic identity, interstate rivalry between TULF

(Tamil United Liberation Front) and territorial settlement of local Sinhala since 1949 on the issue of statehood and thereby there have been ups and down in Indo-Sri Lanka relations ever since. Formation of Liberation Tigers of Tamil Elam (LTTE) in May 1976, a right wing of TULF, a militant group based on formed under the leadership of Velupillai Prabhakaran to create an independent state of Tamil Elam in the north and east of Sri Lanka for Tamil people, remain serious concern now and then.[6]

Paradoxically, India could not normalize relations due to ethnic and political hurdles. Since July 1983, problem became worse when group of Sinhalese with Tamils led serious confrontation despite measures taken by security personnel to prevent the escalation. India's diplomatic initiative by Indira Gandhi Ministry in July 1983 to bring LTTE and Sinhalese on one platform was a constructive step forward. During 1985-1986, both India and Sri Lanka experienced the threatening of LTTE when Sri Lanka suffered serious casualties manifested in form of explosion of several public and private buildings, banks and commercial establishments. It led to serious refugee crisis when large number of Tamils migrated to India following 'chase policy' of Sri Lanka. Despite peace measures, nothing came in concrete. Situation became alarming in May 1987 following genocide attack on ethnic Tamils. Diplomatic initiative of India was the sign of relief when the Government of Sri Lanka showed the spirit of peaceful accommodation. It finally resulted into historical Indo-Sri Lanka Peace Accord on 29 July, 1987 between Rajiv Gandhi and Jayewardene.

Indo-Sri Lanka Peace Accord: Major Contents

After serious of diplomatic initiatives between India and Sri Lanka, the accord became reality where both partners agreed for merger of Tamil majority into a single province besides. Consensus on common referendum where northern and southern provinces of Sri Lanka have to maintain a single Provincial Council to maintain 'violence free zone' is also an important step. Both parties also agreed for elections in the Provincial Council has to be maintained under strict and transparent rule to optimize the maximum accountability. Besides, the important considerations like merger of eastern province with common identity, end of all hostilities, establishment of Independent Charge for General Amnesty, and peacekeeping contingency were given due focus. Other important issues like integrity of ethnic identity, respect for Indian coast guards, navy, common use of Trincomalee Island under military supervision and assurance for intelligence personnel to maintain the harmony of Peace Accord were also considered.

In fact, Peace Accord proved instrumental to relieve the tension and to maintain the harmony at Jaffna, Colombo and Trincomalee Islands. Amidst controversies, India agreed to send some 30,000-defence personnel wing of Indian Peace Keeping Force (IPKF) to respect the accord through relief operations in providing food, shelter, clothing, medicines, and other essential commodities. Peace Accord, however, remained partially fulfilled when the situation became worse in July 1989. Sri Lankan President Prema Dasa showed displeasure over the one-sided role of Indian Peace Keeping Force (IPKF) for not providing full justice to local Sinhalese in defined territories. India opted not to ceasefire despite difference which was evidently seen in Islamabad SAARC Summit in July 1989. Establishment of India-Sri Lanka Peace Committee representing both countries during the National Front Government in early January 1991 to solve vexed ethnic problem worked as wonders.

In November 1991, Sri Lanka agreed to establish Joint Trade Committee bilaterally signed at Colombo during 6th SAARC Summit (21-22 November, 1991). Both countries witnessed some improvement in July 1992 when some 23,000 refugees were peacefully repatriated to India. By the end of 1992, both countries entered into several economic and cultural agreements that virtually characterized the end of previous hostilities. Successive SAARC Summits at Colombo (29-31 July 1998, 1–3 August, 2008), 28–29 April, 2010 (Thimpu-Bhutan), 10–11 November, 2011 Addu City (Maldives), and 9–10 November, 2016 (Islamabad) brought more normalcy between two rival partners. But the fundamental issue of ethnic problems continues ever since.

India-Sri Lanka Fishermen Crisis

Sri Lanka, the land of God, has been blessed by rich resources of fishing. However, due to geo-strategic location, Sri Lanka continues to remain under tight security with high risk factor. These issues are related to disagreement over the territorial rights to the island of Kachchatheevu, frequent poaching by Indian fisherman near Palk Bay in Sri Lankan waters, damaging economic and environmental effects of trawling. There is a greater need to find out permanent solution of problem.

The key issue has been related to Palk Bay with 137 kilometres length and roughly 100 kilometres in width, divided by the International Maritime Boundary Line (IMBL) touching both India and Sri Lanka. However, over

1,00,000 fishermen from Sri Lanka and over 50,000 from India continue to create geographical claims about the fishing sites that decide the social and economic conditions of Indian and Sri Lankan fishermen. But it has wider repercussion over culture, ethnic and refugee issues between Sinhalese (Sri Lankan Tribes) and Tamils that led to serious ethnic conflict in 1983. By some official estimates of Sri Lanka Government, the fishing contributes roughly 30 per cent of export revenue. To avoid complications, India and Sri Lanka agreed to establish Joint Working Group on fisheries to resolve the likely disputes related to detention, illegal arrest, unnecessary harassment and ethnic disputes from both sides: India and Sri Lanka coast guards. Timely assurance was also given that neither side suffer any casualty of life, livelihood, and property.

The real issue is how long trawlers from Tamil Nadu will continue to fish in Sri Lankan territorial waters, and how soon bottom trawling is ended. The official statement after the talks between the foreign ministers refers to "expediting the transition towards ending the practice of bottom trawling at the earliest". An agreement on this is crucial, but in absence of a time-frame, there remains a question mark about the solution of problems. Even Sri Lankan Tamil fishermen are firm on an immediate end to all incursions and are against seized Indian boats being released without legal process, though they agree that the arrested fishermen should be released. For now, Tamil Nadu should show greater understanding of the plight of the Sri Lankan Tamil fishermen, who are economically weaker and yet to fully recover from a devastating war, and agree to a more reasonable phase-out period. Sri Lanka, then, can look at a licensing system under which fishermen from both sides can fish on specified days using sustainable methods and permissible equipment. It is important that all sides recognize that there is a humanitarian dimension. During Modi's visit to Colombo in March 2015 and May 2017, issues like strong political ties, sovereignty of Kachchatheevu island, prospects, poaching and trawling, proposed solutions and seizing opportunity were discussed between Sri Lankan President Maithripala Sirisena with Indian Prime Minister Narendra Modi. Other import issues like development cooperation, commercial ties, shared tourism and economic security, were also discussed. Identification of proper institutional mechanism and collaboration require the effective adoption and sustainability. There is urgent call to arrange for regional guidelines, monitoring of multinational collaboration and technology transfer activities between India and Sri Lanka is increasingly being felt.

Indo-Bangladesh Relations

Geo-historically, Bangladesh (Formerly East Pakistan) has been a part of India during English Rule. In 1971, India has been an active supporter when Mukti Bahini from East Bengal played a significant role against Pakistan in liberation of Bangladesh. It was duly acknowledged by Dhaka Officials when both countries signed Treaty of Friendship, Cooperation and Peace for 25 years (1972-1997), based on 'Soviet Model' where economic and social strengths were considered as pillars of developments. Relations with Bangladesh has been marked as uneven with respect to disagreements of border disputes over Farakka Barrage, Moore island and plight of undocumented migrants. Let us have brief overview of these issues.

Farakka Barrage Issue

It is widely believed that Farakka Barrage is the legacy directly linked with Indo-Pak ties since 1971 during the earliest phase of relations. During the year 1975, geo-political issue was essentially settled by Indira Gandhi Ministry. Unfortunately, Bangladesh media propagated against India while highlighting the Farakka Barrage issue in the UNO. While on India's stand, the issue was taken as positive resulting in bilateral agreement in November 1977. By the virtue of agreement, a Joint River Commission (JRC) was set up to deal long pending issue but JRC failed to arrive at a particular consensus. During 1982, Indira Gandhi with Bangladesh President H.M. Ershad held mutual dialogues under Indo-Bangladesh JRC. It was entrusted with the responsibility of carrying out feasibility study and deciding upon the optimum solution. Thereafter, series of diplomatic initiatives followed through NAM to normalized Farakka Barrage issue. Finally, in November 1985, both countries reached an accord of sharing Ganga Water for a definite period under MoU. In January 1986, India and Bangladesh agreed to study the proposal for an amicable settlement under the Plan of Action for sharing Farakka Barrage Water with other common rivers. Ever since, Ganges Water Treaty determines the water-sharing arrangements between India and Bangladesh.

However, its ability to suitably divide riparian water rights and foster cooperation has limited appeal. India's construction of the Farakka Barrage has soured the bilateral relationship between the two countries. India and Bangladesh face continued pressure to meet rising water demands. There is little effective water agreement to sustain a cooperative bilateral relationship while meeting these demands. Giving the conflicting scenario ever since 2012 over Ganges Water Treaty, there is a serious concern about the plan of action. Both South Asian Partners (India and Bangladesh) are facing serious challenges due to scarcity of food, water and natural disasters. Hence, a greater need is felt to enhance partnership for prospective future. Land Boundary Agreement between India and Bangladesh signed in 2015, represents a significant hope for an agreement to be reached over the Teesta waters where some 21 million are dependent on project. A possible solution both for India and Bangladesh is to redesign the Farakka Barrage by allowing uninterrupted flow so that sediments also are equally divided and fish can migrate. Till the end of 2019, the issue remained unsettled due to political and economic differences.

Issues of Moore Island

Historically, the issue of Moore Island goes to 1971 during the liberation of Bangladesh. However, since 1980s, the question of Moore Island in the Bay of Bengal on the issue of sovereignty remain more controversial. The establishment of Moore Island Joint Commission did not fulfil the mission rather it aggravated the issue in May 1981 that even threatened Indian ship Sandhya deployed for joint survey. Since 2000, New Moore Island is proving like ecological disaster as major areas are getting submerged into water as shown by several satellite images, heading towards global warming.[7]

Bangladesh, a low-lying delta nation of 160 million inhabitants have worst affected experience of global warming. Officials estimate some 19 per cent of Bangladesh's coastal area will be underwater and 20 million people will be displaced if sea levels rise just one metre by 2050 as predicted by some environmentalists. The process of migration began long ago which continues even today. Both India and Bangladesh claimed the empty New Moore Island, which is about two miles long and one and half miles wide. The demarcation of the maritime boundary—and who controls the remaining islands—remains an open issue between the two South Asian neighbours, and the disappearance of the island does nothing to resolve the issue as stated by Indian officials. Till the end of 2019, the issue still remains pending despite several visits of PM Modi and Minister of External Affairs, Shushma Swaraj. Let us hope that the issue will be finally settled by end of 2020.

Refugee Problems

Bangladesh continues to face domestic, regional as well as international problems due to socio-economic instability and political upheavals. Creation of Pak in 1947 and thereafter Bangladesh in 1971 became serious concern for India. The subsequent political developments resulted in the influx of undocumented refugees from Bangladesh to India of diverse categories, especially Chakmas (Buddhists), Bengalis (Muslims), Christians and large number of unidentified Hindus. The United Nations High Commission for Refugees (UNHCR) Conventions (1951) and Protocols (1967) proved temporary relief while NGOs and Human Right Agencies working for the settlements and rehabilitations, were found miserably unsuccessful due to authoritarian policies and unplanned economic developments. Initiatives by both countries to promote bilateral dialogue, large number of academic and intellectual bodies, regional organizations and cultural forums became the imperatives to Human Rights agencies. But the worsening situation between New Delhi and Dhaka Officials left refugees nowhere but to become asylum seekers with no definite goal. Number of political organizations in India blamed the refugees being intruders, terrorists and fundamentalists without giving any solid evidence. The situation is explosive and therefore, there is an urgent need to promote healthy democratic tradition to resettle the problems. India, being the largest democracy and member of various forums should opt flexible approach with no hidden agendas to analyze the refugee's problems in India. By some conservative estimate there are some ten million Bangladeshi refugees living in different parts of India since 1971. Development since 2019 add more serious problem as some 40,000 Rohingya Muslims in India who migrated from Myanmar, *via* Bangladesh, remains a serious concern. Ideal of India is based on the Principle of "*Atithi Devo Bhava*". India has been providing economic assistance to Rohingya Muslims fled from Myanmar's Rakhine Province to Bangladesh (Cox Bazar) by their perilous journey on the humanitarian ground. Let there be partnership between India-Bangladesh-Myanmar to promote humanitarian objectives.

India-Bangladesh Relationship: An Appraisal

Unlike Pakistan and Sri Lanka, India's relations with Bangladesh has been much better despite geo-political differences. On the optimistic side, interpersonal relations and civil society contact groups between the two countries have increased. Both nations need to undergo a change in mindset. At the pessimistic scale, Bangladesh has been struggling to ensure the sustenance and preservation of human security within its borders. India's contribution towards Bangladesh's War of Liberation in 1971 was critical to the latter's birth. There are few fundamental issues between India and Bangladesh, such as land and maritime boundary demarcations, the sharing of waters from 54 common rivers, informal trade, transnational crime, and interference in internal affairs that have adversely affected their relationship.

Findings

India's triangular partnership has to find a suitable place in the international community. Being the immediate neighbours, each nation is unlikely to accept the inferior position *vis-à-vis* the others. Pak's tilt towards China and USA neither affects Bangladeshis nor Sri Lankans, whereas India remains too sensitive in either way. Some critiques have suggested that India should give more focus on economic prosperity by sensibly adopting 'Sustainable Economic Model' to provide stronger and effective security rather than promoting saffron agenda. Clearly, all priorities need peaceful environment where faster democratic growth can be achieved by accepting all communities irrespective of religious and social differences. Given the present influx of global scenario, all four partners: India, Pakistan, Bangladesh and Sri Lanka need to evolve an effective and creative inter-regional dialogue in a simple room of exchange without involving outside elements.

There is a greater need to develop multilateral ties between rival partners without involving any power bargainers for prospective future. Peace, understanding and territorial integrity should match together between India's triangular partners. Several analysts have suggested that India's relationship between these partners is yet to come out from the legacy of communal antagonism, censorship of Indian media, suspicion and common social insecurity. Whereas the mindset of Pak has still not changed and the game of snakes and ladders continues whereas the intervention of third partner make situation more complicated. Dilemmas and differences need to be constructed and created through meaningful dialogue only. For a durable peace and stability of the Subcontinent, there is a need that the leadership of realistically visualizes the future of the region and accepts the ground realities through an optimistic mindset. This process would provide opportunities for enhancing economic development and social integration in the subcontinent spirit for *Aman ki Asha* (hope for peace), shaking hands with same flag, inter-exchange of national flags, spirit of true freedom rebuilding peace, democracy and freedom of press.

Presently, there are several drives or actors from the state, market and civil society that act as a pushing force in the ongoing process of regionalism among these Asian Tigers. Strategic factors like balanced economic development, level of interdependence, and the nature of trade relations are increasingly significant. If peace agendas are judiciously followed, the agreement is likely to bring about economic stability in the member nations. Three powerful neighbours: Pakistan, Bangladesh and Sri Lanka may also facilitate healthy trade as well as investment relationship with India thereby bringing about many structural reforms in the economy of the seven countries. The best option 'South Asia Economic Global Model' with concerted and coordinated efforts can work as wonders, well known by India's decades old partners.

ENDNOTES

1. Nayar, Kuldeep (1995), *Distant Neighbours: A Tale of the Subcontinent*, New Delhi: Vikas Publishing House, pp. 136-37.
2. Narayan, M.K. (2004), "Politics of Proliferation", *World Focus*, Vol. 25, No. 2, February, p. 21.
3. "Self Determination, Terrorism and Kashmir", *JNU News* (New Delhi), Vol. 18, No. 2, March-April 2002, pp. 9-12.
4. Bhat, Sunil, "J&K Administration ends house arrest of Political Leaders in Jammu", *India Today*, 2 October, 2019.
5. 'Sri Lanka' in *Britannica Ready Reference Encyclopaedia* (2006), New Delhi: Encyclopaedia Britannica India Pvt Ltd. Vol. 9, pp. 127-28.
6. Ministry of External Affairs, Government of India, "Visit of External Affairs Minister to Sri Lanka, February 5-6, 2016", press release, February 6, 2016, http://www.mea.gov.in/press-releases.htm?dtl/26330/Visit_ of_External_ Affairs_Minister_to Sri Lank_Febraury_56_2016
7. 'Sri Lanka' in *Britannica Ready Reference Encyclopaedia* (2006), New Delhi: Encyclopaedia Britannica India Pvt. Ltd., Vol. 9, pp. 127-28.

REFERENCES

'Sri Lanka' in *Britannica Ready Reference Encyclopaedia* (2006), New Delhi: Encyclopaedia Britannica India Pvt. Ltd, Vol. 9, pp. 127-28.

"Self Determination, Terrorism and Kashmir", *JNU News* (New Delhi), Vol. 18, No. 2, March-April 2002, pp. 9-12.

"Sri Lanka—Living with Terror", *Frontline*. PBS. May 2002. Retrieved 9 February, 2009.

Bhat, Sunil, "J&K Administration ends house arrest of Political Leaders in Jammu", *India Today*, 2 October, 2019.

Kaur, Kulwant (ed.), *Global Terrorism: Issues Dimensions and Options,* New Delhi: Kanishka Publishers, Distributors, 2005, p. 200.

UN DOC S/726, 21st April, 1948.

V. Suryanarayan and V. Sudarsen, *Between Fear and Hope: Sri Lankan Refugees in Tamil Nadu,* Chennai: T.R. Publications, 2000, p. 43.

15

Indo-Pak Relations and Peace in South Asia

Challenges in Modi Era

Sudhir Singh

Modi government has completed five years of its first term in May 2019. Leaving many political pundits guessing returned in power with larger majority. It is the maiden government after 1984 at the Centre which returned in power with larger majority. In these years Prime Minister Modi has initiated many comprehensive innovations in India's foreign policy. His government has adopted a proactive foreign policy. Modi government has also adopted neighbourhood first policy.

Cooperation and conflict have been the hallmark of the day with China. In the backdrop of Pulwama and Balakot, President Xi came to Chennai for 2nd consecutive summit level talks with PM Modi in October 2019. India and the United States relations have radically changed during last five years. In the republic day celebrations of January 2018, all 10 head of states of ASEAN visited New Delhi. Indo-Japan relations have also improved. Modi has initiated 'Act East' to deal proactively with Southeast and East Asian region. It has also initiated 'Look West' and Modi has visited almost all-important capitals of the Middle East. He has also visited Israel and became maiden Indian PM to do so.

The fact is that China has emerged as powerful country in Asia and trying to emerge as a global power. Modi has assessed that containing China is a must now. Therefore, he is determined to build coalition that will strengthen his bargaining capacity. According to Kanti Vajpayee, eminent Indian foreign policy analyst, "Especially in East Asia where New Delhi has moved unprecedently close to the United States and to Vietnam, Japan and Australia, this coalition strategy is moving India away from its traditional aversion to alliance like relationship."[1] This coalition in reference to Pakistan and China is required. Raja Mohan, another noted expert of Indian foreign policy writes way back in 2003, "Thus on Pakistan, India must have a mix of military and diplomatic options... for a full exploitation of Pakistan's contradictions with its neighbours and the international system and stepping up of Pressures against Pakistan." New Delhi should collaborate with America on transforming the internal dynamics of Pakistan's society.[2] On China, India's warming ties with the United States have forced Beijing to reconsider its own relations with New Delhi." After the Cold War, India had a higher profile in South East Asia, where many nations see New Delhi as maintaining the balance of power in the region. Closer relations with Japan and Vietnam are signs of "new trend of Indian assertiveness; yet India should not directly confront China and become a front-line state in a potential American containment of Beijing."[3]

This kind of coalition building paid during the Doklam crisis in 2017 and the PLA was forced to withdraw partially due to global isolation of China because of meticulous diplomacy of Modi govt. The United States and India came closer since the end of the Cold War. But they have become very close in the aftermath of 9/11 terror attack. Many American strategic leaders have pointed out their finger at Pakistan against nurture and protection of Haqqani network. Haqqani network has killed largest number of U.S. led NATO forces in Afghanistan. The arrival of President Trump has further complicated the problem for Pakistan. President Trump administration has candidly stated that Pakistan is a part of the problem in Afghanistan and could not become part of the solution. In April 2018, maiden time in the history of Pakistan-U.S relations, the U.S. censored Pakistani diplomats to not cross 40 km of area of their office. The prevailing circumstances between Pakistan and the United States have been extraordinarily turbulent and vindicating U.S. tilt towards India. The United States vowed to work with India in preference to China over the next century to promote a "free and open" Indo-Pacific region led by prosperous democracies in October 2017. Former Secretary of State Rex Tillerson delivered his unexpectedly sharp message to Beijing on the same day President Xi Jinping opened the Communist Party congress.

His upbeat speech was designed to set the stage for a visit next week to China's main Asian rival India, and to lay out a vision for a 100-year "strategic partnership" between Washington and New Delhi.[4] One has to note that since independence till recently Pakistan and United States have been close friends. The US' tilt towards India compelled China to a certain extent to give full support to Pakistan. Although it has to be observed that how far China is supporting Pakistan but one thing is clear that Chinese could not support Pakistan at par with the United States.

According to a new research of an Australian think tank report, China is aggressively acquiring devastating military capacity to dominate Asia and larger region within Indo-Pacific. The 104-page report by the United States Studies Centre at the University of Sydney assessed US military strategy, spending and alliances in the region.

Lead author Ashley Townshend told 'This Week in Asia' that the region's changing balance of power should be of concern to all Asian states—including those seeking to maintain good relations with both superpowers—as it was in their interests to deter Beijing from wielding an 'aggressive foreign policy'.[5]

Since 2007 India-United States and Japan have started 'Malabar Naval Exercise' and it is by and large sustainable even today in 2019. Today India has 2+2 dialogue status with Japan and the United States. Maiden time, India and Japan held 2+2 meeting on 30 November, 2019.[6] Enhancing maritime cooperation in the Indo-Pacific region was top agenda of this meeting. It is significant strategically in the backdrop of prevailing trust deficit in South China Sea and East China Seas between ASEAN disputant countries and China and Japan and China respectably. Japanese PM Shinzo Abe and PM Modi met in December 2019 in Guwahati and Imphal and inked many deals.

Arrival of Modi for the second term is all set to accelerate proactive foreign policy. But despite all radical changes in security architecture of Asia, where it has responded with new vigor, it has also sustained some of the fundamental continuity of India's foreign policy. Modi has himself expressed on number of occasions that India will sustain its struggle for the establishment of justice based international order. He has also stressed that to achieve this 'South-South' cooperation will be must. He has raised the issue of democratization in United Nations structure and other global table of governance.

With the end of 1st term of the Modi regime, it will be quite interesting to analyze its relations with Pakistan and peace in South Asia. India-Pakistan relations is the key to peace and tranquility in South Asia. We are aware about the fact that since independence, India-Pakistan relations have been in turbulence. Modi however started his regime with an olive branch to Pakistan. Modi invited his Pakistani counterpart Nawaz Sharif in his swearing in ceremony in May 2014 along with other South Asian counterparts. It was an unexpected move from Modi, who has been considered hardliner. Modi gave signal to Pakistan that he was intended to take out of box steps to resolve thorny Indo-Pak relations. Both Prime Ministers met many times elsewhere and in December 2015 Modi had surprised all concerned when he landed at Lahore to wish happy birthday to his Pakistani counterpart.

Within days Modi's gesture was reciprocated through Pathankot attack. In September 2016, 19 Indian soldiers were killed in terror attack. In response, first time after 1971, Indian army retaliated across the border and surgical strike was instrumental to eliminate many terrorists launching pads and terrorists. This is unprecedented move by Modi government. During his April 2018 London trip Modi has elaborated it and legitimized surgical strikes and stated that positive regime change has taken place in New Delhi and Pakistan will be responded in its own language and mechanism. Modi government has also been successful to convince the whole world that terror factory is being run from Pakistan and it is the epicentre of global terrorism.

China-Pakistan relations have strengthened with the expanding Indian global stature. It has also blocked one of the tributaries of the river Brahamputra, which is bound to impact negatively in lower riparian countries India and Bangladesh. India and Pakistan constitute roughly over 90 per cent of important assets in South Asia. But the open secret is India and Pakistan have fought three and half war since independence and still trust deficit prevails in unprecedented manner. The Army dominates the levers of power in Pakistan and even during democratic regimes; it rules the roost. The Army doesn't want to lose its dominance therefore they have sustained India as hypothetical enemy.

The post-Pokhran (1998) situation has enhanced Indian status at the global level. Boosted with sustainable economic development India has achieved good progress at the strategic level as well. The end of the cold war and post-9/11 situation has further brought Asia as a dominating continent at the global table of governance.

In the backdrop of Balakot attack (February 2019) how India could reformulate its Pakistan policy? There are many divergences and fewer convergences between both traditional rivals of South Asia. How diplomacy could be used to reduce divergences and increase convergences? This focal point will be widely debated within the ambit of this chapter. Afghan situation is interconnected with prevailing Indo-Pak tensions. Afghan government was one of the earliest governments to criticize Pulwama terror attack and appreciated Indian surgical strike on Balakot, which is in Khyber Pakhtunwah province.

The Afghan theater has become violent and within January-July 2015 around 5,000 people have already lost their lives due to terror resurgence. Combined right from 2009 till July 2015, 16,874 people have been killed in terror related violence.[7] Right from January 2015 to July 2015 alone 4,921 people have been killed which is self explanatory. This bloodshed is sustained even today. It is an open secret that Pakistan provides safe havens to terror groups operating in Afghanistan. Under President Trump regime therefore United States has imposed number of sanctions against Pakistan. Since last few years violence has accelerated in Afghanistan. According to the UN, at least 32,000 civilians have been killed and another 60,000 wounded in the last decade, when the organisation began compiling the data. Civilian deaths jumped by 11 per cent from 2017 with 3,804 people killed, including 927 children, and another 7,189 people wounded. It states the actual situation.[8] United States has started dialogue with the Taliban since October 2018 to resolve Afghan tango and willingness to withdraw NATO army (including US one) before the US presidential election scheduled in November 2020. During his July 2019 Washington visit, Imran Khan assured that Pakistan will support in this exercise and the best evidence is that PM went to White House to meet US president along with its army chief, perhaps maiden time in the history of Pakistan-United States relationship. Peace and stability will prevail in Afghanistan even after deal between Taliban and the United States, it is a matter of future. But old trends suggest the point that Pakistan remains part of Afghan tango and could not become part of its solution. President Donald Trump has however cancelled the Afghan peace dialogues just before Afghan presidential elections and that has again left uncertainty on this front. NATO led forces have been containing the menace of terror since October 2001 when 'Operation Enduring Freedom' was launched. The US military have lost 2400 soldiers and allied more than 400, so combinedly NATO has lost above 2800 soldiers while combating against the Taliban and other terror networks.

In May 2019, Modi led BJP returned into power even with larger majority. Over the last five years, Modi met Pakistani leaders many times and expressed the desire to sustain dialogue. But non-state actor's interventions prevented the pace of normalization of relations between traditional rivals of South Asia. In November 2015, after meeting on the sidelines of the climate change summit in Paris, Modi and Sharif announced resumption of dialogue. The two NSAs subsequently met in Bangkok and discussed a range of issues including peace and security (terrorism) and Kashmir.[9] Foreign Minister, Sushma Swaraj then met Sharif and Pakistan's NSA in Islamabad while attending the 'Herat of

Asia' conference. The two sides vowed to resume dialogue with a broader agenda.[10]

Former PM, Yousuf Raza Gillani stated in 2012 when he was PM, "Pakistani military is not within state rather Pakistani state is within Pakistani army." It is vindicated by a noted comment on the intricate relationship between Army and terror networks in the backdrop of November 2017 Islamabad siege, which lasted three weeks by the daughter of a prominent pro army political leader. Imaan Mazari, daughter of Tehrik-e-Insaf leader, Shireen Mazari who is known for her pro army views.

She stated "shame on the army that finances the activities of the terrorists, who have burnt down Islamabad and have plans to burn the entire country" she further added "that the army on one hand spoke of martyrs, but on the other hand disrespected Pakistan's martyrs by making deal with the same terrorists who killed Pakistani soldiers.[11] Pakistani army is doing these nasty works for their own public then what hell they cannot do for India." Anti-India megalomania is the basic philosophy of the army to dominate the system. But in reality, army can do anything to sustain their hegemony.

After May 2018 general election, the government has changed in Pakistan. Imran Khan led PTI has taken over and Khan has become Prime Minister. During election process, the ruling PTI, L-N, PPP and other parties have refrained from their pet rhetoric of anti India megalomania. Sharif had promised during election campaign that if elected he will promote cordial relationships with India. When Nawaz Sharif returned in power after May 2013 elections, he took many small steps to pave the way for reconciliation. His government has released over 350 fishermen in August 2013 as a goodwill gesture. In an interview given to *Telegraph* (London), Prime Minister, Nawaz Sharif asserted that his victory in May 2013 elections as a mandate for peace with India. He further added that "We have been in very unfortunate arm race with India ever since partition and I think we are a very unfortunate country from that point of view. He stressed that trust deficit should end and we both countries must settle all outstanding issues through dialogue and remain with peace and development."[12] Imran Khan also tried to do so at least in perception but he is so weak that he could not take any positive steps.

I must return on the focal issue now. What are the basic irritants between both traditional rivals of South Asia? It keeps on changing but more or less core issues have been sustainable. When Benazir Bhutto's PPP took over in 1988 and she became first women Prime Minister of Pakistan, the Pakistani army took three assurances from her, where she promised not to intervene. Kashmir, Afghanistan and Nuclear issue were the three arenas.

In May 2011, Osama bin Laden was killed at Abbottabad, just few hundred meters away from prestigious Kakul military academy, which is also not far away from Islamabad. The Pakistani commission which was constituted for its investigation has revealed many things which proved the allegation that OBL had a protection from the army. It has also been revealed by the commission that OBL was in Pakistan since his ouster from Afghanistan.

Another issue is Kashmir. Since last 72 years, it has been the core issue between India and Pakistan. Pakistan is claiming over Kashmir due to its religious and geographical proximities. It is also an open secret that despite many wars and cross-border terror in Kashmir, Pakistan has not been able to snatch Kashmir from India. This has helped to the Pakistani military to remain most important and powerful institutions of the country. In May 2014, COAS, Raheel Sharif has stated that the Kashmir is jaguar vein of Pakistan. This process has helped to militarise the country and thus negated fundamental freedom and human rights.

In August 2019, Modi government has scrapped special status of Kashmir while removing article 370. Pakistan adopted all brands of propaganda to catch the fish from the troubled waters but hardly any exclusive support was offered to it. China which is all weathered friend of Pakistan despite visits of high-profile Pakistani leaders were guarded when they suggested to settle the problem on the basis of existing bilateral framework of resolving disputes.

After Pakistani foreign minister's Beijing visit in August 2019 in the backdrop of scrapping of article 370, joint statement stressed "China recognises that the Kashmir dispute must be properly resolved based on the UN Charter, relevant UN Security Council resolutions and bilateral agreement."[13]

According to eminent strategic thinker Pervez Hood-boy, Pakistan status at the global stage has reduced a lot:

> "Third, patrons have their own interests. To call a friendship higher than the Himalayas, deeper than the oceans, and stronger than steel may be good poetry. But patrons act after a cold calculation of losses and gains. China's silence on Kashmir and its climb-down in May (2019) at the United Nations on Masood Azhar's blacklisting shows just how carefully it weighs things. Saudi Arabia, on which Pakistan pins its hopes, went along with India."[14]

The editorial comment of the prestigious Pakistani daily 'Dawn' comments vindicated Pakistan's isolation on this issue.

> "The crisis in India-held Kashmir could trigger global consequences, yet the world has not responded to Pakistan's urgent exhortations with the level of robustness as situation warrants. Instead of full-throated condemnation, there is a language of equivocation. Indeed, some countries, most notably US and UAE, have even gone along with India's brazenly false assertion that stripping Kashmir, an internationally recognised disputed territory, of its special status is an 'internal matter'. Saudi Arabia's bland reaction thus far avoids expressing any opinion whatsoever."[15]

Despite Pakistan's all-round mobilization and British Member of Parliament protest, United Arab Emirates has conferred its highest national award to PM Modi. Pakistani diplomacy has been frustrated after it. It is vindicated with the following statement of Pakistani foreign minister Shah Mehmood Qureshi[16]:

> "International relations are above religious sentiments. The UAE and India have a history of relations in connection with investment. However, I will soon have a meeting with the UAE foreign minister to inform him about the prevailing situation in India-held Kashmir", he said while responding to media queries regarding the grant of the UAE's highest civilian award to Indian Prime Minister Narendra Modi.

Army is all powerful in Pakistan. In the words of former army chief, General Jehangir Karamat, "Whenever there is a breakdown in ...stability, as has happened frequently in Pakistan, the military translate its potential into the will to dominate, and we have military intervention flowed by military rule."[17] Since independence out of 72 years of history, Pakistani army has ruled 32 years and even when it is not ruling it is formulating the policies related to core issues of foreign policy like Kashmir, Afghanistan, United States, China and Nuclear etc. When civilian regime is ruling over Pakistan our empirical experience vindicates that more anti Indian megalomania prevails in the Pakistani system in comparison with the periods directly ruled by the army.

Pakistan has adopted terror as an important instrument of its foreign policy since last many decades and despite loss of more than 70,000 people in terror related violence since 2007, which is more than the loss of Bangladesh war, it is all set to sustain the process. Retired Gen Musharraf's 2018 televised praise of Hafiz Saeed also reflects a changed stance. Declaring that "I am the greatest supporter of LeT", he asserted that "LeT and JuD are both very good organisations of Pakistan" because "I have always been in favour of action in Kashmir and I have always been in favour of pressuring the Indian army in Kashmir."[18] This is a remarkable turnaround—one recalls that Musharraf's government had declared LeT a terrorist organisation and banned it on January 12, 2002.

According to Hoodbhoy "Militant groups operating against Indian rule in Kashmir have always been looked favourably upon by the security establishment—this fact has never been in question. At the same time, Operation Raddul Fasaad (elimination of internal conflict) points to a recognition in army quarters of the serious danger involved; more Pakistani soldiers have been killed by jihadists turned bad than those in four Pakistan-India wars."[19]

Security architecture in Asia has remained turbulent. Deepening Indo-U.S. relations has put Chinese under 'Security Dilemma'. China perceives India as the only challenge in Asia. PM Modi has given exclusive twist to Indo-U.S. relations. Japan, ASEAN and at certain extent Australia has also joined the group in a tacit manner. It is evident through Chinese behaviour on Pakistan front. Till 2013 China was trying to be neutral in Indo-Pak conflict but since the arrival of Modi has taken direct steps to help Pakistan to contain India within South Asia.

Post-Balakot Challenges

In February 2019, suicide terror attacks killed 40 para military soldiers in Pulwama, Kashmir. It created huge public sentiment to teach Pakistan a lesson. PM Modi assured the nation that it will be revenged soon and finally on 26th February early morning, Indian Air Force bombarded HUGI training centre at Balakot, Pakhtunwah province. It was the maiden attack on Pakistani soil after 1971 war. This early morning air force attack on terror training centre had eliminated over 350 terrorists. Next day Air force plane intruded in Pakistani space and crashed but pilot Abhinandan was caught by the Pakistani army. He was released within days.

United States' NSA, John Bolton had stated that India has the right to retaliate and US support India in its fight against terrorism. According to Munir Akram, Pakistan's representative in the United Nations General Assembly:

> "Pakistan is near if not in the eye of the brewing Sino-US storm. Neutrality is not an option for Pakistan. The US has already chosen India as its strategic partner to counter China across the 'Indo-Pacific' and South Asia. The announced US South Asia policy is based on Indian domination of the subcontinent. Notwithstanding India's trade squabbles with Donald Trump, the US establishment is committed to building up India militarily to counter China. On the other hand, strategic partnership with China is the bedrock of Pakistan's security and foreign policy. The Indo-US alliance will compel further intensification of the Pakistan-China partnership. Pakistan is the biggest impediment to Indian hegemony over South Asia and the success of the Indo-US grand strategy. Ergo, they will try to remove or neutralise this 'impediment'."[20]

Challenges Ahead

Pulwama terror attack has created some new challenges for the Modi government. Within days after Pulwama attack, Indian army executed surgical strike on terror launching pads at Balakot which is in the deep Pakistan. It was the maiden attack by India into deeper Pakistan after many decades. The entire world has appreciated this move and accepted that India has also right of self-defense. Through Balakot, India has established Israel type image that if terror groups will attack within days and weeks, it will be duly revenged. The million dollor question is how to cope up with the emerging situations. Sanjay Baru, press secretary of former PM, Manmohan Singh, said "What all this means is that normal relations are unlikely to be restored between India and Pakistan in the near future." Pakistan has refused to establish normal trade relations with India, refused to adhere to the trade liberalization programme of the SAARC and has refused to provide transit rights for Indian goods and vehicles seeking access to Afghanistan and Central Asia. Given this hard reality it is only natural that the Indian government has decided to stay away from the SAARC Summit. More than the supportive decision of Afghanistan, the fact that the Bangladesh, SAARC founder country, has also decided to stay away from Islamabad Summit shows that SAARC has entered a cul de sac. With trade relations frozen in time, with diplomacy derailed by military-supported terrorism and Pakistan's increasing resort to nuclear blackmail, a new era of India-Pakistan cold war has begun. Of course, there is always a risk of a 'hot war' if Pakistan military becomes desperate or Islamic jihadists provoke both countries into direct conflict."[21]

Baru talks about cold war, which has already begun. China has already launched its ambitious CPEC and vowed to support Pakistan. It will be an interesting situation because in previous wars, China had not extended its support to Pakistan. Indian profile has increased many rounds since last two decades and at this juncture many global powers including the United States has indicated their support to India. But given the prevailing situation and long-term gain to India, it is advisable not to go for war. According to eminent strategic journalist Chidanand Rajghatta:

> "Islamabad has only itself to blame for its downward spiral. Cleaved from the same geographic entity, India and Pakistan took different roads to nationhood. The One is going uphill through the tough path of democracy and empowerment and the other on freebies and rental money through security pacts, mainly with the U.S. It is a consequence of the choices Pakistan has made for itself with its embrace of toxic Islamist extremism. So, India should prepare for war by all means, but without firing a shot in anger, it can watch Pakistan stumble along the road to perdition."[22]

Pakistan lacks adequate direction and dedication to develop it properly despite geo-strategically; geo-economically located at the centre of South, South-West and Central Asia. Dominance of the army has further reduced its capability to accelerate its all-round development and maximize the benefits of its geographical location. According to Ambassador, Ashraf Jahangir Qazi, "Pakistan has five neighbours: China, India, Iran, Afghanistan and the US which is a global neighbour. Except for China, Pakistan has relations ranging from unsatisfactory to dangerous with the other four. This places an enormous burden on the China-Pakistan relationship—a burden that, unless addressed, a globally emerging China could find too distracting, onerous and risky to sustain.

This Chinese dilemma has been vindicated through changing Chinese attitude. PM Modi visited China in April 2018 and had six rounds of informal summit talks with Chinese President, Xi Jinping at Wuhan. Both leaders also issued strategic guidance to respective militaries to strengthen communication to build mutual understanding. They also agreed that through greater consultation they will manage their overlapping regional and global interests. They also pledged to build multi-polar, pluralistic and participatory global economic order. They condemned terrorism and pledged cooperation to eliminate the menace. Interestingly, they also pledged to launch common project in Afghanistan.[23] President Xi came for second summit talks to Chennai in October 2019. It has been extra-ordinary embarrassing for Pakistan because of timing.

Ambassador, Ashraf Jahangir Qazi has highlighted hypocrisy of ruling oligarchy regarding their India policy and overall conduct of foreign policy:

> "India is the perennial enemy. But Pakistan seems to believe that merely blaming a blameworthy India, instead of maximizing its longer-term foreign policy options through development, is good enough policy. Both India and Kashmir are inherently longer-term challenges for Pakistan. There are no short-term solutions. Moreover, there are no zero-sum solutions that favour Pakistan. However, a corrupt and dishonest leadership will never speak this truth because it has not got the moral standing to inform the people about diplomatic, economic and military realities. It prefers to deceive them rather than develop the country to a point where it can negotiate with India and solicit international support for its stand on a more equal and effective basis."[24]

SAARC and Modi Government

SAARC was formed in 1985 to promote regional cooperation in South Asia. South Asia is an important region where 1/5 of global humanity lives. It is an area which is deprived in terms of resources and roughly 1/3 population of the region still lives in acute poverty according to any global parameter. SAARC completes 34 years of its formation in 2019. Much after SAARC in 1991, NAFTA was constituted in North America for regional cooperation. The intra-trade in NAFTA right now is over 20 per cent, ASEAN over 50 per cent and EU over 65 per cent but within the ambit of SAARC it is bare minimum and hardly crossed 5 per cent. The whole of South Asia is interconnected region agrarian economy. Due to lack of intra-trade within region, poverty elimination process has been slow. We have old connectivity routes if renovated properly it could be lifeline of trade and tourism in the entire area.

Afghan territory from Wagah border is hardy 500 km, but Pakistan only allows Afghan trucks to bring their goods till the border but not allowing to bring the goods from the Indian side. PM Modi has called for better connectivity across South Asia but it was not duly taken by Pakistan. Annual SAARC summit has also not organized since last many years due to turbulent Indo-Pak relations.

PM Modi has tried his level best to reach out other countries of South

Asia. He visited SriLanka in 2015 and again in 2018 and also in 2019 after returning into power. After assuming the office, his maiden visit was Bhutan. He visited Nepal also twice. He also visited Dhaka once and met his Bangladesh counterpart, Sheikh Hasina Wajed many times. He visited Kabul twice also and vowed India's commitment to sustain reconstruction process in this war-torn country. There are also high-profile visits of our dignitaries in different countries of South Asia. Newly elected Sri Lankan president visited New Delhi in November 2019. These visits have propelled regional cooperation at least with India and other countries minus Pakistan. Indian contribution in the reconstruction of Afghanistan has been immense and even acknowledged globally.

Under Modi regime, serious efforts have been made to accelerate trade, tourism and all possible cooperation within South Asia. Minus Pakistan with rest of South Asia, relationship has grown up and gamut of cooperation has mushroomed since last 5 years of Modi regime. In 2017, India launched a satellite for South Asia but Pakistan refused to come under its ambit. Although it was within the ambit of SAARC, India has already given MFN status long back in 1996 but till date, Pakistan has not reciprocated. It argues that due to bigger in size, Indian economy will swell its economy. But fact remains unanswered that Pakistan has accorded MFN status to China in 2012 and Chinese economy is at least 300 per cent larger than India. If Chinese economy has not been able to swell Pakistani economy then how Indian economy will do so. Although there is a strong demand in the industry sector of Pakistan to accord MFN status to India. It is complimentary to each other as well due to 3300 km long border.

If these developments will be duly implemented then peace and prosperity will prevail in South Asia. India and Pakistan cordial relations will further accelerate other South Asian countries to cooperate with the positive spirit. Under Modi regime, however gamut of cooperation with other countries of South Asia has taken place and through that peace building efforts have been made particularly in Sri Lanka and Nepal. Cordiality with Pakistan is bound to propel the tempo of regional cooperation. Modi government has tried its level best to sustained unilateral process to engage Pakistan. Given the prevailing retrospection in the military establishment which is ultimate boss of foreign policy, one may hope that there will be convergences of ideas between military establishment and civilian regime. I believe then India will be more then eager to grab this opportunity.

Concluding Remarks

Since its inception, Pakistan has perceived India as its immortal enemy. In recent years, Pakistan has witnessed killings of thousands of innocent citizens. This has triggered a small debate in Pakistan that its western border is more dangerous than its eastern border for national security. According to BBC, defence analyst Talat Masood "Pakistan army for the first time has admitted that the real threat is emanating internally and along the western borders and not from India, which was previously considered as number one enemy of the state."[25]

Through emulating China-India model, Pakistan could earn the financial leverage to eradicate its fundamental problems. But again, all powerful army has prevented it to realize. It is an era of globalization and despite rhetoric it is clear that every country has to cooperate to sustain their developmental process. Pakistan could not ensure sustainable development without ensuring peace with India. As nuclear power both countries are aware about the consequences of conflict. As pointed out by E. Sridharan "Explicit nuclearization with a demonstrated missile capability has assured Pakistan's security in a way that reduces the sensitivity to relative gains in the military sphere... Pakistan is more secure vis-à-vis a possible Indian military threat than ever before...Therefore, it has less to fear and much to gain from greater economic engagement with India."[26]

A stronger Pakistan is in the larger interests of India. India has emerged as an Asian power and aspiring for global status. India must shed its elder brother mentality within South Asia and must prove that it is a responsible and peace building country. Through this process India can not only propel its developmental process but also convince the global community that despite all odds it is also abided by reconciliation and international norms in South Asia.

France and Germany fought many bitter wars and both World Wars even they fought from different sides. But they have learnt a good lesson from their bitter experience. The Elysee Treaty of 1963 brought the two rivals closer for progress and prosperity. Both are cooperating in a massive way under the framework of the EU. India and Pakistan could emulate this example under the ambit of SAARC.

Pakistan civil-military conflict has been mainly accountable for the turbulent relationship and it has been sustainable either the country is ruled by the civilians or the generals in uniform. India remains scoring points for both and given the prevailing balance of power it is bound to sustain in foreseeable future as well.

After the completion of the 1st term of Modi government, Indo-Pak relations are still in cold storage despite multiple efforts by Modi government. Pulwama and Balakot has further eroded any hope of reconciliation between both countries in immediate future.

Since last few years, Indian economy has remained fastest growing economy of the globe even leaving China behind. It is expected that India will grow with this pace for a long time to come. Economic development requires durable peace. Even though Pakistan is not reciprocating peace initiates at par with our expectations, Modi government must sustain extending olive branch. It will fulfil larger interest of our foreign policy and within South Asia; our smaller neighbour's will witness the truth. India has already marked its imprint at the global level. Pakistan is a permanent geographical neighbour. Instead of focusing much on Pakistan, Modi government must decentralize its focus in the areas where India's presence has been minimal even today. Modi government has adopted this holistic approach since last five years to deal with Pakistan and must sustain the process. Durable peace in South Asia is conducive for sustainability of growth saga of India and needless to say that it will propel Pakistani and other South Asian economics as well.

ENDNOTES

1. Kanti Bajpai, "Narendra Modi's Pakistan and China Policy; assertive bilateral diplomacy, active coalition diplomacy", *International Affairs*, 93; 1, 2017. p. 70.
2. Raja Mohan, *Crossing the Rubicon: The Shaping of India's New Foreign Policy*, Penguin, New Delhi, 2003, p. 202.
3. *Ibid.*, pp. 101-2.
4. "Warning for China as US hails India 'partnership". *AFP*, October 19, 2017.
5. Bhavan Jaipragas, Chinese missiles likely to cripple Asia-based US forces in event of confiict: report, *South China Post*, Hong Kong, August 18, 2019.
6. Indrani Bagchi, "Maritime cooperation in Indo-Pacific to top India-Japan 2+2 meet", *Times of India*, New Delhi, November 30, 2019.
7. "2014 among deadliest years in AF with 10 k civilian casualties", *The Times of India*, New Delhi, August 9, 2015.
8. "Afghanistan civilian deaths hit record high in 2018", UN, *Aljazeera*, 24 February, 2019.
9. Subhajit Roy, Parveen Swamy and Sheela Bhatt, "India, Pakistan break the ice off camera in Bangkok", *Indian Express*, New Delhi, 7 December, 2015.
10. "India, Pakistan ready for talks", says Sushma Swaraj in Islamabad, *India Today*, 9 December, 2015.

11. "Pro-military leader's daughter roasts Pak army for propping up terrorists", *Times of India*, New Delhi, 2nd December 2017, p. 22.
12. "Blame Game between India, Pak has to stop", *The Indian Express*, New Delhi, August 24, 2013.
13. Naveed Siddiqui, China to "Uphold justice for Pakistan on Kashmir Issue", *Dawn*, Karachi, August 9, 2019.
14. Pervez Hoodbhoy, "Client and Patrons", *Dawn*, Karachi, July 6, 2019.
15. "A Tepid Response", Editorial, *Dawn*, Karachi, August 9, 2019.
16. Shakeel Ahmed, "FM moves to paper over UAE award for Modi", *Dawn*, Karachi, August 26, 2019.
17. Nawaz, Shuja, *Crossed Swords, Its Army, and the Wars Within*, Oxford University Press, Oxford, 2008, pp. xxvoii-xxviii.
18. *Op. Cit.*, No. 11.
19. *Ibid.*
20. Munir Akram, "Pakistan and Sino-Us Cold War", *Dawn*, Karachi, June 9, 2019.
21. Sanjay Baru, "An Indo-Pak Cold War", *The Indian Express*, New Delhi, 3 October 2016).
22. Chidanand Rajghatta, "Pakistan's Road to Perdition", *The Times of India*, New Delhi, 5 October, 2016.
23. Sachin Parashar, "India, China to join hands for Af project", *Times of India*, New Delhi, 29 April, 2018.
24. Ashraf Jahangir Qazi, "Pakistan's Foreign Policy", *Dawn*, Karachi, 30 December, 2017.
25. *Dawn*, Karachi, 9 January, 2013.
26. Sridharan, E., "Improving Indo-Pakistan relations; International Relations Theory, Nuclear Deterrence and possibilities for economic cooperation", *Contemporary South Asia*, Vol. 14, No. 3, September 2005, p. 322.

16
Islamic Micro-finance
A Potentially Viable Tool for Poverty Alleviation in South Asia

Sana Beg

Introduction

South Asia happens to be one of the fastest growing regions in the world. Ironically, it is also home to one of the largest concentration of people living in abject poverty on earth. This is true that there has been evidences of growth in this region, that far exceeds the Sub-Saharan African region, however, still large number of poor are living below the poverty line. And thus, this is a cause of concern and needs deliberate attempts by the governments of these countries to improve the situation of the region. Poverty is a serious problem for most of the countries of South Asia. Extremely poor people suffer from nutritional deficiencies, face disguised hunger, underemployment and social exclusion which all leads to a wide range of health and socio-economic problems. Poverty is not only deprivation of economic or material resources but a violation of human dignity too.

Among the South Asian countries, India has the highest number of people living below the poverty line. It is now widely recognized that the existence of poverty is not because of scarcity of resources but exists as a result of inequality and injustice and thus poverty today is man-made. People living below the poverty line do not have the fundamental human right, the right to a dignified life. Poverty has intensified as a result of exclusion of groups of people on the basis of caste, class, gender, religion etc. However, if right steps are taken by the governments and the public at large, eradication of poverty is possible.

Poverty Alleviation and Micro-finance

In the second-half of the twentieth century, it was recognized that certain deliberate attempts needs to be taken for poverty eradication by people, institutions and governments if any nation really want to develop. Micro-finance too emerged as a tool for poverty eradication. Micro-finance has emerged as an economic development approach intended to address the financial needs of the downtrodden where the commercial banks have failed to reach. Micro-finance has been referred to as the provision of financial services to low-income clients, including the self-employed and low-income entrepreneur in urban, semi-urban and rural areas. According to CGAP (2004), micro-finance or financial services for the poor encompass savings, credit, payment and transfer services, and insurance. Provider of micro-finance services can be non-governmental micro-finance institutions, savings and credit cooperatives, commercial banks, community-based organizations with bank linkages, insurance companies, state banks and others. Yunus (2007) defined micro-finance as a provision of small amounts of thrift, credit and other financial services and products to the rural and urban poor to improve their living standards by increasing their household income and therefore, creating demand for other goods and services. Although initially it showed great potential, but micro-finance have, however, not been able to reach the objectives even after decades of its adoption.

Hassan (2015) have identified three main problems associated with mainstream micro-finance-borrower unfriendly products and procedures, inflexibility and delay, high transaction costs (both legitimate and illegitimate) and lastly often micro-finance being seen as a social obligation rather than a business opportunity. It is being argued that micro-finance are causing huge burden on the poor, leading to vicious cycle of debt, poverty and eventually deaths in some cases. The recent spate of farmer suicides in India, is a case in point.

Islamic Finance and Economics: The Concept

Islam is a religion that is distinct from other religions as it is not just a religion of rituals. It is a rule-based system which specifies rules for all aspects of life. The foundation of Islamic economics is based on economic development and growth along with social justice. It is believed that existence of poverty is not because of scarce resources but because of the result of wastage, extravagant behaviour of the rich and exploitation of a section of the society. Everyone in the Islamic society must be given the same opportunities to access the natural resources gifted by God. If, unfortunately, someone has no work or is not in a position to work then it is the duty of the society to fulfil his or her minimum requirements for a dignified life. Islamic vision of a just society both socially and economically is based on abolishing interest and/or other exploitative elements from the society. All financial activities like lending, borrowing and investing should be based on profit and risk sharing. The Islamic financial system leads to a more sustainable economic growth and fair opportunities for all because of optimal rate of capital formulation and efficient utilization. It is a value-based system aiming for moral and material well-being of the individual and the society at large.

Extremes of wealth and poverty needs to be avoided so much so that Islam prohibits overspending and waste. It lays stress on the fact that after moderate spending necessary to maintain a modest living standard, surplus must be returned to the members of the society who, for a variety of reasons, are unable to work, hence the resources they could have used to produce income and wealth were utilized by the more able. Islam considers the more able as trustee-agents in using these resources on behalf of the less able. The less able get a share in the income and wealth of the more able through a network of mandatory and voluntary levies.

The Islamic financial system creates a balanced relationship between the individual and the society. Self-interest and private gains of the individual are not denied, but they are regulated for the larger betterment of the society. Islamic banking and finance is inspired by the Islamic Economics and are consistent with the principles of Islamic law (*Shariah*). The very reason of existence of Islamic banking is the divined prohibition of taking or giving of interest. Another important tenet of Islamic Banking is profit and loss sharing. Islam also prohibits gambling, speculation and investment in industries like pork, alcohol and pornography. Islamic economics aims to eradicate injustice, inequality, exploitation and oppression of all forms.

Islamic Micro-finance

Islamic micro-finance can be said to represent the meeting of two fast growing financial industries—Islamic finance and micro-finance. It aims at combining the Islamic social principles of caring with the micro-finance's power to provide financial access to the disadvantaged section of the society. In Islam, the economic policy is to secure the satisfaction of basic needs for every individual completely and to enable him to satisfy his luxuries to the maximum possible. Islam looks at every human being individually rather than as the total of individuals who live in the country. The objective of the economic policy in Islam is to ensure the rights of life for every individual and not just to raise the standard of living in the country. Nor is it just to provide means of satisfaction in the society, leaving people free to take from such means as much as they can, without securing the livelihood for each individual. In this respect, economic principles of Islam deal with rules of resource allocation, production, exchange, distribution and redistribution. The central tenet of Islamic economics propagates the equal distribution of resources for the development of the different strata of society and to maximize and utilize the talent of all individuals so that they can contribute towards development of the society as a whole. The Islamic approach to poverty alleviation is more inclusive than the conventional one.

In Islamic micro-finance, the poorest of the poor is given preference for receiving the public support. Zakat and Sadaqah are two important instruments of charity that can play a critical role in poverty alleviation. The main sources of fund in Islamic micro-finance includes external funds, savings of clients and the charitable funds while in conventional micro-finance there is no provision of charitable funds. The main drawback with the conventional micro-finance is high rates (sometimes as high as 30%) charged from the poor people to make financial gains to the micro-finance institutions. On the other hand, Islamic micro-finance are based on profit and loss sharing schemes. Like the Islamic banking, the Islamic micro-financial system provides an array of instruments and micro-finance products that are Shariah-compliant. Instruments of fund mobilisation and financing includes zakah, sadaqah, awqaf, wadiah, qard-al-hasan, mudarabah, musharakah and murabahah.

Micro-savings—The savings of the poor are investments for Islamic Micro-finance Institutions. The profits and losses are shared between the Micro-finance Institutions and the customer, depending whether the investment of deposits are on mudarabah, musharakah or takaful.

Micro-credit—The Islamic Micro-finance institutions allows customers the acquisition of assets that are needed for their productive activity by giving them on rent; the acquisition being financed by products like qard-e-hasaan, murabahah, ijara, salam etc. All these products create debt and the customer pays the price of assets with gross margin.

Micro-lease—In contrast to conventional lease, the risks are very high to the Islamic Micro-finance Institutions takes on the responsibility of all damages involuntary caused to its customer. The modalities of lease contract are defined in advance.

Micro-takaful—Micro-takaful is micro-insurance based on mutual guarantee to protect the borrowers from unpredicted risks. To improve prevention of risks and strengthen the security of borrowers, a number of people contribute to create an insurance fund that compensate borrowers who face some emergency or an undesirable event in their business. The premiums are invested in shariah-compliant investments.

Conclusion

The greatest challenge facing the global development community as the world is well into the third millennium is to attack persistent poverty and overcome the low levels of social and economic development of the poor that constitutes a sizable proportion of the world population. Poverty can be best understood as a situation where people lack the basic needs for survival including food, water, shelter, education and healthcare. Both developed and developing nations have their share of people who are poor and thus because poverty is widespread, eradication of poverty has been on the top of the list of the Millennium Development Goals.

Although almost all countries of the South Asia have been introducing many economic policies for poverty reduction but the living conditions of the poor people continued to deteriorate, unemployment and income disparity increased. The previous poverty reduction strategies improved the general economic conditions such as increasing the Gross Domestic Product (GDP) without improving the living standards of the common people. The two critical elements, i.e. the applicant's reputation as a person of honour and the availability of collateral against which claims can be made in case of default poised important impediments to the poor especially in the rural areas to access into credit market. The poor are usually perceived by the "profit-orientated" banks as high-risk borrowers due to inherent difficulties in assessing their creditworthiness at the same time their inability to provide collateral to pledge against any potential risk. This, lead to a need for a financial system specially for poverty alleviation and thus micro-finance emerged. Micro-finance is a section of a financial system whose main aim is to fight poverty. Micro-finance institutions focus on the poor and low-income earners which are two groups that are highly neglected by conventional banks. However, this too had been only partially successful because of the few drawbacks that the conventional micro-finance.

Islamic finance, as micro-finance, focus on the welfare of the entire society. Islamic finance also encourages the poor to participate in entrepreneurial activities in order to improve their welfare and lay great emphasis on financial inclusion. Islamic micro-finance is a combination of both micro-finance and Islamic finance. However, Islamic micro-finance scores better than micro-finance as it overcomes the limitations that micro-finance faces. The concept of micro-finance is about four decades old but its role in poverty eradication is still doubted. Micro-finance has the drawback of being discriminatory, exploitative with high interest rate and unstable. The biggest issue with the conventional micro-finance system is that it is interest-based meaning that loanees have to pay back loans with interest irrespective of whether their businesses succeeded or failed. Indeed, this is where the largest difference between conventional micro-finance and Islam micro-finance lies; the latter advocates for interest-free financial services.

Thus, the reasons why Islamic micro-finance scores better than the conventional micro-finance to alleviate poverty is because it is interest-free and the redistribution of wealth and risk and profit sharing are its two pillars. The charity based model for poverty alleviation includes Zakah, sadaqah, awqaf, Qard-e-hasan and are the products which can fulfil the basic food and consumption needs for life survival. Their main purpose is to pull out a poor from financial crisis and can be seen as a solution to the challenge of poverty. The risk-sharing and profit-sharing models of poverty alleviation includes products like Murabahah, Musharakah, Mudarabah, Ijarah, Salam, Istisna etc.

Countries in the South Asia that wishes to be one among the developed nations need to introduce Islamic banking and with that Islamic micro-finance without any delay. It is worth mentioning that Islamic micro-finance systems have revolutionized micro-finance by giving it a spiritual, ethical and moral aspect.

> "Wherever we lift one soul from a life of poverty, we are defending human rights.
> And whenever we fail in this mission, we are failing human rights."
>
> —*Dr. Kofi Annan*,
> Former Secretary-General, United Nations

ANNEXURE

Mudarabah is a profit-sharing contract wherein, supplier of money capital contracts with a working partner on the basis of sharing the resulting profits. Losses, if any, are considered loss of capital and borne by the owner of capital. The working partner, in that case, goes unrewarded for its efforts. This is the 'loss' borne by the working partner, a feature of mudarabah which has made some to characterize it as profit and loss sharing or PLS. The sharing contract when applied to farming is called muzara'ah or share-cropping.

Musharakah is a partnership contract. In partnership two or more parties supply capital as well as work/effort. They share the resulting profits according to agreed proportions, but losses are to be borne in proportion to respective capitals.

Murabahah is a sale agreement under which the seller purchases goods desired by a buyer and sells it to him/her at an agreed marked up price, payment being deferred. The higher price paid would leave a margin for the seller in order to reward him/her for expertise in bargaining, better knowledge of market conditions etc.

Ijara is a leasing contract that permits one party (the lessee) to use an asset or property owned by another party (the lessor) for an agreed upon price over a fixed period of time.

Salam is a forward financing transaction, where the financial institution pays in advance for buying specified assets, which the seller will supply on a pre-agreed date.

Istisna is a contract of acquisition of goods by specification or order, where the price is paid progressively in accordance with the progress of a job completion. This is practiced for purchase of an item that is yet to be completed or produced, for example, a house to be constructed where payments are made to the developer or the builder according to the stage of work completed. Istisna differs from ijara in that the manufacturer must procure his own raw materials.

Zakat is one of the five pillars of Islam. An individual who earns more than what he or she consumes in a year must pay Zakat, which is calculated according to his or her level of net worth (essentially a wealth tax). Its obligations are to the community as a whole: they are to be made specifically and directly to the community's less fortunate members. The *Quran* emphasizes the significance of Zakat that it reduces material inequality and enhances brotherhood in the society.

Sadaqah is voluntary social spending. Independent social spending is the best possible way for members of the Islamic social order to promote a more equitable distribution of wealth and resources. People who can donate more than the obligatory Zakat should share their wealth with the less fortunate.

Qard-al-hasan literally means a 'beautiful loan'. It is described as beautiful because it is an interest-free loan granted to a needy where the debtor is obligated to return the principal and the creditor does not put any condition regarding the timing of its return; the terms of this loan is decided by the borrower.

REFERENCES

Abdelkader, I., B., Salem, A.B., "Islamic *vs.* Conventional Micro-finance Institutions: Performance Analysis in MENA Countries", *International Journal of Business and Social Research*, Vol. 3, No. 5, 2013.

Aldosari, B.N., "Islamic Microfinancial System and Poverty Alleviation", *International Journal of Development and Economic Sustainability*, Vol. 4, No. 6, December 2016.

Aslam, M.N., "Role of Islamic Micro-finance in Poverty Alleviation in Pakistan: An Empirical Approach", *International Journal of Academic Research in Accounting, Finance and Management Science*, Vol. 4, No. 4, October 2014.

Beg, S., "Prospects, Problems and Potential of Islamic Banking in India", *International Journal of Accounting and Financial Management Research*, Vol. 6, Issue 3, October 2016.

Beg, S., Mullick, N.H., "Increasing Financial Inclusion Through Islamic Banking in India", *International Journal of Business Management and Research*, Vol. 6, Issue 1, February 2016.

Beg, S., Mullick, N.H., "Islamic Banking and Finance in India: Need of the Hour", *International Journal of Marketing, Financial Services and Management Research*, Vol. 4, No. 4, December 2015.

Chapra, M.U., "Islam and the Economic Challenge", *Islamic Economic Series-17*, The Islamic Foundation and the International Institute of Islamic Thought, 1995.

Dusuki, A.W., "Banking for the poor: The role of Islamic Banking in microfinance initiatives", *Humanomics*, Vol. 24, Issue 1, 2008.

Hassan, A., "Financial Inclusion of the Poor: from Microcredit to Islamic Microfinancial Services", *Humanomics*, Vol. 31, Issue 3, 2015.

Hassan, M.K., Lewis M.K., *Handbook of Islamic Banking*, Edward Elgar Publishing, 2007.

Khan, S.P.K. and Beg, S., "Microfinance: A Powerful Tool for Economic Empowerment of the Poor", *International Journal of Commerce and Business Management*, Vol. 3, Issue 1, April 2010.

Obaidullah, M., Khan, T., "Islamic Micro-finance Development: Challenges and Initiatives", Islamic Development Bank, King Fahd National Library Cataloging-in-Publication Data. *Policy Dialogue Paper No. 2*, 2008.

Samad, M.A., "Islamic microfinance: tool for economic stability and social change", *Humanomics*, Vol. 30, Issue 3, 2014.

Tajudeen Olalekan Yusuf, Abdul Hakeem I. Mobalaji, "The Role of Islamic Micro Insurance in Economic Growth and Development—The Nigerian Experience: A Case Study of Al Barakah Microfinance Bank, Lagos", *International Journal of Business and Commerce*, Vol. 1, No. 10, June 2012.

Yunus, M., "Creating a World without Poverty: Social Business and the Future of Capitalism", *Public Affairs*, New York, 2007.

SECTION IV

Socio-economic Development and Regional Diversities

17

Challenges for Human Development and Governance in South Asia

An Overview

Niharika Tiwari

Introduction

South Asia is a dynamic region with its own politico-strategic importance. The region's strategic situation is such as its geo-political importance has been recognised by the comity of the nations since long. It is located at the crossroads of Asia; this region is adjacent to the China and Central Asia. It also links the West Asia with South East Asia. Since it borders Indian Ocean, one of the most important strategic area of the world is constituted by it. The term 'South Asia' has been defined and demarcated in different ways. According to Mann (2015), South Asia is able to take its place in the contemporary nomenclature of terms denoting the different major regions of the Asian continent alongside that of East Asia, Central Asia and Southeast Asia. However, defining what comprises South Asia as a major region is contentious as, according to the United Nations' geographical region classification, it comprises the countries Afghanistan, Bangladesh, Bhutan, India, Iran, Maldives, Nepal, Pakistan and Sri Lanka, whereas other definitions and interpretations also sometimes include Burma and Tibet, but omit Iran. However, South Asia as a unit of regional cooperation known as SAARC consists of eight countries, i.e. Afghanistan, Bangladesh, Bhutan, India, Maldives, Nepal, Pakistan and Sri Lanka. It is the most densely populated region of the world. It consists of 25 per cent of world population (approximately 1.891 billion) with only 5 per cent of world GDP. It is both the most populous and the most densely populated geographical region in the world.

According to UNFPA's *State of World Population Report 2019*, India is the most populated country of South Asia with 1368.7 million, followed by Pakistan with 204.6 million, third position is occupied by Bangladesh with 168.2 million. Rest of the countries have relatively lesser population, viz. Afghanistan 37.2 million, Nepal 29.9 million, Sri Lanka 21 million, Bhutan 0.8 million and Maldives 0.5 million. Bangladesh is the second most densely populated country of the world after Singapore. Thus, South Asian countries have huge differences on the basis of geography and population both. Although, South Asia faces many socio-economic challenges owing to its huge population, according to UNFPA (2019) report data South Asia seems to have the advantage of 'Demographic Dividend.'[1] As per this report, more than 55 per cent people of all the eight countries of South Asia come under 15-64 age group. The highest position is of Maldives with 72 per cent population and the lowest is of Afghanistan with 55 per cent population coming under working age group. In South Asia, 65.25 per cent (average) population comes under working age group that can boost up the economic growth of the region. Demographic dividend can be converted into demographic opportunity if good health, quality education, decent employment and many other capability enhancing supports are provided to the people.

Challenges for Human Development

The geographical location of South Asia is also very significant as this region is full of natural resources like forest, water, traditional and non-traditional energy sources etc. Notwithstanding the fact that South Asia has been able to achieve higher economic growth in last decades, the people of this region face poverty and deprivation. The South Asian economic structure is still dominated by the primary sector. Therefore, most of the population works in agriculture and related activities. Since agriculture is a seasonal activity people have to face structural unemployment. Added to this, the region has been one of the most poverty ridden regions of the world. According to Multidimensional Poverty Index[2] of Human Development Report 2019, in South Asia 31.0 per cent population comes under multidimensional poverty. If South Asia is compared with the other regions, it holds second position in multidimensional poverty index, the first place is of Sub-Saharan Africa with 57.5 per cent population facing multidimensional poverty. Whereas, merely 1.1 per cent of population of Europe and Central Asia, 5.6 per cent of East Asia and the Pacific, 7.5 per cent of Latin America and the Caribbean, 15.7 per cent of Arab States are multi-dimensionally poor.

The condition of employment, although improving, is still provides a grim picture. According to the World Bank (2019) observations, agriculture continues to employ a majority of the working-age population across the region. This is especially so in Nepal and Bhutan, but the share is high in Afghanistan and India as well. The second most important source of jobs is the services sector. Sri Lanka is the only country in the region where the services sector employs more people than agriculture, and in Bangladesh the two sectors are even. On the other hand, the share of the manufacturing sector is relatively low across all countries in the region, ranging from 3 per cent in Bhutan to 9 per cent in Sri Lanka. In many countries in the region, construction employs as many people as manufacturing.

The World Bank has further observed that, almost all South Asian countries have a very large number of young people reaching working age every year. Between 2005 and 2015, the number of South Asians aged 15 and above grew by 1.8 million per month, a trend that will only moderate gradually over time. In relative terms, the share of the working-age group in the total population increased by over 1 per cent per year in Bhutan, and by around 0.5 per cent in Bangladesh, India, and Pakistan. At the same time, the employment rate decreased on average more than 1.5 per cent per year in Bhutan and India and by more than 0.5 per cent per year in Bangladesh. Since income per capita grew considerably in all these countries from 2005 to 2015, some decline in the employment rates could be anticipated. However, the declines in employment rates are much larger than can be explained by increasing incomes per capita alone. This contrasts with the experience of many East Asian countries like the Philippines, Vietnam, Malaysia, or Indonesia, for which the employment rate even increased between 2005 and 2015.

South Asian region has its exclusive features and issues that are different from the other regions of the world. These issues range from territorial disputes to human security. For instance, if Kashmir issue is continuously jeopardising the political stability of this region, the instances of poverty are much higher in this region as compared to South East Asia, Central Asia etc. The political instability in Afghanistan and the efforts of big powers to establish their hegemony in the region is also considered as one of the most important factors that influences the destiny and direction of the progress in every aspect. Apart from this South Asia plays very crucial role in the economy of other countries. According to ILO Report (2018) *International Labour Migration Statistics in South Asia*, collectively, there were over 38 million South Asian nationals living outside of their countries of origin in 2017—both in other South Asian countries and farther a field. Remittances send back to the origin country in South Asia help poverty alleviation. However, the stock of international migrants living within the sub region has decreased substantially overall over the past six decades, from 17.82 million in 1960, to 11.38 million in 2015 and 10.88 million in 2017. According to UNESCAP (2019), the feminization of migration has also happened in case of South Asia.

Succinctly, South Asian region has internal as well as external factors that occasionally support and more often weaken the human development of this region. Added to this identity based conflicts are also an important feature of this region. These are often generated due to two types of encounters (Pemberton & Nijhawn, 2008); first, between dominant representations and local "micronarratives" giving rise to struggle for economic resources, control over symbolic capital, or influence within or over institutions of governance, second is called "fruitful encounters"—particularly at the level of the so-called "popular" or "vernacular" religious experience—this relationship is often depicted as one of syncretism.

As Thakur and Wiggen (2004) have argued, South Asia needs a regional identity and rationality. They have illustrated the list of the sources of instability in this region enumerated by Niaz Malik who has observed the reasons behind fact that South Asia remains mired in conflicts and tension. The list formulated by Malik consists of varied sources of instability like: inter-state conflict, internal instability, terrorism, drug trafficking, clandestine arms sale, migration, trafficking in women and children, and the spread of HIV/AIDS. Therefore, regional cooperation is necessary to face the multidimensional threat to security (traditional and non-traditional) in South Asia. For example, extreme weather conditions, diseases like Covid 19, terrorism etc. do not respect national borders. Similarly, South Asia as a single interconnected market can attract foreign investments into the region.

The countries of this region have many things in common that help them override the existing diversities. The most important aspect is the common colonial past. While Myanmar and Sri Lanka experienced direct colonial rule. Bhutan, Nepal surrenders many powers to the British Government in India. Consequently, common administrative, political and legal processes and institutions can be found in India, Pakistan, Sri Lanka etc. Apart from this, the countries of this region enjoy geographical proximity, especially with India. But, British colonial past has been instrumental in generating some infamous disputes in South Asia. For instance, Kashmir issue between India and Pakistan, Tamil nationality issues etc. are the British legacies in the region. Apart from this, growing

South Asian economies can emerge as an attractive economic destination. Another important area of cooperation among South Asian countries may be their trade complementarity with each other. This has been observed in case of Bangladesh and Sri Lanka.

The socio-religious composition of South Asia is also very unique and provides a bedrock wherein multiculturalism can flourish. South Asia is inhabited by almost all great religions and their followers. According to Bose & Jalal (2018), South Asia is the source of the world's great religions. Hindus form the majority of India's population, but are distinguished along lines of languages and caste. While the formal adherents to Buddhism may have dwindled in the land of its birth, it continues to flourish in Sri Lanka and the Himalayas as well as in East and Southeast Asia. Some of the greatest cultural and political achievements of Islam have taken place in the subcontinent, where more than half a billion of the world's 1.65 billion Muslims live today. Each of the three most populous countries in South Asia—India, Bangladesh and Pakistan—has over 175 million Muslims, next only to Indonesia as the largest Muslim countries in the world. South Asia also has significant Jain, Zoroastrian, Christian and Sikh minorities.

Common cultural roots provide feeling of oneness among the people of South Asia. For instance, religious practices, rituals etc. are almost similar across the region. The important feature of this region is that religious faith transcends the sovereign boundaries of the countries and give rise to a feeling of solidarity. However, as it has been observed, sometimes religious differences are highlighted and interlinked with the economic issues to harness the political benefits. Moreover, political establishments make religious minorities scapegoats in order to cover up their failures. Added to this, the ethno-linguistic diversity exists across the boundaries.

The disputes between the South Asian countries are basically of two types; the first bone of contention is intra-regional disputes based on territorial disputes like the Kashmir issue that has jeopardised the peace and tranquillity of this region. Another kind of disputes are related to the relation of the countries of this region to the other countries of the world. Despite of all inconsistencies South Asia has many common threads to consolidate itself as a vibrant region:

> The past, present and future coalesce to create an amalgam of actuality and aspiration. The history of South Asia shows that the foundation for creating South Asian unity still exists, though in a dilapidated condition. The base laid by the Mauryan and Mughal

> empires continues to bind the peoples of South Asia together. There are more commonalities in art, architecture, dance, music, religions, cultures and many more things than leaders of the region dare to admit in the face of present realities of equally multifarious conflicts within and across national boundaries. But the present is hardly discrete—it is an intersection where the past and the future meet. The present is more important for what can be done with what vexes the mind rather than what exists (Lal and Kabir, 2010:1).

This region has enough potential to grow as a unit to realise its potential. Especially, its shared past, common cultural threads, and aspiration for democracy and development are the factors that can lead to a unified South Asia. For instance, in case of languages Urdu, Pali, Prakrit, Sanskrit are the common heritage of all the languages. Celebration of diversity is the only option that can escalate the process of prosperity in this region. However, it requires a high level of political maturity and commitment to democratic values.

Globalization and Issues of Governance in South Asia

Globalization has influenced almost every sphere of human life. Not only in the field of economics but governance and human rights discourses have also witnessed new dimensions and approaches. Now the world is relying on think globally act locally. Consequently, the changes and inventions occurring in any area of the world have potential to influence the entire world order. Globalization has integrated entire world and it has established free flow of capital, goods, services, ideas, diseases etc. Since the world in an interdependent world, institutions of governance and the human rights issues all are needed to be put into right context. International organisations, like United Nations, World Bank, International Monetary Fund etc. are the crucial ones. Apart from this, the world has seen economic regionalism in the form of European Union (EU), Association of South East Asian Nations (ASEAN), South Asian Association of Regional Cooperation (SAARC) etc. Forces of globalization have created certain anomalies as it carries the process of homogenization with it. Since the world order is hierarchical and asymmetrical, the socio-cultural values of developed countries are being imposed on developing countries leading to a kind of dissatisfaction among them. For instance, the notion of 'Asian Values' in the context of human rights discourse is an example in this regard.

In this era of globalization, the notion and expectations from governance have got changed, therefore, the governance has been interpreted as good governance after the observations made by World Bank in the context of Sub-Saharan countries. The World Bank came to know that policies and programmes implemented in this area failed to uplift the condition of the people. After research it was observed that it demanded people to be understood at the centre of all the activities and that they should not be seen as a passive recipient of the benefits being extended by the governing institutions, rather they must be treated as active agents.

In contemporary world, democracy based on good governance is being considered as the backbone of any sovereign state. When one talks about a region, like South Asia, the values of democracy that is equality, liberty and justice and the principles of good governance that define the institutional quality and capacity are at the core of the debate. According to Addink (2019:5):

> Good governance is a norm for the government and a citizen's right. Within the concept of good governance, more specific conditions have been formulated. These norms are sometimes linked to the norms of rule of law and democracy, but mostly they have their own contents. Aspects of good governance are properness, transparency, participation, effectiveness, accountability, and economic, social, and cultural human rights. These elements have developed into universal elements of good governance, although other norms or differing terminology might be found in practice as well, but these are accepted across cultures or are applicable across the board. These six basic elements of good governance have been found to be the hard core of the concept.

It has been observed by the World Bank (Lateef, 2016), in case of Sub-Saharan countries that institutions of governance were not able to address the deprivation issues of the people due to the absence of the principles of good governance. Therefore, World Bank developed its own notion of good governance emphasising on the efficiency and reforms that could strengthen economic development of a country. World Bank's (1994) notion of governance consisted of: public sector management, accountability, legal framework for development and transparency and information. However, the definition of good governance enunciated by United Nations Development Programme (UNDP) is more comprehensive.

It includes, institutional qualities that are performance, adaptability, and stability; and the main governance principles that are participation/inclusion, non-discrimination/equality and rule of law/accountability.

If one analyses South Asia through this perspective of governance, there are many principles that are still either missing in many of the South Asian countries or are at an infant stage. For instance, as far as public sector management and transparency etc. are concerned South Asian countries ranking has been very poor. Out of 180 countries' ranking by Transparency International in Corruption Perception Index 2019, Afghanistan ranked (173), Bangladesh (146), Bhutan (25), India (80), Maldives (130), Nepal (113), Pakistan (120) and Sri Lanka (93). Except Bhutan none of the South Asian countries could qualify under top 50 rank. India slipped from 78 to 80 compared to previous year. The main reason behind low ranking of these countries, as cited by Transparency International, is the existing problems in political integrity and governance.

In South Asia, countries have been actively making efforts to develop and strengthen institutions of democratic governance. Since colonial structure is still continuing, the authoritative values are very much prevalent in this region. Bangladesh and India with their parliamentary democracies, Bhutan with its constitutional monarchy, Maldives, Nepal and Sri Lanka, with their democratic republics and Afghanistan and Pakistan with their Islamic Republic have attempted at different levels of governance to address the increasing demands of democratic reforms.

However, governance system in South Asia is still battling with the legacy of colonialism and partition. The wound of partition provided ground wherein many kind of mistrusts thrived among the different communities. Therefore, in South Asia procedural democracy got established to a large extent, the substantial democracy is still far away. The reason seems to be the poor condition of democracy at social and economic fronts. As South Asia has always been an abode to the highest number of poor and impoverished in the world, only second to Sub-Saharan countries. The region has always witnessed the greatest number of poor and the destitute in the world, in some situations even worse than in Sub-Saharan African countries. The UNDP Human Development Reports have consistently placed most of the countries of South Asia very near the bottom in terms of human development measuring educational, health and quality of life standards. Due to rampant corruption and vested political interests and ongoing conflicts in the region, the socio-economic condition of the people is very poor. It gives rise to the worst levels of human deprivation.

Owing to the weaker socio-economic freedom, inequality is generated on the basis of caste, religion, race, gender and class etc. However, the people of this region remain hopeful as social movements are active at grassroots level in almost all the South Asian countries led by women, caste groups, minorities and civil society in general to instil democratic values at socio-economic fronts. For instance, in India Association for Democratic Reforms (ADR) is actively working in the area of electoral and political reforms, People's Union for Civil Liberties (PUCL) is the largest human rights organisation in India. In Pakistan, the iconic human rights activist and Lawyer Asma Jahangir have initiated a very strong movement for human rights of women, minorities and children in Pakistan and co-founded Human Rights Commission of Pakistan. There is a Women's Action Forum (WAF) in Pakistan to campaign against the discriminatory legislations of the government. In Sri Lanka, The Centre for Human Rights and Development has been active since 1997. Similarly, in Afghanistan, Afghanistan Human Rights and Democracy Organisation is an independent not-for-profit organisation working since 2009. It is trying to contribute to the internalization of and expansion of human rights and democratic values with the help of Afghan Young Women leaders, war victims and writers etc.

A peculiar condition is prevalent in South Asia when one examines human rights and democratic processes. In this region, the institutions like election commissions, human rights commissions, women commissions, political parties and media are often divided on political lines and tend to get influenced by ruling political dispensation. The entire efforts to protect and enhance the democratic fabric of the country and protect the human rights of the people lies with the social activists, few media houses and non-governmental organisations.

Dynamics of Human Rights

Human rights and governance both are directly and indirectly interlinked to each other because all generations of human rights can be protected only if governance process is transparent, accountable and responsible or say people-centric. Efficiency and performance of Institutions of governance ensure that human rights of the people of all castes, religions and sexual orientation will be honoured. According to Addink (2019:171):

> Often a distinction is made between civil and political rights on the one hand and economic, social, and cultural rights on the

> other. Some also add collective rights as a third group. The first group is related to restricting the powers of the state in respect of the individual. The second group often requires governments to intervene actively in order to create good conditions for human development, such as employment, education, and healthcare.

South Asia had been the part of the world wars without even being instrumental in the hostilities of the different blocks fighting wars. It had to pay human, material and moral costs. That is why the region put human rights at the highest regards. All the countries have institutions and laws to protect human rights of the people. However, adherence to it is still debatable. Moreover, South Asian society is traditionally duty-oriented and community and social solidarity takes precedence over individual rights. According to Lal and Kabir in South Asia human rights are still not given much importance because:

> The social mechanism of monitoring human rights violations is equally lax for three reasons. Religious affinity, family honour and tribal ties are considered important in the subcontinent. Secondly, liberalism—the ideology that gave birth to the concept of human rights—is not widely understood in the region. Even though the sanctity of an individual's life, liberty, property, identity and dignity are implicit in all faiths, it has not been able to overcome the horizontal division between creeds or the vertical hierarchy of caste. The third barrier to the acceptance of human rights is also the strongest. For reasons of its own, almost every state in South Asia lives under the constant threat of disintegration. This turns the ideology of 'Reasons of State' into an instrument of consolidating power and exercising authority without a due process of law or accountability. The romantic notion of a person being born free only to find fetters all around later in life is as true in South Asia as anywhere in the world. The universal declaration of human rights is hence an important consideration of existence in the region (Lal & Kabir 2010:38).

Protection of human rights has been one of the major challenges in front of the countries of South Asia. Despite of several efforts being made by the civil society organisations and legislations by the governments, the status of human rights is not very plausible in the region. An analysis of the conditions and incidents reveal that human rights of the people of this region are threatened broadly at two levels; first, it is abused by the fellow citizens in the form of sexual violence, human trafficking, child labour, mob lynching, caste and religion-based discrimination and violence etc. The second type of threats come from the political establishment when people tend to raise their voice against the undemocratic, oppressive, discriminatory and authoritative policies and acts of the government. At present, the region is facing both kind of human rights deprivation. In spite of many dissimilarities one common but pessimistic feature that exists in the South Asian countries is that governments strongly believe in crushing the dissenting voices coming from the youth, media and civil society. Since it is being accepted that as long as people's human rights are not respected, the benefits of globalization will give rise to an asymmetrical society. This is happening worldwide as the world is still an unequal one. Notwithstanding the fact that sustainable development cannot be achieved without assuring a dignified life to all to expand their capabilities, the human development is progressing at a slow pace in South Asia.

Human Development in South Asia

Closely related to the notion of human rights is a much wider concept that is human development. The perspective of Human development goes beyond the concept of quantitative calculation of economic growth. It considers health, education and standard of living as the parameters to measure the efforts and seriousness of the governments. Human development attempts to enlarge the choices of the people so that they can realise their full human potentials.

The countries of South Asia have been constantly active to improve their rankings in Human Development Index along with improving the conditions at grassroots level. According to the Human Development Reports, no other region has experienced such a rapid human development progress. South Asia was the fastest growing region (46 % growth over the period 1990-2018), followed by East Asia and the Pacific at 43 per cent. However, South Asia is grappled with multidimensional poverty, gender based discrimination and other kinds of deprivation. Although the basic necessities are getting fulfilled to a certain extent, the next generation inequalities such as around technology, education and climate change are also opening up. According to UNDP[3] (2019):

> And although millions throughout the region have escaped multidimensional poverty, the incidence of multidimensional

> poverty varies enormously across countries—from 0.8 per cent in the Maldives to 56 per cent in Afghanistan. Out of the 1.3 billion multidimensional poor, 661 million are in Asia and the Pacific, which shares almost half of the multidimensional poor living in 101 countries of the world. South Asia alone shares more than 41 per cent of the total number of multidimensional poor. Despite India's significant progress on the multidimensional poverty front in the past decade, it accounts for 28 per cent of the 1.3 billion multidimensional poor.

Thus, human development in South Asia could not leap forward, yet this region has enough potential to achieve better position in terms of human development. Countries of this region are making efforts through various welfare programmes and policies to enhance the human development. For instance, in India Mahatma Gandhi National Rural Employment Guarantee Act (MGNREGA), Right to Food, Right to Education, Ayushman Bharat etc. are the initiatives taken by the government to improve the life standards of the people. Similarly, according to the World Bank[4], in Bangladesh, safety net programmes have been contributing to the reduction of poverty and vulnerability by addressing a range of population groups through different forms of assistance. These include the provision of income security for the elderly, widows and persons-with-disabilities, generating temporary employment for working age and women, and supporting the healthy development of young mothers and children.

According to the Human Development Report 2019, South Asia was the fastest growing region in human development progress with 46 per cent growth during 1990-2018, followed by East Asia and the Pacific at 43 per cent. On the Human Development Index 2019, out of 189 countries, Afghanistan was ranked 170, Bangladesh 135, Bhutan 134, India 129, Maldives 104, Nepal 147, Pakistan 152, Sri Lanka 71. Similarly, in Gender Inequality Index (GII) gender bias is very much visible in the region. 17.1 per cent women held parliamentary seats whereas in Sub-Saharan Africa it is 23.5 per cent, only 39.9 per cent women have reached to at least secondary level of education as compared to 63.3 per cent of their male counterparts. In labour force participation only 25.9 per cent female are there as compared to 78.8 per cent of male. This data illustrate that despite of being the fastest growing region in the world in terms of human development, deep rooted inequalities based on social discriminations, political and economic marginalisation of women and others relatively weaker sections of the society still sabotage the realisation of human development in this region.

Conclusion

While understanding South Asia it can be said that as difference do not ensure conflict, similarities do not ensure cooperation. The region has evolved over a period of time and it has tried to shed certain historical baggages to move forward. For instance, when countries of this region saw that regional cooperation under the SAARC has not been a success they tend to develop bi-lateral trade agreement. Bi-lateral trade between India and Sri Lanka has been an example of the same. Similarly, forces of globalization have compelled South Asia to diversify its society, economy and governance. South Asian countries are making efforts to meet sustainable development goals. Poverty alleviation programmes are running in all the countries. Bhutan is a country that is guided by the Gross National Happiness philosophy. As a fastest growing region, before this Covid-19 pandemic, South Asia has enough potential to convert itself into a dynamic regional grouping. The most important aspect that needs to be addressed, in South Asia, is that countries should come out of historical wrongs that give rise to scepticism and conflicts. Lack of political will-power undermines the progress of the region. Here South Asia can learn lessons from South East Asian countries, who put their political differences at backburner to make ASEAN a success.

ENDNOTES

1. According to United Nations Population Fund (UNFPA), demographic dividend means, "the economic growth potential that can result from shifts in a population's age structure, mainly when the share of the working-age population (15 to 64) is larger than the non-working-age share of the population (14 and younger, and 65 and older)."
2. The Multidimensional Poverty Index (MPI) is published by the UNDP's Human Development Report Office and tracks deprivation across three dimensions and 10 indicators: health (child mortality, nutrition), education (years of schooling, enrolment), and living standards (water, sanitation, electricity, cooking fuel, floor, assets).
3. UNDP (December 9, 2019). Human development in Asia-Pacific region advances dramatically, but unevenly. https://www.asia-pacific.undp.org/content/rbap/en/home/presscenter/pressreleases/2019/human-development-in-asia-pacific-region-advances-dramatically--.html
4. World Bank (29 April, 2019). Social Safety Nets in Bangladesh Help Reduce Poverty and Improve Human Capital URL. https://www.worldbank.org/en/news/feature/2019/04/29/social-safety-nets-in-bangladesh-help-reduce-poverty-and-improve-human-capital

REFERENCES

Addink, Henk (2019). *Good Governance Concept and Context*. Oxford University Press: UK.

Bose, Sugata and Ayesha, Jalal (Eds.) (2018). *Modern South Asia—History, Culture, Political Economy*. London: Routledge.

Hasan, Z. (1964). SOUTH ASIA AS A REGION. *Pakistan Horizon*, 17(2), 161-167. Retrieved June 23, 2020, from www.jstor.org/stable/41392795

ILO (2018). *International labour migration statistics in South Asia*. ILO. Retrieved on June 29, 2020 from https://www.ilo.org/wcmsp5/groups/public/---asia/---ro-bangkok/---sro-new_delhi/documents/publication/wcms_645286.pdf

Lal, C.K. and Nurul Kabir (2010). *Human Rights, Democracy and Governance*. Pearson: New Delhi.

Lateef, K. Sarwar (2016). Evolution of The World Bank's Thinking on Governance. *Background Paper Governance and The Law*. Retrieved June 27, 2020, from http://pubdocs.worldbank.org/en/433301485539630301/WDR17-BP-Evolution-of-WB-Thinking-on-Governance.pdf

Mann, Michael (2015). *South Asia's Modern History—Thematic Perspectives*. Routledge: New York.

Pemberton, Kelly and Michael Nijhawan (Eds.) (2009). *Shared Idioms, Sacred Symbols, and the Articulation of Identities in South Asia*. New York: Routledge.

Thakur, Ramesh and Oddy Wiggen (Eds.) (2004). *South Asia in the world: Problem solving perspectives on security, sustainable development, and good governance*. United Nations University Press: Tokyo.

UNFPA (2019). *State of World Population Report*. UNFPA.

UNESCAP (2019). Situation Report on International Migration in South and South-West Asia. Retrieved June 29, 2020 from https://www.unescap.org/sites/default/files/SDD_PUB_Sit-Rep-book.pdf

United Nations (2019). World Economic Situation and Prospects 2019. Retrieved June 23, 2020, from https://www.un.org/development/desa/dpad/wp-content/uploads/sites/45/WESP2019_BOOK-CH3-5-south-asia-en.pdf

World Bank (1994). Governance The World Bank's Experience. World Bank. Retrieved June 27, 2020, from http://documents1.worldbank.org/curated/en/711471468765285964/pdf/multi0page.pdf

World Bank (March, 2019) Employment in South Asia: A New Dataset. Policy *Research Working Paper 8779*. Retrieved June 28, 2020, from https://openknowledge.worldbank.org/bitstream/handle/10986/31405/WPS8779.pdf?sequence=1&isAllowed=y

18
Post-Development
New Perspective in Development Discourse

Ankit Tomar

Introduction

The idea of development is one of the most hotly debated terms/issues in the 21st century and appears to be the buzzword. Different scholars have different perspectives and views about it. It should be important to acknowledge here that there are various ideas and theories which are associated with the term 'development' and since the 1950s several theories about development are given in opposition to mainstream theories of development. Therefore, to define development is not as simple as it seems to be. Perhaps it is one of those terms that is extremely difficult to define, if not impossible. The beginning of development as a project and as a Western political discourse is often attributed to "the former United States President Harry S. Truman's inaugural address in 1949" (Illich, 1990; Sachs, 2010). It was in this address that "he stated that foreign nations, particularly those that were labelled as 'underdeveloped' would require assistance in order to achieve 'industrial progress' and a raised standard of living" (Illich, 1990: 6). Even Esteva and several others in the *Development Dictionary* refer to "Truman in the 1940s as beginning of the development era" (Esteva, 1992).

The concept of development gained importance after the second half of the twentieth century. It was the time when a large number of countries in Asia and Africa gained political independence. Most of the countries in these continents were impoverished and often described as 'under-developed' or 'developing'.

In the dominant discourse of mainstream development, which has broadly followed the Washington Consensus and modernist thought, the term development was seen as a universal model, usually associated with modernization of a society, increase in economic growth of a country and so on so forth. "The mainstream discourse on development is based on modernization and the Western idea of progress, which creates a Third World made up of disadvantaged and needy populations" (Escobar, 1995). Apart from that the mainstream development has also become an industry in which certain players have long term vested interests. Therefore, the mainstream understanding of development is very problematic and it gives a rise to the idea of post-development which has not only challenged the conventional notion of development but also rejects modernity. The post-development notion of development discourse is about making development more indigenous, localize and fragmented. Furthermore, it argues for moving away from state and including more number of non-state actors like NGOs.

Arturo Escobar who is the most prominent figure in post-development discourse, in his classic post-development text, *Encountering Development*, describes how the dominant development discourse plays out. Apart from that, Escobar also argued that "to 'help' the Third World to become modern and 'progressive', the mainstream development discourse prescribes the help of the First World-countries whose model of development is based on modernity and progress and have the power and knowledge to 'help' the "Third World" (Escobar, 1995). From the post-development perspective, the mainstream thinking of development is an ethnocentric way to look at the world's inequalities, and therefore, development practice based on this discourse only makes the inequalities more pronounced rather than alleviating them.

Escobar in this work also makes a case for 'alternatives to development' which abandon 'the whole epistemological and political field of postwar development'(*Ibid.,* 675). "The alternatives to development offer:

(1) a critical stance with respect to established scientific discourse and ... a rejection of the ethnocentric, patriarchal, and ecocidal character of development models;
(2) a defence of pluralistic grassroots movements, in the belief that these movements, and 'new social movements' in general may be providing a new basis for transforming the structures and discourses of the modern developmentalist states in the Third World; and
(3) a conviction that we must work toward a relation between truth and reality different from that which has characterized Western modernity in general and development in particular *(Ibid.)*.

> Escobar argues that 'development has functioned as a mechanism of power for the production and management of the Third World ... through the systematic elaboration of forms of knowledge concerning all aspects of importance in the life of Third World societies, and through the creation of corresponding fields of intervention...'(*Ibid.*, 676)."

Different Conceptions of Development

The concept of development has undergone many changes over the years. We can understand the term development in its both broader and narrower sense. In the broadest sense of the term, development conveys the ideas of improvement, progress, well-being and an aspiration for a better life. However, the term development is also often used in a narrower sense to refer to more limited goals such as increasing rate of economic growth, or modernizing a society.

Development has become subject of considerable controversy today. The models of development which have been adopted in different countries have become the subject of debate and criticism and alternative models have been put forward. In the initial years, the focus was on catching up with the West in terms of economic growth and modernization of societies that ignores diverse historical currents. According to Escobar, "the problem with mainstream 'development' is that it is external, based on the model of the industrialized world, and what is needed instead are 'more endogenous' discourses" to development (Escobar, 1992: 411).

In the conventional sense development was understood as a top-down ethnocentric, and technocratic approach, which treat people and cultures as abstract concepts. Mainstream notion of development was "conceived not as a cultural process but instead a system of more or less universally applicable technical interventions intended to deliver some 'badly needed' goods to a 'target' population. It comes to no surprise that development became a force so destructive to Third World cultures, ironically in the name of people's interests" (Escobar, 1995: 44). Therefore, the idea of post-development becomes very important as it denounces the Eurocentric view of development and explores the possibilities outside modern (Western) 'development' paradigm.

Emergence of Post-Development

Post-development has its roots in post-modern critique of modernity and has been greatly influenced by the work of Michel Foucault. The emergence of post-development lies in many factors. "It is the result of widespread disillusionment with conventional development and development failure" (Schuurman, 1993b).

Post-development articulates dissatisfaction with the concept and practice of 'Development' that "lead not to the search for alternative versions of it, but to dismissing it altogether and calling for alternatives to development" (Esteva, 1992; Escobar, 1995; Rahnema, 1997). Drawing on the work of Foucault, post-development portrays development as a monolithic and hegemonic discourse that constructs rather than solves the problems it purports to address.

"The idea of moving 'beyond development' may seem unduly radical and unrealistic when contrasted with a well-established and accepted modernist worldview that has long since informed and justified powerful economic and political interests in the pursuit of Development" (Andreasson, 2010: 88). Post-development thinkers not only make a claim about the fundamental problems with the mainstream 'Development' but also suggest the alternative ways to think on it.

Defining Post-Development

The term Post-Development denotes a school of thought in development theory which is fundamentally critical of the very idea of 'development' and promotes alternative ways of thinking and acting beyond this idea. In the words of Jan Nederveen Pieterse, Post-development, "is the most recent radical reaction to the problems or dilemmas of post-war development efforts". Within the new discourse of development, there are new actors playing a role that has become central to the concept of development, they are new social movements, NGOs, various development agencies etc. In the present time then the discourse of development seems to be following two paths. First is that the development discourse has gone outside the realm of state. Secondly, there has been a rejection of conventional paradigm of development and pursuing alternative agenda.

Post-development (PD) was inspired by Ivan Illich and is usually linked to the works of Gustavo Esteva (1987), Wolfgang Sachs (1992), Arturo Escobar (1995) and Majid Rahnema (1997). Sometimes, Vandana Shiva (1989), Gilbert Rist (1997), Serge Latouche (1993) and others are also seen as part of Post-development discourse. Their central aim was to expose 'development' as an ideology originating in the Cold War and thus to pave the way for alternatives. According to Escobar, following are the characteristics of Post-development:

(a) "the interest in alternatives to development, not the interest of alternative development.
(b) a fundamental rejection of the classical development paradigm.
(c) an interest in local culture and local knowledge.
(d) a critical perspective on established scientific discourses.
(e) solidarity for pluralistic grassroots movements" (Ziai, 2007: 100).

Post-development and the call for alternatives to development, assessing the role awarded to new social movements and the implications for social change. There are two most fundamental hypotheses which are put forward by post-development writers. "*Firstly*, the traditional concept of 'development' is seen as a Eurocentric construct where the West is labelled as 'developed' and the rest of the world is perceived as 'underdeveloped'. This constitutes one society as the ideal norm and others as deviations of that norm. *Secondly*, it is argued that the traditional concept of development has authoritarian and technocratic implications" (Parfitt, 2002:7). Post-development writers seek to "dismiss the post-World War II concept of development by reference to its top down authoritarian form, as directed by intrusive state mechanisms and international development agencies" (Escobar, 1995; Esteva and Prakash, 1998b). In short, "along with 'anti-development' and 'beyond development', post-development is a radical reaction to the dilemmas of development" (Pieterse, 1998: 175). Post-development focuses on the underlying premises and motives of development. What sets it apart from other critical approaches is that it rejects development. "It is rejected not merely on account of its results but because of its intentions, its world-view and mindset" (Pieterse, 1998: 175-176).

This Post-structural critique of institutional development's idiom and empirical field, known as post-development theory, draws on and extends Foucault's re-conceptualization of power-knowledge formations as discourse. The essential idea of post-development theory "is to see the discourse on development articulating First World knowledge with power in the Third World" (Peet, 1997: 75). It analyzes development as a significant discourse of power, focusing on "the way in which discourses of development help shape the reality they pertain to address, and how alternative conceptions of the problem have been marked off as irrelevant" (Nustad, 2004:13). Post-development scholars apply Foucault's work on the appropriation of the mind in modern societies to the relation between North and South and argue that development produces post-colonial subjects (cf. Brigg, 2002) permeating the South as a category defined in relation to the North (Manzo, 1991) through the disciplinary and normalizing processes of the development apparatus. The idea of post-development not only denounces the mainstream, Eurocentric notion of development but it also tries to problematize the notion poverty in itself also. An important insight that runs through post-development is that poverty is not to be taken for granted. In the words of Vandana Shiva, "culturally perceived poverty need not be real material poverty: subsistence economies which serve basic needs through self-provisioning are not poor in the sense of being deprived. Yet the ideology of development declares them so because they do not participate overwhelmingly in the market economy, and do not consume commodities provided for and distributed through the market" (Shiva, 1988b: 10).

Post-development takes development as a discourse. According to Escobar, the "discourse of Development, like the Orientalism analyzed by Edward Said, has been a mechanism for the production and management of the Third World... organizing the production of truth about the Third World" (Escobar, 1992b: 413-414). A standard Escobar quote is: "development can best be described as an apparatus that links forms of knowledge about the Third World with the deployment of forms of power and intervention, resulting in the mapping and production of Third World societies" (Escobar, 1996: 213).

Alternatives to Development

Many concerns of post-development are not new, they are shared by other critical approaches to development also. Though post-development share a concern of dependency theory in terms of seeking autonomy from external dependency, but it is not limited only to this rather, it goes further as a power-knowledge regime also. While dependency thinking privileges the nation-state, post-development, like alternative development, privileges local and grassroots autonomy. Post-development is different from alternative development. On the one hand, alternative development belief in redefining, reformulating of a development, whereas on the other hand, post-development seeks for alternatives to development not for alternative development. Escobar who is a prominent post-development scholar is 'not interested in development alternatives, but rather in alternatives to Development'. From post-structuralist perspective, alternative development is rejected because "most of the efforts are also products of the same worldview which has produced the mainstream concept of science, liberation and development" (Nandy, 1989: 270).

The work of Foucault are useful for understanding the operation of power in the post-war development project, and for comprehending how power operates through the World Bank. In this way a critical engagement with post-development can improve our understanding and analysis of development. This chapter offers a closer engagement with Foucault's conceptualization of power as one way of advancing post-development. As Foucault's work has inspired much post-development writing, this is an obvious starting point, albeit one which deserves to be complemented with engagements with indigenous knowledge and other scholarship.

Through its post-structural critique of development, post-development provides a fundamental dismissal of institutional development. According to Arturo Escobar, the deconstruction of development gave rise to post-development. Deconstruction (also deconstruct, deconstructionism, deconstructionist) refers to Jacques Derrida's philosophical methodology which prescribes "the process of breaking down conventionally accepted concepts, categories, and oppositions". More specifically, deconstruction in this chapter critiques the received essence, or what is perceived as natural and normal by the mainstream, of categories, concepts or oppositions.

According to Jakimow, "the 1990s saw the emergence of post-development in response to the failing development industry. This new school of thought was inspired by post-modernist thinking and called for an abandonment of the modernization-as-development paradigm" (Jakimow, 2008). Post-modernism and post-development are both schools of thought that have completely rejected certain aspects of modernism (Muller, 2006). Therefore, one could state that post-development is a school of thought under the umbrella of post-modernism. Post-development critiques modernism as a development model, or modernization-as-development. According to Escobar, "modernization-as-development is legitimated and justified by the idea that knowledge, as we sterner define it, is objective and above those that are in need of developing" (Escobar, 1995).

In critiquing development, post-development thinkers deconstruct development while focusing on the role of power and knowledge in modern development (Müller, 2006). Post-development theorists have declared development obsolete and bankrupt and have called for 'alternatives to development'. As pointed out by Nederveen Pieterse, post-development theory can be distinguished from other critical approaches to development (such as dependency theory, 'alternative development' theory and 'human development') by its insistence that development be rejected entirely, rather than better implemented or altered in specific ways (Pieterse, 2000: 176).

Post-development theorists reject the PWWII development project, rather than development. It could, indeed, be said that they feel that the PWWII development project has not brought about development! Thus, the call for an 'end to development' and 'alternatives to development' is a rejection of the post-World War II attempts to engineer particular changes in the so-called 'Third World' in order to bring about a situation deemed by various development theorists.

Post-Colonial and Post-Structuralist Approach to Development

Both post-colonial and post-structuralist approaches to development are the offshoots of modernity. On the one hand, post-colonial approach to development is a reaction to imperial Europe's colonial practices, while the post-structuralist approach to development is the result of (continuing) failures of modern (industrial economic) development to solve the problems of poverty, inequality and injustice everywhere.

Post-colonialism literally means 'after-colonialism' or 'after independence'. However, according to Radcliffe definition it, refers to "... ways of criticizing the material and discursive legacies of colonialism" (Radcliffe in McEwan, 2008: 124). In this way post-colonial approach challenges the very meaning of mainstream (modern) development discourse. The following is a brief compilation of ideas espoused by post-colonialism:

- integrate indigenous knowledge system;
- criticize destructive modernization and imperialism;
- challenge single-path homogenizing development;
- influenced by Marxist socio-political and economic analyses (e.g. exploitation, class struggles, centre periphery power relations);
- supports diversity of views and priorities (including non-Western views of feminism);
- belief in power relations dynamic; and
- attempts to overcome inequality for non-Western people by linking North-South through fair-trade.

If post-colonialism is a reaction to imperial Europe's colonial practices expressed through its anti-colonial discourses than post-structuralism is a rejection against the hegemony of modern (Western) 'development' concept and practice.

Concluding Remarks

To conclude it can be argued that post-development is the phase which can be understood through different approaches for example post-colonialism, post-structuralism etc. Apart from that this chapter has also made several arguments related with the issue of development. For instance, the idea of development has become one of the important variables or a factor in today's globalized world which impacts on international political economy in so many ways. In this chapter, it has been argued that the notion of development has changed within the paradigm of post-development which challenges the conventional notion of development based on the materialistic conception of development and makes a case for the new ways for thinking about development discourse in terms of post-development which can provide better understanding of development. Furthermore, it has been also illustrated in this chapter that how the idea of development is very much related with power, domination and therefore, a means of controlling others. Besides that, it is also important to note down here that this chapter does not have aim to downsize development *per se*, instead it tries to highlight the potentials of development for empowerment of some societies or states on the cost of others.

REFERENCES

Dasgupta, S. (1985), *Towards a Post-Development Era*, London: Mittal.

Escobar, A. (1985), "Discourse and power in development: Michel Foucault and the relevance of his work to the Third World", *Alternatives*, *10*: 377-400.

Escobar, A. (1991), "Anthropology and the development encounter: the making and marketing of development anthropology", *American Ethnologist, 18* (4): 658-682.

Escobar, A. (1992), "Reflections on 'Development': grassroots approaches and alternative politics in the Third World", *Futures*, *24*: 411-436.

Escobar, A. (1995), *Encountering Development: The Making and Unmaking of the Third World*, NJ: Princeton University Press.

Escobar, A. (1996), "Imagining a post-development era", in: J. Crush (ed.), *The Power of Development*, London: Routledge.

Esteva, G. (1992), "Development", in W. Sachs (ed.), *The Development Dictionary*, London: Zed.

Friedmann, John (1992), *Empowerment: The Politics of Alternative Development*, Oxford: Blackwell.

Kothari, R. (1988), *Rethinking Development: In Search of Humane Alternatives*, Delhi: Ajanta.

Nederveen Pieterse, J. (1991), "Dilemmas of development discourse: the crisis of developmentalism and the comparative method", *Development and Change*, *22* (1), pp. 5-29.

Nederveen Pieterse, J. (1998), "My paradigm or yours? Alternative development, post-development, reflexive development", *Development and Change*, *29* (2), pp. 343-373.

Nederveen Pieterse, J. (2000), "After Post-Development", *Third World Quarterly* *20* (1), 175-191.

Rahnema, M. (1997), "Towards post-development: searching for signposts, a new language and new paradigm", in: Rahnema & Bawtree (eds.), *The Post-Development Reader*, pp. 377-404.

Rahnema, M. and Bawtree, V. (eds.) (1997), *The Post-Development Reader*, London: Zed.

Rist, G. (1990a), "Development as the new religion of the West", *Quid Pro Quo*, *1* (2), pp. 5-8.

Sachs, W. (ed.) (1992), *The Development Dictionary: A Guide to Knowledge as Power*, London, Zed.

Shiva, V. (1988b), *Staying Alive: Women, Ecology and Development*, London: Zed.

19

Enigma of Modernity

Emerging Threats for the Lives beyond Developmentality

Deepika Handa

Introduction

In contemporary times, over the years the Model of Development adopted by the developing countries like India after Independence come under a great deal of criticism, that led us to rethinking about the goals and processes of development in contemporary times. The period of last 200 years of colonialism and imperialism, greatly influenced the nature and character of our priorities of development. The Rapid Industrial growth and development of the Western countries became an Ideal Reference point for most of the Newly Independent countries of Asia and Africa. But now the critics of this so-called Eurocentric Model of development pointed out that this kind of development model proved very costly in terms of Social, Economic and Political Implications. A large number of people have been displaced from their homes and localities because of the construction of Big Dams, Industrial Activities and Mining Projects, that led to the loss of livelihood and increased impoverishment, therefore, this whole process now led us to the debate over the politics of the present development process and its Implications on the Social, Economic, Political and Ecological Aspects of our Society.

Here we have to understand that the discourse of modern development and modernization has been influenced by the monolithic vision of capitalist and industrialist growth. The agenda of colonialism and global capitalism in the present scenario have changed their face and global power structure now uses the phrase like modernization and development to impose its hidden materialistic agenda on Third World countries. The coloniality of power and knowledge in the contemporary times rested upon multiple "creative destructions", often carried out on behalf of "civilizing", liberating, or emancipatory projects, which aimed at reducing the understandings of the world to the logic of Western epistemology. Examples of this were the conversion of the knowledge's of colonized peoples and of the diversity of their cultures and cosmologies to expressions of irrationality, of superstition, or, at best, to practical and local forms of knowledge whose relevance was dependent on their subordination to modem science, perceived as the sole source of true knowledge (De Sousa Santos: 2007). In this discourse of the analysis of the impact of coloniality of power and knowledge Bonaventura De Sousa very significantly pointed out that:

> While the political dimension of colonial intervention has been widely criticized, the burden of the colonial epistemic monoculture is still accepted now-a-days as a symbol of development and modernity. The production of the West as hegemonic knowledge required the creation of another, constituted as an intrinsically disqualified being, a collection of characteristics that were markers of inferiority towards the power and knowledge of the West and, thus, available for use and appropriation by the latter. Colonial alterity as a space of inferiority took various shapes that reconfigured the already existing processes of manufacturing inferiority, based on sex, race, or tradition (*Ibid.*). As a result, three resilient subaltern figures are still with us: the woman, the savage, and nature (De Sousa Santos, 2007: xxv).

In the 1950s and 1960s, theorists of development saw indigenous and traditional knowledge as inefficient, inferior, and an obstacle to development. Current formulations about indigenous knowledge, however, recognize that derogatory characterizations of the knowledge of the poor and the marginalized populations may be hasty and naive. In reaction to Modernization Theorists and Marxists, advocates of indigenous knowledge underscore the promise it holds for agricultural production systems and sustainable development.

Apart from that this whole process of modern development has also severely transformed the nature into an unconditionally available natural resource. The modern model of development is deeply structured and influenced by the Judaeo-Christian belief and the modern reductionist science and technology which see the nature and environment as a commercial object that want to conquest and create mastery over nature. Nature, turned into a resource, has no logic but that of being exploited to its exhaustion. Once nature is separated from human beings and from society, there is no way of conceiving of how they feed back into each other. This concealment prevents the formulation of balances and of limits, and that is why ecology can assert itself only through ecological crisis. This construction of nature as external to society and as a resource—something alien to the peoples the Europeans came in contact with—was one of the core foundations of the capitalistic civilizational model. It followed the requirements of the constitution of the new world economic system based on the intensive exploitation of resources (*Ibid.*).

The modern development and its drive to attain mastery over nature and transform it into a raw material for limitless industrial production required the destruction of nature as commons—that is, something all have access to and responsibility for. The destruction of the commons was essential for the creation of natural resources as a supply of raw materials for industry. A life support base can be shared; it cannot be owned as private property or exploited for private profit. The commons, therefore, had to be privatized, and people's sustenance base in the commons had to be appropriated for feeding the engine of industrial progress and capital accumulation (Shiva, 2010). The treatment of nature as a resource which acquires value only in exploitation for economic growth has been central to the project of development. It is also central to the development crisis. Philosophically, the desacralization of nature entailed the violation of nature's integrity by violating the limits which had to be maintained for the resurgence and renewal of nature's life (*Ibid.*).

So, in this scenario what we have seen is that after the evolution of modern commercial capitalism, the natural biodiversity now transformed into an industrial raw material for the rising industries, which was earlier the natural capital of the two-thirds of humanity that depended on biodiversity as its means of Food, Fisheries, healthcare and crafts. The various components of wild biodiversity now began to be seen as a 'Raw Material' for global capitalist and corporate groups. The present modern commercial age has induced the kind of development process which not only exploited environment, ecology and nature but also limited it as a source of natural resources which can be used limitlessly to gain maximum commercial profit in emerging consumer society (Kothari, 1997: viii). This issue is not simply about the use and abuse of natural biodiversity for commercial purposes but also significantly related with the discourse of modern model of development based on capitalist modernity.

This discourse helps us to understand that how the complex interaction and linkages of power and knowledge not only create hierarchy between different knowledge systems but also transform the inherent nature of various indigenous local knowledge traditions in order to fulfil the commercial concerns of the contemporary capital oriented market economy. This process directly impacts not only balance of nature but also transform the human-nature relationship in a manner that threatens the sustainability of natural resources as well as diverse ways of cultures and living traditions which depends on local ecosystem for their livelihood and identity. The debates related with politics of knowledge now-a-days clearly points out that how from time immemorial the various diverse indigenous local traditions of knowledge have a coherence and logic of their own, that they constitute effective system of production and consumption which maintain ecological harmony while ensuring the social and cultural cohesion of the group. But the modern development discourse based on the sense of superiority of the modern science largely neglected the cultural and social dimensions of these societies, which resulted in the destruction and marginalisation of indigenous forms of culture and social life as well as balance of nature (Marglin, 1990: 24). In this scenario, Vandana Shiva has very relevantly pointed out that how:

> Colonialism is a constant necessary condition for capitalist growth: without colonies, capital accumulation would grind to a halt. 'Development' as capital accumulation and the commercialisation of the economy for the generation of 'surplus' and profits thus involved the reproduction not merely of a particular form of creation of wealth, but also of the associated creation of poverty and dispossession. A replication of economic development based on commercialisation of resource use for commodity production in the newly independent countries created the internal colonies. Development was thus reduced to a continuation of the process of colonisation; it became an extension of the project of wealth creation in modern Western patriarchy's economic vision, which was based on the exploitation or exclusion of women (of the West and non-West), on the exploitation and degradation of nature, and on the exploitation and erosion of other cultures. 'Development' could not but entail destruction for women, nature and subjugated cultures, which is why, throughout the Third World, women, peasants and tribals are struggling for liberation from 'development' just as they earlier struggled for liberation from colonisation (Shiva, 1998: 1-2).

India's people have traditionally recognised the dependence of human survival on the existence of forests. A systematic knowledge about plants and forest ecosystems was thus generated and informal principles of forest management formulated. It has often been stated that 'scientific' forestry and the scientific management of forest resources in India began with the British. When the British colonised India, they first colonised her forests. Ignorant of their wealth and of the wealth of knowledge of local people to sustainably manage the forests, they displaced local rights, local needs and local knowledge and reduced this primary source of life into a timber mine. Women's subsistence economy based on the forest was replaced by the commercial economy of British colonialism. Teak from Malabar was extracted for the King's Navy, and the Sal of Central India and the Conifers of the Himalaya were exploited for the railway system. Although it is always local people who are held responsible for deforestation, it is commercial demands that have more frequently resulted in large-scale forest destruction (*Ibid.*).

But, even after getting independence from British colonial regime, the Post-colonial Indian Nation State continued the legacy of colonial era and waged a war against tribal and indigenous communities in the name of modernization and development. And after the 1990s, the new economic policy of Indian state which is based on economic liberalization, privatization and globalization model of development in India is virtually depriving the tribal people and other agriculture dependent poor people of their traditional means of sustainable livelihood by promoting the unregulated growth of mineral-based industries in the tribal regions of India. In the name of modernization and the country's economic development, the elites in India are taking over the life sustaining resources of the poor and pushing them into a further marginalized state of living as a result of displacing them from their land and homes. Such development serves the interests of these elites while it impoverishes the tribal people and poor peasants in these regions who are dependent on the life sustaining resources of the ecosystems in which they live. The mining and other industries that are taking over the resources of the ecosystems of these tribal people and poor peasants fail to provide them with an improved and sustainable means of making a living. This problem has created increasing conflict between these ecosystem dependent peoples and the elites. The former is fighting to defend their traditional and sustainable forms of subsistence and the latter are intruding into the territory of these people to exploit the land, forests and minerals in their ecosystems. In the name of development and of civilizing, assimilating and mainstreaming the tribal people, the affluent elites are evicting these poor people from their homes and land (Gadgil and Guha, 1995). Mega development projects like multipurpose river dams and large-scale mining generate benefits for the few relatively better off sections of population while marginalizing and excluding the poorer tribal people.

Tribals *vs.* the Modern Environmentalism: The Concerns of the Rights of Tribals for their Livelihood and Identity

If we go deep into the history of forest management and regulation by Colonial and post-Colonial state, then we can see how as compared to pre-colonial times when the forest were in the domains of kings and their kingdoms, the local indigenous tribal people at that time were allowed to inhabit, cultivate, graze their cattle, and make livelihood out of forest resources without any restriction and imposition (Guha, 1993). But after the advent of the Colonial British Government, the tribals were looked upon as 'encroachers' on their own land, not by any formal law of land but by their historical custom. They became illegal in the eyes of those who in actuality had usurped control over the forests illegitimately, using force and power. By early 19th century, the colonial regime was controlling vast tracts of forestland (Gadgil and Guha, 1992). This development was the beginning of the suffering for the tribals in every way, especially their right to livelihoods, besides disturbing the traditional forms of conservation and management of system of forests (*Ibid.*). This was also the time when centralised forest administration or planned forest management started taking its roots in India. Between 1864 and 1865, the first attempt to legislate the Forest Act was made. The enactment of the 1878 Act gave the colonial government immense powers to declare any forest land as 'government land', resulting in reservation of forests. During this process, the tribals agitated, protested and rebelled, only to be suppressed mercilessly (Bandi, 2012).

But this Colonial Legacy to centrally control and encroach upon the forest land which was the common property of the indigenous tribals continued even in post-colonial Indian state policy. The National Forest Policy of 1952 focused on protecting forest resources with centralised control, while exploiting its resources commercially by subsidising traditional community rights and depriving the livelihoods of the forest-dependent people. Creation of national parks and wildlife sanctuaries, following the 1972 Wildlife Protection Act (WPA), the highhandedness of forest bureaucracy through the 1980 Forest Conservation Act (FCA), and the 1991 amendment to the 1972 WPA, further contributed to restricting the movements of the Forest-Dependent People (*Ibid.*).

In this context Ashish Kothari argues that how the policy and practice of Indian State on Protected Areas, National Parks and wildlife sanctuaries was largely influenced by the experience from the Western European American Model, which was primarily based on the 'closure' of natural Habitats to human population (Kothari, 1997: p. 28). The Idea and Concept of PAs (Protected Areas) is actually a urban middle class centric concept in which there is a belief that biodiversity and environment can only be protected by establishing pristine habitats untouched by the humans. But the other side of the story is very different because contrary to the conventional middle class image of PAs as pristine habitats untouched by the human hands the majority of India's PAs have human communities dependent on them for sustenance and Livelihood (*Ibid:* 27). Actually the declaration of PAs and the imposition of Regulations under the Wildlife Protection Act was almost always done without consulting with these communities, and resulted in their rights being terminated or access to basic resources being cut-off without adequate provision of alternatives (Lasgorceix and Kothari, 2009: 37-47). In this debate on PAs *versus* Tribal Rights, Pankaj Sekhsaria has very relevantly argued that the issues question and debates about tribals and conservation are subsumed by the overwhelming belief in the priority of a particular type of Development paradigm in which forest and biodiversity is reduced to commercial concerns and needs of Industrialisation and in order to achieve this goal this paradigm has severely sidelined the issues of tribal rights and their traditional livelihood (Sekhsaria, 2007: 575-577). Thus, it is clearly indicative in this area that policy and politics of the state has largely been driven by the modern worldview in which biodiversity is seen as separate from the human intervention and treated as pristine. The state and its policy has largely failed to identify the fact that the natural resources are meant to be used, and the beauty of human interaction lies in restraint and limits rather than absence (Banerjee, 1998).

The dispossession of the local people of their rights, their resources and their knowledge has not gone unchallenged. Forest struggles have been taking place throughout the country for over two centuries to resist the colonisation of the people's forests in India. The access and rights of the people to forests were first severely encroached upon with the introduction of the Forest Acts of 1878 and 1927. The following years witnessed the spread of forest *satyagrahas* throughout India, as a protest against the reservation of forests for exclusive exploitation by British commercial interest, and their concomitant transformation from a common resource into a commodity. Villagers ceremonially removed forest products from the reserved forests to assert their right to satisfy their basic needs. The forest *satyagrahas* were especially successful in regions where survival of the local population was intimately linked with access to the forests, as in the Himalaya, the Western Ghats, and the Central Indian hills. This struggle was also continued during post-Colonial period by the ecosystem dependent people through the politics of various New Social movements. Due to these struggles Forest policy has undergone pronounced change over the last 30 years. The 1980s witnessed the rise of community forestry, which sought to look first at community needs and then design a local forest programme around them. Ideally, the locals began to be included in all phases of project design, with technical help from professional foresters. In many countries, community forestry coincided with efforts—domestic or external in origin—to decentralize and downsize governments.

Conclusion

At the end by analysing the above argument and theoretical discourses what we have understood is that the question and debates about tribals and conservations of bio-diversity and forest are subsumed by the overwhelming belief in the priority of a particular type of development paradigm in which forest and bio-diversity is reduced to commercial concerns and needs of industrialization. In order to achieve this goal, this paradigm has severely sidelined the issues of tribal rights and their traditional livelihood. But, the dispossession of the local people of their rights, their resources and their knowledge has not gone unchallenged. Forest struggles have been taking place throughout the country for over two centuries to resist the colonization and control on the people's forests in India. And now we have seen that the marginalized tribal indigenous people of India have achieved a milestone success through their political mobilization and struggle in the form of Forest Right Act of 2006. The Scheduled Tribes and Other Traditional Forest Dwellers (Recognition of Forest Rights) Act, 2006, popularly known as the Forests Rights Act (FRA), was enacted in 2007 through the Ministry of Tribal Affairs (MoTA) to correct the 'historic injustice done to forest-dwelling communities'. The Act (interchangeably used for FRA henceforth in the text) gives individual property rights to the tribals and other forest dwellers on the forest lands under their occupation for cultivation and dwelling rights to manage them, and the total ownership rights on Non-Timber Forest Produce

(NTFP)/Minor Forest Produce (MFP), alongside community rights. The significance of this Act is that all these rights would also be applicable in protected areas (sanctuaries and national parks).

The Preamble of the FRA says the Act aims at strengthening the conservation regime of forests. But there are many other Acts directly or indirectly linked to conservation. The most important of them is the Indian Wildlife Act, 1972. This Act supports preservation of forest land with a well-defined objective, namely, preserving wild flora and fauna for protecting biodiversity. The basic constraint to implementing the Act is a lack of coordination between government departments, because each department tries to take a "stand" that is based on its original mandate and objectives of the department and "set of rules" in a given action arena. For example, the Forest Department considers the implementation issue as a continuation of the Forest Conservation Policy 1988, while it is a tribal welfare issue for the department of tribal affairs. The local bodies and survey department perceive their role mainly as a facilitator. Although the Gram Sabhas are the most empowered authority in the implementation process, they seem to wait for directions from the higher authorities. Due to various biophysical and community related factors, the process of implementation got delayed and the signs are that it may drag on in future also. The reasons for this slow-down can be attributed to unawareness of tribal community regarding the provisions of the Act and their inability to articulate their rights. Community rights and conservation duty provisions seem to be completely ignored in the process of implementation of FRA. There has been a growing realisation that without the active participation of the forest dwellers (particularly, forest dwelling STs and other traditional communities), it will be extremely difficult to achieve the main objective of biodiversity conservation. The need of the hour now significantly calls for the active Political Mobilization and participation of tribals and indigenous communities through various social movements so that not only the real benefits of the FRA reach to the tribal communities but the drawbacks and limits of this Act can also be addressed.

Lastly, it is important to mention that the two contrasting perspectives—modern development based on accumulation and appropriation of natural wealth, and the other social community-oriented development paradigm—are still not a settled debate. Although the Forest Right Act, 2006 has provided some important reliefs to the poor tribal, its glaring loopholes continue to pester these ignorant and uneducated tribals. In the light of above discussions, it is important to engage these people with their centuries old local knowledge system of conservation of forests and their resources. In other words, a participatory model of development would not only ensure tribal's democratic rights of ownership of these resources but it will also turn the unequal modern development discourse away from the West-centric to the people-centric development discourse where the hierarchy of knowledge and privileging a particular way of life would be done away with. In short, this chapter argues not only the need of democratic struggles for realizing these rights but also creating an alternative people-centric development model.

REFERENCES

De Sousa Santos, Boaventura, Joao Arriscado Nunes and Maria Paula Meneses. (2007). *Introduction in Another Knowledge is Possible—Beyond Northern Epistemologies*, edited by Boaventura de Sousa Santos. xix-lxii. London: Verso Books.

Kothari, Ashish. (1997) *Understanding Biodiversity: Life, Sustainability and Equity*. Orient Longman.

Lasgorceix, Antoine and Ashish Kothari. (2009). "Displacement and relocation of protected areas: A synthesis and analysis of case studies". *Economic and Political Weekly.*

Marglin A., Stephen. (1990). "Towards the Decolonization of the Mind" in *Dominating Knowledge—Development, Culture and Resistance,* Edited by S.A. Marglin and F.A. Marglin. 1-28. Oxford: Clarendon Press.

Banerjee, Madhulika. (1998). "The Long Road to Khari Baoli: Environment and the Market for Medicinal Plants." Paper presented at the 7th Annual Conference of the IASCP.

Guha, Ramchandra. (1983). "Forestry in British and Post-British India: A Historical Analysis", *Economic and Political Weekly*, Vol. 18, No. 44, pp. 1882-1896

Gadgil, M. and R., Guha. (1992). *This Fissured Land: An Ecological History of India*, Oxford University Press, Delhi.

Bandi, Madhusudan. (2012). Implementation of Forest Rights Act: Undoing the Historical Injustices?, *Working Paper No. 117*, Research Unit for livelihoods and Natural Resources, Centre for Economic and Social Studies: Hyderabad.

Sekhsaria, Pankaj. (2007). "Conservation in India and the Need to Think Beyond Tiger *vs*. Tribal." The Association of Tropical Biology and Conservation.

Shiva, Vandana. (2010). *Resources in the Development Dictionary: A Guide to Knowledge as Power*. Edited by Wolfgang Sachs. 228-242. London: Zed Books.

Shiva, Vandana. (1998). *Staying Alive: Women, Ecology and Survival in India.* Zed Books.

20
Participation of Non-Governmental Organisations in the Social Development
An Analytical Study of Nepal

Ajulka Saxena

Introduction

Nepal is a landlock central Himalayan country in South Asia. Nepal was a monarchy in which the king was sovereign and had entire powers of the state. Nepal suffered tyranny of the monarch since the Shah period. The Ranas turned it into hell for the people. The alienation of people of Nepal created by the Ranas led them separated from rest of the world. The first and second Mass movements of Nepal created the path for democratic republic state and the sole survivor as a Hindu monarch which was the Himalayan kingdom of Nepal since September 25th, 1768 got ended on May 28th, 2008. Nepal has never been brought into the British colonial rule. There have always been political instabilities in Nepal because of change of rule from monarchy to democracy and democracy to monarchy. The monarch was always confined to itself instead of thinking about citizens and taking care of them by making developmental policies by which the citizens could be able to attach themselves with the rest of the world through the path of progress and development. In Nepal, the natural calamities which occurred there, destroyed the economy and the poor people completely. Hence, there was a great need for a civil society to raise its voice in favour of the common people. This entire scenario paved the way in the construction of civil society. Later on, civil society, self-help groups and liberalization paved the way for the emergence of mushrooming of NGOs serving for different sectors.

Objectives

This study attempts to address the following key research objectives:

- To assess the role of NGOs in social development in Nepalese society.
- To study the factors responsible for the genesis and mushrooming of NGOs in Nepal.
- To find out the relevant data regarding working of NGOs and their local and foreign funding.
- To reveal out the impact of works dispensed by NGOs in Nepal.
- To investigate the relationship between the government and NGOs in Nepal in special reference to the Social Welfare Council.

Methodology and Literature

Both Qualitative and Quantitative methods have been brought to use for this study. I have conducted the study upon the NGOs of Nepal through a direct visit to the desired NGOs of Nepal for primary data collection. Hence, the method of data collection has been primary and secondary both. The primary data has been collected through going to various national NGOs, their main offices in Kathmandu and other branches in other areas of Nepal, their projects, their annual reports and activities in different sectors. Also, rehabilitation centres, reformatories and areas where their projects have been executed. In order to find out the relationship between the government and NGOs and their monitoring, the Social Welfare Council and the District Administrative office have also been visited.

The secondary data collected from various sources like, books, articles from various national, South Asian and international journals, different government websites, the World Bank website etc. Only four national NGOs which are registered in the Social Welfare Council of Nepal have been observed and studied. Statistics and data charts regarding different sectors in which NGOs work have been given from the Social Welfare Council of Nepal.

Genesis of Civil Society in Nepal

Discussing civil society in Nepalese context, it is worthwhile to mention that the extant notion of civil society in Nepal is a fairly one. The contemporary revival of this idea of civil society owes much to the series of political movements and struggle for democracy in country. In Nepal, the contemporary civil society emerged from oppositional politics. The Shah dynasty created grounds for a monarch which did not give rights to its people instead made an ally with the British when India was a colony after being defeated by the latter. This very scenario led the British have lots of legitimate rights over Nepali territory through the treaty of Sugauli, 1816. The Monarch became absolute with the emergence of the Ranas who ruled till 2008.

The Ranas separated Nepali people from rest of the world but could not stop them of knowing the cultural and political movements in other parts of the world especially in India. Many political, cultural, social, economic and educational organisations were made to help people during black days. During the time of absolute monarchy, Nepali citizens created some civil society groups and self-help groups to help one another. But with the extension of Ranas' tyranny over people, a strong civil society emerged parallelly. "*Discussing civil society in Nepalese context, it is worthwhile to mention that the extant notion of civil society in Nepal is a fairly one. The contemporary revival of this idea of civil society owes much to the series of political movements and struggle for democracy in country.*"

The hereditary post of the Prime Minister and suspension of fundamental rights repelled people completely. The decade of 1980s brought liberal policies introduced in Nepal through which many civil society groups and self-help groups turned into NGOs. Also, since 1990, Nepal had been facing political instability, the civil war, the quest for people's rule, the utmost poverty, violation of human rights gave genesis to the civil society which includes self-help public and private groups, NGOs in particular. Hence, a huge movement stood up to retaliate the monarch in 1996 known as the I Mass Movement. This movement showed the true colours of democracy to Nepali citizens. Although, the movement could not last long because of having no experience of democracy. The Rana ruler again stood up and vested all the powers into him led the II Mass Movement which became decisive to root out the Ranas and establish democracy. And Nepal became a democratic republic after 250 years of slavery under the Monarch. This entire movement had the inclusion of various civil society groups, NGOs and INGOs, citizens, Communist Party of Nepal and other influential political leaders. The movement, therefore, assumed the test of fostering democratic rights of the people and the creation of a responsible government. The legitimacy of the Nepalese state, therefore, rests on its embeddedness in society which can "*either cede a measure of its autonomy to the state through voluntary consent, or withhold it, thus denying it any sense of legal or moral standing*" (Fox, 1995: 6). A new constitution had come into force to decide Nepali citizens' future. Though there are still instabilities in the politics of Nepal but NGOs and other civil society groups have been made the development partners of the government in order to develop Nepal. Panday says, "We find that the civil society has to contribute even in empowering the state in the interest of social transformation, if by empowerment we can mean building the capacity and legitimacy of the state to address the issues of social concern" (Panday, 1999:131). In reference to the civil society, there are still a lot of social problems, political crisis and economic scarcity lying in Nepal. Now the main work of civil society is to keep an eye upon the government and make Nepal subtle and stable from all aspects.

Emergence and Expansion of NGOs in Nepal

A non-governmental organization (NGO) is a social organization motivated to work in sectors like religion, socio-cultural, economic, educational, environment, women, children etc. irrespective of any political ideology and belief. It is a non-profit social institution established formally after registering at the Chief District Officer's office and affiliated with the Social Welfare Council (SWC) of Nepal to work for the socially and economically backward people. In the Panchayat Regime, the Social Welfare Council was known as the Social Services National Coordination Council which had a tight control, regulation and supervision on the political and the social participation of NGOs by the Queen who was the chairperson. The presence of International NGOs was also regulated by the Royal Palace. During this period, it was illegal for anyone to engage in the development activities in Nepal without the government's permission. I found NGOs got genesis in Nepal at the time of British rule to serve the people. There was only one NGO in 1927. Under the Panchayat Regime, there were only 4 NGOs in 1951. The number of NGOs grew slowly to 10 in 1960. During 1977-78, only 17 NGOs were registered in the then founded SSNCC [Social Service National Coordination Council] which increased to 37 in 1987. Only a few large NGOs, such as the Nepal Red Cross Society and the Nepal's Children Organization had country-wide network and the rest remained at the local level with small coverage. But the mushrooming of NGOs started from 1987 onwards when Nepal started facing the frequent social and political transition. In 1990, there were 220 NGOs. In 1991-92, the number of NGOs increased from 393 to 1,210 in 1993. By 2006-07, the total number of NGOs registered with the SWC reached 24,804. The number of non-governmental organizations (NGOs) working in Nepal has grown significantly since the 1990s due to a range of factors. A total of 39,759 NGOs and 189 international non-governmental organizations were registered in Nepal between 1977 and 2014 and 39,763 [which is sector-wise yet not updated at SWC] in 2015 in various sectors, including health, agriculture, poverty alleviation, and good governance. Despite thousands of NGOs and significant amounts of foreign aid, Nepal remains one of the poorest countries in South Asia. The case of Nepal indicates that aid and donor support alone are insufficient for sustained development.

Nepal as a low-income country, has weak governance; poor resources and high unemployment. There are inadequate national budgets to support universal health and education coverage and rely on the support of private organizations. Hence, Nepal has become fertile land for the growth of NGOs. Here, NGOs implement programmes providing various services (for example, healthcare, education, microfinance, agricultural products, livelihood activities) or work as an advocate for empowerment, community participation, and democracy (for example gender equality, right-based approach, marginalization issues). The rapid increase in the number might have been favoured by the restoration of a multi-party democracy in 1990 from the one-party Panchayat government in Nepal. The political ideology of a country needs to favour the functioning of NGOs, if they are to flourish. An NGO needs to be registered at the District Administration Office with necessary information that includes name and address, objectives of the organization, source of funding, and names of any management committee members. The organization needs to be affiliated with the Social Welfare Council of the Government of Nepal, and its programme and any foreign aid needs the approval of the Council.

Reasons of Rise of NGOs

The liberal policies implemented by the World Bank in the Third World countries have led the latter encourage and implement privatization. The free exchange of trade and globalization have paved the way to create an international trade in which the foreign and international agencies establish their firms in different countries for economic boost up. But this has given them a right to interfere in the internal politics of the very country which is a threat to its sovereignty. Also, the corrupt bureaucracy and red-tapism are also one of the reasons to create more development firms and agencies to dispose the works. It is also needed that there has to be a government which promotes NGOs and their works. These criteria have been fulfilled by the Nepali society and the government. Also, the government has been and is still unable to do all the development works and meet the necessities of Nepali society as it is still busy to get the country out of couple of centuries losses made by the monarch. Hence, it promotes NGOs and their activities in different sectors.

Position of NGOs in Nepal

NGOs' position in Nepal is very sound. There are more than one lakh NGOs working in different sectors but many of them are not registered. Presently, the registered number of NGOs is 49,265 which shows a hike of 9,506 NGOs in Nepal as registered ones, according to one of the officials *Mr. Pradeep Yadav* from the Social Welfare Council of Nepal (SWC). The site is under the process of updation. Hence, it shows 39,759 NGOs registered with the SWC. There are many NGOs in Nepal which were established at the time of emergency or a sudden need but do not get registered with the SWC and dissolved when the task was done.

Uprety cites nine types of civil society organizations working actively in Nepal. They are—

1. NGOs
2. Religious organizations
3. Trade unions
4. Social and cultural groups
5. Identity-based associations
6. Professional associations
7. Networks
8. Federations
9. Trusts

NGOs and Other Sectors Associated with Social Development

Table 20.1 shows the number of NGOs registered with Social Welfare Council between 1977 and 2014 in different sectors.

Table 20.1: No. of NGOs registered with SWC between 1977-2014

Sectors	*Number of NGOs*
AIDS and abuse control	98
Child welfare	1,149
Community and rural development	25,403
Educational development	517
Environmental protection	1,451
Handicapped and disabled	758

(Contd.)

Sectors	Number of NGOs
Health services	875
Moral development	1,146
Women services	2,967
Youth services	5,395
Total	**39,759**

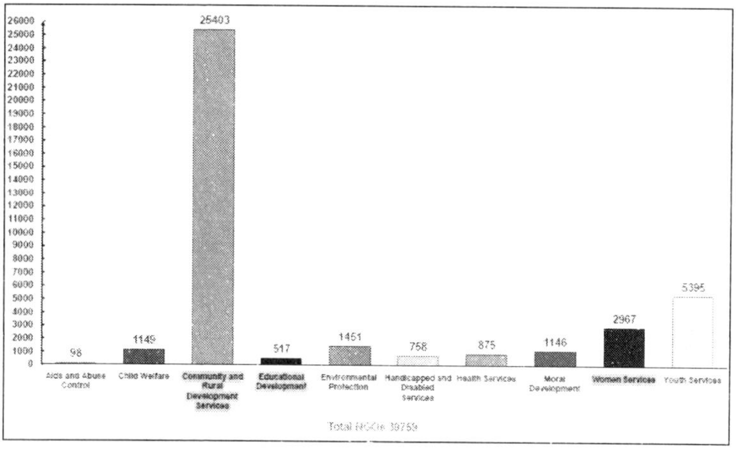

Fig. 20.1: NGOs Affiliated with SWC by Sector [2034-2071, Asadh/1978-July, 2014]
Source: The Social Council of Welfare, Nepal. www.swc.org.np

Fig. 20.2 shows NGOs affiliated with SWC, Nepal by all regions.

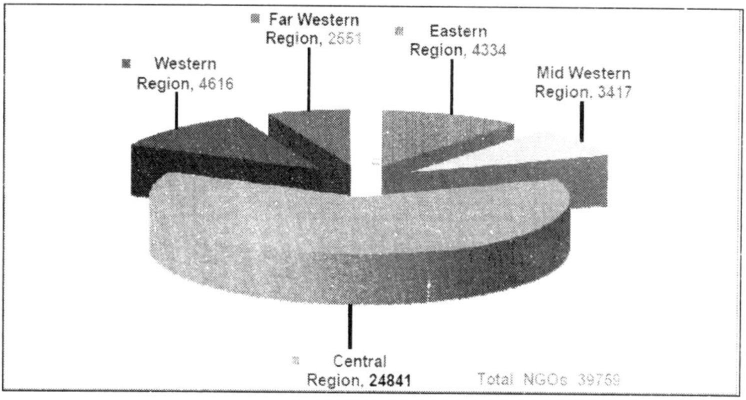

Fig. 20.2: NGOs Affiliated with SWC by Region [2034-2071, Asadh/1978-July. 2014]
Source: The Social Council of Welfare, Nepal. www.swc.org.np

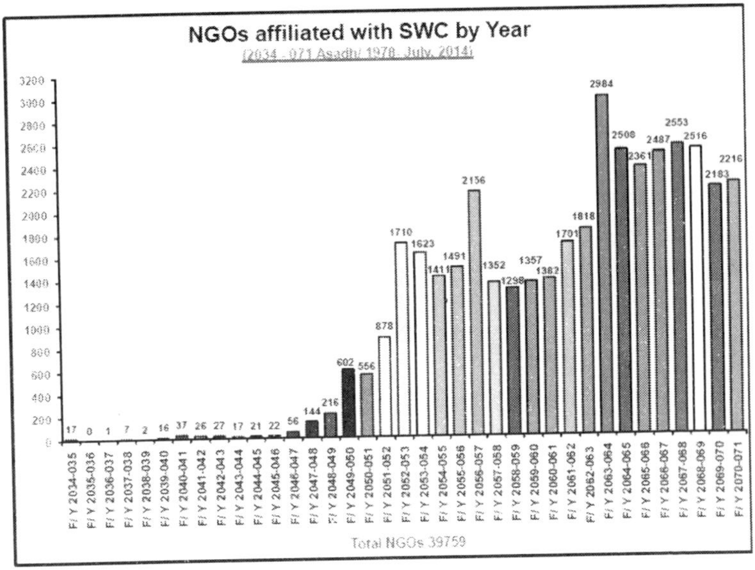

Fig. 20.3: NGOs Affiliated with SWC by Year [2034-071, Asadh/1978-July, 2014]

Source: The Social Council of Welfare, Nepal. www.swc.org.np

Fig. 20.3 shows the division of NGOs according to the five regions, Nepal is divided within and year-wise growth of NGOs registered in the SWC respectively.

The Association of Social Welfare Council of Nepal with NGOs in Nepal

The Social Welfare Council of Nepal is a national level governing body to keep account of all the registered NGOs and INGOs. The SWC being a kind of first and foremost government agency established in the South Asia which became inspiration for other South Asian countries to establish such agency in order to keep accounts of NGOs and control over them as well. The SWC keeps an eye upon working culture of NGOs, their sources of funding (foreign and local), their annual budget, their functions and their running projects. It was very first set-up by the king himself to keep control upon NGOs when there was absolute Monarchy and the king had fear to be overthrown by the increasing power of Nepali civil society and voluntary organizations. Therefore, the Social Service National Coordination Council was established to keep control over NGOs and their foreign funding sources. Mainly it kept control over activities done by NGOs. Now the work of the SWC is to keep all the NGOs, INGOs and VSOs under one shed through getting them registered in it. Having power of registration, re-registration and rejection of NGOs, it certainly influences the working culture of NGOs and monitors their activities. The administration of the SWC curtails the increasing powers of private voluntary organizations and instructs them to be within the legal fences. All the registered NGOs and INGOs have to abide by the laws and regulations set up by the SWC in order to be having legitimacy. The Social Welfare Council of Nepal is known to work under the Ministry of Women, Children and Senior Citizen for welfare of people of Nepal through leading all the registered NGOs and INGOs to the legal and transparent path in order to be socially and politically accountable. It not only gives assistance to the government but also instructs VSOs to coordinate with the government.

There are some specific works done by the Council—

1. The Council effectively conducts its functions for the social welfare and development.
2. The Council coordinates among the social welfare organizations and assists them.
3. The Council evaluates, monitors, controls and checks the functions, funding and budgets of the registered NGOs and INGOs.
4. The Council helps the NGOs and INGOs in their establishment, development and expansion and makes them strong.
5. The Council works as a coordinator and mediator between the government and NGOs.
6. The Council gives its valuable advices to the Government of Nepal in the formation and execution of policies and programmes.
7. The Council establishes treasury to conduct and commence various social service programmes.
8. The Council advocates social services to be provided by different local, national and international stakeholders to Nepal. For such purpose, it encourages national and foreign investors and social service organizations to invest in the inclusive development of Nepal.
9. The Council keeps records of all the works, projects, funds and information about NGOs and INGOs.
10. It also encourages entities to research and study about the social welfare.

11. The Council conducts surveys on the projects led by NGOs in the area of their execution through the Secretary concerned with that area for revealing out the real contribution of such particular NGO.
12. The Council also holds pacts with native, foreign and international organizations and countries for the purpose of social welfare of Nepal.
13. The Council also seeks and receives financial assistance and contribution by various international agencies and countries.
14. At the time of natural disaster or any other emergency, it seeks the financial help of the various concerned countries and spends that amount systematically.
15. The Council also does verification works regarding the assets of NGOs and INGOs.
16. Through annual evaluation, inspection and audits, the Council tightly controls on the expenditure and functions of NGOs.

The District Administrative Office and the Registration Process of NGOs

The District Administrative Office is directly associated with the SWC in order to keep a watch upon the registered NGOs at the local level. It is the smallest unit of the SWC. Any NGO registered with the SWC has to get itself registered with this Office in order to get legal status and SWC's certificate. The process of re-registration is followed by all registered NGOs in order to get their licence renewed.

NGOs and the Government

Government's role is very important in the establishment of NGOs and their mushrooming. The monarch earlier did not let NGOs flourish while it established Social Service National Co-ordination Council of Nepal (SSNCC) to keep a tight watch upon the establishment and activities of NGOs. The Queen herself would preside over the authority and the SSNCC was run by the palace itself. With the establishment of democracy, liberal policies and social, political and economic instability in Nepal, NGOs got the opportunity to flourish. The countries which mediated between the monarch and the other allies of popular support let their international agencies establish in Nepal at the same time when other foreign and international agencies either established their branches in Nepal or raised immense funds to the NGOs and CSOs of Nepal. The Social Welfare Act of 1990 was implemented to re-organise the process of legal status of NGOs which later gave emergence to the Social Welfare Council of Nepal out of the SSNCC. During data collection from Nepal, the chairman of SWC mentioned NGOs being the development partners of the government. But the funds raised to NGOs became the cause of distress of the government as many cases came out regarding corruption of NGOs' representatives, their expenses and misuse of distributed funds by the foreign collaborations. The guidelines of the SWC were renewed and implemented strictly upon NGOs. Now the scenario is different as the government still finds NGOs it is development partner but on the other hand, the foreign funds raised to NGOs are given to the SWC directly which is distributed by the SWC to the concerned NGOs according to the need of their projects and activities. This very idea leads them towards more transparency and accountability towards people. Other than that, NGOs' projects and funds are audited by the concerned officer from the District Administrative Office and a team of the representatives of the fund raising foreign/international authority. Undoubtedly, NGOs have been bringing the resources to poor Nepal to settle down the basic issues and economy. They have started playing role in the political development through crucial advocacy of main rights and lobbying in favour of execution and implementation of new and existing laws.

Participation of NGOs in Social Development in Nepal

"Until 1990, international organizations and multilateral donor agencies were mainly supporting government programmes. NGOs were marginalized and the significance of NGOs in nation building was shadowed due to government policy. When the country entered in the democratic era, the role of civil society organizations began to be realized in the public arena. The government of Nepal has considered NGOs as its development partner while on other hand, people [particularly those suffering from poverty, illiteracy, poor health and other forms of socio-economic problems] are also expecting efficient roles and better services from NGOs."

The role of NGOs in social development is very crucial as most of the NGOs are associated with the social welfare and development works. NGOs are very important for their roles played in the areas of education, human resources, rural and urban development, sustainable development, economic and healthcare facility and environmental conservation. In Nepal, there are many INGOs which have played a crucial role in building the infrastructure. Foreign welfare agencies or NGOs work in collaboration with regional or national NGOs in order to fulfil the basic and special needs of the society. In Nepali society, many NGOs have been playing their role in formation of the democratization.

"In Nepal, most of developed countries' overseas development offices are present, like the World Bank, Asian Development Bank, and various international non-governmental organizations. Overseas development agencies such as the Danish Development Agency are helping the conservation of forest, training for forestry conservation, are working for the Cleaner Kathmandu Project, and much more. Bilateral donors Australia, Canada, China, Denmark, Finland, France, Germany, India, Japan, The Netherlands, Norway, Switzerland, United Kingdom, United States of America and multi-lateral donor ADB, EC, FAO, IFAD, ILO, IMF, UNICEF, UNDP, UNESCO, UNHCR, UNIDO, UNFPA, WB, WFP, WHO are all working for and helping Nepal." William writes, "They illustrate and show the evidences of global change, cultural change, and socio-economic change from various sources and encourage locals to participate and cope with the changing environment. NGOs role of advocacy for and with the Poor is the one of the major roles for global transformation" (William, 1991).

In the same series, one of the national NGOs which has been covered during the primary data collection is Maiti Nepal. It is important to mention about this particular NGO which is necessary to make this research from general to particular.

Maiti Nepal

Fig. 20.4: Logo of Maiti Nepal.

Maiti Nepal's Logo

Maiti Nepal is one of the largest national NGOs of Nepal which has been serving in the field of women and children related issues, disaster management, human trafficking and political advocacy for human rights.

It is important to notice that since 1993, this NGO has been constantly working upon the improvement of Nepali women and their rights. The Chairperson and founder of Maiti Nepal Anuradha Koirala has been awarded with CNN Hero, UN award, and many more for the role she has been playing. Also, she was appointed as the governor of the Bagmati Pradesh (Kathmandu, Nepal) from 2018 to 2019. She is the very first person from an NGO to be a governor of a Nepali province. The very issues which Maiti Nepal has been raising and trying to resolve is very acute and related to the very idea of equality, democracy and human rights. Maiti Nepal works in Nepal and India. There is a branch office of Maiti Nepal in New Delhi to collaborate with its Nepali branch and rescue team who rescue human trafficking Nepali women and girl victims from India and its borders. Also, Maiti has established its office at the international airport, Kathmandu where its representatives can coordinate and communicate with its rescue team and other welfare organizations in order to rescue victims. As Nepal has been facing a severe human rights violation through women and girl trafficking not only inside but out of the country especially India and China. It is noticed that the monarch, civil war, political, social and economic instabilities have made the condition of women and girls the worst. They are the real sufferers of Nepali society. When the government could become stable, it indulged in welfare works and development of infrastructure of the country. Urbanization was one of its main aim. Hence, gender disparity got broadened and they became highly marginalized. Meanwhile, the mushrooming of NGOs in different sectors became essential for women and girls when NGOs related to women and girls' issues were established and started working in far rural and town areas of Nepal. Issues related to women and girls were then brought into light. The decade of 1990 and 2000 are the witness of such NGOs working for human rights and social causes in different sectors parallelly. Maiti is one of them. Maiti Nepal has some very specific facilities and activities which make it a social, political and economic non-governmental organization which has been spreading awareness among the Nepali communities, rescuing girls from being trafficked, providing safe migration to those who have been trafficked once and advocating for human rights to be upheld. Being so vociferous about these serious concerns, Maiti Nepal has become a listed member of the United Nations Economic and Social Council.

There are numbers of activities done by Maiti Nepal in different sectors—

Various Programmes Run by MAITI Nepal

Names of the Programmes executed by MAITI Nepal
1. Awareness and Advocacy
2. Prevention and Protection
3. Transit Homes
4. Prosecution and Legal Counselling
5. Rescue and Re-patriation
6. Re-integration and Rehabilitation
7. Women and Rehabilitation Homes
8. Child Protection Programmes
9. Education Sponsorship

There are 13 districts where Maiti Nepal organizes its activities—

1. Kanchanpur
2. Banke
3. Nawalparsi
4. Nuwakot
5. Sunsari
6. Parsa
7. Mukwanpur
8. Kathmandu
9. Kailali
10. Rupandehi
11. Morang
12. Ilam
13. Jhapa

Maiti has its head office in Kathmandu from where it gives commands for getting its activities organized. There are number of tasks Maiti Nepal is indulged in. Maiti Nepal has an agenda of social and political aspects both as it has an entire team to work inside and outside of Nepal to rescue the women and girls from trafficking. Also, it has a team of lawyers and public prosecutors to file their cases and run the trial free of cost. Maiti has a team of trained counsellor for counselling of women and girls who go through the trauma of violence and mental and physical abuse. During the visit to Nepal, I visited a number of rehabilitation homes, hospices, transit home, half way home to evaluate the condition of girls and women. All basic facilities are provided to them. There are certain periods of their stay at rehabilitation homes. Other than that, their parents are also counselled by trained counsellor and the victims are prepared to face and fight the trial in the court. The period of their stay varies from 15 days to 3 or 6 months in the rehabilitation houses. They are made trained in art and craft or some small-scale industrial work to live their livelihood by their own. Being a social NGO, Maiti Nepal canvasses about the importance of human rights in streets, town and other far areas where awareness lacks. It has several vans and teams at different places to canvass through songs, awareness rallies, distribution of leaflets and posters. Maiti Nepal seeks support from different agencies like parliamentarians, law makers, its counterparts in India, other NGOs working in the same sector, schools and colleges.

During the year 2017-18 Maiti Nepal thoroughly worked for the human rights and could be successful in achieving new statistics regarding its activities in the area of women and girls related issues.

2017-18 Annual Report and Ground Reports of Maiti Nepal Show its Data

Cases	*Number of Cases*
Total Interception	3,919
Migrants Informed at Borders	1,57,121
Victims Rescued	273
Human Trafficking Cases Initiated	30
Women Trained at Prevention Homes	147
Women Trained at Rehabilitation Homes	128
Girls/Women who Returned Directly from Borders	1,138
Missing/Found	2,444/320

Also, Maiti Nepal has Information and Counselling Centres established in every district where its branches are placed, where people come for community mediation, child abuse, women violence and human trafficking related issues and get them registered. Also, Maiti Nepal conducts students' awareness programmes at school and college through workshops and meeting gatherings. Maiti Nepal has conducted hundreds of *door-to-door awareness programmes* about women violence, sexual abuse and safe migration. For knowing the legalities about human trafficking, Maiti Nepal conducts workshops and orientation programmes on human rights and human trafficking in collaboration with police, other NGOs' representatives, public prosecutors and judges. Maiti Nepal's Centre at

Kathmandu is very large in area where Kathmandu based rehabilitation home and prevention home is located. There is also a training centre in which women and girls learn to be self-dependent through learning courses like, sewing, beauty parlour, handy-crafts, candle making etc. Maiti Nepal has rescued girls from Mumbai, Kolkata, Agra, Punjab, Rudrapur and Sikkim from India and other gulf countries like Kuwait, Jordan, Dubai, UAE, Saudi Arabia and many more other places. Many projects have been successfully led by Maiti Nepal and the most recent is **'ACTIVE' (Action at Community on Trafficking Intervention and Violence End),** which has covered four different districts where awareness programmes, workshops, rallies from school students especially girls and college students have been conducted. The main motive of this project is to spread legal and social awareness about women violence, human trafficking and child abuse. Maiti Nepal has given the facilities to all its victims of free trial and legal counselling. Also, families of such victims have been provided free psychological counselling along with victims themselves.

Transforming Nepal through NGOs

In Nepal, transformation is taking place in every sector such as in political sector, economic sector, social sector, and cultural sector. NGOs are key stakeholders to bring change in Nepal. Particularly transformation can be noticed in the following:

(i) NGOs have been bringing social changes in Nepali people's lives through various awareness programmes held in various suburb areas where still government's policies are unreachable.

(ii) One of the main works done by NGOs of Nepal is political advocacy and legal lobbying through which Nepali people have come to know about their rights and got aware how they can be saved.

(iii) NGOs play a vital role in boosting up Nepal's economy. Since, SWC has associated NGOs with its development works, they have emerged as fund raising machine for building infrastructure and rural and urban development.

(iv) NGOs have emerged as one of the environment conservation players now through making their marks in community forestry programmes through people's participation at rural level.

(v) Business and Industrial sectors have been getting enriched through NGOs as NGOs get major amount of their funding from foreign or international fund-raising agencies which prepare the grounds for big multi-national companies to be set up in Nepal which directly boosts the economy.

(vi) The cultural sector has become diverse as earlier there was Monarch which levied Hindu orthodox upon people but now Nepali people are allowed to follow any religion.

(vii) More than 250 INGOs are set up in Nepal which respectively, play their role in economic development under the supervision of the SWC. There are some flyovers constructed in Nepal by INGOs.

(viii) 29,500 NGOs work in area of Community and Rural Development which is one of the most essential sectors to be considered for rural people's development where government is still making efforts to make its marks.

(ix) There are 1569 different NGOs registered with the SWC working in Environment Sector. They seek people's and government's support and participation in environment conservation.

Weaknesses of NGOs and Their Counter

NGOs in Nepal are not out from controversies as still there are more than one lakh NGOs and only 49,000 are registered with the SWC which clearly shows that more than half number of NGOs are not registered and get their funds from the fund-raising agencies and spend them by their own. No audit, no monitoring and zero control from any government authority lead them to be unaccountable, corrupt, opaque and ambiguous. The registered NGOs get funds forwarded by the SWC by the concerned funding agency though non-registered NGOs get themselves funds directly from the fund-raising agency. This entire process can make them corrupt as there is no agency to control over the expenses done out of the provided funds. In an open-ended interview with me, Mr. Anand Thapa, the director of INGO Section in the Social Welfare Council of Nepal said, "Some NGOs in Nepal emerge at the time of need. They don't get themselves registered in the SWC and get a good amount of funds. After some time, they get dissolved when the task is done." This shows how some of the NGOs have been originating only for the sake of monetary gain. There is a grave need to register all the NGOs small or large in the SWC. A tight and keen watch has to be levied over this issue. Also, representative of the SWC has to go for project auditing with the district administrative officers in order to check the reality on grounds at the site of the project execution.

Conclusion

It is noticed widely that NGOs since 1990s have been participating in social, cultural political and economic development of Nepal. The government also has started considering them as their development partners. The role of the SWC has become very crucial with respect to its monitoring upon NGOs works and activities. But there is still a need of proper coordination and channeling between the government and NGOs which sometimes, becomes chaotic in execution of activities. However, the new regulation by which the SWC gets all the funds from the funding agencies then it diverts to the concerned NGOs according to their need and expenses will definitely bring some changes.

REFERENCES

Alejandro Quiroz Flores, Lecturer, University of Essex. (2017, April 10). *The key role of NGOs in bringing disaster relief in Nepal.* Retrieved April 14, 2017, from http://theconversation.com/the-key-role-of-ngos-in-bringing-disaster-relief-in-nepal-40883.

Bhandari, M. (2014). "Civil Society and Non-Governmental Organizations (NGOs) Movements in Nepal in terms of Social Transformation." *Pacific Journal of Science and Technology*, 177-189.

Bhatta, C.D. (2007). "Civil Society in Nepal: In Search of Reality." *Nepalese Studies*, *34*, 45-57.

Bhattachan, K.B. (2004). *NGOs in Nepal: Non-governmental Organizations Challenges and Opportunities.*

Dahal, D.R. (2001). *Civil Society in Nepal Opening the Ground for Questions.*

Dhakal, T.N. (2006). *Challenges of Civil Society Governance in Nepal.*

Fox, L., Helweg, P., and Hansen, G. (1997). *Advocacy Strategies for Civil Society: A Conceptual Framework and Practitioner's Guide.* Unpublished paper for USAID.

Giri, A., Khatiwada, P., Shrestha, B., and Chettri, R.K. (2013). "Perceptions of government knowledge and control over contributions of aid organizations and INGOs to health in Nepal: a qualitative study." *Globalization and Health*, 9(1), 1.

Green, A., and Matthias, A. (1995). "Where do NGOs fit in?" *Development in Practice*, *5*(4), 313-323.

Kamat, S. (2004). "The privatization of public interest: theorizing NGO discourse in a neoliberal era." *Review of International Political Economy*, *11*(1), 155-176.

Karkee, R., and Comfort, J. (2016). "NGOs, Foreign Aid, and Development in Nepal." *Frontiers in Public Health*, 4.

Ghimire, Harihar (2008). *NGO/INGO centred approach: An alternative approach to development.*

Mercer, C. (2002). "NGOs, civil society and democratization: a critical review of the literature." *Progress in Development Studies*, *2*(1), 5-22.

Pallari Help Nepal! List of NGOs assisting earthquake assistance and relief. Retrieved April 14, 2017, from http://www.oneindia.com/feature/ngo-list-nepal-earthquake-2015-contribution-help-1734702.html (2015, May 02).

Panday, D.R. (1999). *Nepal's failed development: Reflections on the mission and the maladies*. Kathmandu: Nepal South Asia Centre.

Rijal, Y.R. *Nongovernmental Organizations in Nepal: Roles and Policy Issues*.

Sharma, M.L., Peacock, O., and Gopal, K. (2003). *Globalisation, democracy and governance in South Asia: Issues and Alternatives* (Vol. 39). Kalinga.

Sharma, P., Guha-Khasnobis, B., and Raj Khanal, D. (2014). *Nepal Human Development Report 2014*. GoN (Government of Nepal) and UNDP (United Nations Development Programme), Kathmandu.

T. Louise Brown, (1996). *The Challenge to Democracy in Nepal: A Political History*, pp. 1-2, Routledge, p. 111.

Tek Nath Dhakal, *Challenges of Civil Society Governance in Nepal, JOAAG,* Vol. 2, No. 1, p. 63.

Ulvila, M., and Hossain, F. (2002). "Development of NGOs and political participation of the poor in Bangladesh and Nepal," *Voluntas: International Journal of Voluntary and Nonprofit Organizations*, *13*(2), 149-163.

Uttam Uprety, "A Reflection on the legal framework for civil society in Nepal", *The International Journal of Not-for-profit Law*, Vol. 13, Issue 3, June 2011, http://www.icnl.org/research/journal/vol13iss3/art_3.htm, pp. 1-26.

William, C. (1991). *Non-government initiatives: The urban poor and basic infrastructure services in Asia and the Pacific*. Asian Development Bank, Manila.

Wright, G.W. (2012). "NGOs and Western hegemony: cause for concern and ideas for change." *Development in Practice*, *22*(1), 123-134.

SECTION V

Mainstreaming Gender and Minorities

21

Good Governance a Prerequisite for Securing Women Rights

Experiences From India and Turkey

Anisur Rahman and *Sana Ahmed*

Introduction

All human beings as a member of human society have some rights whether male or female to survive and making life better that is why they are called human rights. Rights are the conditions and protections which are entitled to every human being and without which no individual can realize its best self. The government must protect the rights of every citizen through proper governance in the country. Without understanding the human beings and the government, it is difficult to achieve the development of the country as well as of its citizens in a sustainable manner. Both good governance and human rights gained prominence and are important phenomena. Francis Fukuyama defined "Governance as the ability of the government to formulate and execute policies and to deliver services despite that government is democratic or not."[1] The term Governance was popularized in the 1980s when economic reforms gave prominence to the process and manner of governing and also because of the failure of Structural Adjustment Programmes (SAPs).

World Bank in 1989 used the term Governance in "Sub-Saharan Africa—From Crises to Sustainable Growth" and explained as it "an exercise of political power to manage nation's affairs."[2] It was a major theme of the Annual Development Economic Conference, but president Barber Conable was the first to use the term good governance and who referred it as the "public service that is efficient, the reliable judicial system, and administration accountable to its public". Later the concept of good governance was further developed through World Bank's publications such as 1992 "Governance and Development"; 1997 World Development Report "State in a Changing World" and 1990s Comprehensive Development Framework further suggested that for ensuring good governance government have to embrace accountability, transparency, effective and efficient bureaucracy, active civil society, the participation of the citizens, decentralization, respect for human rights. Participation, accountability, transparency, corruption control, effectiveness and rule of law are the major characteristics of good governance identified by the World Bank.

Ernest Barker defined "Rights are the external condition necessary for the development of the capacities of the personality of the individual."[3] Human rights are those basic values without which people cannot live in dignity and are those conditions of life that allow us to fully develop. As stated by United Nations, "human rights ensure that a human being will be able to fully develop and use human qualities such as intelligence, talent, and conscience and satisfy his or her needs."[4] The concept of human rights was defined after Magna Carta, the first document that talks about the freedom of people. It was signed by King John of England in 1215 which gave some concessions to the English people. For granting rights to the English citizens, a Bill of Rights in 1689 was passed by parliament which suspended the powers of crown granted rights to the people like no person required to pay tax, no unusual punishment, no interference of the crown in the freedom of people etc.

American and French revolutions also played a significant role in the foundation of human rights as it initiated an era of democratic revolution. After drafting its constitution in 1787, the US granted many rights to its citizens like the right to vote, freedom of the press, freedom of expression etc. which was followed by French Declaration in 1789 which recognized various rights of citizens like the right to equality, property rights, and the right to liberty, transparency, and accountability of governance. The Universal Declaration of Human Rights (UDHR) mentions in Article 1 of the Charter that promotion and the encouragement of human rights and freedoms for all without discrimination as to sex, language, race, or religion is one of the primary purposes of the UN. For maintaining peace, security, and assuring people their equal rights, UN General Assembly adopted the Declaration in 1948 which included civil, political, economic, and cultural rights and declaring human rights at the universal level. For making human rights a binding law and to monitor the obligation of state parties to the concept UN adopted two covenants in 1966—the International Covenant on Civil and Political Rights (ICCPR) and the International Covenant on Economic, Social and Cultural Rights (ICESCR).[5] Collectively, the UDHR, ICCPR, ICESCR are known as the International Bill of Rights.[6] Inherent, not exchangeable, universality, equality, and feasibility[7] are the characteristics of Human rights.

This chapter tries to explain that good governance is the precondition for women's rights and also the constitutional measures adopted by the government to grant women equal rights in India and Turkey and also further explained the status of women's rights in the respective country after so many constitutional measures or provisions. It is very necessary to explain the evolution of good governance and human rights in India and Turkey.

Evolution of Good Governance and Human Rights in India and Turkey

Good Governance in India and Turkey

The concept of Good governance in India is very old. In ancient times, rulers were bound to follow *'Raj Dharma'*, for ensuring good governance. The concept was defined in the ancient Indian texts especially in Kautilya's *Arthashastra* which defined the rights and the duties of the king to establish a welfare state and for achieving good governance, it stated that the "happiness of king lies in the happiness of his people, in their welfare his welfare, and whatever pleases his people he shall consider as good."[8] In the 1990s, the issue of governance became a primary concern in India. World Bank's concept of good governance was adopted in the five-year plans for its successful realization.

The Ninth Five Year Plan (1997-2002) includes a chapter "Implementation, Delivery Mechanism, and Institutional Development" that studied the weakness in the implementation and the formulation of these plans. The problem of decentralization, accountability, and assessment and monitoring of policies was also raised. The Tenth Five Year Plan (2002-2007) in its Chapter "Governance and Implementation" defined governance as all the functions performed by the state, civil society and market to empower citizens through participation in the country's political, economic and social activities and also highlights the universal features of good governance that are the exercise of legitimate political power, transparency, equality, participation and accountability towards people. Eleventh Five Year Plan (2007-2012) and Twelfth Five Year

Plan (2012-2017) also define good governance as essential for the proper functioning of any society. 73rd and 74th Constitutional Amendments and Right to Information Act are also adopted to achieve good governance through decentralization. It ensures the efficient use of resources and focuses on the proper delivery of services to its citizens and also provides social authority to the system. Even in the present government, World Bank's concept is considered as an utmost important concept for improving the quality of governance as Prime Minister Narendra Modi on 6th March, 2018 said that transparency and accountability for democratic and participative governance, as they help to build the trust and improve the impact of government schemes.[9]

Good governance was first introduced in the West Asian region by World Bank in its report "Better Governance for Development in the Middle East and North Africa" in 2003 called for the improvement of 'good governance' in Arab countries as an indispensable precondition for economic growth and it also stated that the issue of good governance is not a political issue, but a development issue because good governance has a main role in promoting economic development and in offering essential social services."[10] In 1980s, Turkey also adopted the Structural Adjustment Programmes (SAPs) for its development but it proved to be a complete failure which led the country to face serious issues like the problem of legitimacy, representation crises, lack of participation, and inefficiency of the government to meet the needs of its citizens etc.

Turkey has adopted various elements of the concept such as participation, decentralization, equality, transparency in its governing structure. Turkey is a democratic, parliamentary, secular, and social republic governed by the rule of law in which all three branches of government—the legislature, executive, and judiciary—are independent of one another. Executive power is exercised by the elected president while legislative power is vested in the Grand National Assembly and judicial power shall be exercised by the independent courts. Citizens got a universal adult franchise immediately after independence in 1923, with the right to representation from 1933 onwards. For ensuring overall the development and participation Turkey adopted decentralization under the European Charter of Local Self-Government for the welfare of its citizens and also improving the quality of governance at every level.

For curbing corruption which is an important characteristic of ensuring good governance, Turkey beacme a member of many international organizations such as the Financial Action Task Force, the Group of States against Corruption (GRECO), the International Anti-Corruption Academy

(IACA), and the Open Government Partnership Initiative (OGPI). Good governance in Turkey can be seen through the policies, constitutional amendments, and laws the government adopted. Both countries have adopted good governance in their governing structure according to their own political, economic, cultural, and social settings.

Human Rights in India and Turkey

The protection of human rights in India was also realized in the ancient period. The Vedic period was based on a norm '*Dharma*' which explains the duties of a person that should be performed. Various scriptures like *Bhagavad Geeta* embody human rights values in which one chapter is dedicated to *Karmayoga* means the *Yoga* of Work which talks about the obligation of performance of duty without any selfish interest and for the welfare of the world. As Kautilya in his *Arthashastra* has prescribed the duties of the king and said that whatever pleases his subjects shall be considered as good; in the happiness of his subjects lies his happiness[11] with harmlessness, freedom forgiveness are his duties to all for a welfare state.

After Independence, constitution-makers had to draft a constitution that meets the desires of Indian people. So after the commencement of a new constitution on 26th January, 1950, the natural laws rights were incorporated in Part III (Fundamental Rights) and Part IV (Directive Principles of State Policy) which granted basic human rights to the people for the development of their personality. The procedure of Judicial Activism and Public Interest Litigation is also a means to protect the basic rights of people. India signed two important Covenants of UN, i.e. International Covenants on Civil and Political Rights (ICCPR) and the International Covenant on Economic, Social, and Cultural Rights (ICESCR) in 1966 introducing human rights as a concept. For the protection and promotion of human rights, a separate Act was adopted by the Constitution of India known as the Protection of Human Rights Act in 1993, it protected the rights related to equality, liberty, life guaranteed by the Constitution. It also set up the Human Rights Commission both at the national and state level. There are various other international conventions or declarations signed by the Indian Government like Convention on Elimination of All Forms of Discrimination Against Women (CEDAW) in 1980, Child Rights Convention (CRC) 1992, Hague Convention 1958 etc.

As far as the evolution of human rights in Turkey is concerned, it can be traced back when Turkey was under the Ottoman Empire. At that time, certain types of rights were given to minorities like they have freedom of religion, right to life, property rights. A new constitution was adopted in Turkey in 1876, which mentioned basic human rights in Articles 8 and 26.[12] Turkey's then-President Kemal Mustafa Ataturk immediately, after independence in 1923, adopted a written constitution and introduced various fundamental rights like right to equality, liberty, right to education, new inheritance law, right to vote and equal representation etc. Major rights were introduced by the government when the Constitution was once again amended in 1982 which guarantees more fundamental rights like the right to property, freedom of religion, freedom of expression.

There are three human rights mechanism active in the world: (1) European Convention on Human Rights (1953); (2) American Convention on Human Rights; (3) African Charter on Human and Peoples Rights. Turkey follows the European Convention as it is the most developed and there is an European Council with its European Court of Human Rights (ECHR) that is the only human rights court in the world. Turkey is also the founding member of the Council. The seriousness of introducing institution for safeguarding human rights in the country was started getting realized from 2000 onwards when they signed both UN Covenants, that is ICCPR and ICESCR. Provincial and District Boards of Human Rights (2003), Human Rights Presidency (HRP) (2001-2012), Human Rights Delegations, Supreme Boards of Human Rights[13] are the various institutions to protect and promote Human rights in the country. Another important law was passed by the Turkish government, i.e. Turkish Human Rights and Equality Institution[14] in 2016 by replacing the Turkish Human Rights Institution of 2012 to improve the functioning of law. Other conventions like Convention on Elimination of All Forms of Discrimination Against Women (CEDAW) 1985, Optional Protocol to the International Covenant on Civil and Political Rights 2004, European Convention for the Prevention of Torture and Inhuman Degrading Treatment or Punishment, 1995, International Convention for the Suppression of Terrorist Bombing, 2002, Grand National Assembly also established a Committee for Human Rights Inquiry and further promoting, developing and safeguarding human rights in the Republic of Turkey.

Relationship between Women Rights and Good Governance

According to the Beijing Platform for Action, the goal of equality, development, and peace cannot be achieved without the active participation and the inclusion of women in decision-making at all levels of governance.[15] Sustainable development is very important for which the government must work progressively to secure the rights of individuals. Human rights represent a set of values that guides the government's functions. The accomplishment of human rights can be realized only in a favourable environment that is provided by the government. There are three types of obligations enforced by human rights on states, i.e. the obligation to protect, respect, and fulfil. Women's rights are the human rights as Vienna Declaration and the Programme of Action 1993 stated that "human rights of women are integral, undeniable and inseparable part of the universal human rights and also put emphasis on the elimination of gender-based violence." So, without good governance, women's rights cannot be protected sustainably. The notion of human rights enlightens the effort of good governance which includes various legal state institutions, actors, political and administrative processes accountable for fulfilling the rights and needs of the population. Good governance enhances women's rights when the state expands its capacity to fulfil its liability to provide essential goods and services such as health; right to education; food etc. and these services should be accessible. In modern times, the State has undertaken the task of providing adequate protection and reasonable opportunities to everyone for the full development of individual personality.

Good governance is a process of creating sound, legitimate, and accountable legislative, judicial, and administrative institutions in which citizens can fully empower and participate in the decisions that affect their lives. Good governance and human rights are the means of social transformation. Women are the disadvantaged section of society as they have never enjoyed equal rights as compared to men. So for enhancing equality there is a need for human rights and good governance. Good governance and women's rights are supposed to be interdependent and to ensure effectiveness government must address the differing needs of its citizens whether male or female. The government must enable and empower the disadvantaged section of the society, i.e. women by granting them rights for the development of themselves and to be active participants in the governing process of the country for sustainable development. The purpose of good governance is not only to provide basic amenities to the people but a life, which is qualitative and dignified in the real sense[16] and also acts as a method to enhance citizen's potential to assert human rights.

Constitutional Provisions for Women in India and Turkey

Various provisions were introduced by the founding fathers of the Constitution for empowering and securing women's rights. Constitution of India guarantees rights for women in Article 14 which is right to equality before the law; Article 15 prohibits discrimination irrespective of religion, sex, caste etc.; Article 16 which guarantees equality of opportunity in terms of employment under state offices and also outlaws discrimination in terms of sex; Article 19 assures freedom of speech and expression; Article 21 allows women to live a decent life with liberty.

The above are fundamental rights which are enforceable by law but the Constitution also guaranteed certain rights in Directive Principles of State Policy under Article 39 which provide equal pay for equal work for men and women; Article 42 assures that there will be a good humane condition for labour and also include maternity leave. Several Amendments and Acts were also introduced by the government like Article 243 under 73rd and 74th Amendment Act in which one-third seats are reserved for women in Panchayats and Municipalities; according to Women's Reservation Bill 33 per cent of seats are reserved for women in Lok Sabha; Protection of Women from Domestic Violence Act, 2005; National Commission for Women Act, 1990; The Prohibition of Child Marriage Act, 2006; Juvenile Justice (Care and Protection of Children) Act, 2000; Bonded Labour System (Abolition) Act, 1976; Contract Labour (Regulation & Abolition) Act, 1979; Inter-state Migrant Workmen (Regulation of Employment and Conditions of Service) Act, 1979; Child Labour (Prohibition and Regulation) Act, 1986; Relevant provisions of Indian Penal Code, 1860; Relevant provisions of Code of Criminal Procedure; Family Courts Act, 1984[17]; and also Women Reservation Bill, 2010.

At the advent of Independence, the need for empowering women in Turkey was addressed by the government, and several provisions were introduced in the Constitution again and again. Article 10 of the Turkish Constitution envisages equality before the law and stated that men and women have equal rights. Women above 18 years are entitled to vote, representation and to engage in political activity under Article 67 of the Constitution; in Article 42 educational rights are granted; Turkish Civil Code came into being in 2002 that guarantee equality amongst men and women in terms of the divorce, custody of child and inheritance of property, raising the legal age of marriage to 17 and also passed the Family Protection Law 2007 for establishing family courts in every district; in 2005 Turkish Penal Code was also passed with a view of combating violence against women. These three articles were introduced to stop violence and protect victims mainly children and women.

Employment Act of 2003 in Turkey was also drafted to control or improve the working condition of employers or employees. For increasing education among women, the government has collaborated with several international organizations to launch many educational projects like "Support to Basic Education Programme" (SBEP); "Mother and Daughter in School" etc. In Turkey, most of the welfare activities are performed by the government in collaboration with civil society organisations like Turkish Organization of University Women (TÜKD); Women for Women's Human Rights (WWHR); Flying Broom (UçanSüpürge); Women Entrepreneurs Association of Turkey (KAGIDER); KAMER Foundation; TÜSAID (Turkish Industrialist's and Businessmen's Association); MUSIAD etc.

Status of Women Rights in India and Turkey

The Constitution of both the countries guaranteed rights through various provisions introduced from time to time. Health, education, employment, politics, protection from violence are the main areas in which the status of women's rights is measured because in some areas women's rights are still violated. In India, everyone has franchise through a vote and be a part of the decision-making process. In reality, however, women participation in politics was influenced by their male influencers not only when they are casting their vote but also in terms of representation in political activity.

Education in the lives of women plays a very crucial part as it helps them to be self-reliant. Among women literacy rate is the lowest in India, 65 per cent as compared to 82 per cent of males in 2017-18. In terms of employment, women's status is very poor, their participation in labour force fall from 36 per cent in 2005 to 26 per cent in 2018. Most of them performed unpaid work as 95 per cent of them worked in an unorganized sector or are unpaid work and also more than 47 per cent of women are agricultural labourers as most of them are illiterate there is a wage gap as men are paid more than women for the same job. Crime against women is the most prevalent practice in India. According to the National Crime Records Bureau (NCRB) data, there were 89,097 cases related to crimes against women registered in 2018. Out of these registered cases, 31 per cent are related to cruelty by husbands or relatives, 22 per cent of cases were of kidnapping or abduction and 10.3 per cent are comprised rape cases.

Turkey is among the first in the West Asian region to grant the right to equality and the right to vote to women immediately after its independence in 1923. Women have the right to vote and representation since 1930 and 1934 but their political representation does not portrait a good picture. In 2019, 17.4 per cent of women are in parliament as compared to 15 per cent in the 2015 election. In 2019, 22.1 per cent of ambassadors are women in the Ministry of Foreign Affairs. Only 43 women are provincial and district mayors in 2019 elections and there is only 104 out of 600 lawmakers in Turkish parliament are women. In terms of education, the literacy rate among females in Turkey is very high that is 90 per cent as compared to India. The economic empowerment of women is very low in the country. As per the International Labour Organization database 2019, merely 33 per cent of women are a part of the labour force out of which 26 per cent are agricultural labourers. Like India, violence against women is very prevalent especially domestic violence against women has increased to 75 per cent over the past 15 years as 40 per cent of women in Turkey experienced some sort of violence in their lives. From 1st January to October 20th, 2019, 302 women were killed in 324 days after being subjected to violence.

Conclusion

Good governance and human rights are concerned with the relationship between the State and its citizens. State capacity and services are linked. The government's relationship with its citizens is strengthened by good governance and through which they can enjoy human rights for the development of their potential and personality. In both India and Turkey, women are disadvantaged and they are dependent on government efforts for safeguarding their freedom and rights. That is why both the countries have introduced good governance in their governing process which in turn guarantees human rights through various constitutional amendments and acts in political, economic, social, and cultural spheres where women are highly discriminated. The chapter has highlighted the efforts of the government for promoting and protecting women's rights in education, politics, employment, health. Both India and Turkey have made numerous policies, laws and also signed international agreements and conventions for safeguarding the rights of women. As per the governing structure of each respective country participation of women is good in areas like politics in India while in Turkey women are great in numbers in terms of education. In both the countries percentage of violence against women is very high. Though they have introduced various policies and laws for promoting and protecting the rights of women, the result does not seem satisfied as the status of women rights is still discriminatory and human rights violation is very high. The government should also involve men and women both while making the policies and also tried to change the mindset of the people.

ENDNOTES

1. Francis Fukuyama, "What is Governance?", *Centre for Global Development*, Washington, 2013, p. 3. https://papers.ssrn.com/sol3/papers.cfm?abstract_id=2226592 (accessed on 9th July, 2020).
2. World Bank, "Sub-Saharan Africa—from Crises to Sustainable Growth", 1989, p. 55. http://documents.worldbank.org/curated/en/498241468742846138/pdf/multi0page.pdf (accessed on 10th December, 2018).
3. Abdulrahim, P. Vijapur, *Human Rights in International relations*, MANAK Publication, New Delhi, 2010, p. 19.
4. "Human Rights Background" https://www.theadvocatesforhumanrights.org/uploads/ch_2_2.pdf (accessed on 30th June, 2020).
5. Abdulrahim P. Vijapur, "Human Rights in International relations", *Manak Publication*, New Delhi, 2010, p. 53.
6. *Ibid.*
7. Md. Kamruzzaman and Shashi Kanto Das, "The Evaluation of Human Rights: An Overview in Historical Perspective", *American Journal of Service Science and Management,* Vol. 3, No. 2, 2016, p. 6. https://www.researchgate.net/publication/318851323_The_Evaluation_of_ Human_Rights_ An_Overview_in_Historical _Perspective (accessed on 30th June, 2020).
8. Dr. Dinesh Arora, "Good Governance: A Study of the Concept in Indian Context", p. 6. http://paperroom.ipsa.org/papers/view/33195 (accessed on 20th November, 2018).
9. NDTV, "Transparency and Accountability Must for Good Governance, says PM Modi", March 2018. https://www.ndtv.com/india-news/transparency-accountability-must-for-good-governance-says-pm-modi-1820460 (accessed on 31st January, 2019).
10. Gamal M. Selim, *The International Dimensions of Democratization in Egypt: The limits of Externally-Induced Change,* Springer, 2015, p. 69.
11. Dr. Dinesh Arora, "Good Governance: A Study of the Concept in Indian Context", p. 6. http://paperroom.ipsa.org/papers/view/33195 (accessed on 20th November, 2018).
12. Akif TÖGEL, "Ottoman Human Rights Practice: A Model of Legal Pluralism," *Yildirim Beyazit Law Review*, 2016, p. 211. https://papers.ssrn.com/sol3/papers.cfm?abstract_id=2844399 (accessed on 12th July, 2020).
13. BicanŞahin, "Mechanisms of Human Rights Protection Anatomy of Human Rights Regime in Turkey", *European Liberal Forum*, 2016, p. 15. https://

www.liberalforum.eu/wp-content/uploads/2018/09/rapor-ing.pdf (accessed on 8th July, 2020).

14. *Ibid.,* p. 15.
15. Colleen Lowe Morna, "Gender and Governance: A Proposed World Bank Action Plan", p. 2. http://www.gdrc.org/gender/governance/wb.pdf (accessed on 21st April, 2020).
16. B.M. Sharma and Abhishek Sharma, "Development, Good Governance and Human Rights", *Indian Journal of Public Administration*, Vol Lx, No. 2, April-June 2014, p. 228. https://journals.sagepub.com/doi/abs/10.1177/0019556120140202?journalcode=ipaa (Accessed On 21st April, 2020).
17. Dr. Vibhuti Patel, "Gender Equality and Human Rights", 2018. https://www.researchgate.net/publication/328879183_Gender_Equality_and_Human_Rights_by (accessed on 21st April, 2020).

REFERENCES

Arora, Dinesh, *Good Governance: A Study of the concept in Indian Context*, p. 6. http://paperroom.ipsa.org/papers/view/33195 (accessed on 20th November, 2018).

Chaudhary, Renuka, "Human rights, women rights and culture in India", *International Journal of Advanced Research and Development*, Volume 3; Issue 1; January 2018. http://www.advancejournal.com/download/1044/3-1-196-224.pdf (accessed on 21st April, 2020).

Evolution of Human Rights and Its Place in India, https://shodhganga.inflinet.ac.in/jspui/bitstream/10603/151828/9/09_chapter%25204.pdf (accessed on 8th July, 2020).

Fukuyama, Francis, "What is Governance?", *Centre for Global Development*, Washington, 2013, p. 3. https://papers.ssrn.com/sol3/papers.cfm?abstract_id=2226592 (accessed on 9th July, 2020).

"Human Rights Background" https://www.theadvocatesforhumanrights.org/uploads/ch_2_2.pdf (accessed on 30th June, 2020).

Kamruzzaman, Md. and Das, Kanto Shashi, "The Evaluation of Human Rights: An Overview in Historical Perspective", *American Journal of Service Science and Management*, Vol. 3, No. 2, 2016, p. 6. https://www.researchgate.net/publication/318851323_The_Evaluation_of_Human_Rights_An_Overview_in_Historical _Perspective (accessed on 30th June, 2020).

Lokanadham ,Sujatha, "Gender issues: relevance to good governance", *Journal of Research in Humanities and Social Science*, Volume 2, Issue 12, 2014. http://www.questjournals.org/jrhss/papers/vol2-issue12/H2125457.pdf (accessed on 21st April, 2020).

Morna, Lowe Colleen, "Gender and Governance: A Proposed World Bank Action Plan", p. 2. http://www.gdrc.org/gender/governance/wb.pdf (accessed on 21st April, 2020).

Murphy, Teri and Vibe, Christina Maria, "Gender Mainstreaming: Turkey's Policies and Practices in Peace Building Initiatives," *Policy Brief*, October 2013. https://kasaum.ankara.edu.tr/files/2013/02/Gender_Mainstreaming-2013.pdf (accessed on 21st April, 2020).

NDTV, "Transparency and Accountability Must for Good Governance, says PM Modi", March 2018. https://www.ndtv.com/india-news/transparency-accountability-must-for-good-governance-says-pm-modi-1820460 (accessed on 31st January, 2019).

Özgür H. Çınar and Tolga Şirin, "Turkey's human rights agenda", Routledge Taylor & Francis Group, 2017. https://www.tandfonline.com/doi/full/10.1080/23760818.2017.1350354 (accessed on 10th July 2020).

Patel, Vibhuti. *Gender Equality and Human Rights*, 2018. https://www.researchgate.net/publication/328879183_Gender_Equality_and_Human_Rights_by (accessed on 21st April, 2020).

Şahin Bican, "Mechanisms of Human Rights Protection Anatomy of Human Rights Regime in Turkey", *European Liberal Forum*, 2016, p. 15. https://www.liberalforum.eu/wp-content/uploads/2018/09/rapor-ing.pdf (accessed on 8th July, 2020).

Saikia, Krishna Ishan, "Good Governance and Human Rights: International and National Perspective", *International Journal of Advancements in Research and Technology*, Volume 2, Issue 7, 2013. https://www.ijoart.org/docs/GOOD-GOVERNANCE-AND-HUMAN-RIGHTS-INTERNATIONAL-AND-NATIONAL-PERSPECTIVE.pdf (accessed 21st April, 2020).

Selim, M. Gamal, *The International Dimensions of Democratization in Egypt: The Limits of Externally-Induced Change*, Springer International, 2015.

Sharma, B.M. and Sharma, Abhishek, "Development, Good Governance and Human Rights", *Indian Journal of Public Administration*, Vol. lx, No. 2, April-June 2014, p. 228. https://journals.sagepub.com/doi/abs/10.1177/0019556120140202?journalcode=ipaa (Accessed on 21st April, 2020).

TÖGEL Akif, "Ottoman Human Rights Practice: A Model of Legal Pluralism", *Yildirim Beyazit Law Review*, 2016, p. 211. https://papers.ssrn.com/sol3/papers.cfm?abstract_id=2844399 (accessed on 12th July, 2020).

Vijapur, P. Abdulrahim, *Human Rights in International Relations*, Manak Publication, New Delhi, 2010, p. 53.

World Bank, "Sub-Saharan Africa—from Crises to Sustainable Growth", 1989, p. 55. http://documents.worldbank.org/curated/en/498241468742846138/pdf/multi0page.pdf (accessed on 10th December, 2018).

22
Women Empowerment and Local Self-Governance in Jammu & Kashmir

Tabasum Firdous

Women in Kashmir: Status and Empowerment

Kashmir is one of the most volatile regions in entire South Asia. Since the outbreak of militant insurgency and subsequent armed conflict termed as 'proxy war' unleashed from across the border by Pakistan, thousands of people have been killed in the mindless violence. These three decades of violence have deeply affected peoples' livelihood, their living environments, health, eating habits, their work and workplaces, their access to education and so on. However, it is the women of Kashmir who have felt its impact most severely. The short and long-term effects of armed conflict have made Kashmiri women-folk the most vulnerable group for more reasons than just violence. Women suffer in many ways due to continuous violence in Kashmir valley. Be it the economic deprivation, displacement, poverty or gender-based violence, the costs of conflict are borne disproportionately by women. In the absence of an earning member in the family, women are forced to earn a livelihood and feed the family which is not easy being part of traditional conservative societies and also due to the shrunk economic opportunities in the wake of the conflict. Widows, especially, are often unable to provide for themselves and their families due to cultural and religious restraints, lack of education etc. Women are not always able to obtain meaningful employment and are, therefore, unable to provide for their families.

Firstly, Jammu & Kashmir belong to South Asia that is highly conservative region. Now, it is not a hidden phenomenon that women in conservative societies are most vulnerable to exploitation and suppression. This is the case with Kashmiri women as well. *Secondly*, the state has been victim of Indo-Pak conflict and has been sandwiched between orthodox religious orientations, particularly of Hinduism and Islam. This has resulted into regional variations of status of women within the state. For instance, Jammu region has Hindu majority population and bears influence of rest of India in terms of societal and cultural sense. Contrarily, Kashmir valley is a Muslim dominated province reflecting influences of Central Asia, Iran as well as Saudi Arabia and Pakistan in contemporary times. Saudi and Pak influence over the societal set-up of Kashmir valley is the result of religious literature of Wahhabism and other orthodox organizations, developed in Arab world and Pakistan. Easy accessibility and preaching based on such literature have helped in spreading and maintaining restrictions over women in valley with religious sanctions. Also, continuity of political nature of conflict between India and Pakistan with religious provocations has resulted in preventing modern outlook regarding humane treatment of all sections of society including women. Armed resistance, as instigated on the name of religion, thus, acts as a hurdle before women emancipation. Following it, conflict and orthodox religious interpretations have proved more antithetical to the status of women in Kashmir valley.

Thirdly, the continuity of cultural and traditional practices favouring and promoting women subordination are also responsible for the suppression of women in Kashmir. *Fourthly,* language as a tool for preserving women subjugation has maintained *status quo* among larger chunk of Kashmir society regarding women subordination. *Fifthly*, economic dependence and less employment opportunities in service sector, like rest of India, are also responsible for pushing women-folk under male-dominance. *Sixthly*, domestic terror based on economic compulsions, religious sanctions and societal norms also play their part in women subjugation. *Seventhly*, harassment of women in Kashmir by civilian, militants, police and paramilitary forces since early 1990s has helped in promoting patriarchic norms with 'Man-the-protector' as a forced necessity. *Finally*, physical power of men with provocations under psychological and sociological compulsions based on conflict and economy respectively are structured and linked in a way that women emancipation from the evil patriarchic designs is difficult to be achieved.

Under such circumstances, there is an urgent need to empower women. In the light of this, though several programmes have been started, yet these have not achieved the anticipated positive impact on the status of women. The female population of Jammu & Kashmir State slashed down from 47.15 per cent of the total population in 2001 to 46.88 per cent in

2011. As per details from Census 2011, Jammu & Kashmir has population of 1.25 crore over the figure of 1.01 crore in 2001 Census. Total population of Jammu & Kashmir as per 2011 Census is 1,25,48,926 of which male and female are 66,65,561 and 58,83,365 respectively indicating a reduced sex ratio of 883. The corresponding figures of male and female as per Census 2001 were 53,60,926 and 47,82,774 respectively indicating sex ratio of 892. Women thus constitute about 47 per cent of the total population of the State. Women are significant contributors to the growing economy. The total workforce in 2001 was 37.54 lakh workers consisting of 26.80 lakh males and 10.74 lakh females. This workforce consisted of 26.09 lakh main workers and 11.45 lakh marginal workers. Work participation rate amongst females was 22.45 in 2001. A sectoral breakdown of women workers reveals that 56 per cent women are cultivators, 5 per cent are agricultural labourers and 10 per cent workers in the household industry (Muzamil Jan, *Women Development in Kashmir: An intervention through cooperation*, Srinagar, 2011). Women development, no doubt, has been part of the development planning for all the governments. These initiatives have helped in improving the status of women in various spheres to a great extent, yet the imbalance exists.

As mentioned earlier, Jammu & Kashmir which is a border state of India situated in the Himalayas is faced with a protracted conflict which has touched almost every single life in the region, women and children are most hit by this mindless violence. In the absence of stability in the region, hundreds and thousands of women (there is no authentic data to support the claim but the data given by Kashmiri separatist leaders suggest that over 30,000 women have become widows due to conflict) continue to suffer. Widows and half-widows (the women whose husbands have simply gone missing and they do not know their status whether they are dead or alive), in particular are suffering a lot in the absence of adequate sustenance. Due to illiteracy, limited knowledge, skill and resources at their disposal, they are engaged in informal and unorganized sectors where the wages are very low. Low income degrades their quality of life and lowers their standard of living.

Keeping in view the fact that the women of Jammu & Kashmir have suffered badly during the last 27 years of bloodshed and violence, their economic empowerment through their capacity building can be one of the most important option to help and bring out these women from their economic distress. Given the fact that hundreds of thousands of women in Jammu & Kashmir have lost their male bread-earners in the family and they have to fend for themselves and their children, capacity building of these women is the only way to help the women in distress. No doubt the state government has launched various programmes in the past few years which support women to take up new ventures and start self-employment, more efforts are required for the capacity building of these women.

Taking cognizance of women empowerment as one of the main focused area, the Jammu & Kashmir Government has launched various schemes for self-employment of the women. Various programmes which support women to take up new ventures and start self-employment have been initiated by Jammu & Kashmir State Women Development Corporation, Jammu & Kashmir Social Welfare Department and Jammu & Kashmir Rural Development in the past few years. The Jammu & Kashmir State Women Development Corporation established in the year 1991, is the channelizing agency for implementation of the schemes for social and economic upliftment of the women living below the poverty line. Few of the JKWDC schemes which are benefiting women include Empowering Skilled Young Women Scheme, Swayam Siddha and Social Welfare Department.

Empowering Skilled Young Women Scheme (ESW) that forms a part of Sher-i-Kashmir Employment and Welfare Programme was launched by Jammu & Kashmir State Women Development Corporation on 8th of March, 2010 on International Women's Day. Women entrepreneurs belonging to different districts of the state can establish gainful income generating units on nominal interest rate of 6 per cent on select trades of readymade garments, aromatic medicinal plants, boutique, fashion designing, cosmetic shop, DTP, Medical Health Care, Mushroom Cultivation and Floriculture/Agriculture etc. The Jammu & Kashmir Women Development Corporation is raising loan from National Minorities Development and Finance Corporation (NMDFC) and releasing the term loans to female beneficiaries for starting income generating units. Besides, there are schemes financed by National Backward Classes Finance and Development Corporation (NBCFDC) and National Handicapped Finance and Development Corporation (NHFDC) under which loans are advanced to females of backward classes for setting up of their income generating units and handicapped respectively (Shahzada Akhtar, *Kashmir Women Empowerment and National Conference*, Jay Kay Books, Srinagar, 2009). Training centres for skill development of artisans/women beneficiaries are set up under these schemes and thereafter, women are brought under micro credit net to display and sell their products in exhibition-*cum-melas* which are organized by the State Women Development Corporation, both inside and outside the State. These meets give opportunities to women to sell their products.

Political Participation of Women

Women-folk in Jammu & Kashmir is a weak section expected to remain under consistent supervision and control of men. Women are at receiving end of much of the socio-political, economic and cultural aspects. Ill-treatment and harassment of women is a common phenomenon. Women are also the victims of domestic violence. In relation to political affairs, women in Jammu & Kashmir have been kept out of mainstream politics throughout history. Even in terms of voting, women are being used as instruments of exploitation as the male-folk in Kashmir felt threat of militants if they vote. Thus, they assure support to their candidates and parties while directing women-folk of their families to vote accordingly. This trend has been used by males, particularly in rural areas where people are most vulnerable to militant threats. Thus, women have no choice to think and vote according to their own calculations. All this serve to deepen miserable conditions of women who are experiencing inequality, exclusion, alienation and violence in Jammu & Kashmir. Now, it is only the political empowerment of women-folk that can assure women emancipation from exploitation, harassment, violence, inequality and alienation. It, thus, becomes imperative to analyze the status of political empowerment of women in Jammu & Kashmir.

The seeds of women political participation in Jammu & Kashmir can be traced from Naya Kashmir Programme of Jammu & Kashmir National Conference released in 1944. After independence, women were also encouraged for party membership. However, despite many such initiatives by government, women participation remained very low. However, the role of women in Jammu & Kashmir politics slightly changed since 1972 Assembly elections. In this election, as many as eight women candidates contested elections for the first time. Out of these eight candidates, four won the elections as well. However, the other four candidates lost their deposits. In 1977 elections, comparatively, there was a high number of contestants. However, women participation was again low as only four women candidates contested out of which only one candidate managed to win a seat reserved for women. Out of seven women contestants in 1983 elections, not a single candidate won any seat, and five lost their deposits. In 1987 elections, there were 13 women contestants, but only one candidate won the seat in Legislative Assembly. One interesting feature in relation to women political participation was that all the thirteen woman candidates contested from Jammu and no one contested from Kashmir valley. This is significant in relation to Muslim United Front (MUF) influence by religious doctrines that dominated pre-election scene in Valley.

The 21st century state system, with the focus from governance to good governance, introduced many new mechanisms to meet the interests and ensure inclusive security of the people. One of the significant tools to ascertain good governance is the decentralization of power up to the local levels. Thus, the Panchayati Raj Institutions (PRIs) Act as means to secure the spirit of good governance. The disadvantaged sections of the society like Scheduled Castes, Scheduled Tribes and Women got a space *via* these institutions to promote their interests.

Feminists supported the trend of decentralization, as they demanded equal representation of women at all levels of government. The active political participation of women ensured a way for their influential role in the decision-making process. Women representation in PRIs has the potential not only to liberate women from the rigid social customs in which male dominance is prevalent, but also to resolve their domestic problems collectively. Thus, the changing trend from governance to good governance also paved way for women empowerment while focusing equal rights and representation of women in decision-making process.

However, what strikes to the mind is the question that whether women represent themselves freely and adequately in these institutions. Women empowerment in developing societies is a major concern as the influence of male population, particularly in political arena, limits their role in decision-making and its implementation.

Panchayat System

The Panchayat system is not a new phenomenon in India. However, women remained entirely excluded in traditional scheme of local institutions. Political participation of women in independent India was also insignificant at all levels including Panchayati Raj Institutions. It was only in early 1990s that the government recognized women as another disadvantaged section seeking solution to their discrimination. Now, women are being elected to the local government institutions as a result of 73rd and 74th Amendments to the Constitution of India that mandate the reservation of seats for women in these local bodies of governance. Women representation in PRIs has brought their experiences in governing the civic society of India. This also helped the state system to focus the issues of poverty, inequality and gender injustice at the grassroots level.

The State of Jammu & Kashmir is not different with rest of country *vis-à-vis* women empowerment and representation in political arena. The state witnessed the promulgation of Panchayats by Maharaja Hari Singh only in 1935. However, the tough qualifications for voters and representatives made it difficult for women to participate in that system. The changes in socio-economic scenario following the post-1947 developments created an environment for reactivation of the Panchayati Raj system and the Government in 1951 replaced the Panchayat Act of 1935 with a new Act. Following the recommendations made by Balwant Rai Mehta Committee for devolution of power to lower levels through Panchayats, the state government took a lead by passing the Jammu & Kashmir Village Panchayat Act of 1958, repealing the earlier Acts. However, the Panchayati Raj system remained dysfunctional over a long period. Then, it was after two decades that the State Government introduced an innovative concept of 'Single Line Administration', with the basic aim to secure people's participation through their representatives in the developmental process. This developmental strategy in no way proved helpful to the Panchayati Raj system, but explored the human potential available at the grassroots level that led to the introduction of Jammu & Kashmir Panchayati Raj Act, 1989.

The Preamble of the Jammu & Kashmir Panchayati Raj Act, 1989 states: "Whereas it is expedient to promote and develop Panchayati Raj in the State as an instrument of vigorous local self-government to secure effective participation of the people in the decision-making process and for overseeing implementation of development programmes" (Rural Development Department, 2011: 1). The salient features of the Act include: Three tier-system of Panchayat institutions; reduction of voting age from 21 to 18 years; direct election of the Sarpanchs; constitution of Panchayati Adalat (Panchayat Courts); empowering panchayats to prepare plans and implement schemes for poverty alleviation and employment generation, agriculture and allied activities, rural industrialization, health, universalization of elementary education etc. Meanwhile, it was only in 2001 that the State government, despite inhospitable security environment, succeeded in conducting Panchayat elections. However, the PRIs as set up for the democratic decentralization of development administration witnessed only insignificant women representation. The state government took a bold step in 2004 while amending the Panchayati Raj Act of 1989 on the lines of 73rd Amendment Act to the Constitution of India providing 33 per cent reservation of seats for women in these local governance institutions.

Local self-government institutions act as a means to good governance. It was the same realization that led the state government to carry out 2004 Amendment to ensure better governance. However, the government again failed in conducting Panchayat elections in the state. The coalition government formed by JKNC-INC in 2008 under Omar Abdullah strongly encouraged the establishment of local self-government and announced to conduct elections for the same purpose. As a result, the government succeeded in conducting elections for the Panchayati Raj Institutions in 2011. Out of 143 blocks, Kashmir province had 77 blocks with 2164 Sarpanch Constituencies (out of 4130 total constituencies) and 15,959 Panch Constituencies (out of 29,719 constituencies) (Chief Electoral Officer 2011: 2). The people of Jammu & Kashmir vigorously participated in these elections to choose their representatives.

The most significant feature of 2011 Panchayat elections in the state was the participation of women, not only as voters but also as the candidates to represent women in state administration. More than ten thousand women were elected in these local democratic institutions as Panchs and Sarpanchs. The analysts rightly put these elections as milestone in empowering women of the state. Nevertheless, there are certain issues prevalent in the state of Jammu & Kashmir that act as hindrance in the way of empowering women.

Generally, it is argued that women reservation in PRIs has enhanced their representation but not provided genuine empowerment to them. Some are of the opinion that women reservation in PRIs has actually empowered male members of their families, as they indirectly influence the decision-making in these local governance institutions (Singh, 2013: 1). Thus, it is a significant issue to analyse and explore the role of Kashmiri Women in the functioning of PRIs. There is a need to unveil the extent of the decision-making power of women in PRIs and the problems they are facing.

One of the significant issues in relation to women empowerment in Kashmir is the recent attacks on elected Panchayat representatives and its impact on women status and their political participation. Militants have attacked and killed several Panchs and Sarpanchs in Kashmir division including women representatives. The then Director General of Police, Ashok Prasad said "Our investigations have revealed that militants carried out attacks on Panchs and Sarpanchs like in Kulgam and Sopore etc., as they are soft targets.... We are assessing the situation in different areas at various levels to frame a strategy for ensuring security to Panchs and Sarpanchs" (Panchayat Raj Updates, 2013: 2).

After recent attacks on elected panchayat members, Army has increased patrolling across Kashmir to ensure security among panchayat leaders. However, these attacks have prompted scores to flee their homes as well as resign from the task to represent people at local levels. Bashir Ahmad Malik, Valley Secretary of the Jammu & Kashmir Panchayat Conference stated: "They (Sarpanchs and Panchs) have gone to live with their relatives in other places or districts. The fear is spreading to other areas as well.... I have been receiving calls from our members from various parts of the Valley, saying that they are scared. Many of us are planning a rally in Srinagar to publicly announce our resignations" (Panchayat Raj Updates, 2013: 2).

Thus, women representatives in Kashmir are facing social, political and economic as well as security challenges in dealing affairs at local level. There are various issues and concerns in relation to women empowerment and Panchayati Raj system in Jammu & Kashmir raising certain queries. For instance, whether the reservation of seats in Panchayati Raj Institutions provides genuine empowerment to women in Jammu & Kashmir or it acts as a means to promote the interests of male population *via* women representation? What is the role of women representatives in actual decision-making process in PRIs? What is their role in mobilizing funds under various schemes? What is the impact of security related issues on the social life of women representatives in Jammu & Kashmir?

The author is conducting a survey in relation to the impact of social conservatism and security issues on women empowerment in Kashmir to explore the response of women elected representatives. Taking into consideration the conservative mindset of people acquitting the male domination as well as the impact of security related issues on the status and empowerment of women in Kashmir, some of the women representatives expressed their concern in handling the affairs of people as well as facing the ill-treatment at domestic level. For instance, the interaction with Dilshada Bhat, Panch, Sangram (Sopore), helped in revealing various problems women face at local level governance. She talked about illiteracy of Women Panchayat Representatives and its effects on the smooth functioning of the system, the patriarchal mind set up of the society as hindrances on their way, teasing of Women Elected Representatives by the males etc. She also talked of the insecurity they feel with the treatment of some locals and various groups (who were not willing women to participate in elections). For her, "security of life is the first priority. Only then, government can expect us to work properly as Panchayati Raj Representatives."

Another women representative Raja Begum, Panch, Sumbal Batmahalla (Bandipora) expressed same concerns with the addition of her tale that political participation led to the killing of her brother 12 years before, but no one came forward to provide any help after that unfortunate incident. Syeda Wani, Panch, Bandipora, Ward No. 7, is of the opinion that male Sarpanchs never allow the Women Panchs to work as per their capacity and potential. According to her, "Sarpanchs never take into consideration the consent of Women Panchs for any policy, programme and decision". She also shared her experience of hardships while dealing with bureaucracy and other officials of government departments. She also talked of the impact of women participation in Panchayats on their family lives. In her opinion, "Women are now facing the problems in their families as they spend time in local issues at the cost of their family affairs. However, there is no one to consider such sacrifices of women." Khaata Begum, Panch, Kralkuth Kunzar shared her views that "Women is the victim of domestic violence, lack of basic necessities of life as safe drinking water, health related issues etc.... I participated in the Panchayat elections with the hope to address these problems. However, I have faced lot of problems on the part of administration.... There are only promises in the hands of politicians and administrators. They are not willing to concretize these promises. They delay every time, whatever task we raise before them to address." She also talked of the funds to Panchayats and said, "Women Elected Representatives know nothing about such funds or schemes because of the male dominated society and system. There is no willingness on the part of administration to share such information to the Women Panchs."

Some women elected representatives also talked of the ways to challenge the male dominance and other problems women are facing. For instance, Syeda Wani, Panch, Bandipora, Ward No. 7 expressed her role as a bold woman to challenge the problems created by male representatives. She talked of her courage to face the bureaucracy and male Panchs and Sarpanchs to get her demands fulfilled. She also expressed her role in mobilizing other local women to support her in promoting their issues.

All this invokes the sense to work out a comprehensive strategy on the plight of women representatives in Jammu & Kashmir Panchayati Raj system and come out with the policies to strengthen the position of women in the evolving democratic set up of the country. The participation of women representatives in Panchayat meetings, formulating plans, mobilizing funds under various schemes as well as identifying beneficiaries of their localities is quite dissatisfactory. Reservation in quantitative terms will never prove beneficial in empowering women until the male dominated society will change its attitude from domestic to higher institutions of governance.

Thus, there should be awareness campaigns, seminars and workshops for providing adequate information to the women representatives regarding their role, power and significance in establishing the democratic set-up from grassroots level. The government has to focus the development of research institutions in a way to undertake gender-related research in the state of Jammu & Kashmir. The legal inculcation of women empowerment, as a goal of Panchayats, to address as a special local issue is also the need of hour. Nonetheless, there should be legal provisions for special training programmes to build capacity of women and train them in handling the issues pertaining to their localities.

REFERENCES

Bryson, Valerie. (2003). *Feminist Political Theory*. New York: Palgrave Macmillan.

Chief Electoral Officer, Jammu & Kashmir. (2011). 'Schedule for General Elections to Panchayats, 2011'. 18 March.

Heywood, Andrew. (2007). *Politics*. New York: Palgrave Macmillan.

Muzamil Jan, *Women Development in Kashmir: An intervention through Cooperation*, Jay Kay Books, Srinagar, 2011.

Panchayat Raj Update. February 2013. New Delhi: Institute of Social Sciences, vol. XX, no. 2.

Rural Development Department, Jammu & Kashmir. (2011). *Panchayati Raj Act, 1989 and Panchayati Raj Rules, 1996*. Srinagar: Government Press.

Shahzad Akhtar, *Kashmir Women Empowerment and National Conference*, Jay Kay Books, Srinagar, 2009.

Singh, Prof. Ranbir. (February 2013). "Our Panchayats, Our Future", *Panchayat Raj Update*, Institute of Social Sciences, New Delhi, vol. XX, no. 2.

23

Role of Media in Political Objectification and Sexualization of Female Body

A Post-colonial Discourse

Anusha Halim

> "It is far more difficult to murder a phantom than a reality."
>
> —*Virginia Woolf*

> "Cinema is a beautiful medium that reaches out to millions. Through film, we can implant idea in people's mindsets which can bring about significant changes."
>
> —*Kangana Ranaut, Bollywood actor*

Feminism, a movement which started in the late nineteenth and early twentieth century to liberate women and to achieve a common goal of equality of sexes has failed miserably in these two centuries. If we were to ask ourselves, can we really say women are free? We may have broken through legal and material hindrances but Media has weighed us down through the set images it has made of women. Media and power have always been synonymous. Media has the power to reach out to millions of people at the same time in no time. Media is not just a source of entertainment but works as a culture shaper in a way. Cinema, one of the major forms of media, as we can see rules the minds of billions whether it is through films or soaps or songs or advertisements. As strong as a medium Media is, it has a big responsibility for the amount of audience it caters to. But what is more intriguing and common in all these is the role and projection of women. Since time immemorial, women have been a subject of constant attention. Cinema has always been a matter of debate among teens, adults and old ones because of the way they significantly affect our mundane life. And it would not be wrong to say that they act as a source of *masala* in our lives, especially the women actors. Media, if not always, has mostly tried to objectify women. For example, why is it necessary for the Axe deodorant makers to show that applying this particular perfume will attract women? Women are used as a prop in most of the advertisements, for instance, the most recent ad of Sunny Leone is where she is seen on a beach in minimum clothes in the most erotic form to publicize the use of flavoured condoms. It is, however, the need of the hour to inform people about the use of various protective measures, but what does not make any sense here is the usage of Leone's body in the advertisement. She is not used to spread awareness but only as a marketing instrument. Luce Irigaray in *This sex Which Is Not One* writes,

> "Women, in this sexual imagery, is only a more or less obliging prop for the enactment of man's fantasies….But such pleasure is above all a masochistic prostitution of her body to a desire that is not her own and it leaves her in a familiar state of dependency upon man. Not knowing what she wants, ready for anything, even asking for more, so long as he will 'take' her as his 'object' when he seeks his own pleasure" (Irigaray, 1985: 25).

Naomi Wolf in *The Beauty of Myth* writes,

> "The sexual revolution promoted the discovery of female sexuality; 'beauty pornography'—which for the first time in women's history artificially links a commodified 'beauty' directly and explicitly to sexuality—invaded the mainstream to undermine women's new and vulnerable sense of sexual self-worth" (Wolf, 1991: 10).

Media, if it is informative at one point, it surely is deceptive most of the time. For example, propagating creams to whiten the skin, popular advertisements that we all see everyday, are nothing but a lie and many ads have been banned due to making wrong promises. Advertisements in South Asia are not only derogatory but are sexists as well. The progressive attitude that some of the ads boast about are mostly regressive. In these ads, working women are also expected to do their household work which is not wrong if their male counterparts invest just as much time in their house. After all, is it not the responsibility of both? One such Surf Excel ad shows a working woman coming late at home who is expected to wash clothes, cook and clean the house while at the same time husband is seen sitting on a couch, asking for coffee and relaxing. Some ads in the name of propagating their products show a fair and pretty woman taking shower while some profess that using a certain cream will make them fair and insinuate that fairness is directly related to getting hired in for a job. Such ads mostly inseminate self-hatred, self-loathing, physical obsession and fear of ageing. Advertisement like these not only gives away wrong information but also sets a wrong precedent for women by calling a fair girl beautiful while completely dismissing the duskier ones propagating the idea of not sharing responsibilities between partners. Wolf writes,

> "We are in the midst of a violent backlash against feminism that uses images of female beauty as a political weapon against women's advancement: the beauty myth. It is the modern version of a social reflex that has been in force since the Industrial Revolution. As women released themselves from the feminine mystique of domesticity, the beauty myth took over its lost ground, expanding as it wanted to carry on its work of social control" (Wolf, 1991: 10).

One of the earlier ads of Mercedes-Benz where they used women's breasts to give away the idea of comfort which did not just shamelessly objectify and commodify a woman's body but also took away her right to be human. What else would the display of women's body parts such as breasts, thighs, or buttocks mean, if not commoditization of her body. The nonsensical use of female body in most of the movies is just a decorative muse, while in ads, showing a man and a woman in the same shirt but in a different pose altogether where a man's shirt buttons are all closed while women's all wide open is nothing but a political tactic in order to increase sales rate and profit. Byerly and Ross in their book *Women and Media: An Introduction* mention that,

> "The macro-level is associated with finance and investment, and the macro-level with relations of production, including the day-to-day decision-making concerned with policy-making and creation of products. The micro-level is associated with media content, particularly the representation of women as subjects and the coverage of issues relevant to women's lives" (Byerly & Ross, 2006: 76).

Women in any society have to fight for her rights, be it in the West or India. In the writings of the post-colonial literature, women are seen on the periphery, they remain subaltern because of the way they have been treated in a patriarchal society. Suniti Namjoshi, a feminist fabulist, in her fable 'The Mothers of Maya Diip', highlights two different societies, one where there are no men just women and all of them are addressed as mothers. Namjoshi here presents us with a dystopian world in which these women live in a lesbian society and to give birth, they milk young boys of their semen and drown them in the sea which highlights the problematic issue of girl-killing in our society. On the other hand, there is another society, which does milk the boys of their semen but instead of killing them, they keep them and designate them as mothers, again a problematic situation because in the process they are manipulated into living as what they are not, stripping away their identity. The twist comes in when a young girl named Jyanvi enters this place and she falls in love with a woman who is a part of this dystopian set-up named Saraswati who is also a mother. The problem comes when Jyanvi refuses to take care of Saraswati's child and just wants to be her lover. Namjoshi questions this matriarchal society which outcasts Jyanvi because she does not fit in the conventional idea of being a mother. Namjoshi, through her work tries to show the problems with the matriarch rule and is directly emphasizing the problems that are there in the patriarchal world.

Charlotte Perkins Gilman's work, 'If I Were a Man', projects a woman who fantastically turns into her husband and finds out that she has 'pockets', that she is now financially independent. Gilman, like Virginia Woolf shows the importance of letting a female work, she might be much more talented than the man, but the patriarchal society decided otherwise and devoid her of any chance altogether. Gilman goes on to make people understand the loss of identity with which a woman suffers when she is not even considered worth giving chance. She is expected to fit in the roles of a daughter, a wife, and a mother and if she deviates from these assigned stereotyped roles, she is to be only considered a prostitute.

> "Margaret Gallagher's (1979) UNESCO-funded study emphasized the underlying reason why women's image would continue to concern women for decades to come: 'The... media are potentially powerful agents of socialization and social change-presenting models, conferring status, suggesting appropriate behaviours, encouraging stereotypes' " (Quoted in Byerly & Ross, 2006, p. 17).

Concentrating on the projection of women in ads, we see that a woman only gets married when she is taken to a jewellery shop because, of course, it's a womanly trait to look pretty and be materialistic. This is not just limited to the ads but songs as well. "Chitiya Kaliya" loosely translated as *White Arms,* became an instant hit and one of the loved songs for the young generations, is another example, where Jacqueline Fernandez (Indian actor) is seen dancing on the streets, showing off her white arms, and asking her man to take her to movies, shopping and the like instead of doing it all of that herself. There are various songs where women are compared to an Indian sweet that is '*Jalebi*', or a firecracker that is '*Patakha*', or is even compared to a 'bomb'. And these are only the decent ones. One such singer whose popularity rests on objectifying women is Honey Singh, an Indian Rapper. One of his songs that went viral is 'Blue eyes', which not only reduces women to a mere object through words but also through video. The woman is seen not as a human but only as a body to be used for sexual gratification, her body is compared to a bomb, an explosive used to kill people, a nasty comment is made on the way she is dressed up, and to grab her attention the man is luring her by showing off her white Ghini Car, not only this the girl is then subtly asked if she would like to go to a club or to the man's house.

Another very disturbing characteristics of Bollywood are its 'Item' numbers. As normal as this word 'Item' sounds, one would be surprised that this particular word is used in relation to women who dance off wearing minimal clothes and the only reason for casting these women in the film is to add spice. The most disturbing part of this whole show is that film industry projects it in a way that whatever that is being shown in the dance, be it twenty children dancing with a half-dressed female lead or forceful sexual acts, are enjoyed by women. And for a particular part of society, this is the ultimate truth that whatever that is shown by the media is gospel truth and hence, it later governs their actions. Now this only results in sexism, but also contributes to the collective psyche of men and they assume that only the women who stay at home are chaste and those who do not are impure and are available for them. Because media through its films, ads or soaps show women as weaker sex, this then plays a larger role in issues like low pay, freedom of choice, difficulty in getting equal career opportunities or education. As Ritupurna Chatterjee writes,

> "[i]t will be highly presumptuous to assume that Hindi cinema is the root cause of a spike in sexual assaults. But Bollywood and regional cinema in equal parts, because of their reach, scope and

> influence, have a larger role to play in assuming responsibility for the message it sends out to millions of audiences—some highly impressionable" (Yasin, 2013).

Television soaps comparatively have adopted a very progressive attitude by propagating a woman's career, widow re-marriage, by showing resistance towards child marriage and the like yet they fail to realize the loopholes and continue to be very dogmatic. One very popular show feature on Star Plus; "*Yeh Hain Mohabbatein*", loosely translated as "It is Love" is well-liked, and is run in almost every household in India and Pakistan. This television soap is a story of a woman who faces problems in getting married because she is infertile; she has been rejected several times before getting married. And eventually marries a divorcee who has a child. She is settled with a man who is not even interested in her and the only reason he and his family accept her is because of his daughter who loves this female. The female protagonist who hails from a good family, is beautiful, financially sound but due to one biological weakness which is not even her fault makes her settle in a relationship where the man is not concerned with her being. The situation of women from before has not changed much. Women of today are still expected to do the job designed for her at home, even if she is working outside without complaining. In the age of media where people seldom read history books, it becomes highly insensitive and irresponsible to present a distorted version of anything. When talking about representation, "Padmavat" by Sanjay Leela Bhansali, a film loosely based on the epic poem by Malik Muhammad Jayasi calls itself a historical drama yet misrepresented history by portraying Khilji's character inappropriately. Khilji who according to historical records was a tyrant but a great administrator is shown as a one-dimensional character that is a 'lustful barbaric meat eater'. The history of Khilji has not just been turned upside down but has been distorted. This particular film has not only altered Mughal history but has invoked Islamophobia, homophobia and is gender biased which has contributed to the already fixed generalization that all Muslims are terrorists. Be it the much talked about omission of Taj Mahal from history books by Uttar Pradesh government or the controversy of declaring Taj Mahal, a Temple and not a Tomb or be it sending every Muslim to Pakistan, if he or she points to one fault either of Indians or its system. In the age where Indian politicians are trying to divide India using its religious diversity, Media then becomes a weapon and hence, should be conscious enough to fight back the communalism and show the unbiased version of history or life. Rana Safavi, a remarkable author and historian in an interview says,

> "Lot of people have written historical fiction and they have been taken as actual truth. We are in the age of twitter, we are in the age of hundred and forty characters, we definitely do not want to read books, seeing videos and consuming movies is far easier. So, the visual medium is the most successful and which has the biggest reach. So the filmmakers and people who make videos have a lot of responsibilities that they should not show anything which so completely distorts history....because they (protagonists) both belong to different religions, that sets up a clash of civilizations which is not what Jayasi definitely wanted because his book starts with *Bismillah-ir-Rahman-ir-Rahim*" (Safavi, *Hindustan Times*, 2018).

Safavi in her interview further mentions that Jayasi has talked about Mansarovar, a lake fed by the Kailash glaciers, and goes on to say that the world has been made by Allah for Muhammad, the last Prophet. Safavi mentions how beautifully Jayasi combines it all to create a unity between Chistees and Nathpanthis and she goes on to say that Bhansali has missed the entire point of the poem '*Padmavat*'. She says,

> "The poem *Padmavat* is a fight between Ishq-e-Haqiqi which is divine love and Nafs (ego). ... Khilji was no doubt cruel and tyrant but he was not a barbarian. He was in fact a very astute administrator, his agrarian and land and market reforms have been followed by many, in fact his land reforms were followed by Akbar and Sher Shah because he cuts off the intermediary between the cultivator and the State and took direct tax from them. So, he reduced the burden on them as well as increased taxation because he needed to maintain an army" (Safavi, *Hindustan Times*, 2018).

Safavi further adds that he did all these things because,

> "he needed to defend his borders and strengthen the army. The Mongols were standing just at the doorstep of the Delhi Sultanate, and they had already devastated most of Central Asia, in fact Baghdad, Samarqand and all these places had been destroyed by the Mongol horde and it is under Alauddin Khilji that he kept

> Delhi safe that art and culture flourished, men of learning came here and Delhi in fact started to be called Baghdad of the east" (Safavi, *Hindustan Times*, 2018).

Bhansali's film only showed a part of Khilji's character of his being a tyrant and a bisexual, all the while dealing with the subject insensitively, but forgets to keep the rest which makes it highly stereotypical. Another failed character of Malik Kafur played by Jim Sarbh has been turned into a "lovesick buffoon". Bhansali has failed to acknowledge that Kafur was in fact a very successful General who not only handled the Deccan campaign but the Mongol campaign as well. Its main female lead played by Deepika Padukone, she kills herself along with many other women in order to protect their honour. Bhansali could have portrayed a strong character by making her fight but he succumbed to the stereotypical image of women being weak. Such portrayal of one-dimensional caricature not only contributes to the hatred but also strengthens the very idea of stereotype.

Media is only making films, soaps and advertisements which show women as either damsels in distress or item numbers or somebody who is a heartbreaker or a mother or a slut. Women are either shown in the light of White or Black. What they fail to realize is that women are more than their face, body or colour. It is equally disturbing to see young women doing everything in their power to look flawless by opting face-lift surgeries, breast enlargement, starving themselves to get a zero figure due to the nailed down image that media has made of women by showing that only flawless women gets a job or a man to like them. Advertisements are using women as goods, they are used as a bait for their profits, setting unjust standards for other women and men to follow. The beauty which every man and woman is striving for keeps changing and with every decade new standard come up. Earlier beauty was all about being fair skinned, people with darker skin were associated with the working class and fair with an elite, voluptuous body is considered to be a sign of fertility and now people pay to get tan skin and spend hours in gym to get that perfect slim body. Irigaray writes,

> "Why are men not objects of exchange among women? It is because women's bodies—through their use, consumption, and circulation—provide for making social life and culture possible, although they remain an unknown 'infrastructure' of the elaboration of that social life and culture" (Irigaray, 1985: 171).

Media shows women as damsels in distress, always in need to be of help and protection just like most of the Disney movies. We tell stories of princesses to our daughters which make them believe that they need their prince charming to protect and rescue them which later in life results in weaker psyche in young girls and does not let them take charge of their lives.

But the media, as a wonderful and dangerous weapon that it is, forgets that what it shows in reel becomes a real life tragedy for many. For instance, projecting stalking as romance. The 2015 Bollywood Blockbuster Film, "Tanu Weds Manu Returns", starrer R. Madhavan, is seen following a girl who is his wife's look-alike. It showed Madhavan (Manu) in all its innocence, as a victim of the story and her wife as a vamp, while neglecting the fact that the wife (Tanu) in the movie has been expected to follow the rules set by the patriarchal society. Tanu, who is different from a conventional woman, is left alone by her husband while the love interest of Manu shifts to another girl whom he stalks. 'Stalking' which is a crime in many countries is shown as a romance in the film; Manu stalks this new girl (Kusum). The film is well-liked by people across the country and beyond, the director, however, without realizing sends a message of stalking as a normal act and that it should be followed by any man who wishes to woo a girl. And if this was not enough it also encourages 'kidnapping' which is a crime all-over the world. It does not only put a normal friendship in a bad light but also conveys that 'kidnapping' is okay. It boasts that kidnapping should be done if the girl you wish to marry does not reciprocate your feelings; you have the authority to kidnap her and make her yours by force. The character of Deepika Padukone from a 2012 movie 'Cocktail' is of a girl who drinks, has had relationships, and not very conventional so to say according to Indian standards, undergoes a complete transformation in order to be accepted by his love interest. Another one such movie, which again was a huge success, is a 1993 film, 'Darr' loosely translated as 'Fear', where we see Bollywood's romance king Shahrukh Khan in love with Juhi, which in reality is a movie of a stalker and a psychopath who is in dire need of medical treatment. Next on the list is Kundan's character from the 2013 film 'Ranjhana', another hit, is a story of an innocent boy who loved a girl with all his heart and died without getting his love reciprocated and the blame of his unrequited love is finally put on the girl. Meanwhile, we see audience's coming out from the theatre, crying their hearts out while young girls curse Zoya (Sonam Kapoor) for not loving the hero back. What slips from the minds of these young people is that Kundan was nothing but a psychopath who followed Zoya everywhere and could never accept and come to terms with the fact that she also has rights to choose whom she loves. The idea of romance, relationships, independence, beauty, and acceptance in these films is nothing but dark. The image that the media has created of women is the reason why we are in dire need of women empowerment.

It is now a high time for us people to understand the difference between chivalry and cheapness, between love and stalking, between being moody or taking space, between weak and strong, between progressive and selfish, understanding what lies within and what lies beyond and not everything that media shows should be followed blindly. Harassment is not love, for what this generation falls prey to. One must understand that the idea of beauty differs, it is not fixed but is very much relative and what after all beauty is and should we give this idea of beauty so much power so as to ruin lives. As women, we do many things which give us the satisfaction of approval from others, but in order to earn the respect of people we change ourselves, where our greatest weakness lies. As Kangana Ranaut stated in The World Summit in London that, "You have to be confident of who you are. Others' opinions of you will always shift." Because we are not our hair or lips or body, because we are more than just spice, because we are HUMAN.

> "Thus, women's secrets I've surveyed
> And let them see how curiously they're made,
> And that, tho' they of different sexes be,
> Yet in the whole they are the same as we.
> For those that have the strictest searchers been,
> Find women are but men turned outside in;
> And men, if they but cast their eyes about,
> May find they're women with their inside out"

—*The Works of Aristotle in Four Parts*, 1822, p. 16.

REFERENCES

Byerly, Carolyn M. and Karen Ross. *Women and Media: A Critical Introduction.* Malden: Blackwell Publishing Ltd., 2006. Print.

Irigaray, Luce. "This Sex Which Is Not One". *This Sex Which Is Not One*. Trans. Catherine Porter and Carolyn Burke. Cornell University Press, 1985. Print.

Irigaray, Luce. “Women on the Market”. *This Sex Which Is Not One*. Trans. Catherine Porter and Carolyn Burke. Cornell University Press, 1985. Print.

Namjoshi, Suniti. *The Mothers of Maya Diip*. The Women’s Press Limited, 1989.

Safavi, Rana. “Islamophobic, homophobic and sexist: why Bhansali’s Padmaavat is problematic.” *Times, Hindustan*. Online video clip. YouTube. YouTube, 1 Feb. 2018. Web. 9 Mar. 2018. <https://www.youtube.com/watch?v=1b8wdnufXoc>.

Wolf, Naomi. “The Beauty Myth.” *The Beauty Myth: How Images of Female Beauty Are Used against Women*. Vintage, Clays Ltd., St Ives Plc, 1991. Print.

Yasin, Sara. *X index: The Voice of Free Expression*. 21 January, 2013. 16 October, 2015 <https://www.indexoncensorship.org/2013/01/bollywood-india-gender-women-new-delhi-salman-khan/>.

BIBLIOGRAPHY

Byerly, Carolyn M. and Karen Ross. *Women and Media: A Critical Introduction*. Malden: Blackwell Publishing Ltd. 2006. Print.

Green, Germaine. *The Female Eunuch*, Great Britain: MacGibbon & Kee Ltd., 1970. Print.

Times, Hindustan. “Islamophobic, homophobic and sexist: why Bhansali’s Padmaavat is problematic.” Online video clip. YouTube. YouTube, 1 Feb. 2018. Web. 9 Mar. 2018. <https://www.youtube.com/watch?v=1b8wdnufXoc>.

Namjoshi, Suniti. *The Mothers of Maya Diip*. The Women’s Press Limited, 1989.

Riach, Graham K. *An Analysis of Gayatri Chakravorty Spivak’s Can the Subaltern Speak?* Routledge, 2017.

Richardson, Angelique. *Women Who Did: Stories by Men and Women, 1890-1914*. Penguin Books, 2005.

Wolf, Naomi. “The Beauty Myth.” *The Beauty Myth: How Images of Female Beauty Are Used against Women*. Vintage, Clays Ltd., St Ives Plc, 1991. Print.

Yasin, Sara. *X index: The Voice of Free Expression*. 21 January 2013. 16 October 2015 <https://www.indexoncensorship.org/2013/01/bollywood-india-gender-women-new-delhi-salman-khan/>.

24

Gender and Media

Interrelationship between Construction, Stereotype and Impact

Shah Alam

We live in a mediated, consumption-oriented society, where the stories produced and disseminated by media institutions play an essential role in deciding the worthiness of the issues. The media informs the masses and keeps us updated by taking the follow-ups and moulding people's opinions by distinctly teaching them. Individuals learn a great deal from how images of women and men are portrayed in the media. Besides other socializing influences such as family and peers, the media helps form perceptions of gender roles and can shape the behaviours that stem from those perceptions. How individuals shape their social characters, how they come to differentiate between genders, colour, ethnicity, race, caste—even urban or rural—is shaped by objectified texts presented by media for audiences that are increasingly biased by the social construction of gender. In short, the media has a strong position in controlling our social realities. Research offers compelling evidence suggesting that men and women are far more similar than being different across a wide range of domains. Our gendered perceptions can lead us to believe that men and women inhabit different characteristics, which can trigger self-fulfilling prophecies confirming these expectations. While the difference in gender is rooted in biology, how we perceive and perform gender is rooted in culture. The social milieu influences the manifestation of present attitudes and behaviours, but it is also a powerful shaping force throughout the lifespan. According to Byers & Dell (1992), we reckon culture—as a procedure through which people share and discuss the meanings of our social experiences, social relations, and, therefore, ourselves. This chapter looks into the relationship between gender and media and how media portrays gender in response to its construction and stereotype. It also investigates how mediated communication represents the social construction of gender and ultimately shapes our understanding of the same.

Media and (de)construction of Gendered Identities

Media plays a dominant role in people's everyday lives. It influences how we see ourselves and the world to some extent. In different forms of media, images of men and women are represented in different ways and with different characteristics. The media has a substantial impact on culture, shaping societal structures and operations. Dominant media forms profoundly assist in constructing gender norms. The codes displayed by advertising and other media platforms are associated with representing male and female attributes. These gender codes shape how society views gender and assists in determining what acceptable gender performance is. The media's reinforcement of gender stereotypes, codes, and gender displays shapes how society perceives and constructs genders. Eliminating negative gender stereotypes is essential to achieving gender equality, and the media are central to promoting this change.

Gender is not formed at birth; this self-identification of being male or female is constructed through cultural and social attributions. Media platforms set these social and cultural attributions as ideals for gender performances. In today's world, mass media works as a primary tool that introduces and encourages individuals to be a part of a gendered world (Krijnen & Van Bauwel, 2015). The societal standards set by media organizations shape male and female characteristics to be identified by the social pattern. Within the media, men are constructed to be influential, aggressive figures, embracing financial stability, and dominant control. At the same time, the media projects women to be constructed as nurturing figures, concerned with family and sustaining feminine beauty. These gender assumptions often display negative representations that create hurdles for women in developing and reaching their true potential within society. In her work "Women, work and social rights", Celica Benoit believes that gendered stereotypes make it more difficult for women workers to be seen with seriousness. Benoit also states that male colleagues are more respected in these companies, for they are perceived as more dedicated workers (Cecilia M. Benoit, 1999). Benoit's findings reveal that the media's influence constricts both men and women, as the sexes are forced to conform to gendered ideals.

Following in the wake of the political liberalization, women's advocacy organizations created a potential new space that did not previously exist under the one-party system. These organizations spearheaded the struggle for women's liberation, which can be seen as the beginning of a women's movement. The significance of a women's movement is seen in a cognitive space filled with the interaction between different groups, organizations, and institutions (Eyerman and Jamison, 1991). This position falls into a broader category of recent research on culture and social movements influenced by post-structuralism and post-modernism, extending the perspective of movement culture as a process in interaction with other institutions. It focuses on the new symbolic codes created by groups that challenge the *status quo* and are expressed through different forms of public discourse (Taylor and Whittier, 1995). The mass media is only one arena for public discourse, but it is the central one for social movements because it is the only site that provides a potentially shared public discourse (Gamson and Modigliani, 1989). The media plays a decisive role in the broader dissemination of ideas, issues, and actions because it allows new ideas and issues to be discussed as part of the public agenda, as opposed to in more closed circles. In this way, the media helps redefine collective identities.

These gender codes become slowly acculturated within mass media and marketing. These days, many advertisers portray men and women with stereotypical gender norms and roles. In many advertisements, women are often displayed in a sexualized nature that exposes females as vulnerable, defenceless figures (Jhally, 1989). Men are generally displayed in advertisements symbolizing power and status. Male advertisements use a body that displays and conveys men as dominant and aggressive (Jhally, 1989). This body language in advertisements allows companies to construct gender identity and reinforce gender norms. Making advertisements that construct gender enables these companies to effectively market, as they can invoke through these products.

There are many advertisements marketed towards children, which exposes gender identities and roles. Such advertisements develop a sense of gender identity in children's minds by conforming to gender roles. Psychologist Lawrence Kohl perceives gender identity as constructed within the early stages of childhood. Mass media messages display masculine and feminine characteristics as the norm for society. These norms leave a substantial impact on children at their young age as they have an intense yearning to fit in and feel accepted amongst their peers. These masculine and feminine characteristics constructed by media messages, become acculturated into modern culture and are manifested to society as the standard practice for men and women. It becomes apparent that gender is socially and culturally constructed through media outlets. These media forms are incredibly influential and can alter how society perceives gender.

While representations of women always have been central to feminist media critique, feminist media studies have gone through considerable changes and critique since feminism took off in the early sixties. This entails a movement away from a monolithic view of women as unconditional victims of sexist media. Cultural studies associated with the Birmingham School have been an essential influence in redefining feminist media studies and rethinking media influence in general. According to Liesbet van Zoonen (1994), the most fruitful research has been carried out at the junction of cultural and feminist studies, which has given rise to inquiries that reach far more profound and broader than the original limited agenda of matters such as stereotypes and sex-role socialization. In particular, Stuart Hall's encoding/decoding model (1973) for the production of meaning has been an essential influence in feminist media research and has inspired some of the main issues in this thesis. The model states that the construction of meaning is framed between producers and audiences based on some sort of negotiation. The tensions and contradictions in the production are acknowledged and reverberated in media texts, which can no longer be seen as consistent entities carrying singular meaning. Texts are characterized as 'polysemic' (Morley, 1980), which carries contradictory, divided, and plural meanings, which opens the possibility of cultural resistance in the reception.

An essential element in the cultural studies tradition is that the construction and taking of meaning do not happen in a vacuum; instead, meaning production must be understood as situated in a specific historical and social context embedded in existing power formations. This gives rise to how gender constructions in the media discourse can be related to the context in which they are produced—political, economic, social, or cultural. Therefore, the media and its producers can operate within different and sometimes contradicting discourses; feminist versus commercial; modern *versus* traditional; official *versus* popular discourses.

Both cultural and feminist studies have had the ambition to produce a cultural critique that contributes to a better understanding of the relationships between power and exclusion. However, research carried out in the junction of cultural and feminist studies have been criticized for reconstructing the dominant gender discourse rather than analyzing its dynamics (van Zoonen, 1994). In handling the complexity in the media discourse, which entails both dominant representations and alternative and perhaps challenging definitions of gender, the support is found in feminist post-structuralism. The approach provides a focus on the media as a site for conflict and contestation in which the definition of gender is subjected to continuous discursive struggle and negotiation. The media, as it represents only one discourse and practice, is in itself a product of multiplicity, sometimes entailing contradictory cultural definitions of femininity, which positions the individual subject in different, overlapping, and competing ways.

A central element in post-structuralism is that the dominant discourse tends to produce its opposition. Therefore, the disciplinary power of discourse prescribing and restricting gender identities and experiences can be resisted and subverted. Post-structuralism carries a strong liberal element, crucial in a cultural struggle of women's emancipation and in explaining social change. From this perspective, women's/gender NGOs spearheading the struggle for women's liberation can be viewed as 'communities of discourse' engaged in the enunciation of new cultural codes that might contest dominant representations and prevailing notions of gender (Taylor and Whittier, 1992).

Feminists have increasingly shown an interest in culture and representation, in which a cultural struggle is shaping the nature of femininity and masculinity (Michèle Barrett, 1992). Prevailing definitions of gender are being contested in both the symbolic realm of mass communication and at the more mundane level of everyday life, characterized by routine and ordinary activities, thoughts, and feelings (van Zoonen, 1994). This renewed attention to culture is probably a consequence of both a general turn towards culture in the social sciences and the development of feminist post-structuralism, focusing on gender as a cultural construct constituted in social and cultural practices and discourses.

Stereotypical Transformations and the Impact of Media

Gender stereotypes are generalized views or preconceived notions. Individuals categorized into different groups and categorized as women and men and are assigned specific characteristics and roles limited to their sexes. Stereotypes are descriptive, in which members of a particular group are perceived to have the same attributes regardless of individual differences. They are prescriptive as they set the parameters for what societies deem to be acceptable behaviour. Stereotyping becomes more complicated when it is used as a vehicle to degrade and discriminate against women. Gender stereotyping is the exercise of ascribing to an individual woman or man specific attributes, characteristics, or roles owing to their membership in the social group of women or men. A gender stereotype is a belief which may cause its holder to make assumptions about members of the subject group, women and men. Contrary to it, gender stereotyping is the practice of applying that stereotypical belief to a person.

A stereotype becomes deleterious when it limits women's or men's capacity to develop their potentials, pursue their prospective careers, and make choices about their lives and life plans. Any type of stereotypes can be harmful. For example, it is based on the stereotype that women are more nurturing than child-rearing responsibilities often fall exclusively on them. Gender stereotyping also becomes wrongful when it leads to the violation of human rights. The CEDAW Committee highlighted how traditional attitudes by which women are regarded as subordinate to men perpetuate widespread practice involving violence and coercion.

Women's image and the role played by them in the media are heavily influenced by existing social and cultural norms, including gender stereotypes. When visual means of communication predominate, the stereotypical images of women and men influenced by the media can subvert the progress made in pursuit of gender equality. Nevertheless, the media are a means of power and influence in promoting social values and shaping social opinions. Hence, it can be one of the most robust tools to advance the cause of gender equality. The messages propagated by media leave a significant impact on how social and cultural norms concerning gender are perceived and evolve. In such cases, gender-neutral portrayals of women and men can be crucial in promoting and strengthening social awareness of gender equality and preventing and eradicating gender discrimination.

As per gender-stereotypical perceptions, women are expected to be dependent, weak, incompetent, emotional, fearful, flexible, passive, modest, soft-spoken, gentle and caretakers. In contrast, men are supposed to be powerful, competent, relevant, logical, decision-makers, aggressive, focused, energetic, and assertive. The stereotypical notions are deeply engulfed in the social consciousness, which leads us to believe these notions are basic norms. In the social set-up, where a patriarchal society flourishes, 'son preference' is an age-old gender bias. The male of the family is expected to bear the responsibility of carrying forward the legacy of the family. On the other hand, girls or women are generally regarded as '*Parayadhan*' or others' property. The dowry given to the groom ensures that daughters are often seen as an 'economic liability'.

Sex (being male or female), is essentially a question of biology and genetics, while gender is the cultural and social codes and conventions associated with either sex. The identification of dichotomy between sex and gender has become increasingly crucial as feminist and masculinist criticisms have sought to question the conventional and established perceptions in which we are brought up to think of men and women. Feminist and masculinist critics argue that the ideas and traits associated with gendered roles are not issues of biological determination, but social and cultural conventions. Being born a woman or a man does not necessarily mean being either a housewife/homemaker or a professional working outside of the home. Gender is perhaps the primary category we use for sorting human beings, and it is a crucial issue while discussing the representation. The concepts of gender are associated with the elements of one's identity, which are established societal norms.

Media seems to be an essential way of establishing these identities to modify or even define them. Through visibility, media makes us grow up with an awareness of what constitutes appropriate characteristics for objects and humans. It is straightforward to recognize that typically masculine means robust, hard, sweaty, and typically feminine, supposing fragility, softness, and fragrance. Feminist thinkers believe that there is a significant and long-lasting influence of the media in either challenging or perpetuating existing gender norms. Liesbet van Zoonen explores how feminist theory and research contribute to the broader interpretation of multiple roles of media in gender construction in contemporary societies. Media as an instrument and means for gender sensitization can only be utilized when the full influence of media on gender construction is understood.

The social milieu, which can influence the reflection of people's attitudes and behaviours, can also serve as a powerful medium in shaping their perceptions throughout the lifespan. Bussey and Bandura (2004), in their work on a social-cognitive approach to gender development, suggested that "the mass media and ongoing input from parents and peers offer pervasive cultural modeling of gender roles." These are only children who assimilate cultural models. Research on the possible selves suggests that throughout our lives, we continue to draw hoped for and feared selves from the categories made salient by the individual's particular socio-cultural and historical context. These fears and hopes are also influenced by the models and images provided by the media and by the individual's immediate social experiences.

Gender stereotyping indicates the process through which gender roles are perpetuated in the socialization of individuals. It refers to preconceived ideas, whereby males and females are arbitrarily assigned characteristics and roles determined and limited by their sex. Gender stereotyping forces individuals to adhere to a predetermined gender role because of their sex and regardless of their natural predisposition. It may limit the development of their natural talents and abilities, resulting in a waste of human resources. More generally, it influences the formation of gender identities among young people, influencing their educational choices, and consequently, their future professional and private lives. Gender stereotypes that diffuse the mass media may have direct consequences for women's intellectual performance and career aspirations. Davies, Spencer, Christine and Iserman (2009) theorized that sexist media depictions might activate stereotype threat conditions. Women may fear being negatively evaluated based on a prevalent stereotype and may consequently dis-identify with or underperform in domains in which they are not expected to do well. Stereotypical representations of gender in the mass media also interact with racial stereotypes to affect individuals' perceptions and behaviour.

Along with other 'socialization agencies', such as the education system, and family, the media play a pivotal role in providing the 'symbolic materials' (images, role models, values, and narratives) that individuals are likely to use of constructing their identity. Dennis McQuail conceptualizes such a phenomenon in terms of the 'negotiated influence of media' in its four-phase account of the development of thinking about media effects. In his view, the media use a social constructivist tool: they construct meanings and offer them to the audience members, who negotiate and incorporate them within their meaning structures. Therefore, the meanings are constructed by the audience members through a mediation process that is mostly influenced by the receivers' social context.

Although the audiences are free to accept or refuse media contents and meanings, it is the media system that has the power to decide which gender role models will be visible and which ones will not, as described by the classic agenda-setting theory which underlines the ability of the media to influence the significance of issues on the public agenda. TV current affairs programmes, radio dramas, music videos, songs, magazines, adverts, and websites represent authoritative sources of gender information that might reinforce or challenge our ideas about gender.

This makes the role of media a particularly ambivalent one. The media, especially mainstream, commercial media, aim to attract as much audience as possible. Therefore, they tend to 'play safe', emphasizing shared values, using a simple language, and providing an often simplistic, stereotyped representation of social reality, groups, and phenomena. Stereotypes are common and widespread because they help us understand complicated processes, reduce uncertainty, and provide a sense of security. Nevertheless, stereotyping in any field is a way of thinking that preserves from social change, and gender stereotyping is no exception to this.

It is crucial to mention that women are not a homogenous group with the same experiences. However, they do experience what we call intersectionality: multiple and varying degrees of disadvantage and marginalization that may vary from context to context, and from woman to woman. However, these experiences are organized around the demographic markers of gender, age, class, sexual orientation, and physical and other disabilities. This intersectionality element makes it difficult to talk about "women" in general, but it forces us to grasp the complexity of the challenges women face. It is also important to acknowledge that social change's aim cannot focus on the "individual". It is not about improving women's position in the media on an individual or a particular group basis, but about improving their status as a social group. Therefore, although women are not just "one category," they are neither individuals devoid of social context.

Conclusion

Media's most significant role has always been linked to a watchdog and informing the citizenry so that participation in public affairs and decisions can be realized through democratic deliberation. The underlying conditions of democratic, mediated public deliberation are access to and exercise of citizenship rights, namely social, economic, cultural, and political rights. This means that public deliberation, at whose centre the media are firmly grounded, can be democratic only when speakers, viewpoints, and experiences consort equal respect and space, and where equality of dialogue partners is guaranteed.

The media continue to be considered the fourth pillar, despite wakeless changes in media landscapes and the enormous role the market plays in everyday management and content production. Moreover, despite the dominance of consumer-oriented discourse within and about today's media—discourse that characterizes communication as a business—is the fundamental principle of serving democratic values and democratic deliberation that guides public policy expectations and follows international standards tools of human and civil rights.

The role played by media in addressing gender issues has been of long-lasting concern when considering the process of moving towards gender-inclusive society. This role can be identified mainly through two interrelated fronts, by representing and narrating gender and gender roles through content programming, design, and production, media shapes and reinforces stereotypes and prejudices about women and men. These are also reinforced on a second front by the current structural organization of mass media and communications. The fact that women are still in the minority in media professions disadvantages them not only as producers of meaning but also as technologists and decision-makers.

In order to educate the public and to have an educated public, the news authors and the media representatives have to have a holistic image of what discrimination is, what gender equality is, and further how they have to represent the gender in media. Initially, a problem of consciousness, gender equality, and gender representations in media, as a general way of getting the information in our days, has become so important in the public sphere, that it is crucial to point out some aspects regarding women, men, and their public image. This public image transported by the media content and significances to the readers, viewers, and listeners contribute to educating the public in the sense of observation and traces some inequalities perpetuated by the media.

REFERENCES

Barrett, M. (1992). "Words and things: materialism and method in contemporary feminist analysis." In Barrett, M. and Phillips, A. (eds.), *Destabilizing Theory.* Cambridge: Polity Press.

Benoit, Cecilia M. (1999). *Women, Work and Social Rights: Canada in Historical and Comparative Perspective.* Canada: Pearson Education.

Bussey, K., and Bandura, A. (2004). "Social Cognitive Theory of Gender Development and Functioning." In A.H. Eagly, A.E. Beall, and R.J. Sternberg (Eds.), *The Psychology of Gender* (pp. 92-119). The Guilford Press.

Byers, J., and Dell, C. (1992). "Big differences on the small screen: Race, class, gender, feminine beauty, and the characters at 'Frank's Place'." In Lana F. Rakow (Ed.), *Women making meaning: New feminist directions in communication* (pp. 191-209). New York: Routledge.

Davies, Paul G., Steven J. Spencer, Christine Logel and Emma Iserman. (2009). "The perils of double consciousness: The role of thought suppression in stereotype threat", *Journal of Experimental Social Psychology.*

Eyerman, Ron and Jamison, Andrew (1991). *Social Movements: A Cognitive Approach*. Cambridge: Polity.

Gamson, W.A., and Modigliani, A. (1989). "Media discourse and public opinion on nuclear power: A constructionist approach." *American Journal of Sociology*, *95*, 1-37.

Hall, Stuart. (1973). *Encoding and Decoding in the Television Discourse*. Birmingham: University of Birmingham.

Jhally, S. (1989). "Advertising, gender and sex: What's wrong with a little objectification?" In R. Parmentier and G. Urban (Eds.), *Working papers and the proceedings of the centre for psychosocial studies*, 29.

Krijnen, T., and Van Bauwel, S. (2015). *Gender and Media: Representing, Producing, Consuming.*

"Lesbian Feminist Mobilization." In Aldon D. Morris and Carol M. Mueller (eds.), *Frontiers in Social Movement Theory,* pp. 104-129, New Haven: Yale.

Morley, D. (1980). *The 'Nationwide' Audience: Structure and Decoding*. London: BFI.

Taylor, Verta and Nancy Whittier (1992). *Collective Identity in Social Movement Communities*.

Zoonen, Liesbet van. (1994). *Feminist Media Studies*. London: Sage Publications.

25
Changing Discourse of Nationalism and the Status of Minorities in Bangladesh

Saiyad Md. Shahnawaz

The study of nationalism is prerequisite to analyse the evolution and nature of a nation. It has been an important tool to mobilise various sub-identities into one national symbol for political autonomy and self-determination.[1] In the view of Richard Handler, "Nationalism is an ideology concerned with boundedness, continuity, and homogeneity encompassing diversity."[2]

The idea of nationalism has been very much in evidence since the seventeenth century British rebellion against monarchy[3] and eighteenth century French Revolution of 1789.[4] However, "initially on the principle of nationality there was no attempt to fashion a general theory applicable to all cases, or to resolve the antinomies of each issue in a coherent and systematic manner."[5] But after the Second World War, nationalism became a subject of intense study influenced by the process of decolonization and the establishment of new states in Third World countries.[6]

Nationalism: Conceptual Understanding

Nationalism has been defined by a number of scholars. But these conceptual frameworks have different in terms of the contents and the characteristics of nationalism. In the Western context, nationalism is seen as a consciousness among a community leading to its self-determination and political autonomy. The Marxist on the other hand linked nationalism to the class struggle.[7] However in Indian subcontinent, both the Western and Marxist interpretation of nationalism is relevant. Here, nationalism is viewed as a symbol of unified struggle during patriotic movement against the colonial rule initially, but its discourse changed after the independence from the British Colonial Empire.

Nationalism as a concept is one of the mostly debated notions at the international arena and it has been defined by many authors; however, there is no comprehensive definition applicable to all situations. This is due to the fact that humanity is divided into nations, each nation has its own character, history and destiny.[8] So, its characteristics depend upon many other entities like ethnic, cultural, linguistic and religious identities of a specific community residing in a particular nation or state.

Basically, nationalism is an ideological and a political movement which can emerge in many forms. It is the subject of extensive and contextual interpretations. Smith in his work "Ethno-Symbolism and Nationalism" identified some key motifs and themes of 'nationalism'; those are autonomy, territorial unification, social solidarity, sorority, unique cultural identity, home land pride, feeling of indigeneity, continuity, proud feeling on glorious historical past and destiny etc.[9]

The above thematic characteristics defined by Smith suggest that, "nationalism can be defined as an ideological movement to attain and maintain autonomy, unity, authenticity as well as dignity on behalf of a population for the continuity of earlier culture towards glorious destiny."[10] It denotes that 'nationalism' is not simply a mobilization of shared sentiment or consciousness but an active movement to attain and maintain the nation imagined by political elites and nationalist leaders.[11]

Nationalism is seen as a state of mind of human beings; a manifestation of certain ideological goals which they wish to realize through united efforts. For John Hutchingson, "there are two distinctive and sometimes competing types of nationalism; a political nationalism that has as its aim of autonomous state; and a cultural nationalism that seeks a moral regeneration of the community"[12] in order to create a self-sustaining and unified nation. Sometimes both of this kind of nationalism is concerned with the welfare and autonomy of the nation.[13] However, after achieving political nationalism; when the cultural nationalism aims to the regeneration of the community, nationalism based on religion emerged which leads to discrimination and marginalization of religious minorities in a democratic state.

Hutchinson viewed that, "nationalism is believed to be strongly rooted in the thoughts and behaviour of people"[14] and Ishtiaq Ahmed opines that, "nationalism has been looked upon as a political doctrine of self-determination."[15] In this context nationalism is seen as a distinct phenomenon that combines the thought and behaviour of people in the process of self-determination.

Ernest Gellner believes that "nationalism is an explicable and inevitable natural corollary of certain salient conspicuous traits of modern or modernizing societies."[16] He perceived nationalism as a political principle, which holds that the political and national unit should be congruent.[17] Moreover, he points out that, "nationalism can be a sentiment or the feeling of anger aroused by the violation of principle, or the feeling of satisfaction aroused by its fulfilment."[18] Furthermore, he adds that the nationalist principle can be violated by several reasons such as lack of political control over boundaries of nations, the ruler's decision to favour particular groups, by which an intolerable sense between groups emerges.[19] Kohan saw nationalism as:

> "the giving of a specific political structure to certain inherent similarities among a particular group of people based on language, religion, customs and so forth. He defined nationalism as an idea that fills a man's brain and heart with new thoughts and new sentiments, and drives him to translate his consciousness into deeds of organized action. He argued that the growth of nationalism is the process of assimilation of the people into a common politicized form."[20]

Juergensmeyer in his book *Religious Nationalism Confronts the Secular State* (1994) viewed the emergence of Pakistan as an excellent example of the religion serving as a basis of nation-formation.[21] In line with Juergensmeyer; Anderson argues that, "nationalism is not a matter of politics or reason, but emotion, more akin to a religious feeling shared among individuals who otherwise possess little in common besides imagined emotional ties".[22] In context to the emergence of Pakistan, it can be presumed that the religion was only the factor which united the people from two separate territories (1200 miles) demanding single sovereign state (Pakistan). Besides religion (Islam), the people of both sides (East Pakistan & West Pakistan) had nothing similar. They had not only territorial distance separated by India, but they were also vastly different from one another in terms of ethnicity, traditions, cultures, rituals and many more things.

It is clear from some of the above stated definitions that nationalism has been viewed as a process through which an ethno-cultural identity moves towards self-determination. It took roots as a demand for self-determination since the end of the eighteenth-century French "Revolution of 1789."[23] It was due to the rise of nationalism that many empires with heterogeneous cultural groups got disintegrated and new independent states emerged with homogenous cultural identity. The ultimate goal of nationalism in Third World was to achieve statehood. In this way, nationalism in the Third World can be viewed as a process to unite the people on the basis of ethno-cultural identities and then to claim its sovereign rights over a particular territory.

Louis Snyder saw nationalism and national movements as a struggle against feudal or imperialist powers Marxisth theoretician.[24] Number of scholars have viewed nationalism in the context of developing countries and have tried to define it accordingly. There are many scholars who consider nationalism as a struggle against the colonial rule.[25]

In Third World, nationalism played a very effective role during freedom struggle of many countries. However, the nature of nationalism was not the same in every state due to the unique identity of its people and political elites. As a result, in some states, nationalism united people on the basis of composite culture and ancient tradition; while in other places, ethno-cultural and linguistic identities were very effective instruments to combine the aspiration of people. In all cases, the role of nationalism was to unite different segments of society into one, irrespective of varieties of identities.[26]

It can be said that nationalism is an ideological phenomenon adhered by a group or a community for the attainment of a political objective. Nationalism may have both negative and positive implications. For instance, Bangladesh represents a similar case. The 'Bangalee' nationalism espoused by the 1972 Constitution of Bangladesh requires Bengaliness to be the primary identity of the citizenry. On positive note, it united all the Bengalee speaking people from East Pakistan to be united against the West Pakistani oligarchy. In effect, it presupposes either the extermination of the cultural identity of the non-Bengalis or their submergence in the larger collectively. This implicit coterminality between citizenship and nationhood is resisted by minority nationalists. For example, Chakma leader Manabendra Narayan Larma refused to be identified as Bengali. He resisted on Bengaliness for Bangladeshi citizenship[27] and argued that: "I am a Chakma, not a Bengalee. I am a citizen of Bangladesh, a Bangladeshi. You are also a Bangladeshi, but your national identity is Bengalee...They (Chakmas) can never be Bengalee."[28] Just after 15 years of existence as a sovereign state, the Eighth Amendment (1988) to the Bangladeshi Constitution shifted ecthno-cultural nationalism to territorial nationalism by replacing 'Bangalee' with 'Bangladeshi' as the primary identity of citizenship. Again, the Fifteenth Amendment (2011) reverted back to 'Bangalee Nationalism' as of 1972.[29] So, with change in ruling regime, nationalism in Bangladesh changes from Bengali to Bangladeshi (nationalism) and *Vice Versa*.

Nationalism in Bangladesh

Nationalism in Bangladesh is a unique case to study. The people of Bangladesh are still searching their identities as Muslims, Bengalis or Bangladeshis. So, there is a need to observe the nationalism in Bengal from prior to the British era in order to understand nationalism in context to historical events.

In the view of Sanjay Bhardwaj, at the beginning of 13th century, "society in Bengal evolved with syncretic values emphasised on religious inclusion and tolerance among the people in relation to a wide range of influences that included Buddhism, Hinduism, Islam, Sufism and Tantrik cultures, each of which had been accommodated within indigenous tribal cultures."[30] He further opined that these syncretic values promoted, "a unique Bengali Muslim identity different from other Islamic culture, where Muslims and Hindus could venerate common deities and holy men (*Pirs*), and pay tributes to the same shrines (*Mazars*)."[31]

During the period of British-India the sense of separate identity is raised into the mind of the people in this region. The Muslim rulers and Sultans created misconceptions among Muslim middle class against the Hindus of Bengal. Their backwardness was manipulated by Muslim elites to create a sense of a separate identity ('Muslim Nationalism' instead of 'Bengal Nationalism'). As a result, Bengal was firstly partitioned in 1906 on the basis of religious identities. Later, the traumatic upheaval of India's Partition based on two-nation theory (Pakistan for Muslims and India for Hindus) sowed the seeds of religious nationalism in Indian subcontinent. The symbol of religion provided the most powerful basis of political identity and action during the movement for Pakistan. As a result, the British-India was divided into two separate states, namely India and Pakistan in 1947.

Following the initial jubilation of nationhood, the Pakistan state did not attempt to resolve problems inherent in uniting a culturally pluralistic, ethnically diverse and geographically divided society. It was assumed that the imagined national unity achieved from religious identity would somehow contain the complex ethnic, linguistic and cultural differences that existed within Pakistan. But the emergence of Bangladesh in 1971 in the name of secular and Bengali nationalism broke the religion-based state ideology of the Pakistani period (1947-1971).[32] Religious nationalism was unable to provide the physical integrity of the new nation-state for long. Unlike West Pakistan, East Pakistan had a long tradition of syncretistic cultural practices; as a result religious identity was overridden during the springing up of Bengali nationalism, that eventually led to the creation of Bangladesh in 1971.

The Emergence of Bengali Nationalism

Some of the main reasons for the emergence of "Bengali Nationalism" in East Pakistan were the lack of Bengali political participation in official decision-making processes, and the colonial-style economic exploitation of East Pakistan by the central government in the West Pakistan. As a result, a national movement eventually culminated in an armed conflict, following the Pakistani Army's brutal crackdown in March 1971.[33]

Following Partition, Pakistan failed to develop adequate nation building policies to integrate East Pakistan into the idea of Pakistan. It became increasingly evident to the East Pakistani elites that partitioning Bengal on the basis of religious identity had only been understood by the West Pakistani elites as a political strategy to achieve authority over territory. There had been no genuine vision of how Pakistani's nation building could actually include Bengalis. In addition, there was an imbalance in the distribution of power among different groups within the nation-state.[34]

The national elites, Punjabis and migrants from North and West India were ethnically and linguistically minority in numbers but they controlled the political system of Pakistan. Inevitably, the concentration of political power and economy excluded the indigenous inhabitants, especially the Bengalis. In fact, Bangla speaking people constituting the major segment of the Pakistan were in minority in power sharing.[35] The feeling of subordination and marginalisation prepared the base of "Bangla Nationalism". Table 25.1 shows the languages spoken in undivided Pakistan.

Table 25.1 irrefutably indicates that the overall Bengali speaking people were 55.8 per cent in comparison to 7.2 per cent of Urdu speaking people, even knowing this fact the political elites in Pakistan took the decision to make Urdu as a National language. However, Urdu speaking people were merely 14.6 per cent in West Pakistan too; 67.6 per cent people were Punjabi speaking people. The recognition of Urdu as the only state language of Pakistan, which was not spoken by even 1.5 per cent of East Bengal laid out the foundation of language movement.

Table 25.1: Languages Spoken in Pakistan[36]

Language	*East Pakistan*	*West Pakistan*	*All*
Bengali	99.0%	0.1%	55.8%
Urdu	1.3%	14.6%	7.2%
Punjabi	Nil	67.6%	29.5%
Sindhi	Nil	14.2%	6.2%
Pasto	Nil	8.9%	3.9%
Balochi	Nil	2.9%	1.3%
English	0.8%	2.1%	1.4%

Source: Pakistan Census, 1961, Compiled by Young, 1979: 480.

Language Movement and Bengali Nationalism

The language movement of 1952 was the first mass movement in the East Pakistan based on secular characteristic. It highlighted the connection between cultural rights and emancipation from autocratic regime. It inevitably led to the struggle for self-determination and finally, the Liberation War of 1971.[37]

Since, the basis of the emergence of Pakistan was religious nationalism demanding separate land for Muslims. The recognition of Urdu as the only State language sowed the seed of conflict between the West and the East Pakistani elites (scholars and political leaders). Muslim elites from West Pakistan opined that Urdu (spoken by 1.3% in East Pakistan and 14.6% in West) should be the *lingua franca* because of its reputation as the cultural symbol of Indian subcontinental Muslims. However, Bengali Muslims resisted, arguing that the new nation (Pakistan) had more Bengali speakers (55.8% overall and 99% in East Pakistan) than Urdu speakers (7.2% overall and 14.6% in West Pakistan). Furthermore, Bengali Muslims regarded Urdu as the language of the elites, not the language of the majority of Muslims.[38] Many attempts were made by Bengali leaders to persuade the central government to make Bengali as one of the state languages but all proposals were rejected.[39]

When we look back in February 1948, the rulers of the Constituent Assembly stipulated that English and Urdu would be the only two languages of the Assembly. This sparked off the already brewing language movement in East Bengal.[40] Consequently, on 26 February, 1948, the "All Party State Committee of Action and in the same month the East Pakistan Muslim Students League (EPMSL)[41] (with Sheikh Mujibur Rahman as its Organising Secretary) were formed in the eastern province, which organized a *hartal* to protest the government's policy on language."[42]

This was the first mass movement by the Eastern Provincial Bengali people unitedly against the Western Pakistani oligarchy. During this demonstration for the recognition of Bangla as a state language many students were beaten up by the police. A compromise was worked out subsequently by the Committee of Action (COA) and the government of Nazimuddin.[43] Later on 21 March, 1948, Muhammad Ali Jinnah visited Dhaka, where he declared publicly that:

> "For official use in this province, the people of the province can choose any language they wish. The question will be decided solely in accordance with the wishes of the people of this province alone, as freely expressed through their accredited representatives at the appropriate time and after full and dispassionate consideration. There can, however, be only one *lingua franca*—that is, the language for intercommunication between the various provinces of the state—and that language should be Urdu and cannot be any other. The state language, therefore, must obviously be Urdu, a language that has been nurtured by a hundred million of this subcontinent, a language understood throughout the length and breadth of Pakistan and above all a language that more than any other provincial language embodies the best that is in Islamic culture and Muslim tradition and is nearest to the language used in other Islamic countries. It is not without significance that Urdu has been driven out of the Indian Union and that even the official use of the Urdu script has been disallowed."[44]

After the visit of Jinnah by 1951, the language movement was in dormant position. Again, on 26 January, 1952, Khawaza Nazimuddin in course of his visit to Dacca (Dhaka) announced that Urdu alone should be the State language of Pakistan.[45] With this statement, the movement sprang up again. 'All Parties Central State Language Action Committee' was immediately formed on January 30, 1952. This committee called a general strike throughout East Pakistan on February 21, 1952. To resist the province-wide mass protest and general strike, Nurul Amin, (the then Chief Minister of East Bengal) banned all processions and rallies on February 21, 1952 and imposed section 144. On the same day, students demonstrating near the University and Medical College were killed by the police.[46] After this brutal incident, the whole Eastern province appeared to have risen in rebellion.

The supreme sacrifice of students laying down their lives protecting mother language on 21 February (popularly known as Ekushey) is recognised as the Martyr's Day (Shaheed Dibash) in Eastern Province. This historic incident encouraged the beginning of a movement to glorify Bengali language and ethnicity as well as a symbol of resistance and the beginning of the struggle for independence.[47] Consequently, Bengali blood and the electoral verdict of 1954 provincial election forced Ali Bogra to accept Bengali as a State language on 7 May, 1954. The collective memory of language movement, with the numerous forms of commemoration has to the beginning of a secular-linguistic Bengali nationalism.[48]

The language movement sowed the seed of a strong fervour in cultural unity. The fundamental base of this spirit was a strong lingo-cultural awareness among the East Pakistan's people. The religion believed to the common bond between the two wings of Pakistan could not end the demand for the separate land for Bengali People.[49]

The Language movement motivated the vivacity of Bengali nationalism. In the successive struggles and movements throughout the fifties and the sixties, it was this spirit that inspired the people leading eventually to the emergence of a free nation in 1971.[50] Table 25.2 shows chronological development of Eastern Province of Pakistan towards imagined glorious destiny of self-determination.

Table 25.2: The Political Movement of East Pakistan[51]

Period	*Leading Groups*	*Major Issues of Nationalism*
1947-54 Muslim League dominant	Landlords, lawyers, students	Recognition of Language and provincial autonomy.
1954-58 Emergence of Regional Parties and coalition politics	Lawyers, students, workers, Bengali businessmen	Economic disparities and parity of representation in public services.
1958-69 Centralised polity of Ayub Khan and frustration of regional elites.	Lawyers, teachers, students, Bengali businessmen, workers, organized peasants	Economic disparity, Bengali language and culture, regional participation, full regional autonomy symbolized in the six-point demands.
1969-71 Against Yahya Khan's regime, mass-movement, election, aggregation crisis and disintegration of Pakistan	Students, workers, organized peasants, guerrillas, armed personnel, Bengali civil servants, teachers, lawyers, Bengali businessmen	Economic disparity, maximum autonomy, complete independence for East Pakistan, Bangladesh movement.

The struggle of national liberation in Bangladesh was the movement against the West Pakistani oppressive regime. The people of East Pakistan were being oppressed by the West Pakistan due to their cultural difference not the religious one. So, the essence of Bengali nationalism was based on secularism on as all the people of the East Pakistan unitedly protested against the imposition of Urdu as the only state language of Pakistan. It was Direndranath Datta (a member of Hindu community), who firstly forwarded an amendment proposal at the Constituent Assembly of Pakistan (CAP) on February 25, 1948 for adopting Bangla as one of the official languages.[52] Later, all the people irrespective of religion caste and class joined the movement demanding equal status of Bangla as the state language.

Bengali Nationalism

Bengali nationalism sprang up demanding the protection of lingo-cultural identity of the East Pakistani people. The uprising that gave the incentive to the language movement of 1952 was a strong demonstration in retaliation to brutal attack on the language and indigenous culture of the Bengalis by the non-Bengali rulers from the then Pakistan. Besides language, the people of East Pakistan were discriminated in every sphere of life. They were marginalised even in governmental jobs, bureaucracy, army and other services related to the state affairs.

In 1966, out of a total 1,14,302 government officials, only 27,648 (24.18%) were from East Pakistan. By 1970 only 3 (15%) Bengalis out of 20 had attained the rank of secretary at the highest bureaucratic level. Similarly, Bengalis representation in the army was less than 7 per cent and there were only 2 (5.71%) lieutenants-general and major-generals out of 35. Furthermore, most of the defence budget was spent within West Pakistan, leaving East Pakistan with largely unprotected borders.[53]

Majority of posts and all the key positions in East Pakistan were held by the West Pakistanis; even the President used to appoint either a senior West Pakistani military official or a puppet East Pakistani who had direct access to the central ruling clique as the Governor of East Pakistan. Moreover, the West Pakistani officials posted in the East Pakistan used to consider themselves socially and racially superior. Neither they bothered to develop any real bonds with the local people nor did they develop the region.

The feeling of inferiority among the East Pakistani people alienated them from the West Pakistan. Consequently, the cultural similarity among the East Pakistani spurred the sentiment of self-determination and Bengali nationalism. Later, the intellectuals from the East Pakistan instilled the spirit of Bengali nationalism into the mind of common people. They even inspired the people to mobilise against disparity and repressive measures of the Pakistani rulers.[54] As a result many intellectuals were killed by Pakistani military and their collaborators.

The most important political party propagating the idea of largely extended autonomy and later the independence of the East Bengal was 'the Awami League.'[55] Following the independence in 1971, the government under Awami League led by Sheikh Mujib-ur-Rahman incorporated the principles of nationalism, socialism, democracy and secularism as the fundamental Principles of Sate Policy and probity of governance in Bangladesh.[56] According to Bina D'Costa:

> "interestingly, within three years of independence, Mujib himself failed to uphold his principle of secular nationalism. He started to attend religious gatherings, and gradually dropped the nationalistic slogan '*joy Bangla*' from his speeches. Most importantly, the Islamic nationalist parties—including the Jama'at-i-Islami, several factions of the Muslim League, the Nizam-i-Islami and the Jamiat-e-Ulama-e-Islam—had earlier been considered Pakistani Army collaborators, and thus had been banned, eventually co-opted. On 30 November, 1973, a general amnesty was granted to all collaborators, with the exception of those who were charged with murder, rape and arson."[57]

The above step taken by Mujib paved the way to the resurgence of Islamist group and political parties in Bangladesh. Consequently, the assassination of Sheikh Mujib-ur-Rahman on 15 August, 1975, followed by the military takeover on 30 November, 1976 by Maj. Gen. Zia-ur Rahman ushered a new era of nationalism in Bangladesh.[58]

Bangladeshi Nationalism Leading to Ascendancy of Islamist

The promise of Bangladesh developing into a secular democratic nation strengthened by the spirit of Bengali nationalism was rudely thwarted by assassination of Mujib-ur-Rahman.[59] The change of regime in Bangladesh also changed the basic ideology of nationalism; explicitly turned it towards religion.

Zia-ur-Rahman and the Politics of Islamisation: In order to do away with the ideology of Awami League after the failure of the Mujib government in 1975; Zia preferred a contrasting model of nationalism in Bangladesh. In his new establishment he strengthened the element of religious nationalism that was in the interest of the majority Muslims. It also consolidated his position among Muslims because he needed the support of majority Muslims and military juntas in order to remain in power. However, on many occasions; Zia himself defined his concept of Bangladeshi nationalism, "as something positive, indeed to take advantage of emotions within the country to create institutions of self-reliance, the ability to stand on one's own feet, and a commitment to develop one's own resources."[60] He informed the country's religious minorities that they had nothing to fear by the change in wording in the provisions of the Constitution. He was merely determined to steer a course away from that establishment led by Sheikh Mujibur Rahman's secular 'Bengali nationalism'. Zia's way was of distancing Bangladesh from its Hindu and Indian influences because Bengali nationalism was a lingo-cultural unification of Bangla speaking people which he thought resemblance with the West Bengal of India.[61]

In way to legitimize his rule further, Zia adjusted secularist position to meet conservatives demands, at home as well as abroad. Firstly, just a day after assuming office as the President of Bangladesh on 21 April, 1977; he incorporated Islamic ideals into the constitution. By the proclamation of Order No. 1 of 1977, the ideal *"Bismillah-ar-Rahman-ar-Rahim"* (a phrase mostly used by Muslims) was added at the beginning of the Constitution (above the preamble).[62] Through the same proclamation, Article 8, clause 1; the principle of secularism was dropped from the Constitution; substituting 1A and 2 by: "the principles of absolute trust and faith in the Almighty Allah, nationalism, democracy and socialism meaning economic and social justice, together with the principles derived from them… shall constitute the fundamental principles of state policy (Art. 8.1)."[63] Absolute trust and faith in the Almighty Allah shall be the basis of all actions (Art. 8.1A).[64] Further, by the Fifth Amendment to the Constitution (1977), there were many changes in the Constitution of Bangladesh:

- Article 6 clause 2 which stated that citizens of Bangladesh were to be known as Bangalee as a nation was substituted by, "the citizens of Bangladesh shall be known as Bangladeshis.
- Article 9, which pledge the unity and solidarity of Bangalee Nationalism was removed.
- Article 12, through which communal political parties were banned in Bangladesh, was dropped from the Constitution.

- A new clause was inserted in Article 25 to strengthen, consolidate and preserve the fraternal relationship between the Muslim states on the basis of Islamic solidarity.
- Article 38 of the Constitution which banned the communal activities within Bangladesh was revoked in May 1977.[65]

Besides constitutional changes there were educational and administrative changes during Zia's rule:

- Islamiat as a subject was included to class I to VIII as a compulsory paper for Muslim students only and from class IX to X as a supplementary subject.
- The Bengali slogan "Joy Bangla," was replaced by "Bangladesh Zindabad".
- The Second Parliament of Bangladesh began its session with recitation from the holy *Quran* only; while previous recitations used to be made from the holy books from all religions.[66]

The above changes consolidated Zia's power base among Muslims of Bangladesh. And the constitutional commitments to follow friendly relationship with Muslim nations were generally regarded as preconditions to Bangladesh's active participation in the Islamic World Conference. These constitutional commitments assured Bangladesh large amounts of economic aid from oil-rich Muslim countries, particularly from Saudi Arabia.[67] Indeed, Zia took advantage of the emotions of majority Muslim within Bangladesh and turned the sentiment of 'secular Bengali nationalism' to 'religious Bangladeshi nationalism'.

Due to Zia's politics of Islamisation, Bangladesh has seen a phenomenal rise of Islamist political parties and organisation with Islamist agenda. According to one account, in 1970, the numbers of Islamist parties were 11, while the number has been rose up to 100.[68] In the view of Ali Riaz, "the executive orders between 1976 and 1979 removed the ban on forming political parties based on religious ideology and allowed those individuals who collaborated with the Pakistani army in 1971 to participate in politics."[69]

The functioning of Islamist in political arena heightened the ascendancy of Islamist in Bangladesh. According to Muhammad Ghulam Kabir, "Zia-ur-Rahman, successfully changed the image of Bangladesh from a liberal Muslim country to an Islamic country."[70] Further, Lowrenz Ziring viewed that, "the proclamation order of 1977 emphasized Bangladesh's ethos as a land for Muslims."[71]

In September 1978, Zia founded the Bangladesh Nationalist Party (BNP), which worked to reinstate Islamic element into Bangladesh politics.[72] "It was clearly stated in the party constitution that Islam had a pivotal role to play in public life, thus implying that it had a role in politics and public policy as well."[73] The Bangladesh Nationalist Party (BNP) defines Bangladeshi nationalism as "Religious belief and love for religion are a great and imperishable characteristic of the Bangladeshi nation... the vast majority of our people are followers of Islam. The fact is well reflected and manifest in our stable and liberal national life."[74] This indicates that the ideological base of the Bangladeshi Nationalism was Islamic Nationalism. And BNP manipulated Bangladeshi Nationalism for political gain because it was well aware that majority of the people of Bangladesh are the followers of Islam. Here, religion was used as primordial Identity of Bangladeshi people in order to mobilise them against its opponent political party Awami League's ideology as secular party.

Politicking Islam and the Ascendency of Islamists in Bangladesh: After the assassination of Zia-ur-Rahman on 30 May, 1981, General H.M. Ershad grabbed power on 24 March, 1982. Ershad made Bangladeshi nationalism more rigid towards religion (Islam). He promoted the economic aid and foreign assistance for the development of mosques and madrasas.

In comparison to Zia, Ershad brought about more changes in the education system. In December 1983, he assumed presidency and tried to make Arabic a compulsory subject alongside Islamiat, but he could not do so because of the mass protest. However, he encouraged *madrasa* education and declared Friday a full holiday and changed name of the 'Red Cross' to 'Red Crescent'.[75] Islam was declared the state religion with the provision that other religions may be practiced in peace and harmony in the republic.[76] After this proclamation, there was mushrooming of political parties with Islamic affiliations during his tenure by December 1990. His main objective behind all these efforts was to please Islamists and politick religion. In 1990, Ershad had to step down after the mass protest to instal democratic government in Bangladesh.

Islamisation in democratic way: During 1991 first Parliamentary election after long standing military coup, all political parties adopted every means to satisfy Islamist in order to come into power. They used religious symbols, sentiments or appeals to win over voters, even a Hindu candidate by the name Dhiren Bagchi, the candidate from the Zaker Party (of the Peer of Atroshi) was pseudonymed Maulana Dhiren Bagchi.[77] Moreover, all the leading Political Parties misrepresented the 'the first

Qalimah'. The Bangladesh Nationalist Party (BNP) advertised in their manifesto the Qalimah as, "*La ilaha Illallah, Dhener Shinde Bismillah*" (there is no God but Allah: Vote for the Paddy-Sheaf in the name of Allah), the Jamat-i-Islami's slogan was, "*Vote Diley Pally, Khusi Hobe Allah* (Allah would be happy with you if you would vote for Scale).[78] And, the Awami League (AL) came up with the slogan, "*La ilaha illallah, Naukar malik tui Allah* (There is no God except Allah and the both belongs to Allah).[79] The AL during this election (1991) tried to assure that the secularist principles of 1972 would not be restored. According to Anwar Hussain, "even the prophet was brought in the business of electioneering by the Freedom Party when they raised the slogan, "*Vote Dile Kurale Khusi Hobe Rasule"* (Prophet will be pleased if you Vote for axe).[80]

This election of 1991 was well-briefed as free and fair; however religious symbolism played a very significant role. Jamaat-e-Islami (JI) won 18 seats and become apparent as the kingmaker and supported BNP (140/300 seats) to form the government. The AL won 88 out of 300 seats with 30.08 per cent of vote share, though in terms of voting percentage AL was slightly behind BNP (30.81) but in seats comparison, it was big margin.[81]

It was not merely the defeat of AL but the victory of Islamists over secularists and Bangladeshi nationalism over Bengali nationalism. Due to this defeat, the AL began to take steps towards Islamisation, keeping intact its secular ideals officially. In the process, the champion of the liberation struggle (AL) and anti-liberation force (JI) made a formal alliance in 1994 before the 1996 general election. As a result, the ideological dichotomous alliance got the majority of seats and formed the government. However, the AL-JI alliance lasted only four years and in 1998, JI rejoined the BNP in order to fight 2001 election unitedly. Ultimately, even a decade of democratic rule could not change the political discourse in Bangladesh.

By 2001 election, there were no major changes in the manifesto of significant political parties. The main cause of the inclination towards Islamisation was majoritarian interest. All the leading political parties were following the way only to fulfil the interests of Muslims in order to grab power. There were ideological differences among them but they all were representing similar dogma during 2001 General Election (Table 25.3).

Due to more rigid religious faith BNP-led alliance influenced the sentiments of Muslims more than any other political parties and groups. Consequently, BNP-Led four party alliance emerged as victorious and won 216 out of 300 seats in 2001 election. Among the above political parties, the inclination of AL towards religious discourse surprised everyone because

Table 25.3: Declaration in Manifestoes of Major Political Parties During 2001 Election[82]

Political Parties	*Declaration in 2001 Manifesto*
Bangladesh Nationalist Party (BNP)	Will not enact any law contrary to Islam.
Jamat-e-Islami (JI)	Will convert the People's Republic of Bangladesh into Islamic Republic.
Awami League (AL)	No law will be enacted, which will be inconsistent with the dictates of the Qur'an and Hadith.
Jatiya Party (JP)	Existing laws would be brought in line with the principles of the Quran and Sunnah,...religious education would be made compulsory at all levels.
Left and Liberal Parties	Work towards restoration of secular ideals.

the party was formerly had secularists credential and regarded as the champion of the Liberation War of 1971 against religion-based ideology.[83] The main highlight of the successive regimes was that they rehabilitate Islamists in political as well as public life. Top two leaders of JI (alleged war time criminals in 1971) became ministers under 2001 ruling regime. From 2001 to 2006, there was an unprecedented government support to the Islamists in Bangladesh.

It is unfortunate for the people of Bangladesh that have lost their millions of lives in order to restore democracy, secularism, socialism and lingo-cultural nationalism against Islamic based ideology of Pakistan but the resurgence of Islamists made situations feel like Pakistan again. There are many political parties in Bangladesh that are working on the Islamists agenda to make Bangladesh an Islamic State. Due to the similar ideology, beliefs, objectives, and practices; it is difficult to differentiate between them. However, Table 25.4 tries to categorise them on the basis of taxonomical identity.

There has been a remarkable rise of Islamist political parties and organisations in Bangladesh since 1990. According to Ali Riaz, "Islamist parties were 11 in 1970 that rose up to 100 by 2006."[85] The Islamisation of politics and ascendency of Islamist in Bangladesh terrified religious minority the most. The shift from cultural nationalism to religious one created a sense of insecurity among religious minorities.

The politics of nationalism and religious identity in Bangladesh made the situation unfavourable for religious minorities to survive. Even years after independence there is the lack of consensus among political parties for the national identity of their homeland. There is always tussle between Bengali *versus* Bangladeshi identity of its people. The proponents

Table 25.4: Religion Based Political Parties/Groups in Bangladesh[84]

Political Parties	*Distinguishable Traits*
Bangladesh Jamaat-i-Islami (JI)	Pragmatist/opportunist: Want to establish Islamic social order in society through the state, believe in "Islamic revolution".
Jamiyat-e-Ulama-e-Islam, Khelafat Andolan, Ahle Hadith, Islamic Morcha, Khelafat Mojlish, Nejam-e-Islam, Islami Oikkya Jote (IOJ)	Idealist and orthodox: Want a pure Islamic state. Support base is largely within qwami madrassah.
Zaker Party, Islami Shahontantra Andolan (Islami Andolan Bangladesh), Bangladesh Tariqat Federation	Pir (preacher of Islam) centric and mazar based. Aim to establish a state based on traditional Islam and sharia. Weak support base.
Hizb ut–Tahrir Bangladesh	Urban elite-centric: Want to establish Khelafat. Highly educated middle-class leadership, yet to take part in elections.
Harkatul-Jihad al Islami Bangladesh (HuJi-B), Jameat-ul-Mujahideen Bangladesh (JMB), Jagrate Muslim Janta Bangladesh (JMJB), Hijbul Tawheed, Shahadat-e-Al Hikma.	Militant Islamists who aim to establish an Islamic state in Bangladesh through Jihad.

of 'Bengali Nationalism' declared that it accommodates all the people of Bangladesh, however non-Bengali, tribal and hill people feel alienated with this identity too. As per Amena Mohsin views, "Bangladeshi nationalism points out that it is territorial. It separates the Bengalis of Bangladesh and Bengalis of West Bengal (India), which is precisely lacking in Bengali nationalism."[86] However, the Bengali nationalism explicitly had a territorial dimension because it spurred in the Eastern Wing of Pakistan, which had a territorial boundary after 1947 partition. Moreover, the Bangladeshi nationalism, as it evolved in 1975, was in essence a re-assertion of Muslim identity for Bengalis in Bangladesh.[87]

Conclusion

The study is about the growth and relevance of nationalism in ideologically polarized politics in Bangladesh. Though, there is no universally applicable definition of nationalism because of the diversified nature of states and their inhabitants but this study found that nationalism mobilises people on the basis of ethno-linguistic, cultural, racial and various other identities into single national symbol for political autonomy and self-determination.

There are basic themes and motives to achieve nationalism; some of them are political autonomy, territorial unification, social solidarity, sorority, historic territory, cultural identity and glorious destiny.

Nationalism has been viewed as a process through which an ethno-cultural identity moves towards self-determination. In Bangladesh, it has been observed that the notion of nationalism changes with the change in regimes. Initially, the sense of deprivation and subordination among the East Bengal people led to the Bengali nationalism. It was the political manifestation of ethno-lingual sentience of the East Pakistani people. Thus, Bengali nationalism was rooted in the manifestation of pride in the historical, cultural and linguistic heritage of Bangladesh.

In short, we can say that after achieving political nationalism, when the rise of cultural nationalism is to revitalize the particular community, a nationalism based on religion emerges which discriminates against religious minorities in a democratic nation. When cultural or religious nationalism arises in any country after attaining freedom, it means that it will promote the majoritarianism and the religious minorities will be marginalised. This happens only when the country's ruling regime loses control of its internal and external terrain. For example, when the situation on the border is not right and the internal economic situation is beyond control, then some kind of nationalism emerges by putting the dust in public eyes in order to make the ruler remain in power. The effect of social disharmony also affects the economy that make the ruler more nationalist and the situation keep worsening until regime change. The most noticeable thing here is that when the economy is weak, the majority suffers the most. That is why, I believe that patriotism (*Desh Prem*) is better for any nation than nationalism (*Rashtrvad*). Patriotism has the simple meaning of "love to all who live in the country".

ENDNOTES

1. Craig Calhoun, "Nationalism and Ethnicity", *Annual Review of Sociology*, 19 (1993): 211-39, www.jstor.org/stable/2083387.
2. Richard Handler, *Nationalism and the Politics of Culture in Quebec*, (Madison: University of Wisconsin Press, 1988), p. 6.
3. Craig Calhoun, *Nationalism and Ethnicity*, p. 212.
4. Umut Ozkirimli, *Theories of Nationalism*, New York: Palgrave, 2000, p. 12.
5. Anthony D. Smith, *Nationalism and Modernity*, London and New York: Routledge, 1998, p. 10.
6. Umut Ozkirimli (2000), *Theories of Nationalism*, p. 13.

7. Louis L. Snyder, *The Dynamics of Nationalism*, New Jersey: NJ. D. Van Nostrand Company, 1964, p. 12.
8. Anthony D. Smith, *Ethno-Symbolism and Nationalism: A Cultural Approach*, London and New York: Routledge, 2009, p. 61.
9. Anthony D. Smith, *Ethno-Symbolism and Nationalism*, pp. 62-63.
10. Anthony D. Smith, *Nationalism and Modernity*, London and New York: Routledge, 1998, p. 61.
11. *Ibid.*
12. John Hutchingson, *Modern Nationalism,* London: Fontana, 1994, p. xiii.
13. Anthony D. Smith, *Nationalism and Modernity*, p. 66.
14. John Breuilly, "Reflections on Nationalism", *Philosophy of the Social Sciences* 15, no. 1 (March 1985): 65–75. doi: 10.1177/004839318501500106, p. 73.
15. Ishtiaq Ahmed, *State, Nation and Ethnicity in Contemporary South Asia*, London: Pinter, 1996, p. 7.
16. Ernest Gellner, "Nationalism" Theory and Society, Vol. 10, No. 6 (Nov., 1981), pp. 753-776, www.jstor.org/stable/657332, p. 753.
17. Ernest Gellner, *Nations and Nationalism,* Oxford: Basil Blackwell, 1983, p. 1.
18. *Ibid.*
19. *Ibid.*
20. Michie Jonathan, *Reade's Guide to the Social Studies,* London and Chicago: Fitzroy Dearborn Publisher, 2001, p. 1099.
21. S.L. Sharma (2002), "The Discourse on the National Question in South Asia", in *Nation and National Identity in South Asia, (eds.)* S.L. Sharma and T.K. Oommen New Delhi: Orient Longman, 2002, p. xvi.
22. Jonathan Michie, (eds.) *Reader's Guide to the Social Sciences*, London and Chicago: Fitzroy Dearborn Publisher, 2001, p. 1099.
23. Umut Ozkirimli (2000), *Theories of Nationalism,* p. 12.
24. Louis L. Snyder, *The Dynamics of Nationalism*, New Jersey: NJ. D. Van Nostrand Company, 1964, p. 12.
25. Anthony D. Smith, *Theories of Nationalism,* London: Holmes & Meier, 1983, pp. 8-9.
26. Anthony D. Smith, *Theories of Nationalism,* pp. 8-9.
27. Tanweer Fazal, (ed.) *Minority Nationalism in South Asia*, Oxon: Routledge, 2013, p. 3.
28. *Ibid.*
29. *Ibid.*
30. Sanjay K. Bhardwaj, "Contesting identities in Bangladesh: a study of secular and religious frontiers", Working Paper, 36. *Asia Research Centre, London School of Economics and Political Science,* London, (7 October 2011), http://eprints.lse.ac.uk/38640/.
31. *Ibid.*
32. Taj I. Hashmi, "Failure of the 'Welfare State': Islamic Resurgence and

Political Legitimacy in Bangladesh", in Shahram Akbarzadeh and Abdullah Saeed (eds.) *Islam and Political Legitimacy,* London: Routledge Curzon, 2003, p. 102.

33. Bina D'Costa, *Nation Building, Gender and War Crimes in South Asia,* Oxon: Routledge, 2011, p. 90.
34. *Ibid.*
35. *Ibid.*
36. *Ibid.,* p. 87.
37. Kabir Chowdhury "Of History, Nationalism and Poetry", in Geeti Sen (ed.), *Crossing Boundaries,* New Delhi: Orient Blackswan, 1997, p. 104.
38. Sufia M. Uddin, *Constructing Bangladesh: Religion, Ethnicity and Language in an Islamic Nation,* New Delhi: Vistar Publication, 2006, p. 124.
39. Sufia M. Uddin, *Constructing Bangladesh.*
40. A.M.A. Muhith, *Bangladesh: Emergence of a Nation,* Dhaka: University Press, 1992, p. 85.
41. Talukder Maniruzzaman, *The Bangladesh Revolution and its Aftermath,* Dhaka: University Press, 1988, p. 54.
42. Sufia, M. Uddin, *Constructing Bangladesh,* p. 124.
43. Muhith, *Bangladesh: Emergence of a Nation,* p. 54.
44. Sufia, M. Uddin, *Constructing Bangladesh,* pp. 124-125.
45. M. Waheeduzzaman Manik, "Formative Phase of the Language Movement", *The Daily Star*, (21 February 2012), available online at, http://archive.thedailystar.net/suppliments/2012/21st%20February%202012/page2.htm.
46. Noruddin Mohammad Burhan, "Language movement and Bengali nationalism", *The Financial Express*, (21 Feb. 2013), available online at, http://www.thefinancialexpress-bd.com/old/print.php?ref=MjBfMDJfMjFfMTNfMV8xODdfMTYwODgz.
47. Sufia (2006), *op. cit.*, p. 125.
48. Talukder Maniruzzaman, *The Bangladesh Revolution and its Aftermath,* Dhaka: University Press, 1988, p. 58.
49. Noruddin Mohammad Burhan (2013), "Language Movement and Bengali Nationalism", *The Financial Express*, Dhaka, 21 February, 2013, available on Internet at, http://www.thefinancialexpress-bd.com/old/index.php?ref=MjBfMDJfMjFfMTNfMV8xODdfMTYwODgz, (12-02-2013).
50. *Ibid.*
51. Bina D'Costa, *Nation Building, Gender and War Crimes in South Asia,* Oxon: Routledge, 2011, p. 91.
52. Noruddin Mohammad Burhan (2013), *op. cit.*
53. Bina D'Costa (2011), *op. cit.,* p. 90.
54. Muazzam Hussain Khan, "Killing of Intellectuals", *Banglapedia: National Encyclopedia of Bangladesh*, (2012), http://www.banglapedia.org/HT/K_0330.htm.
55. Talukder Maniruzzaman (1988), *op. cit.*, p. 19.
56. Article-8, "The Constitution of The People's Republic of Bangladesh", "*Part*

ii-Fundamental Principle of State Policy", available on Internet at, http://bdlaws.minlaw.gov.bd/pdf_part.php?id=367.
57. Bina D'Costa, *op. cit.*, p. 107.
58. Bertil Lintne, "Religious Extremism and Nationalism in Bangladesh", (2002), http://www.asiapacificms.com/papers/pdf/religious_extremism_bangladesh.pdf.
59. Kabir Chowdhury, "Of History, Nationalism and Poetry", in Geeti Sen (ed.), *Crossing Boundaries,* (New Delhi: Orient Blackswan, 1997), p. 108.
60. Franda, Marcus, "Ziaur Rahman and Bangladeshi Nationalism", *Economic and Political Weekly*, Vol. 16, No. 10/12, (March, 1981), http://www.jstor.org/stable/4369609, p. 375.
61. Lawrence Ziring, *Bangladesh: From Mujib to Ershad,* Delhi: Oxford University Press, 1992, pp. 127-128.
62. M. Anisuzzaman, "The Identity Question and Politics", in Rounaq Jahan (ed.), *Bangladesh: Promise and Performance*, Dhaka: University Press, 2002, p. 59.
63. Gokulesh Sharma, *Constitution of SAARC Nations*, New Delhi: Deep & Deep Publication, 2008, p. 470.
64. Gokulesh Sharma, *Constitution of SAARC Nations*, p. 470.
65. M. Anisuzzaman (2002), *op. cit.*, p. 59.
66. *Ibid.*
67. *Zillur* R. Khan, "Islam and Bengali Nationalism", *Asian Survey*, Vol. 25, No. 8 (August, 1985), http://www.jstor.org/stable/2644113, p. 849.
68. Ali Riaz, and Ali Raji, "Who are the Islamist?", in Ali Riaz and C. Chritine Fair (eds.) *Political Islam and Governance in Bangladesh,* Oxon: Routledge, 2011, p. 46.
69. Ali Riaz, "The Politics of Islamisation in Bangladesh", in Ali Riaz (ed.), *Religion and Politics in South Asia*, London and New York: Routledge, 2010, p. 48.
70. Muhammad Ghulam Kabir, *Changing Face of Nationalism: The Case of Bangladesh,* New Delhi: South Asian Publishers, 1994, p. 201.
71. Bruce Lawrence, *Shattering the Myth: Islam Beyond Violence,* Princeton, NJ: Princeton University Press, 1998, p. 127.
72. Bina D'Costa (2011), *op. cit.*, p. 107.
73. Ali Riaz, *The Politics of Islamisation in Bangladesh*, p. 57.
74. Meghna Guhathakurta and Willem van Schendel, (eds.), *The Bangladesh Reader: History, Culture, Politics,* Durham and London: Duke University Press, 2013, p. 332.
75. Meghna, *The Bangladesh Reader.*
76. Gokulesh Sharma, (2008), *op. cit.*, p. 469.
77. Syed, Anwar Hussain, "Religion and Ethnicity in Bangladesh Politics", in Verinder Grover (ed.) *Bangladesh: Government and Politics,* New Delhi: Deep and Deep Publication, 2000, p. 383.

78. Zakia Soman and J. Dhabi, *Peace and Justice,* New Delhi: Pearson India, 2010, p. 51.
79. *Ibid.*
80. *Ibid.*
81. Ali Riaz (2010), *op. cit.*, p. 54.
82. Ali Riaz, *Religion and Politics in South Asia,* p. 59.
83. Ali Riaz, *Religion and Politics in South Asia*, p. 60.
84. Ali Riaz, Religion *and Politics in South Asia,* p. 56.
85. *Ibid.*
86. Amena A. Mohsin (2004), *op. cit.*, p. 474.
87. *Ibid.*

26

Women in Electoral Politics of South Asia

With Special Reference to India

Niaz Ahmed and *Md. Misbahuddin Ansari*

Introduction

Women's participation in electoral politics is a valid indicator of the efficacious growth of democracy in any country of the world today. Women's participation in decision-making is essential for women's interests to be incorporated into governance. Political participation derives from the freedom to speak out, the ability to take part in the conduct of public affairs; assemble and associate; to campaign and the opportunity to register as a candidate, to be elected and to hold office at all levels of government.[1] Women's Political participation can be defined as those actions of women by which they seek to influence or to support government and politics. South Asian society is extremely multicultural and multidimensional. Different South Asian states have different notion of women's political participation. Most of the South Asian countries are democratic and India is the largest democratic country in the world which is located in the region. South Asia is unique in the context that the region has three Islamic republics as Afghanistan, Pakistan, and Maldives, and two secular democracies with a Hindu majority as India and Nepal, and two democracies with Buddhist majority as Sri Lanka and Bhutan, and one secular democracy with Muslim majority as Bangladesh.[2]

Since the last 60 years, political systems have become diverse from democracy in India and Sri Lanka with varying degrees of authoritarian tendencies to outright military dictatorship, theocratic autocracy and democracy in Bangladesh and Pakistan.[3] Nepal has made a democratic transition from a monarchy that was overthrown by a Maoist revolution but faces problems of consolidating its democratic base. Maldives is a small island country in the region and was declared a republic in 1968, bringing an end to more than 800 years of monarchy. Afghanistan has had a long history of coups, monarchy and dictatorship and is now an Islamic Republic. The first woman Prime Minister in the world was from South Asia, the state of Sri Lanka.[4] There were many women heads of state as well as government from the region such as Chandrika Kumartunga and Sirimavo Bhandaranaike in Sri Lanka, Indira Gandhi and Pratibha Patil in India, Benazir Bhutto in Pakistan, Khaleda Zia and Sheikh Hasina in Bangladesh.[5]

In India, women have largely plucked to acquire the critical mass required to introduce gender perspectives in political decision-making processes at higher levels and to promote gender-friendly legislation.[6] Despite having clear-cut constitutional commandment for providing equality to women in the public sphere, including electoral politics, prejudice and discrimination against women in India continue even after 70 years of independence. Affirmative action for women and different disadvantaged groups has been enshrined into the Constitution. In 1992, through the 73rd Constitutional Amendment Act, Indian government enacted the reservation of a minimum of one-third of seats for women within all of India's locally elected governance bodies commonly referred to as Panchayati Raj Institutions.[7] This study would reveal what kind of women's participation in Indian politics is going on. It would try to analyze the government policies and the role of political parties for the empowerment of women in the political sphere.

Political Participation of Women in South Asia

In South Asia, women's representation in different political institutions remained underrepresented despite having different socio-political rights. South Asian women have made tremendous progress on different development indicators such as educational attainment, financial resources, labour market participation, and equal inheritance rights.[8] As far as literature is concerned, elite women participate in the mainstream political sphere in South Asia.[9] Women's participation and contribution to political processes has been increasing both at the mainstream and grassroots levels. Women's representation in the national parliament is presently 7.33 per cent, and a woman Prime Minister.[10] Several women mayors have been elected. Since 1991 with the restoration of democracy in Nepal, women's political representation is growing. Women issues have been given priority in the mainstream as well as local levels. Women leaders from different political parties have started raising their strong voice for women's rights.

Despite having different military regimes women's representation in Pakistani politics is growing significantly.[11] It had also a woman Prime Minister. Different political parties have women wings for women's political empowerment. In Sri Lanka, the representation of women in political institutions is very low in the mainstream as well as the grassroots level. As far as data is concerned 12 women are in Parliament out of 225 total Parliamentarians. In Afghanistan despite having Islamic republic women's representation in political sphere is gaining day by day. Maldives is a small country, where women participation in the political institution is very low. Women's participation in South Asian Parliament is mentioned in Table 26.1.

Table 26.1: Women's Participation in South Asian Parliament

Country	*Name of Parliament*	*Total Member*	*Women Member*	*Percentage of Women*	*Year of Election*
India	Lok Sabha	543	78	14.6	2019
	Rajya Sabha	243	24	9.8	2019
Bangladesh	Parliament	300	22	7.33	2018
Nepal	Pratinidhi Sabha	275	90	32.73	2017
	Sanghiya Sansad	58	22	37.93	2020
Pakistan	National Assembly	323	69	21.36	2018
	Senate	104	20	19.23	2018
Sri Lanka	Parliament	225	12	5.33	2019
Maldives	People's Majlis	87	4	4.6	2019
Afghanistan	House of People	249	68	27.2	2019
	House of Elder	68	19	27.94	2019
Bhutan	National Council	25	4	16	2018
	National Assembly	47	7	14.89	2018

Source: Inter Parliamentary Union (IPU).

Table 26.1 illustrates women's representation in different political institutions of South Asia. It is seen that Nepal, Afghanistan, Pakistan have more women representatives in their national politics. Female participation in mainstream politics of Bangladesh, Sri Lanka and Maldives has been very low.

Women's Political Participation in India

India is the largest democratic country in the world and a large number of women have participated in political sphere. In ancient times, women enjoyed considerable freedom so far as social, political, and educational activities were concerned and thus enjoyed a status and prestige in society. In homes, women were given superior position to that of men, as they were treated as the embodiment of goddess of wealth, strength and wisdom.[12] That time women enjoyed equality and were respected both in the family as well as society. But in the medieval period, there was a gradual decline in the position and status of women in India. At that time, the spread of Islam provided a healing touch to the degradation of women.[13] During the Mughal era, women's position in socio-economic and political sphere had been also good and they occupied different socio-political positions. In the British rule, women position was not so good, but after different reforms of various social customs, women also occupied a good position.[14] In the time of Indian National Movement under the leadership of Mahatma Gandhi, women's political participation had been remarkable. Indian women entered the open field of politics.[15]

India became an independent democratic republic since 1947. First national election held in 1952, from that time women's participation in political field have been visible. Since independence time women's participation in political and social life is increasing day by day. The Constitution of India establishes a parliamentary system of government, and guarantees its citizens the right to be elected, freedom of speech, freedom to assemble and form associations, and vote. The Constitution of India in 1950 officially granted adult suffrage to all. Prior to universal suffrage, provincial legislatures had granted women the right to vote. This is enshrined in Article 326 in the Constitution of India.[16] India is a parliamentary system with two houses: Lok Sabha the Lower House and Rajya Sabha the Upper House. In both houses women's representation is also visible since its formation. Table 26.2 shows female representation in the elections of Lok Sabha since 1952 to 2019.

Table 26.2 shows that in the first Lok Sabha election of 1952, only 43 women contested and 22 of them were elected to the House out of 499 total members and their percentage were 4.41. Day to day female representation in the Lok Sabha is increasing. In the 17th Lok Sabha Election of 2019 there are 543 members and 78 of them are women and their percentage has increased to 14.6 per cent. In the said election 724 women contested from different political parties. Rajya Sabha is the Upper House of Indian Parliament, where women's representation in the House is also visible (See Table 26.3).

Table 26.2: Women's Representation in Lok Sabha Since 1952–2019

Year of Election	Total seat	Women Contested	Women Elected	Percentage of women
1st/1952	499	43	22	4.41
2nd/1957	500	45	27	5.40
3rd/1962	503	70	34	6.76
4th/1967	523	67	31	5.93
5th/1971	521	86	22	4.22
6th/1977	544	70	19	3.29
7th/1980	544	142	28	5.15
8th/1984	544	164	44	8.9
9th/1989	517	198	27	5.22
10th/1991	544	325	39	7.17
11th/1996	543	599	39	7.18
12th/1998	543	274	43	7.92
13th/1999	543	278	49	9.02
14th/2004	543	355	45	8.03
15th/2009	543	556	59	10.86
16th/2014	543	636	61	11.23
17th/2019	543	724	78	14.6

Source: Election Commission of India Report.

Table 26.3: Women's Representation in Rajya Sabha Since 1952–2019

Year	Total Seats	Number of Women	Percentage of Women
1952	219	16	7.3
1957	237	18	7.6
1962	238	18	7.6
1967	240	20	8.3
1971	243	17	7.0
1977	244	25	10.2
1980	244	24	9.8
1985	244	28	11.4
1990	245	38	15.5
1996	223	20	9.0
1998	223	19	8.6
2004	245	27	11.1
2009	245	22	8.97
2014	245	29	11.83
2019	245	24	9.8

Source: Election Commission of India Report.

Table 26.3 highlights female representation in the Upper House of Indian Parliament. In 1952, women member of the House were only 16 out of total 219 members and their percentage was 7.3. Gradually, female representation to the House is increasing and in 2014 their representation has increased to 29 out of total 245 and their percentage was 11.83. And finally, in 2019 female representatives were 24 where the total member of the house were 245. From the very beginning women have been largely participating in the voting process. Their voting rate is going closer to that of men. Table 26.3 reveals female voting percentage in the Lok Sabha elections since 1952.

Table 26.3: Women Voting Percentage in Lok Sabha Elections (1952–2019)

Year of Election	*Female Voting Percentage*	*Male Voting Percentage*	*Difference with male voting rate*
1st/1952	37.1	53	15.9
2nd/1957	38.8	56	17.2
3rd/1962	46.6	63.3	16.7
4th/1967	55.5	66.7	11.2
5th/1971	49.1	60.9	11.8
6th/1977	54.9	66.0	11.1
7th/1980	51.2	62.2	11.0
8th/1984	59.2	68.4	9.2
9th/1989	57.3	66.1	8.8
10th/1991	51.4	61.6	10.2
11th/1996	53.4	62.1	8.7
12th/1998	58.0	66.0	8.0
13th/1999	55.7	64.0	8.3
14th/2004	53.3	61.7	8.4
15th/2009	55.8	60.2	4.4
16th/2014	65.6	67.1	1.5
17th/2019	68.0	68.3	0.3

Source: Election Commission of India Report (ECI).

Table 26.3 shows that from the first general elections women participation has been increasing gradually. In the election of 1952 female voting rate was 37.1 per cent and in the 4th general election of 1967 their voting rate has been increased to 55.5 per cent. Male turnout during that same period was 53 per cent in 1952 and 66.7 per cent in 1967. In 2014 parliamentary general election women's voting rate was 65.6 per cent compared to 67.1 per cent turnout for men. India ranks 20th from the bottom in terms of representation of women in Parliament. Again, in the 17th general election of 2019, female voting rate was 68 per cent and their counterpart male voting rate was 68.3 per cent.

Role of Political Parties

Political parties are the main actors in the field of politics. Political Parties are regarded as the gatekeepers of democracy as well as political participation.[17] Political parties are generally considered as the most important institution which influences women to enter into politics. India has a multi-party system with 8 registered national parties and 48 other regional and state parties and also number of unregistered parties.[18] Here the discussion would be only the prominent national parties and its policies for the promotion of women's political participation. Indian National Congress (INC), Bharatiya Janata Party (BJP), and Communist Party of India (CPI) are predominantly national political parties, which are playing role in Indian mainstream as well as grassroots politics since very long time. All these parties have their women wings for the capture of women votes. All India Mahila Congress or Mahila Congress is the women wing of the Indian National Congress.[19] It is represented by the Pradesh Mahila Congress in all the states of the Indian Union. BJP Mahila Morcha is the Women Wing of the Bharatiya Janata Party. National Federation of Indian Women is the Women Wing of Communist Party of India (CPI). All political parties talk about women's empowerment but in praxis there is no special facility for women's political empowerment within the party. Following are some policies of national political parties for the promotion of women's political participation.

The Indian National Congress-led UPA established an independent Ministry of Women and Child Development in 2006 for the empowerment and upliftment of women.[20] The Ministry is taking care about different issues related to women and children. The Indian National Congress is committed to the enactment of the Women's Reservation Bill to reserve 33 per cent of all seats in the Lok Sabha, and in all State Legislative Assemblies for women. But the Bill has not been approved yet. The Indian National Congress policy is to open an Academy for Political Empowerment to provide elected women representatives legal and administrative education and develop their leadership skills.

Bharatiya Janata Party has various policies for women empowerment. However, the party organizes different programmes related to women issues only for gaining women votes. But in the ground reality, the party does not have any clear-cut policy towards women's political participation. Communist Party of India has also many policies for the empowerment of women. The party also organizes different programmes for women related issues and also awareness related issues. But there is no special reservation policy for women within the party structure.

Role of Indian Government/Government Policies

The Constitution of India is the most vital document which talks about the political equality of Indian citizen whether men or women. From the time of independence, Indian government makes many policies for the empowerment of women in socio-political field. Women are becoming a part of political life since independence. Following are the important policies of Indian government which specially emphasize on women's political participation.

The National Policy for the Empowerment of Women (NPEW), 2001, was formulated by the Government of India, which laid down a comprehensive progressive policy for the advancement, development, empowerment of women in all fields.[21]

Women's Reservation Bill (The Constitution 108th Amendment Bill) was passed by the Rajya Sabha but the Lok Sabha has not yet voted on the Bill. It proposes to amend the Constitution of India to reserve one third (33) per cent of all seats in the Lok Sabha, and in all state legislative assemblies for women.

Indian government also implemented the United Nations Convention on the political rights of women (1952), which means women are also a part of political life.[22]

The Ministry for Women and Child Development was established as a department of the Ministry of Human Resource Development in the year 1985 to drive the holistic development of women and children in the country. In 2006, this department was given the status of a Ministry, with the powers to formulate plans, policies and programmes; enacts/amends legislation, guiding and coordinating the efforts of both governmental and non-governmental organizations working in the field of Women and Child Development.[23]

The Indian government launched 'Ujjawala' a new comprehensive Scheme in December 2007 for prevention of trafficking and rescue, rehabilitation and re-integration of victims of trafficking and commercial sexual exploitation.

Women's reservation of not less than one-third of total seats for the direct election to local bodies; Panchayats and Municipalities, articles 343(d) and 343(T) of The Constitution of India. These rights are successfully working in Indian grassroots politics.

'Beti Bacho, Beti Padhao' (Save the girl, educate the girl) is a movement which was launched by Indian government on 22 January, 2015, aimed at eradicating of female feticide and raising awareness on welfare services intended for young Indian girls. It is also an important scheme of Indian government for women socio-political empowerment.[24]

Hindrances to Women's Political Participation

The Constitution of India grants universal suffrage with equal rights to both men and women. Despite having different socio-political rights, women are facing lots of challenges and difficulties to come into politics. Following are the major factors which are responsible for the hindrances of women's political participation in India.

Male Dominated System: India is predominantly male dominated society. In every field we have seen that male part is in the key position. Even in society, polity and economy men are regarded superior to women. Women are not given full facility in every field, especially in politics. But things are changing. Presently, we saw the representation of women in political arena.

Lack of Economic and Political Resources: In India, the significant factor that constrains women's political participation is the lack of material resources available to them. Indian politics is about money, power and political networks. It is almost impossible to contest any election without adequate finance and access to political know-how and training. Because women are less integrated within powerful political and economic networks, it is even more difficult for them to participate in large numbers or to play an important role in political decision making. Women are economically disempowered and gender prejudices discourage them from cultivating political contacts early on in their education and careers to prepare them for political roles in the future. Some parties have a separate women's wing but rather than empowering women or expressing their solidarity these often marginalize women further. In Kashmir, the Muslim Khawateen Markaz (Muslim Women's Organization) is the only women's party within the Hurriyat Conference (an amalgam of separatist groups).

Social and Cultural Norms: Societal and cultural norms imposed on women often stop them from entering into the politics. They have to accept the dictates imposed on them and bear the burden of society. They also bear their deprivation and undermining status thinking as a culture of the society. The society is full of prejudices and women are the victim of poor awareness. Lack of participation of women in community-based activities is also one of the major constraints.

Religious Orientation: Indian society is deeply religious orientated society. Orthodox religious norms and practices often hinder the participation of women in the politics. Religious orientation or affiliation came up as a very strong determinant in restricting women from politics. In a society dominated by orthodox religious beliefs priests are at predominant positions. They often discourage women to participate in the politics.

Violence against Political Women: Violence against women is also a source of hindrances of women's political participation in India. Violence against those women who choose the political path is an increasing concern. The assassination of Indian Prime Minister Indira Gandhi in 1984 and Pakistan Prime Minister Benazir Bhutto in 1997 are the example of violation against political women.

Conclusion

Succinctly, it can be concluded that women's participation in politics is really an important aspect in South Asia, especially in India. India is the world's largest democratic country where almost half of the population is women. But women's political participation is still low in comparison to other European countries. Many changes are happening in India for various radical movements in the context of the empowerment of women. Nobel Laureate Amartya Sen in his book, '*India: Economic Development and Social Opportunity*' mentioned that Women's empowerment can positively influence the lives not only of women themselves but also of men, and of course, those of children. The Indian government is also helping through the use of various policies for the empowerment of women, especially in the political sphere. Women's representations in Indian grassroots political institutions are comparatively more than the mainstream political institutions. Indian political parties are using women only as a vote bank without addressing their real demands and aspirations. Women's participation is increasing in India as well as in South Asia, but their representation in key positions of decision-making bodies is still very low.

ENDNOTES

1. Pranab Kumar Panday, *Women's Political Participation in Bangladesh,* New Delhi: Springer, 2013, 1.
2. Andrea Fleschenberg and Claudia Derichs, *Women and Politics in Asia: A Springboard for Democracy?* LIT Verlag: England, 2012.
3. *Ibid.*
4. Rounaq Jahan, "Women in South Asian Politics", *Third World Quarterly,* 9, no. 3 (July 1987), p. 849.
5. Jahan, *Women in South Asian Politics*, p. 858.
6. V.S. Ganesamurthy, *Empowerment of Women in India: Social, Economic and Political* (New Delhi: New Century Publications, 2008).
7. K.S. Saxena, *Women's Political Participation in India*, New Delhi: Jain Book Agency, 1999.
8. Marit Haug, Aadne Aasland and Berit Aasen, "Attitudes Towards Women's Participation in Local Politics in South Asia", *Forum for Development Studies,* (2019), p. 4.
9. Nankyung Choi, "Women's Political Pathways in Southeast Asia", *International Feminist Journal of Politics,* (2018), p. 7.
10. Farah Deeba Chowdhury, *Women's Political Participation in Bangladesh: An Empirical Study*, Universal Press Limited, 2013.
11. Huma Yusuf, *The Evolving Role of Women in Pakistani Politics*, Expert Analysis, Norwegian Peace Building Resource Centre: NOREF, 2013.
12. Raj Bala, *The Legal and Political Status of Women in India,* New Delhi: Mohit Publications, 1999, p. 250.
13. "Towards Equality", *Report of the Committee on the status of Women in India,* New Delhi: Government of India, 1985, pp. 43-44.
14. S.S. Mathur and Anju Mathur, *Socio-Psychological Dimensions of Women Education,* New Delhi: Gyan Publishing House, 2001, p. 25.
15. S.R. Bakshi (ed.), *Advanced History of Modern India,* Vol. 4, New Delhi: Anmol Publications, 1995, p. 226.
16. Indian Constitution, Art. 326.
17. *Handbook on Promoting Women's Participation in Political Parties,* Warsaw: ODHIR, 2014, p. 15.
18. Election Commission of India Report, Government of India, 2019.
19. Data has been adapted from the following source, https://inc.in
20. Government of India Report, 2007.
21. *Ibid.*
22. *Ibid.*
23. Government of India Report, 2008.
24. Government of India Report, 2016.

Index